MW01626133

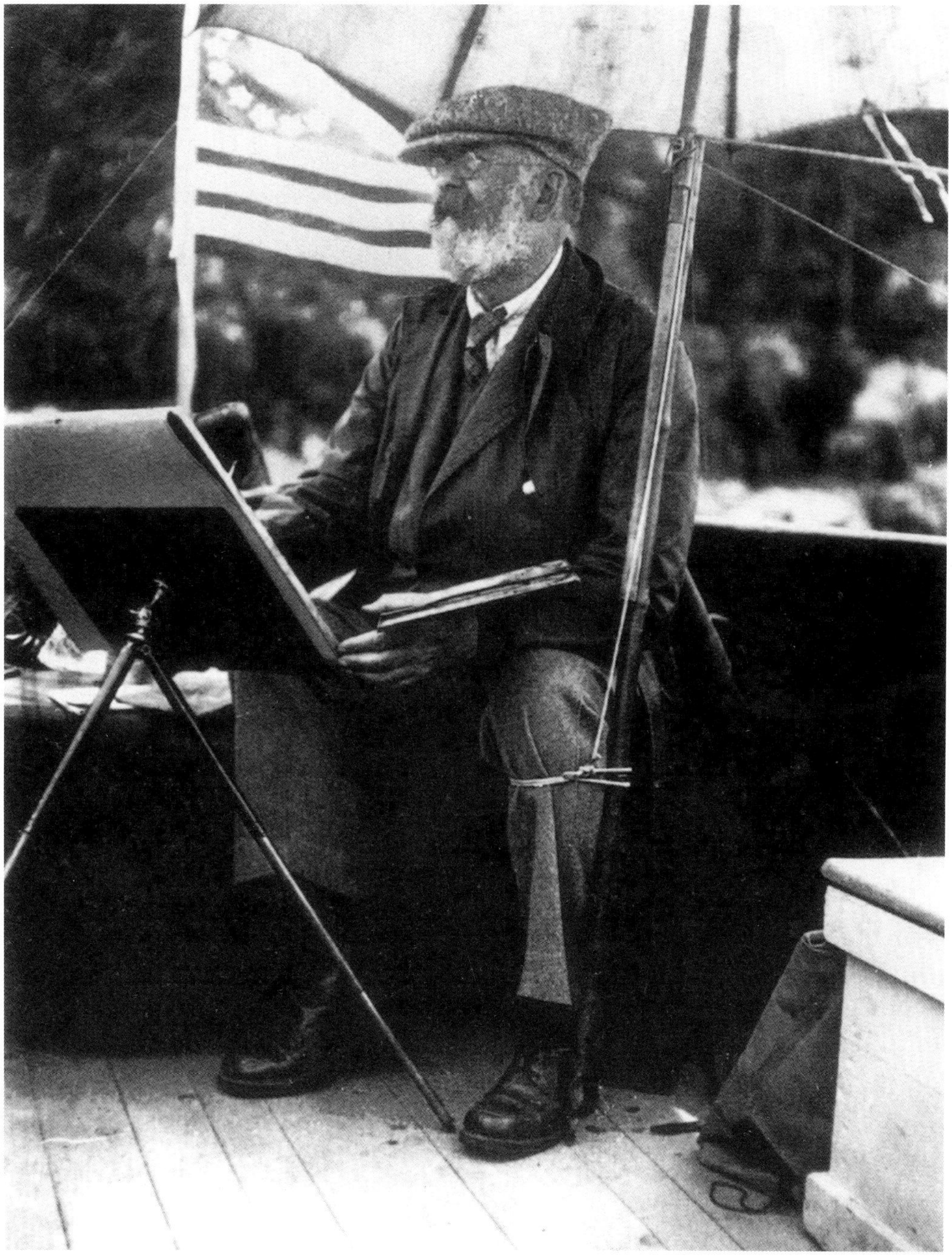

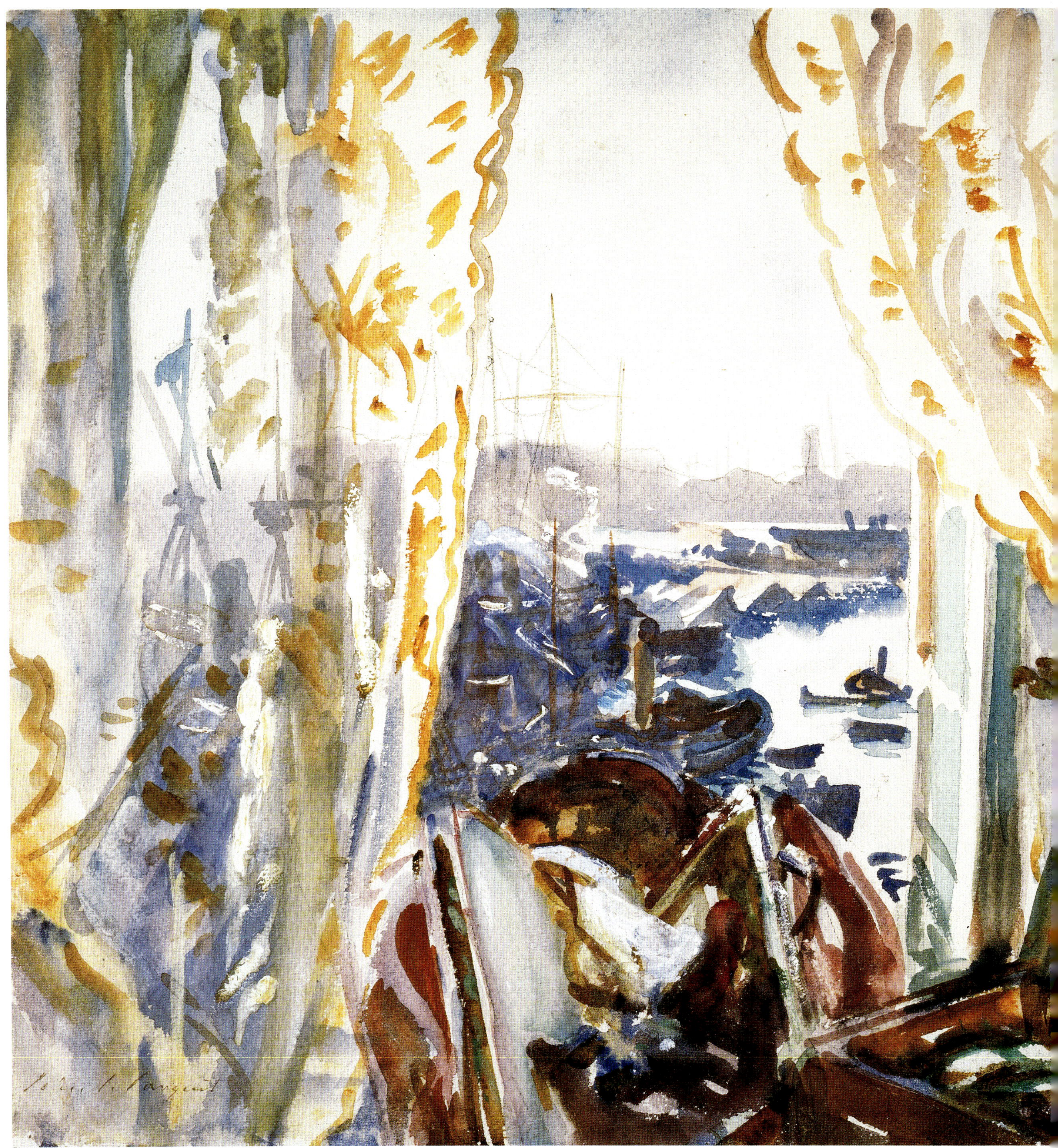

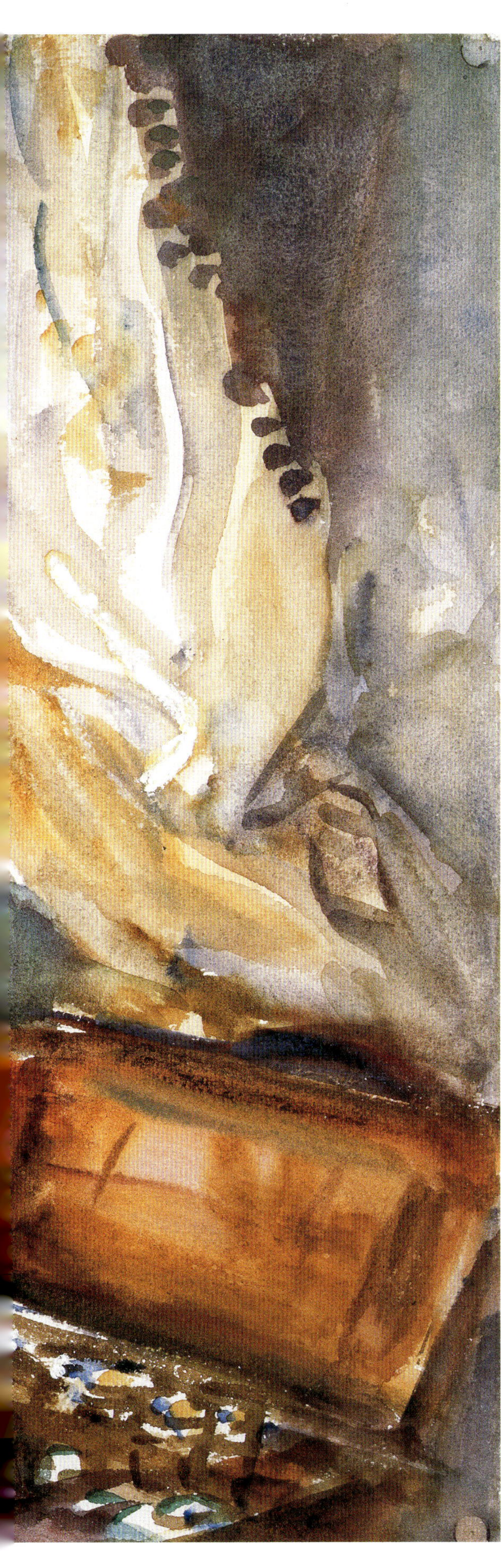

Carl Little

The Watercolors of John Singer Sargent

Picture Editor & Designer: Arnold Skolnick

UNIVERSITY OF CALIFORNIA PRESS
Berkeley • Los Angeles • London

A CHAMELEON BOOK

University of California Press
Berkeley and Los Angeles, California

University of California Press Ltd.
London, England

Published by arrangement with
Chameleon Books, Inc.

Produced by Chameleon Books, Inc.
31 Smith Road
Chesterfield, Massachusetts, 01012

Production director / designer: Arnold Skolnick
Design associate: KC Scott
Printed in China

5 6 7 8 9

Library of Congress Cataloging-in-Publication Data

Little, Carl.
The watercolors of John Singer Sargent / by Carl Little ; designed by Arnold Skolnick.
p. cm.
Includes bibliographical references and index.
ISBN 978-0-520-21970-0 (pbk.; alk. paper)
1. Sargent, John Singer, 1856–1925—Criticism and interpretation.
I. Title.
ND1839.S32L58 1999
759.13—dc21 98-31212
CIP

(half-title)

Sargent painting a watercolor aboard Dwight Blaney's Yacht "Norma," Ironbound Island, Maine Photograph, 1921–22
Courtesy, the Blaney Family Archives

(frontispiece)

View from a Window at Genoa after 1900
Pencil, watercolor and oil on paper
15 3/4 x 20 3/4 in. (40 x 52.7 cm.)
Trustees of The British Museum, London
Presented by Mrs Ormond

Acknowledgments

The author owes an enormous debt to the many individuals whose scholarship has guided the writing of the present book. Biographers Evan Charteris, William Howe Downes and Stanley Olson have provided detailed accounts of Sargent's life that allow us to come to terms with the context of his art nearly seventy-five years after his death. Monographs by Patricia Hills, Richard Ormond, Donelson Hoopes, Martin Hardie, Carter Ratcliff, Trevor Fairbrother and Warren Adelson, among others, and numerous excellent focused essays on Sargent's technique, highlight the achievements of this artist in more than one medium.

Many individuals deserve special thanks: Isabelle T. Eaton at the Isabella Stewart Gardner Museum in Boston; Mike and Ben Blaney; the author's brother David Littie, for copying Sargent material from his art library; the staff of the Northeast Harbor Library and the Thorndike Library at College of the Atlantic; Christopher Huntington for forwarding an article on Sargent's Rocky Mountain sojourn: Sunne Savage Neuman, who tracked down some key Maine watercolors; Charlene Woodcock at the University of California Press for her faith in this project; and, as ever, the enthusiastic and sharp-eyed designer, Arnold Skolnick, who knows how to obtain images trans-Atlantic style.

Finally a personal salute to the author's family, Peggy, Emily and James, who have survived another book with understanding, and to Romeo, who made the supreme sacrifice.

—Carl Little

To everyone at the museums who allowed me access to their extraordinary collections of Sargent watercolors I give my wholehearted thanks: Ruth Jenson from the Brooklyn Museum of Art; Mary L. Sluskonis, Museum of Fine Arts, Boston; Julie Zeftel and Deanne Cross, the Metropolitan Museum of Art; Isabelle T. Eaton, the Isabella Stewart Gardner Museum; Nancy L. Swallow, the Worcester Art Museum; Pamela Stuedemann and Hsui-ling Huang, the Art Institute of Chicago; Melody Ennis, Museum of Art, Rhode Island Shool of Design; Elizabeth Gombosi, the Fogg Art Museum; Nancy Stanfield, the National Gallery of Art; Jeanne Chvasta, the Dallas Museum of Art; Mell Ellis, the New Britain Musem of American Art; Stacey L. Sherman, the Nelson-Atkins Museum of Art; James Crawford, the Canajoharie Library and Art Gallery; Cheryle T. Robertson, the Los Angeles County Museum of Art; Douglas W. Evans, the Westmoreland Museum of American Art; Nancy S. Jackson, the Tacoma Art Museum; Liv Henson, the Cincinnati Art Museum; Cristina Segovia, the Corcoran Museum of Art; and Linda Best, Mead Art Museum.

We are also grateful to our colleagues "across the pond" who provided access to their collections: Pauline Allwright at the Imperial War Museum and Cristina Cinaccarini and Tom Hughes at the British Museum in London, and Suzanne M. Wynne at the Fitzwilliam Museum in Cambridge.

Special thanks to the people at Christie's Images, Art Resource and the Bridgman Art Library; Thomas J. Hosier from R.H. Love Galleries; and Richard L. Feigen from Richard L. Feigen & Co.

Forever thanks to Fred Kline, Judith Friebert, Marion Wheeler, Patricia Hill, to the Blaney Family; and special thanks to Sunne Savage.

—Arnold Skolnick

John Singer Sargent, Watercolorist *6*

Notes *18*

Selected Bibliography *19*

•

Studies and Portraits *20*

Venice *34*

North Africa and the Middle East *52*

In the Mountains *66*

Gardens, Fountains and Statuary *90*

Italy, Spain, Greece and Great Britain *104*

Florida *123*

World War I *133*

The Canadian Rockies and New England *149*

•

Sources of Quotations *160*

Index of Watercolors *160*

John Singer Sargent, Watercolorist

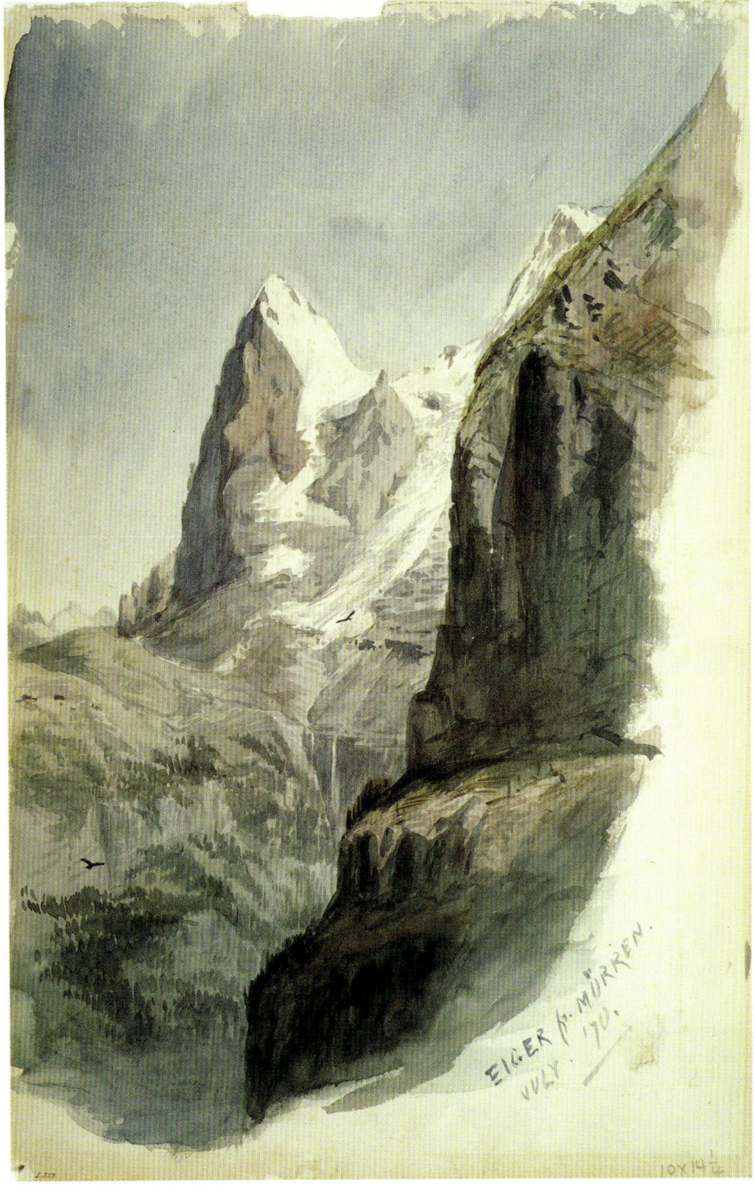

The Eiger from Murren 1870
Watercolor
14 3/4 x 10 1/4 in. (37.4 x 26 cm.)
Gift of Mrs. Francis Ormond,
Courtesy, Museum of Fine Arts, Boston

John Singer Sargent was born in Florence, Italy, on January 12, 1856, the second child of FitzWilliam and Mary Newbold Singer Sargent. At the time of his birth, his father, a retired surgeon, and his mother, an amateur artist, had removed themselves from their native America, from Philadelphia, to recover Mary Sargent's health following the death of an infant daughter. The family settled into a nomadic existence, moving with the seasons through Europe, with extended stays in France, Spain, Italy, Germany and Switzerland.[1]

"This locomotive disposition," wrote Evan Charteris, Sargent's friend and biographer, "was not the expression of a family fidgety in habit, but had economy as well as enlightenment for its aim."[2] As a more recent biographer, Stanley Olson, put it, Sargent received "an education by *Baedeker* and *Murray's*,"[3] a reference to two popular guidebooks of the time. Later in life, the artist would emulate his parents' peregrinations, hosting a kind of moveable painting party made up of family and friends.

Sargent's earliest experiences in art relate to watercolor, and the medium played a significant role in the shaping of his technique. Critics and art historians of his time tended to treat the watercolors as of marginal importance in Sargent's oeuvre. As this book demonstrates, his work in watercolor ranks high both in his mastery of the medium and in the interest he invested in it.

The artist's mother, a watercolorist of some skill (as Winslow Homer's had been), encouraged her son to pursue his artistic inclinations from an early age, providing him with art supplies, including sketchbooks. He also received training in music, which became a lifelong passion.

Mrs. Sargent watched over her son's progress, reporting his advances to relatives. "He sketches quite nicely, & has a remarkably quick and correct eye," she wrote her mother-in-law in October 1867 when John was eleven years old. "If we could afford to give him really good lessons, he would soon be quite a little artist."[4]

At the same time, Mrs. Sargent taught her son how to observe the world around him. During their travels, she was indefatigable in pointing out the particulars of the family's surroundings, elements of architecture and landscape. This constant study would leave an indelible mark on the artist's sensibility and remain the modus operandi that guided his work as a watercolorist.

From his earliest days, Sargent seemed fixed on the reality of his surroundings. "The usual fancies from history and mythology, which even the gravest artists in boyhood have turned to, do not appear to have engaged his attention," wrote Charteris.

> He was much more taken up with things there before his eyes, the shadow of an oleander on a wall, the attitude of a fellow-traveller in a railway carriage, the bronze figures round the tomb of Maximillian at Innsbruck, a country cart, a statue, or a corner of architecture—any detail, in fact, of the visible world.[5]

The family's often lengthy excursions, like the training runs of a marathoner, turned Sargent into a lifelong man of the world and an outdoorsman, able to hike great distances in the Alps, for example, or undergo primitive transportation and accommodations in the pursuit of subject matter in North Africa, the Canadian Rockies or the Carrara Mountains in Italy. "Painting was more than an art to Sargent," Charteris observed, "it held the exhilaration of a sport as well; his quarry was a suitable subject, his trophy the creation of a thing of beauty."[6]

Sargent's first formal artistic schooling came at the age of thirteen in the studio of Carl Welsch, a German-American landscape painter based in Rome. The teenager is known to have copied his teacher's watercolors. He also attended classes at the *Accademia delle belle arti* in Florence and drew from plaster casts at the Albertium in Dresden. Where American artists of his day—and nowadays, for that matter—might dream of study on the Continent at some point in their career, Sargent reaped this experience as a youth.

The young artist also had the opportunity to study the Old Masters in all their original glory, visiting museums and churches, soaking up the genius of the great painters of the past. "I have learned in Venice to admire Tintoretto immensely and to consider him perhaps second only to Michael Angelo and Titian," Sargent wrote in a letter dated March 22, 1874.[7] While not trained as an art historian, he wrote and conversed in depth on art all his life. He wrote perceptive appreciations of a number of artists, including Ignacio Zuloaga, Hercules Brabazon and Sir Joshua Reynolds.

At eighteen, the artist enrolled in the atelier of Carolus-Duran in Paris. Carolus-Duran (1838–1917) was a fashionable portrait painter of the day who preached an aesthetic based on the work of the Spanish master Diego Velásquez (1599–1650). *"Velásquez, Velásquez, Velásquez, étudiez sans relache Velásquez,"* he is reported to have told his students.[8]

One of Sargent's studio mates later recalled the presentation of the youthful painter's work the first day in Carolus-Duran's studio. "We were astonished at the cleverness shown in the water-color and pencil work," he recounted, "and [Sargent's] debut was considered a most promising one."[9]

Most promising indeed: in the fall of 1874, on his first attempt, Sargent passed the *concours*, the rigorous examination that was a requisite to enrollment in the *École des beaux-arts*, a rare achievement for a non-native. His colleagues were quick to recognize his skill; the American painter Julian Alden Weir wrote his mother from Paris in October 1874, "I met this last week a young Mr. Sargent, one of the most talented fellows I have ever come across; his drawings are like the old masters, and his color is equally fine...."[10]

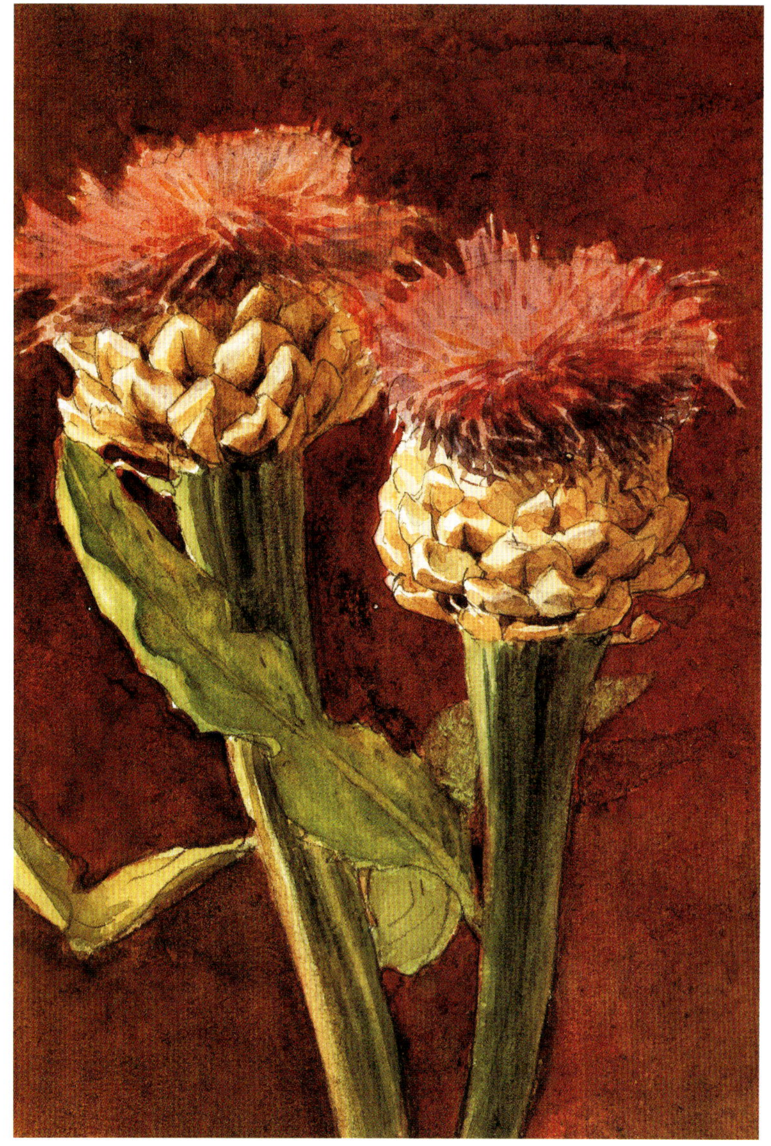

Thistles N.D.
Watercolor on paper
6 1/2 x 4 1/2 in. (16.5 x 11.4 cm.)
The Metropolitan Museum of Art,
Gift of Mrs. Francis Ormond, 1950 (50.130.141aa)
Photograph © 1978 The Metropolitan Museum of Art

Through his training with Carolus-Duran and studies with Léon Bonnat,[11] Sargent developed into a master portraitist and genre painter. He was only twenty-one years old when he painted his first formal portrait and he quickly became a regular exhibitor at the annual Paris Salons.

Sargent gained success early, with such canvases as *Fumée d'Ambre Gris*, 1880 (Sterling and Francine Clark Art Institute), and *El Jaleo*, 1882 (Isabella Stewart Gardner Museum). Displayed to critical acclaim at the Salon in Paris, the paintings were based on memories of trips to Spain

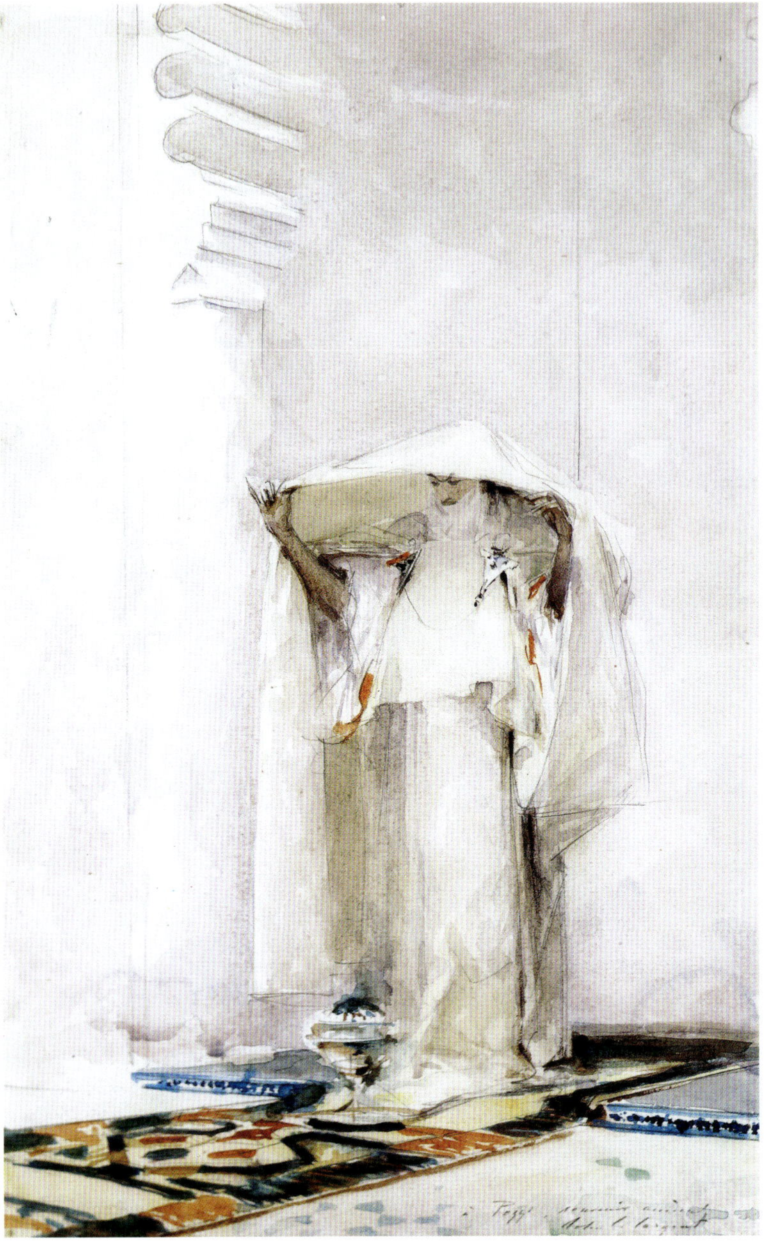

Incensing the Veil 1880
Watercolor on paper, 12 x 7 3/4 in. (30 x 20 cm.)
Isabella Stewart Gardner Museum, Boston

In the Tyrol 1911
Watercolor over graphite on white wove paper
10 1/16 x 19 11/16 in. (25.5 x 50 cm.)
Courtesy of the Fogg Art Museum, Harvard University Art Museums, Gift of Sir Joseph Duveen
© President and Fellows of Harvard College

and Morocco in 1879–1880.

In Madrid, following Carolus-Duran's imperative, Sargent had made copies of the works of Velásquez in the Prado (in his formative years he also copied works by Hals, El Greco, Goya and Degas, among others). Further south, across the Straits of Gibraltar, Tangier provided him with his first exposure to the Arab world. "....The aspect of the place is striking, the costume grand and the Arabs often magnificent," he wrote to a friend. [12]

Watercolor played a distinct role in the creation of Sargent's early masterworks. The artist turned to the medium at various stages of composition, rendering sketches that ranged from loose studies to more finished works. The watercolor *Incensing the Veil*, for example, is a near perfect, although less-detailed, copy of the finished painting *Fumée d'Ambre Gris*. One would assume that the watercolor served as a compositional study for the oil painting, but it may have been a faithful replica executed for an admirer.[13]

With *El Jaleo*, Sargent used watercolor in preparation for the final canvas, which was more than eleven feet long. Drawing on memories of Spanish dance halls, he recruited a professional artist's model, Marie Renard, in Paris to pose for the central figure.[14] The many *El Jaleo* studies testify to the special care Sargent took to render every detail of the dancer's gesture—the graceful outstretched left hand, the akimbo arm, the dramatic turn of the head—as she gives herself to the music.

Along with success, Sargent gained champions, in particular the writer Henry James who would sing his praises almost unabated in the course of their long friendship. James's admiration began almost at once, as testified to in this passage from a letter written from Paris in 1884:

> The only Franco-American product of importance here...strikes me as young John Sargent the painter, who has high talent, a charming nature, artistic and personal, and is civilized to his finger-tips. He is perhaps spoilable—though I don't think he is spoiled. But I hope not, for I like him extremely; and the best of his work seems to me to have in it something exquisite.[15]

Not everyone shared James's enthusiasm: Sargent's portrait of Virginie Gautreau, shown at the Paris Salon in 1884, was greeted for the most part with outrage by the public and critics, causing a scandal that rocked the city and struck a blow to the artist's reputation. Viewers and members of the Gautreau family were shocked by the straightforward manner in which the fashionable woman was portrayed—and by her décolletage and the lavender coloring of her skin. The reviewers pointed to certain technical flaws, but the true basis of their critiques was offended public morality.

When the painting was purchased by the Metropolitan Museum of Art many years later, the title was changed to *Madame X* following Sargent's instructions. Subsequent opinions of the portrait have mellowed. Today, the painting is considered one of the artist's most remarkable likenesses.

On the heels of this disastrous showing, and with the encouragement of his new friend James, Sargent fled Paris for London. Initial visits across the channel led to a residency in England. It was not long before he moved into 13 Tite Street in Chelsea, recently vacated by James McNeill Whistler. Sargent resided there until his death in 1925.

Sargent was a plein air painter[16] from an early age, habituated to working out of doors, but the rustic charms of rural England inspired him to increased activity in the field. On seasonal retreats to Broadway in the Cotswolds, the artist painted away from the studio as much as possible, and partook in boating parties and al fresco picnics with friends and family.

The writer Edmund Gosse (1849–1928) captured the painter in action, in an oft-cited account of Sargent wandering into the English countryside and selecting a motif seemingly at random. "His object," wrote Gosse, "was to acquire the habit of reproducing precisely whatever met his vision without the slightest previous 'arrangement' of detail, the painter's business being, not to pick and choose, but to render the effect before him, whatever it may be." [17]

At the same time, Sargent "shut the once-useful and well-thumbed texts of Carolus, Velásquez and Hals, and opened another, entitled Claude Monet."[18] Much has been written about his debt to the Impressionists, in particular his good friend Monet, and yet the majority of commentators qualify the aesthetic connection. The painter and art critic Fairfield Porter, for example, noted that the Impressionists' light was "light interpreted" while Sargent's light "was one thing he understood and could give you his feeling for." [19]

Sargent's impromptu approach to subject matter, as described by Gosse, along with his eye for light, came into play during his many visits to Venice. He had made several trips to this fabled city in the company of his parents, but it was in the early 1880s that he returned as a mature artist. "There is plenty of work to be done here," he wrote to his friend Vernon Lee (née Violet Paget) in October 1880. [20]

The roster of artists who have painted Venice is long and impressive, ranging from Canaletto in the early 1800s to Richard Estes in the 1980s.

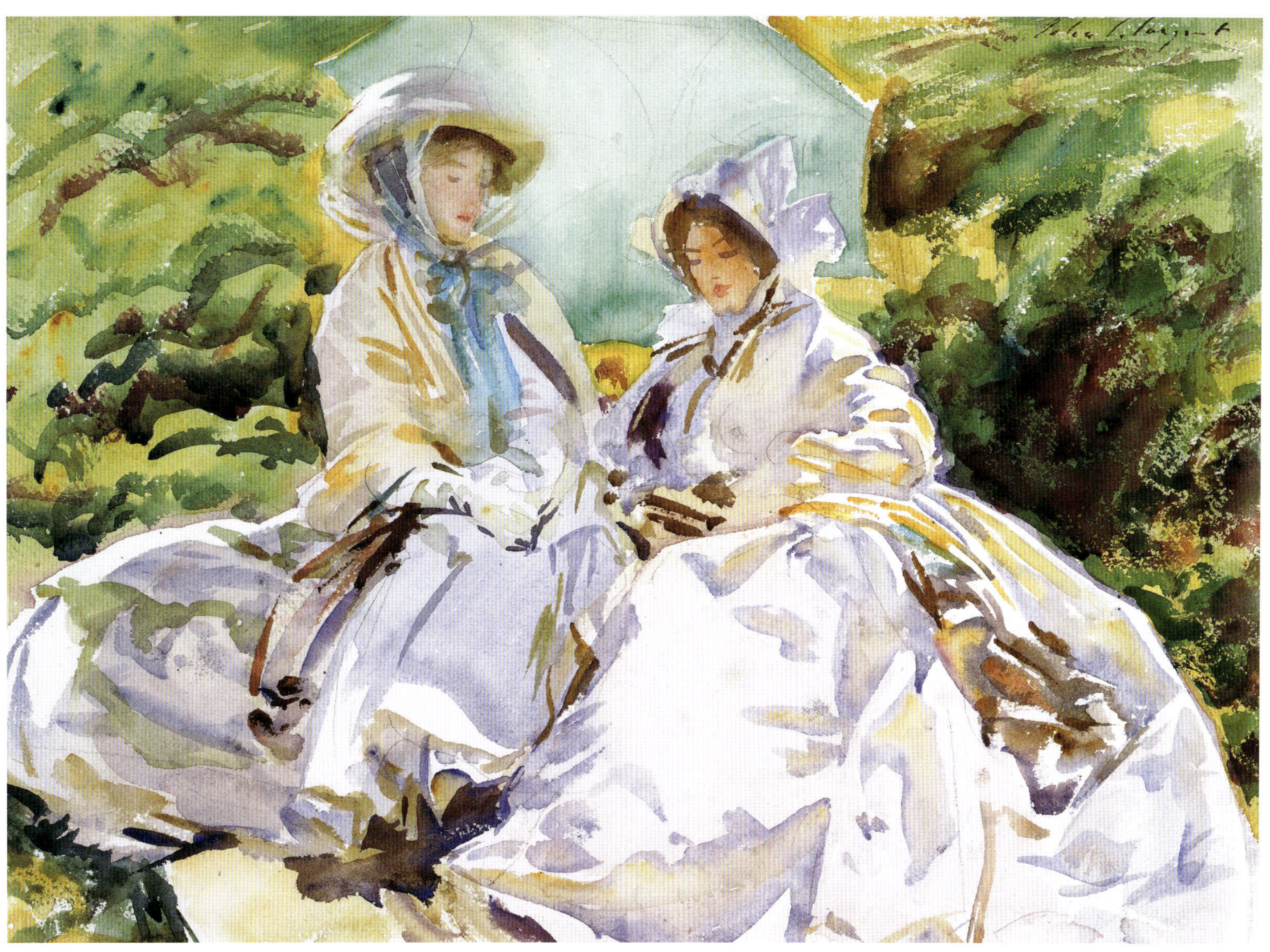

In Sargent's time, Whistler, Monet, Childe Hassam and Maurice Prendergast were among those who spent time there, rendering in their signature styles the people, architecture and ambiance of this marvelous "bride of the sea."

Another Venice painter was watercolorist Hercules Brabazon (1821–1905), who has often been cited as an influence on Sargent. In the appreciation he wrote at the time of a Brabazon exhibition in 1891, Sargent might have been speaking about himself:

> Immediate sensations flower again in Mr. Brabazon's [watercolor] drawings, with a swiftness that makes one for a time forget that there has been a medium. Those who look principally for suggestions of Nature in pictures will be grateful....[21]

Built on water, on a great network of canals, Venice was magical, a place of romance and intrigue.[22] Using the highly portable medium of watercolor, Sargent painted far and wide, often from a gondola, which explains the unusual perspective of many of his images. Over the course of his visits to the city, he returned to specific motifs again and again. The gondoliers, who created dynamic diagonals poling their sleek boats along the canals, were among his favorite subjects.

Drawn to architecture as a subject since his early days, Sargent painted the palaces, churches and other baroque edifices in the city with great fluency, frequently focusing in on a single section of a facade. He could model the steps of an entrance to a building with the accuracy of a sculptor. He painted famous sights, such as the Rialto and the Bridge of Sighs, as well as less traveled spots.[23]

It is as if Sargent took one of those complex views of Venice by Canaletto and separated out the various elements: people seated on some stairs, gondoliers taking a siesta, the tangle of ship's rigging along the waterfront. He sought detail. As Henry James so eloquently put it, "Wonderfully light and fine is the touch by which the painter evokes the small Venetian realities."[24]

If Sargent was not, as he once stated, interested in *vedutas* (views), at times he would open wide the angle of his vision to encompass the city's grand thoroughfares. His greatest interest lay in objects—ships, mooring posts, bridges—and in urban fragments—corners of buildings, edges of canals.[25] At the same time, the play of light and shadow in Venice inspired marvelous effects, the surface of the water represented by a flurry of lively brushstrokes.

These Venice watercolors were acclaimed in their day. A reviewer writing for the *London Illustrated News* in 1903 resorted to something like hyperbole to express his awe:

> If some of his oil-portraits seem more alive than the people who sat for them, so these water-colour drawings of Venice seem almost brighter than the brightness of Europe's most radiant and ethereal city. The waters are wetter than water. Everything is given with the intensity of a dream. One wonders whether Mr. Sargent's visual power is greater than normal, since he seems to see things more vividly than they are seen by others.[26]

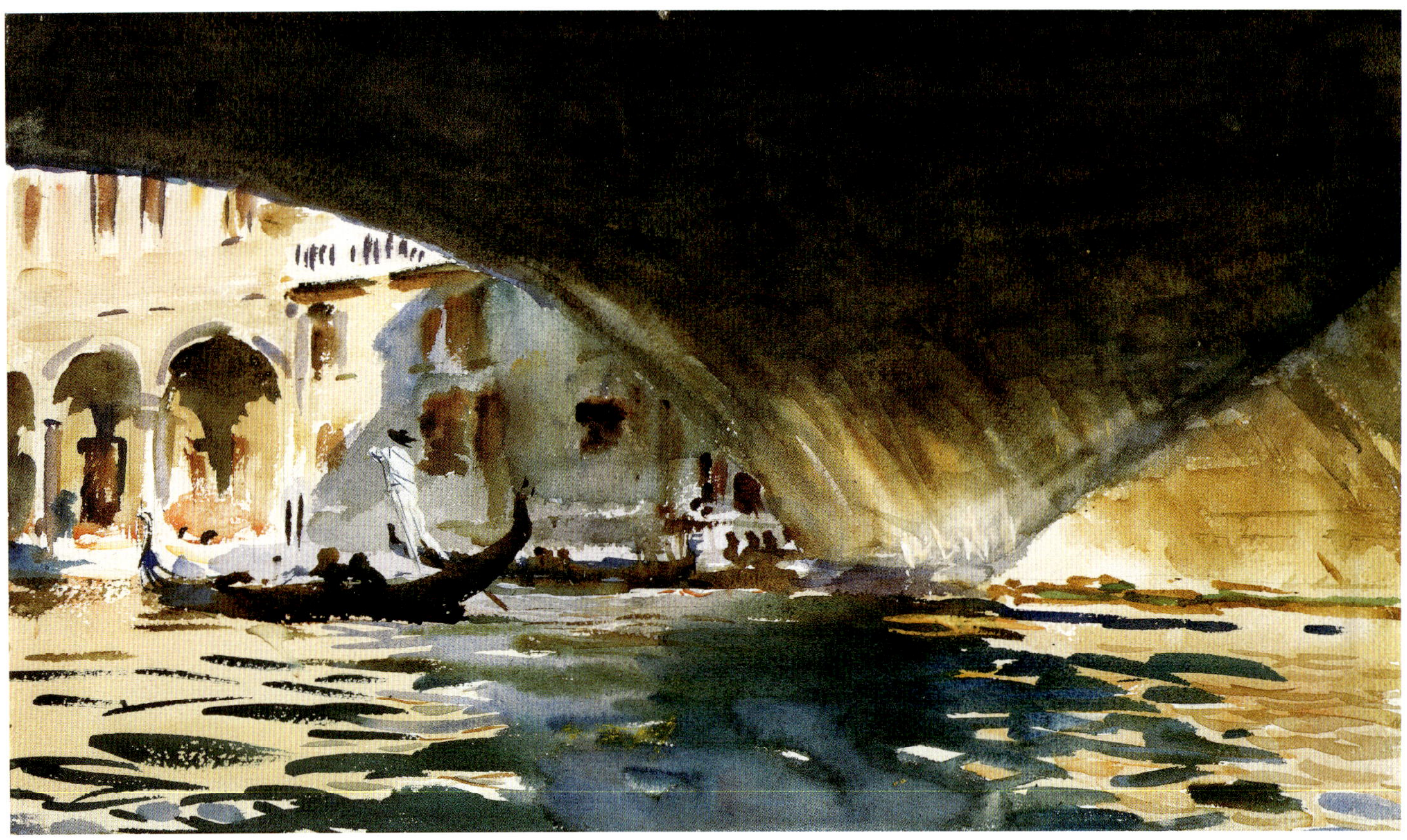

Under the Rialto Bridge c. 1909, Watercolor over graphite on paper, 10 7/8 x 19 in. (27.6 x 48.4 cm.)
Hayden Collection, Courtesy, Museum of Fine Arts, Boston

One of Sargent's earliest memories was of a cobblestone of brilliant porphyry that caught his eye during a walk in Florence—it so delighted him that he asked his nurse to revisit it on their daily walks.[27] This eye for bright elements in his surroundings remained with him all his life and is nowhere more apparent than in the remarkable watercolors made around Europe after 1900. Indeed, an image of colorful pavements in Sicily seems a direct manifestation of that early fascination.

The subject matter of Sargent's watercolors from his travels across the Continent displays enormous variety. On a holiday to the Greek island of Corfu in the Ionian Sea, the artist set up his tripod easel in front of a stand of olive trees, fascinated by the gnarled beauty of their trunks and the way the strong Mediterranean light played among the twisting branches.

On Majorca, the largest of Spain's Balearic Islands, the skeleton of an abandoned ship, linens hanging on a clothes line and pomegranates in thick foliage were among the motifs that caught Sargent's eye. The latter is a tour de force of watercolor, the handling as lush and full as the subject itself.

The perspective in the watercolors is often dramatic or unexpected, as when Sargent painted the precipitous slopes of the Carrara Mountain quarries, accented with the rubble of marble mining. Unlike the commonplace panorama where the artist has simply set himself down in front of an attractive vista, these landscapes transport the viewer into the scene in a most direct manner.

Unusual shapes had great appeal to Sargent, whether the curving jetty at San Vigilio above Lake Garda or gourds hanging like odd-shaped pendants on Majorca. He was also attracted to gardens, fountains and statuary; these subjects stand among his most poetic, calling up places that seem to be situated outside of time.

As he had in the company of his mother, Sargent picked out individual elements from his surroundings upon which to focus. A group of sphinxes on a terrace of the palace of La Granja at San Ildefonso near Segovia, Spain; statues raked by sunlight at the Villa di Marlia in Lucca, Italy; a fountain in the Piazza Navona in Rome—he never tired of rendering such features of his sunlit environment.

The artist's letters are full of reports of painting prospects. In the summer of 1913, he wrote from Lake Garda, "we have discovered a nasty little pension on a little promontory, which is otherwise paradise—cypresses, olives, a villa, a tiny little port, deep clear water and no tourists." [28] In a letter from 1917, he rhapsodized, "....I should like to spend a summer at Frascati and paint from morning to night at the [Villa] Torlonia or the [Villa] Falconiere, ilexes and cypresses, fountains and statues—*ainsi soit-il* [so be it]—amen."[29]

Sargent also continued to copy, as if his training as an artist were a lifelong enterprise. Viewing a ceiling decoration by Tiepolo in Milan, he drew a freeform rendition of a section of the mural, a tribute to one of his favorite artists.[30]

As testified to by these watercolors, Sargent's activities as an artist were continuous. Painting was at the core of his existence. "To some of us," wrote his friend Vernon Lee in 1926, "he seemed occasionally to paint to the exclusion of living." And yet Lee recognized, as did Sargent's family and friends, that the artist's life "was not merely in painting, but in the more and more intimate understanding and enjoying the world around him."[31]

In 1926, a year after Sargent's death, Adrian Stokes, who had accompanied the artist to the Alps, described what had inspired his late friend to paint a particular watercolor:

> Sargent's watercolors...usually record, with the utmost directness, something that had excited his admiration, or appealed to his artistic intelligence. That may have been the clearly defined and exquisite edge of some rare object; or the way in which a dark thing, when opposed to vivid light, is invaded by it and loses local color; or the change that seems to occur in the color of things along the edge where they meet.[32]

Sargent practiced this way of seeing during his many sojourns in the mountains of Switzerland, Austria, Italy and France. From 1900 to 1915, he spent a part of nearly every summer or autumn in elevated climes, ranging in his travels from the Simplon Pass and the Val d'Aosta to the Dolomites and the Tyrol. Chamonix, Saas Fee, Purtud, Giomein, Breuil, Isère, Colfuschg—he and his entourage settled in remote places to relax and, in Sargent's case, to paint to his heart's delight.

Eliza Wedgewood, one of a group of friends who accompanied the artist around Europe in the early 1900s, outlined the schedule of a typical day in Sargent's company:

> Every autumn we spent together the routine was the same—breakfast generally 7.30, afterwards work literally all day till the light failed. At rare intervals an excursion—if very hot a siesta after the midday meal, but work was the order of the day....After dinner [piano] duets and chess & early to bed.[33]

Sargent believed in this kind of regimen. "Above all things," he would exhort his students at the Royal Academy Schools in London, "get abroad, see the sunlight, and everything that is to be seen...."[34]

More than simply an escape from a stuffy studio in London (and portrait seekers knocking on his door), the mountains also offered Sargent motifs of great appeal. Chalets, streams, pine forests and peaks all inspired his watercolor brush. While he might turn out a rendering of such classic and dramatic subjects as the Matterhorn or a mountain fire,[35] he could also paint a lovely watercolor of a fence, attracted by the warm color of the worn wood and the workmanship of its construction.

Among the most remarkable alpine watercolors are studies of mountain brooks and streams. In these paintings, Sargent frames small sections of the landscape, removing them, as it were, from the greater context of their mountainous surroundings. In doing so, he highlights the configurations of rocks, the way the sun accents the water. The appeal of such subjects equals the visual pleasure derived from Monet's water-lily studies.

Tiepolo Ceiling—Milan c. 1904
Watercolor and graphite on white wove paper
14 x 9 15/16 in. (35.6 x 25.2 cm.)
The Metropolitan Museum of Art,
Gift of Mrs. Francis Ormond, 1950 (50.130.25)

Likewise, a simple crucifix in the Tyrol appealed to his sensitive eye. Painted in 1914, as the first rumblings of World War I were being heard, this watercolor and other pictures of the time "reflect," notes biographer Richard Ormond, Sargent's "sombre and premonitory mood."[36] In another painting, the grave markers in a Tyrolese graveyard add dark decorative accents to a haunted setting.

These alpine sojourns were social times, and Sargent enjoyed depicting his co-travellers at their various activities. Women in bonnets and voluminous dresses find cover from the sun under parasols, while an artist friend works at his easel by the edge of a stream or a youthful figure bathes in a stream.[37] Sargent understood the truth of something an early traveler, Conrad Gesner, wrote about the Alps: "Let us then conclude that from walks in the mountains undertaken in the company of friends the highest of all pleasures and the most charming of all delights of the senses are obtained."[38]

Sargent was a true Edwardian, accustomed to the good life that the era afforded the wealthy. He was full of wit and was cosmopolitan through and through. He made an excellent living from his work, but his prosperity led not to decadence, but to expressions of generosity to others.[39]

A lifelong bachelor, Sargent surrounded himself with family and friends, and his sexual energy was apparently channeled into his work, whose almost tactile sensuousness can be admired particularly in his later watercolors and oils. His fame, as well as a distinctive belly and beard, made him the perfect subject for the greatest social cartoonist of the time, Max Beerbohm, who drew no less than seventeen caricatures of the artist.[40]

As a sought-after portraitist, Sargent captured the likenesses of many of the luminaries of his time, the well-to-do, the socially connected. He also painted famous writers (Henry James, Coventry Patmore, Robert Louis Stevenson, William Butler Yeats), actresses and singers (Ellen Terry, Ethel Barrymore, Eleonora Duse), political figures (Theodore Roosevelt, Woodrow Wilson) and artists (Monet, Paul Helleu).

When executed in watercolor, the society portraits often display a wonderful informality. While he tried—sometimes unsuccessfully—to avoid commissioned oil portraits in the last decades of his life, Sargent enjoyed rendering his family and acquaintances in quick sketches that capture the leisurely pace of their lives.[41]

Sargent painted reclining subjects, not stiff and posed like an odalisque, but truly relaxed—even his World War I soldiers are shown napping. He was especially fond of drawing his companions as they slept, stretched out in an Alpine meadow or on a cot. Whereas he was often put to the test with wide-awake sitters during formal portrait work (he was known to bribe children with candy), these sleepers posed no such problem: they were the perfect models. What is more, they displayed a figural dynamism that attracted the artist, one that was far removed from the artificial aesthetic of the drowned Ophelia of Pre-Raphaelite fame.

The portrait of Henrietta Reubell seated before a screen is a masterwork of watercolor portraiture.[42] A beautiful balance is maintained between specific details—facial features, the feet of a chair, parts of the background screen—and the overall loose rendering of the setting. Indeed, if one blocks off certain sections of this work, one confronts abstraction.

Equally remarkable, the watercolor portrait of Mrs. Isabella Stewart Gardner (1840–1924), doyenne of Boston's cultured society, attests to Sargent's ability to capture the character of his subjects. "Mrs. Jack," as she was called, was painted in Fenway Court, shrouded in white, grim-visaged yet stately, her death only two years off.

These and other portraits testify to the truth of observations made by one of Sargent's students, Julie Heynemann, who jotted down her impressions of the master. She wrote:

> He [Sargent] showed how much could be expressed in painting the form of the brow, the cheekbones, and the moving muscles around the eyes and mouth, where the character betrayed itself most readily; and under his hands, a head would be an amazing likeness long before he had so much as indicated the features themselves.[43]

Sargent's was a democratic eye; while portraits of the well-to-do in England, France and America garnered him the most acclaim and financial rewards, he also painted with great feeling people of other classes and nationalities. *The Tramp* (originally titled *The Vagrant*), for example, is powerfully expressive—and belies those critics who at times scorned Sargent for the lack of depth in his oil portraits.

In a similar manner, the workers in the marble quarries at Carrara, Italy, subject of a series of watercolors from 1911, take on heroic proportions. These paintings serve as a tribute to the men who risked their lives on a daily basis to cut the white stone out of precipitous mountainsides. In one especially fine watercolor Sargent shows three *lizzatori*, as the quarrymen were called, engulfed by the thick rope with which they conveyed the stone.[44]

On a trip to Lebanon and Syria in 1905–06, Sargent painted a striking series of watercolor portraits of Bedouins, desert nomads whose dark features and costumes appealed to his eye.[45] Drawn to the exotic much as Eugène Delacroix and earlier painters had been, Sargent found himself caught up in another world. An itinerant soul himself, the painter must have felt a special kinship with these desert wanderers who conjured up the mystery one associates with the legends of Arabia.

Sargent had made his first trip to America in 1876, at twenty. While thoroughly Europeanized—he spoke fluent French, Italian and German—he always considered himself American, and on this trip obtained official citizenship. "As for the question of nationality," he wrote to fellow expatriate James McNeill Whistler in 1895, "I have not been invited to retouch it and I keep my twang. If you should hear anything to the contrary, please state...that I am an American."[46]

Following this initial visit, Sargent returned to the United States on many occasions, at times for extended visits. In the late 1880s he established close ties in the city of Boston through portrait commissions, family connections and friendships started in Europe. An exhibition of his paintings at the St. Botolph Club in December 1888 received high praise from the critics. The reviewer from the *Daily Advertiser* stated, "No American has ever displayed a collection of paintings in Boston having so much of the quality which is summed up in the word *style*."[47]

In the course of a year-long stay in America in 1890, Sargent was commissioned to create murals for the Boston Public Library, a project that would occupy him off and on until the final panels were installed in 1919. He would also execute decorative designs for the Museum of Fine Arts and the Widener Library at Harvard.

In the summer of 1916, instead of returning to Europe as had been his habit for a respite from the ongoing mural work at the Boston Public Library, Sargent headed west, to the Canadian Rockies. He was, after all, a man of the mountains, having spent many seasons in the Alps.

Following a visit to Glacier National Park in Montana, Sargent traveled by rail to Seattle, then to Field, British Columbia, with Twin Falls in Yoho National Park his ultimate destination.[48] The accommodations—tents—were far from the Edwardian digs or even the Alpine hostelries to which Sargent was accustomed. He sent a somewhat comic account of the situation to his cousin Mary Hale on August 30:

> ....It was raining and snowing, my tent flooded, mushrooms sprouting in my boots, porcupines taking shelter in my clothes, canned food always fried in a black frying pan getting on my nerves, and a fine waterfall which was the attraction of the place pounding and thundering all night.[49]

Despite these conditions, Sargent managed to turn out several oils and a fine set of watercolors. He painted the tents that had done little to keep him dry, as well as a lovely picture of Lake Louise. Biographer William Howe Downes wrote of these works that the "swift and confident character of the handling and finality of the impression...go very far to place these studies in the top most rank."[50]

Extending his American visit, Sargent traveled to Florida in February 1917 in order to paint a portrait of John D. Rockefeller, Sr. Writing to his friend Ralph Curtis, Sargent reported, "Here I am in a temperature like a Turkish bath about to begin work on the Old Gentleman who looks like a medieval Saint."[51]

When not involved with this duty, Sargent took to watercolor with enthusiasm, turning out a series of fresh and lively studies of Florida scenes. Again his curiosity led him to an unusual assortment of subjects. In a marvelous study of alligators, he proves himself a painter of natural history of the first rank, equal to the challenge of depicting these amphibious reptiles with their prehistoric look. With equal finesse, he effectively rendered a profusion of spikey palmettos.

Sargent was especially taken by the luxurious grounds of his childhood friend James Deering's Italianate palazzo, Vizcaya, in Miami, which reminded him of some of his favorite haunts in Europe. Except for the distinctive Floridian foliage, a view of shady paths with statues might easily be mistaken for a retreat in Italy.

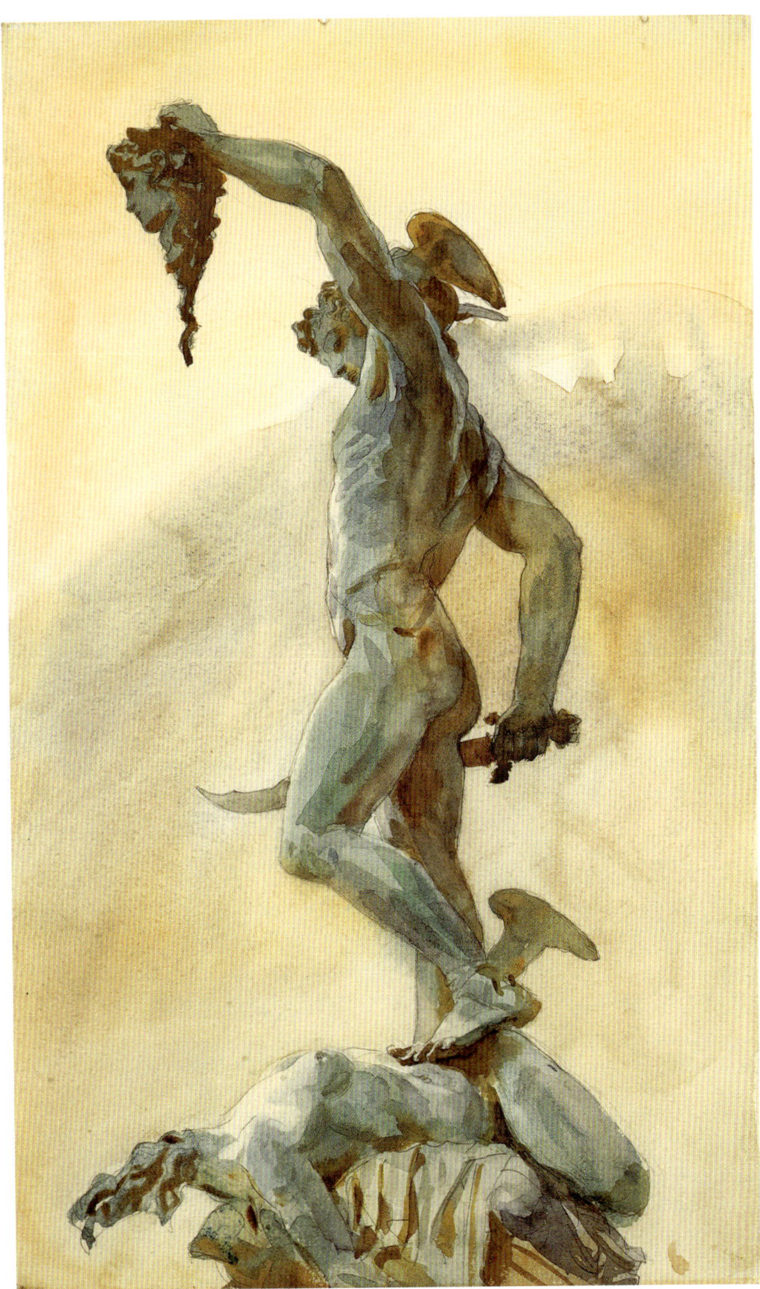

Sketch of Cellini's 'Perseus' N.D.
Watercolor over graphite
14 3/8 x 8 15/16 in. (36.5 x 22.8 cm)
National Gallery of Art, Washington,
Gift of R. Horace Gallatin

Upon his return to England in 1918, Sargent was commissioned as a war artist by the Ministry of Information. Earlier, in October 1916, he had written to his future biographer Evan Charteris expressing his interest in the conflict:

> If the accursed [war] is still going on, which God forbid, when I get back in two or three months, I shall feel tempted to go out and have a look at it....But would I have the nerve to look, not to speak of painting? I have never seen anything in the least horrible—outside of my studio. [52]

Sargent entered the war somewhat naively. He is known to have once surmised to General Fielding that there was "no fighting on Sundays." [53] And he had to be asked by the American military to camouflage the umbrella that served to keep the sun off his painting surface.

Despite this somewhat nonchalant attitude toward one of the most brutal conflicts in recorded history, the artist went to work, seeking the material, the special scene, that would fulfill his commission to produce a single canvas that would sum up the war, specifically the interactions of British and American soldiers. This painting, titled *Gassed* (Imperial War Museum), a large frieze-like work that Sargent completed in his studio in London, satisfied the committee, and yet the watercolor "notes" he took during his "sightseeing tour" of the western front in France are more dynamic. [54]

Sargent visited Berles au Bois, then Arras, Ypres and Peronne, using his watercolors to capture a variety of war scenes. He depicted camouflaged tanks, soldiers filching fruit, highlanders (Scottish troops) dozing on a grassy knoll, the dim interior of a hospital tent. In his hands, a destroyed sugar refinery became a complex study of twisted metal. And he was taken with the vision of masses of men on the move: "In this Somme country," he wrote in October 1918, "I have seen what I wanted, roads crammed with troops on the march. It is the finest spectacle the war affords, as far as I can make out." [55]

Perhaps his greatest war picture is *Crashed Aeroplane*, 1918. Here he

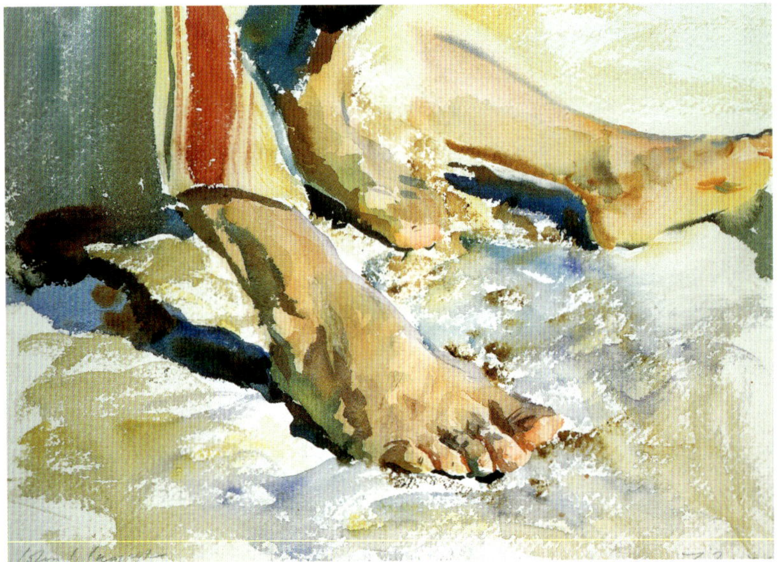

Feet of an Arab, Tiberius N.D.
Watercolor on paper
10 x 14 in. (25.4 x 35.6 cm.)
Courtesy Christie's Images

captures the everyday quality of the conflict: in the foreground, farmers harvest wheat, seemingly oblivious to the skeleton of an airplane that has crashed in a nearby field.[56] The image recalls the opening lines of W. H. Auden's "Musée des Beaux Arts":

> About suffering they were never wrong,
> The Old Masters: how well they understood
> Its human position; how it takes place
> While someone else is eating or opening a window or just walking dully along....[57]

The palette in this painting is somber; browns dominate.[58] This watercolor seems a precursor to the sober landscapes of Andrew Wyeth. By contrast, the watercolor *Tommies Bathing, France*, 1918, with its bright coloring, harks back to Sargent's portraits of friends and family in the Alps or the figural studies from his sojourn in Florida.

In the summers of 1921 and 1922, Sargent was the guest of the painter Dwight Blaney (1865–1944) at his home on Ironbound Island off the coast of Maine. Blaney was a member of the Boston School, a so-called "gentleman painter."[59] Like his renowned friend, he was an accomplished watercolorist who enjoyed working en plein air.

A large island by Maine standards, roughly three miles long by two miles wide, Ironbound lies in the middle of Frenchman Bay, about midway between Bar and Winter Harbors. The first rusticators—summerfolk—had arrived around the time of the Civil War. Blaney maintained a summer studio on the island and hosted artist friends, among them, Sargent, Childe Hassam and Ross Sterling Turner.

At least one oil, a portrait of Blaney painting at the edge of the forest, and a number of watercolors resulted from Sargent's visits to Ironbound. He painted several views of the island, including the impressive wharf which at low tide loomed large out of the chill waters of the Gulf of Maine.

Sargent was obviously taken with the ambiance of the place. As was his habit, while others were relaxing he painted. In his portrayal of the Blaney family on the veranda of their Ironbound home, he depicts the ladies (Mrs. Blaney and the two daughters, Margaret and Elizabeth) busy and comfortably knitting, while the mustachioed patriarch sits in a semi-reclined position with his long legs stretched out before him, taking in the view.

"These [Ironbound] pictures," wrote art historian Lloyd Goodrich, "were Sargent at his least formal—far more sympathetic, both humanly and artistically, than his commissioned portraits of the rich and fashionable." Goodrich praised their "visual freshness," the product of an "infallible eye and unerring hand, that were Sargent's most attractive gifts."[60]

Sargent worked actively in watercolor to the end of his life. He made several watercolor studies while staying with his cousin Mary Hale in Bar Harbor, among them views of Sand Beach (now a part of Acadia National Park) and Somes Sound. In 1924, he created a number of aquarelles aboard the yacht *Constellation*, owned by Bayard Thayer, including a portrait of Commodore Herbert Mason Sears in sailing garb holding binoculars.[61]

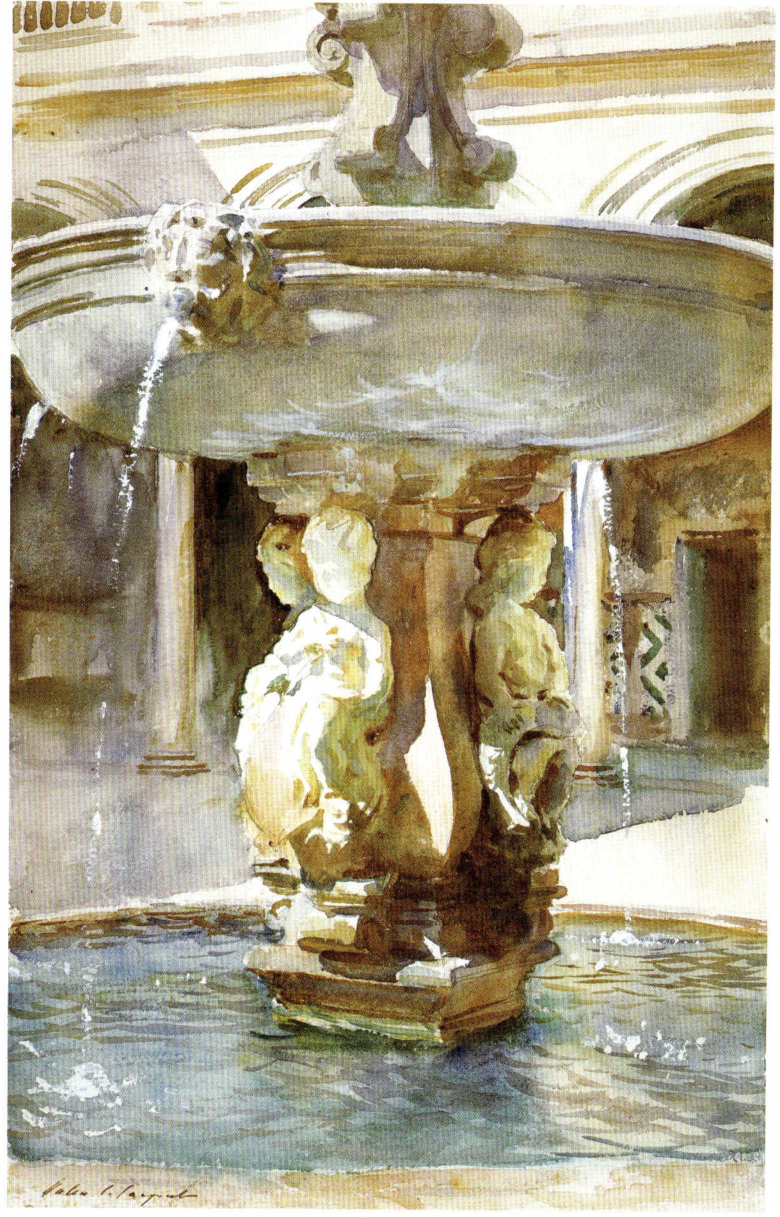

Spanish Fountain 1912
Watercolor on paper
21 1/16 x 13 in. (53.5 x 33 cm.)
Fitzwilliam Museum, University of Cambridge
Photograph © Fitzwilliam Museum, University of Cambridge

The artist died in his sleep at his home in London in April 1925, on the eve of returning to America to install his panels in the Widener Library at Harvard. "The bedside lamp was on," biographer Olson recounts,

> Voltaire's *Dictionnaire philosophique* lay open beside him on the bed, his spectacles pushed from his eyes. He had fallen asleep reading, and suffered a heart-attack in his sleep, a graceful, undramatic departure from life. He was sixty-nine years old, the same age as his father.[62]

Tributes to Sargent's genius were printed on both sides of the Atlantic. One of the finest was written by A.J. Philpott of the *Boston Globe*. "[Sargent] was not of the schools," he wrote. "He was eclectic, bigger than any school. He moved in a sphere apart. He was a law unto himself in art. Sargent is gone, but he will always rank with the immortals in art."[63]

We have come a long way in recognizing Sargent's achievements in watercolor. When one considers that an early monograph on his work, published in 1924 as part of the "Distinguished American Artists" series, reproduced only oils and made not a single mention of watercolor in the text,[64] one realizes the mindset certain historians have had toward the medium. Portraits in oil received the most commentary and were widely reproduced, with a few genre and landscape subjects mentioned in passing.

Other limners of art history categorized Sargent's watercolors as mere studies or, worse, as "holiday" or "off duty" work, not to be taken too seriously. True, the artist utilized this flexible and portable medium to render sketches of sitters and to record his seasonal travels. Yet in the course of Sargent's later life, after 1900, watercolor became central to his artistic vision.

Not everyone accepted the oil-over-watercolor-hierarchy. Indeed, certain commentators went so far as to claim supremacy for the latter in the body of Sargent's overall work. "It is suggestive to note, by the way, that...he [Sargent] is, indeed, more felicitous in his handling of this medium than in his oil paintings," wrote critic Royal Cortissoz, reviewing an exhibition of watercolors at Knoedler in New York in 1909.[65] It could be argued that Sargent's oils owe the freshness and spontaneity of their execution to his formative studies in watercolor.

Sargent is sometimes faulted for his facility with watercolor, but such a criticism fails to take into account his lifelong experience with the medium and his ongoing experimentation with technique. He was, if you will, reared a watercolorist, and his ability to tame the difficult medium, displaying marvelous control even as he let the paints wing across the paper, cannot but elicit admiration—and adulation: artists of his day, and later generations, modeled their approach on his, sometimes rather shamelessly.[66]

A number of commentators, as well as Sargent himself, have written about the documentary nature of the artist's watercolors. He was

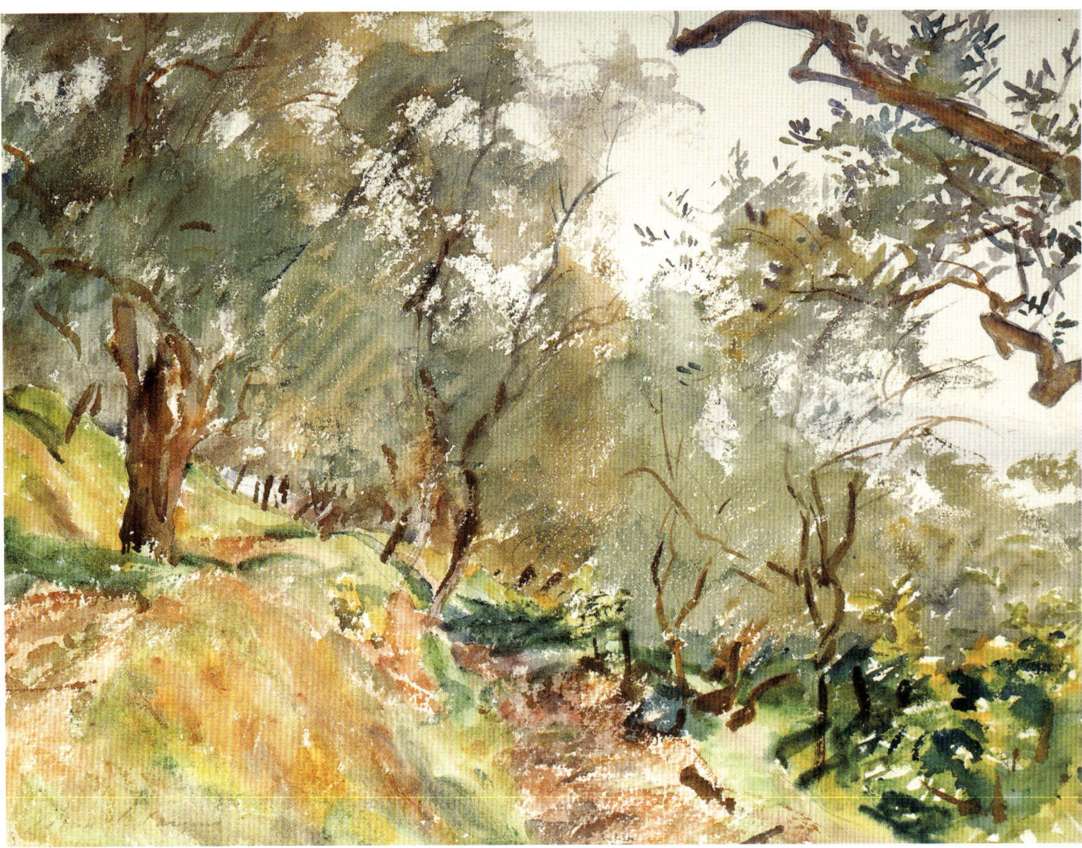

Trees on a Hillside, Majorca 1908
Watercolor on paper
22 x 26 in. (55.9 x 66 cm.)
Collection of the Canajoharie Library and Art Gallery

virtually a tourist all his life, and his watercolors served as souvenirs of his travels. He gave many away as presents to friends and family. While he was known to paint the occasional postcard view—the Alhambra, the Sphinx, the Grand Canal—more often Sargent sought out less traveled routes, side streets, out-of-the-way alpine valleys.

While photography probably did not play much of a role in his watercolor work, Sargent was known to use a camera to record a scene. At times, the relationship between an extant photograph and a finished canvas is unmistakable. His aquarelles sometimes seemed to be produced with the swiftness of a camera shutter. As Richard Ormond describes the process, "Most of his watercolours were painted in a single session, in one continuous process, with the usual accompaniment of sighs, grunts, and windy sizzling sounds from between his lips."[67]

In discussing Sargent's daily routine, historian Martin Hardie compared him to Constable. "[Sargent] was a 10 to 4 painter; and like the work of Constable, his water-colours seemed at times to his contemporaries too startling and forceful, too 'top o' the morning' in their assertive satisfaction with life, almost brutal in their domineering strength." [68]

Hardie took exception with Evan Charteris, who claimed that Sargent did not habitually turn to "the opaque method" when working in watercolor. "It would be more true to say that Sargent nearly always used an opaque method," the former wrote.[69] Subsequent analyses of the watercolors have borne out the truth of this statement.[70]

Sargent limited his painting equipment to a folding tin box of colours. He was satisfied with this simple arrangement: "I find 'box colour' very useful and I use a great many different brushes, keeping my fist full when I work."[71] It is a distinct tribute to the painter that he could create such a rich and varied palette, with certain favorite hues such as blues and browns predominating, from a modest selection of colors.

The artist was known to use pencil to draw in light outlines of the objects in his watercolors. Blank sections of the paper were utilized to great effect, but he also employed friskets—stencils—and resist, a masking substance, to block out sections of his compositions. His Florida watercolors testify to his arsenal, which included "variations in wet-and-dry washing, the combination of opaque and transparent paints, calculated reserving of the existing color or the blank paper from later washes, and adulteration of the paint by additives, as well as all the subtractive methods used by Homer."[72]

Commentators have expressed awe at Sargent's feats in watercolor. Adrian Stokes, who spent two summers painting with Sargent, used a musical analogy—quite fitting as the artist was a highly skilled pianist and connoisseur of music:

> The rapidity and directness with which he worked was amazing. . . . His hand seemed to move with the same agility as when playing the keys of a piano. That is a minor matter; what was really marvelous was the rightness of every touch. . . .[73]

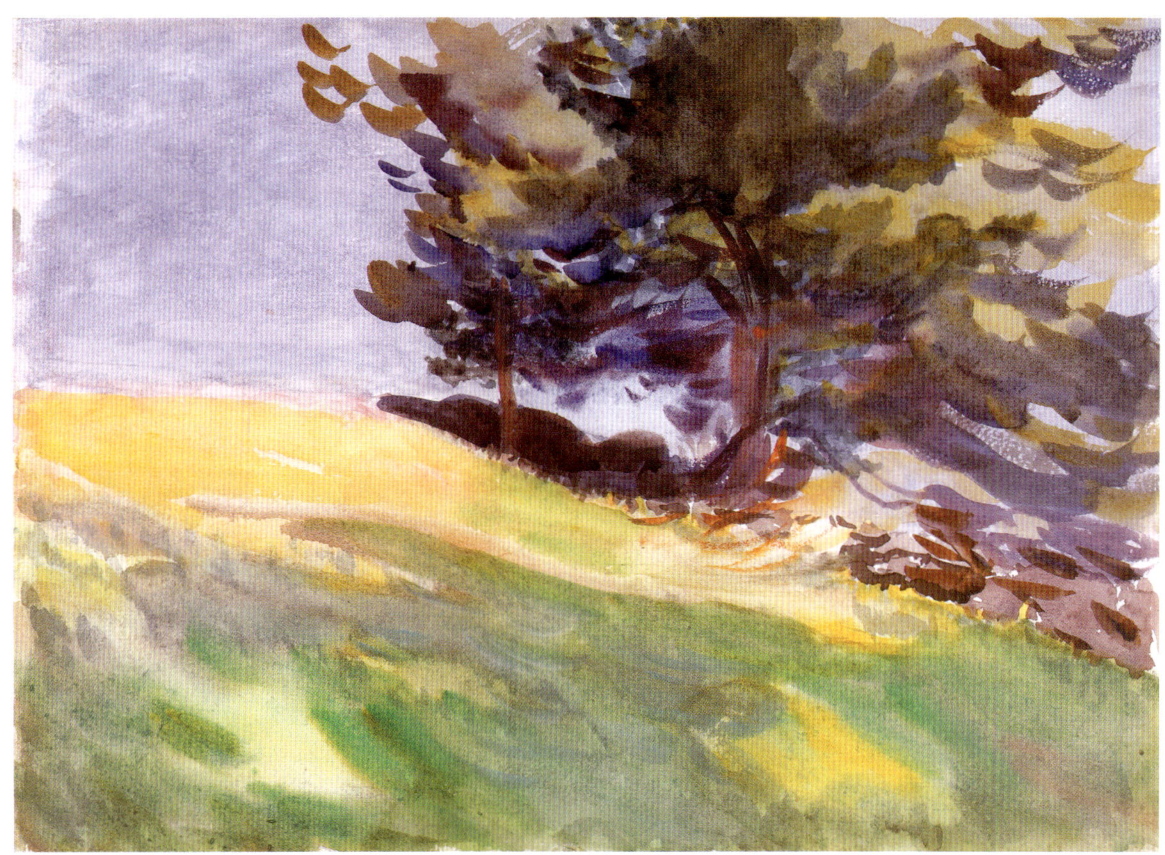

Near June Street 1890
Watercolor on paper
9 3/4 x 13 1/4 in. (24.7 x 33.6 cm.)
Mead Art Museum,
Amherst College
Amherst, Massachusetts
Museum Purchase 1947.113

The artist himself tended to underplay his work in this medium. Charteris describes Sargent's "utmost reluctance…for the purpose of sale, to pull out any one of the water-colours which used to lie in their frames, jammed one against the other, in a large rack on the floor of his studio." He would also make lighthearted fun of the paintings, at times giving them humorous titles.[74]

Yet Sargent came to recognize the value of these works, especially in light of a string of substantial museum purchases in America. The Brooklyn Museum, the Metropolitan Museum of Art, the Worcester Museum of Art and the Museum of Fine Arts in Boston acquired watercolors en bloc after 1900, when the artist was at the height of his powers. He also exhibited them on a regular basis at the Royal Water-Colour Society, the Boston Society of Water Color Painters and other venues, as well as in commercial galleries.

Recent studies of Sargent's oeuvre have devoted increased attention to his watercolor work. His experiments in watercolor technique have been analyzed and praised by scholars and historians of the medium, his fearlessness, both in his methods and his ability to master any subject, recognized.

More than simply an element of the artist's overall genius, watercolor represented liberation from the numbing labors of portraits and commissions.[75] Sargent's bold manner with the medium led Fairfield Porter to relate his work to contemporary abstraction. "A passage of drapery in a Sargent portrait or a scratched background in a Sargent watercolor," he observed, "relates to certain American abstract painting more closely than do Cézanne, Picasso or even Monet."[76]

Sargent's brash approach continues to find an admiring audience among today's painters (Eric Fischl being a prime example). While he appeared immune from the movements that swept the art world at the turn of the century,[77] he couldn't help but experience the excitement of the new. It is through his watercolors that Sargent warrants the label "modernist" and, at times, revolutionary.

Notes

1. Sargent was once described as "an American born in Italy, educated in France, who looks like a German, speaks like an Englishman, and paints like a Spaniard." Cited in Wendy Watson, *Altered States: Conservation, Analysis, and Interpretation of Works of Art* (South Hadley, MA; Trustees of Mount Holyoke College, 1994).

2. Evan Charteris, *John Sargent* (New York: Charles Scribner's Sons, 1927), p. 10.

3. Stanley Olson, *John Singer Sargent: His Portrait* (New York: St. Martin's Press, 1986), p. 18.

4. Ibid., p. 18.

5. Charteris, p. 13.

6. Ibid., p. 46. Charteris also notes that the artist "appeared to escape the fatigues of more normal humanity; at the end of a long day's work his mind would be serene and cool, his temperament buoyant; he would show no sign of fag in brain or limb." (p. 227).

7. Ibid., p. 18.

8. Ibid., p. 28.

9. Olson, p. 33. "It was said that as a student he could make one brush stroke count for five and cover a canvas with paint before the other students were well started." "Art in America" *in Modern Times* (New York: Museum of Modern Art, 1934), p. 24.

10. Olson, p. 46.

11. Bonnat has been described as "a great admirer of Ribera and the Spanish tenebrists." David Sellin, *American Art in the Making* (Washington: Smithsonian Institution Press, 1976), p. 66.

12. Charteris, p. 50.

13. "It is difficult to discover [*Incensing the Veil*'s] exact status in relation to the canvas, *Fumée d'Ambre Gris*, which [Sargent] exhibited at the Salon of 1880….The composition is virtually identical. There is nothing sketchy about the water-colour, though there is, naturally, more detail in the large canvas." Philip Hendy, *European and American Paintings in the Isabella Stewart Gardner Collection* (Boston: Trusties of the the Isabella Stewart Gardner Museum, 1974), p. 227.

14. "According to the American painter Walter Gay, who lived mostly in Paris, the model for the dancer [in *El Jaleo*] was Marie Renard, a professional who posed for him and many well known artists, and another American painter, Kenyon Cox, lent his hands for those of the guitarist." Ibid., p. 221.

15. Olson, p. 106.

16. "The outdoor study was intended to record the experience of a specific and contingent moment rather than the precise details of a determined form." Brochure for *In the Light of Italy: Corot and Early Open-Air Painting*, essays by Philip Conisbee, Sarah Faunce, Peter Galassi, Vincent Pomarded and Jeremy Strick (Washington: National Gallery of Art, 1997).

17. Charteris, p. 77.

18. Olson, p. 149. Sargent first met Monet at the second Impressionist exhibition at Durand-Ruel in Paris in 1876. "*'Est-ce vraiment vous, vous, Claude Monet?'*" he timorously enquired…." ("Is it really you, you, Claude Monet?"). Olson, p. 150.

19. Fairfield Porter, *Art In Its Own Terms* (New York: Taplinger, 1979), p. 203.

20. Olson, p. 94.

21. Richard Ormond, *John Singer Sargent: Paintings, Drawings, Watercolors* (New York: Harper & Row, 1970), p. 70.

22. See, for example, G. A. Henty's *The Lion of St. Mark: A Tale of Venice*, 1889.

23. Ormond notes that the artist "almost never altered a scene or building, or its proportions, to suit his composition, scrupulously adhering to observed fact." Ormond, p. 75.

24. Henry James, "John S. Sargent," *Harper's New Monthly Magazine*, 75 (October 1887): 689.

25. In this regard, Sargent brings to mind Edward Hopper, who also inventoried his surroundings. He told Alfred Barr, director of the Museum of Modern Art, that he didn't want to include watercolors in his 1933 retrospective because "they're too much like Sargent's." Alfred Barr, *Edward Hopper Retrospective Exhibition* (New York: The Museum of Modern Art, 1933), p. 13.

26. Linda S. Ferber and Barbara Dayer Gallati, *Masters of Color and Light: Homer, Sargent, and the American Watercolor Movement* (Washington: The Brooklyn Museum of Art in association with Smithsonian Institution Press, 1998), p. 123.

27. Olson, p. 8.

28. Charteris, p. 171.

29. Ibid.

30. Sargent considered Tiepolo "the first of decorative artists." Charteris, p. 53.

31. Ibid., pp. 254-255.

32. Susan E. Strickler, ed., *American Traditions in Watercolor: The Worcester Art Museum Collection.* (New York: Abbeville Press/Worcester Art Museum, 1987) p. 136.

33. Olson, p. 239. "Sargent usually set off early in the morning, climbing up precipitous paths in search of the right location, while his Italian valet, Nicola, carried his equipment. Once he had chosen a suitable spot, he sat down on a stool to paint, surrounded by a series of protective umbrellas, which made him look 'like a newly hatched chicken surrounded by broken egg shells.'" Ormond, p. 68.

34. Charteris, p. 188.

35. "Sargent did not paint his landscapes as illustrated diaries. He wrote to Henry Tonks in 1920: 'As you know enormous views and huge skies do not tempt me.'" Ormond, p. 69.

36. Ibid., p. 119.

37. As Stokes recounted: "He [Sargent] did not confine himself that summer [of 1909] to landscape. Now and then groups of his friends posed for him with gaily coloured shawls and sunshades so arranged as to make, with rocks and distant mountains, telling colour schemes. These were painted sometimes in oil, sometimes in water-colour, always with astonishing vitality…." Warren Adelson et al., *Sargent Abroad: Figures and Landscapes* (New York: Abbeville Press, 1997), p. 72.

38. Cited in Max Knight, *Return to the Alps* (New York: Friends of the Earth, 1970), p. 39.

39. "….He was undoubtedly prosperous—perhaps the most prosperous painter of our time, or of any time, in Great Britain. Abundance hampers talent more often than does privation, but, as a man, Sargent remained simple and unspoiled; and the water-colours made during the years of his greatest success as a fashionable painter of portraits show that material prosperity never dulled the spiritual edge of his soul." Martin Hardie, *Famous Water-Colour Painters, VII—J.S. Sargent, R.A., R.W.S.* (London: The Studio Ltd., 1930), p. 1.

40. Olson, p. 210.

41. "Sargent had been brought up in the school of the *portrait d'apparat*, and portraits were best for him when they reflected the natural attitudes and surroundings of the person." Donelson F. Hoopes, *American Watercolor Painting* (New York: Watson-Guptill, 1977), p. 46. Sargent's disdain for portraiture would grow over the years; his attitude might be best summed up in these sentiments from a letter to Ralph Curtis: "No more paughtraits whether refreshed or not. I abhor and abjure them and hope never to do another especially of the Upper Classes." Charteris, p. 155. He was also known to have said, "A portrait is a picture in which there is just a tiny little something not quite right about the mouth." Charteris, p. 157.

42. It was Reubell who introduced Sargent to Henry James. Olson. p. 106.

43. Charteris, p. 183.

44. "….For days on end he lived in a shed among the Carrara Mountains, travelling to his work in a basket slung on ropes across a wide ravine, and

subsisting on the food of the workers." Charteris, p. 46. "Sargent was not interested...in making a social comment," notes Annette Blaugrand, "but in using them [the Carrara laborers] as vehicles for other visual interests, such as the plasticity and decorative arrangement of the rope they carry." Patricia Hills et al., *John Singer Sargent* (New York: Whitney Museum of American Art, 1986), p. 231.

45. "Sargent's most interesting studies [from his trip to the Middle East] were of a tribe of Bedouins, with whom he appears to have lived and travelled for a time." Ormond, p. 70.

46. Olson, p. 247. It was the elder Whistler who had expressed enthusiasm over the young artist's watercolors and drawings. Charteris, p. 21.

47. William Howe Downes, *John S. Sargent, His Life and Work* (Boston: Little, Brown, 1925), p. 26.

48. Harvard design professor Denman Ross had sent Sargent a postal card of the Twin Falls, suggesting that it might make a fine subject for a painting. See Bruce Hugh Russell, "John Singer Sargent in the Canadian Rockies: 1916," *The Beaver* (December 1997-January 1998): 4-11.

49. Charteris, p. 204.

50. Downes, p. 71.

51. Olson, p. 254.

52. Charteris, p. 207.

53. Ibid., p. 211. Olson provides this amusing vignette from the artist's wartime experiences: "Once a guardsman levelled his rifle at Sargent, who was busy sketching, and asked who he was; Sargent looked up from his work and calmly gave his name. 'The hell you are! I know the sergeant. Come along.'" Olson, p. 258.

54. Sargent's war pictures seem tame compared to, say, the series painted by George Bellows.

55. Olson, pp. 260-261.

56. British artist Paul Nash painted a similar work, *Bombers in the Corn* (Tate Gallery, London).

57. W. H. Auden, *Collected Shorter Poems, 1930–1944* (London, n.d.), p. 19.

58. "A color range of sullen beauty" is how art historian Donelson Hoopes describes Sargent's palette in this painting. *American Watercolor Painting* (New York: Watson-Guptill, 1977), p. 67.

59. Blaney's biographical entry in the catalogue for the exhibition "The Bostonians" at the Museum of Fine Arts in Boston, 1986, begins, "Gentleman painter of landscapes and seascapes in oil and watercolor."

60. James Carpenter, Lloyd Goodrich, et. al., *Maine and its Role in American Art* (New York: The Viking Press, 1963), p. 116.

61. David McKibbin, *Sargent's Boston* (Boston: Museum of Fine Arts, 1956), p. 63.

62. Olson, pp. 268-269.

63. Downes, p. 108. Richard Ormond concurs: "He remained...an independent figure, without a programme or a following. He made no attempt to found a school, or to collect disciples around him in the manner of Whistler." Ormond, p. 53.

64. *John Singer Sargent*, compiled by Nathaniel Pousette-Dart, introduction by Lee Woodward Zeigler (New York: Frederick A. Stokes Company, 1924), p. viii. "The sixty-four paintings herein reproduced illustrate the varied characteristics of this artist's work"—not if there are no watercolors.

65. Ferber and Gallati, p. 129. "The view is even entertained that they [his watercolors] will do more than his oil paintings to maintain the level of his fame." Charteris, p. 223.

66. "Dodge Macknight built his career as a watercolor painter essentially on Sargent's example, adding his own sometimes daring use of rather strident color to otherwise routine landscape compositions." Susan E. Strickler, p. 35. "Emulation of the artist," notes Annette Blaugrand, "has served both to perpetuate Sargent's watercolor style and to debase it with inferior interpretations." Hills et al., p. 249.

67. Ormond, p. 70.

68. Another example of his sunlight temperament was recounted by Henry Tonks who accompanied Sargent during his stint as a war artist: "I never could persuade him to work in the evening when the ruined town [of Arras] looked so enchanting; he worked systematically morning and afternoon." Charteris, p. 211.

69. Hardie, p. 3.

70. See in particular Susan E. Strickler , pp. 57-64.

71. Ibid., p. 60.

72. Ibid., p. 57. Annette Blaugrund provides a similar inventory of Sargent's methods in discussing his Carrara watercolors: "These works are a compendium of watercolor methods, demonstrating such reductive techniques as scraping, wiping out, and waxing, used in combination with gouache and transparent layering to achieve the glistening effects of sunlight on stone." Hills et al., p. 231.

73. Critic Royal Cortissoz once called Sargent "a Paganini of the brush," a reference to the virtuoso Italian violinist. Sue Welsh Reed and Carol Troyen, *Awash in Color: Homer, Sargent, and the Great American Watercolor* (Boston: Museum of Fine Arts, 1993), p. L.

74. "On another occasion in the Simplon when he had done a water-colour of recumbent figures, with his easel fixed in a depression of the ground, he called the result 'A Worm's Eye View.'" Charteris, p. 178.

75. "Watercolor released Sargent from the constraints of 'correct' pictorial formulas that he observed in his commissioned works." Strickler et al., p. 34. Hoopes puts it more forcefully: "The watercolors are free of the taint of servitude to the demands of international society, and possess a powerful technique which cannot be faulted for superficiality...." Hoopes, p. 20.

76. Fairfield Porter, p. 204. "Sargent's sophistication, as well as audacious compositions, lack of finish, and anti-purist approach to technique that characterized his watercolors, were compatible with the international interests and the vogue for...abstraction in progressive American art circles." Reed and Troyen, *Awash in Color*, p. L.

77. Sargent was openly disdainful of certain schools, including the Post-Impressionists. "The fact is that I am absolutely skeptical as to their having any claim whatever to being works of art, with the exception of some of the pictures by Gauguin that strike me as admirable in color, and in color only." Charteris, p. 192.

Selected Bibliography

Adelson, Warren. *Americans in Venice, 1879–1913.* New York: Coe Kerr Gallery, 1983

——. *John Singer Sargent, His Own Work.* New York: Coe Kerr Gallery, 1980

Adelson, Warren, et al. *Sargent Abroad: Figures and Landscapes.* New York: Abbeville Press, 1997

Charteris, Evan. *John Sargent.* New York: Charles Scribner's Sons, 1927.

Downes, William Howe. *John S. Sargent, His Life and Work.* Boston: Little, Brown and Company, 1925.

Fairbrother, Trevor J. *John Singer Sargent.* New York: Harry N. Abrams, Inc., Publishers, in association with The National Museum of American Art, Smithsonian Institution Press, 1994.

Ferber, Linda S. and Barbara Dayer Gallati. *Masters of Color and Light: Homer, Sargent, and the American Watercolor Movement.* Washington: The Brooklyn Museum of Art in association with Smithsonian Institution Press, 1998.

Hardie, Martin. *Famous Water-Colour Painters, VII—J.S. Sargent, R.A., R.W.S.* London: The Studio Ltd., 1930.

Hendy, Philip. *European and American Paintings in the Isabella Stewart Gardner Museum.* Boston: Trustees of the Isabella Stewart Gardner Museum, 1974.

Hills, Patricia, et al. *John Singer Sargent.* New York: Whitney Museum of American Art, 1986.

Hoopes, Donelson F. *American Watercolor Painting.* New York: Watson-Guptill, 1977.

——. *Sargent Watercolors.* New York: Watson-Guptill, 1970.

Kilmurray, Elaine, and Richard Ormond. *John Singer Sargent.* Princeton University Press, 1998.

McKibbin, David. *Sargent's Boston.* Boston: Museum of Fine Arts, 1956.

Mount, Charles Merrill. *John Singer Sargent, A Biography.* New York: W.W. Norton, 1955.

Olson, Stanley. *John Singer Sargent: His Portrait.* New York: St. Martin's Press, 1986

Olson, Stanley, et al. *Sargent at Broadway: The Impressionist Years.* New York: Universe/Coe Kerr Gallery, 1986.

Ormond, Richard. *John Singer Sargent. Paintings, Drawings, Watercolors.* New York: Harper & Row, 1970.

Ratcliff, Carter. *John Singer Sargent.* New York: Abbeville Press, 1982.

Reed, Sue Welsh, and Carol Troyen. *Awash in Color: Homer, Sargent, and the Great American Watercolor.* Boston: Museum of Fine Arts in association with Bulfinch Press, Little Brown and Company, 1993.

Strickler, Susan E., ed. *American Traditions in Watercolor: The Worcester Art Museum Collection.* New York: Abbeville Press/Worcester Art Museum, 1987

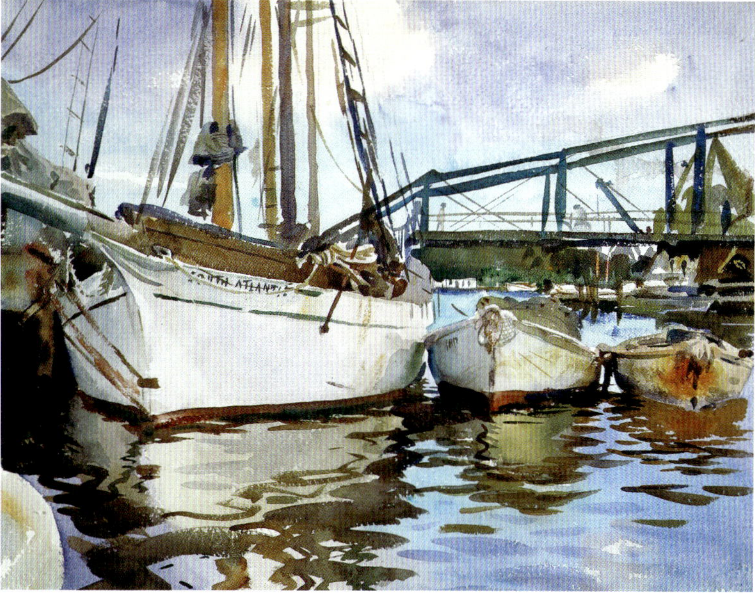

Boats at Anchor 1917

Watercolor over graphite on off-white wove paper

15 3/4 x 20 7/8 in. (40.1 x 52.9 cm.)

Worcester Art Museum, Worcester, Massachusetts

Sustaining Membership Fund, 1917.90

Studies and Portraits

In the late 1870s, when Sargent was establishing himself as a painter in Paris, watercolor played an important role in the preliminary stages of a number of his oil paintings. He employed the medium as a means to an end, turning out swift yet careful studies of the figures that would eventually appear in the finished canvases. Besides their obvious aesthetic appeal, these watercolors provide an important record of the artist's process, especially in portraiture, his forte.

Later, Sargent would utilize watercolor to render portraits of his family and friends. He rarely lost sight of the likeness; the figures in even his most informal pieces can be identified. It is often the casual setting—an alpine meadow, a room in a mountain hostelry—that lends these works their special appeal. More straightforward portrayals, such as that of the elderly Mrs. Gardner, are marked by an unerring eye for features and clothing—and a profound feeling for the subject.

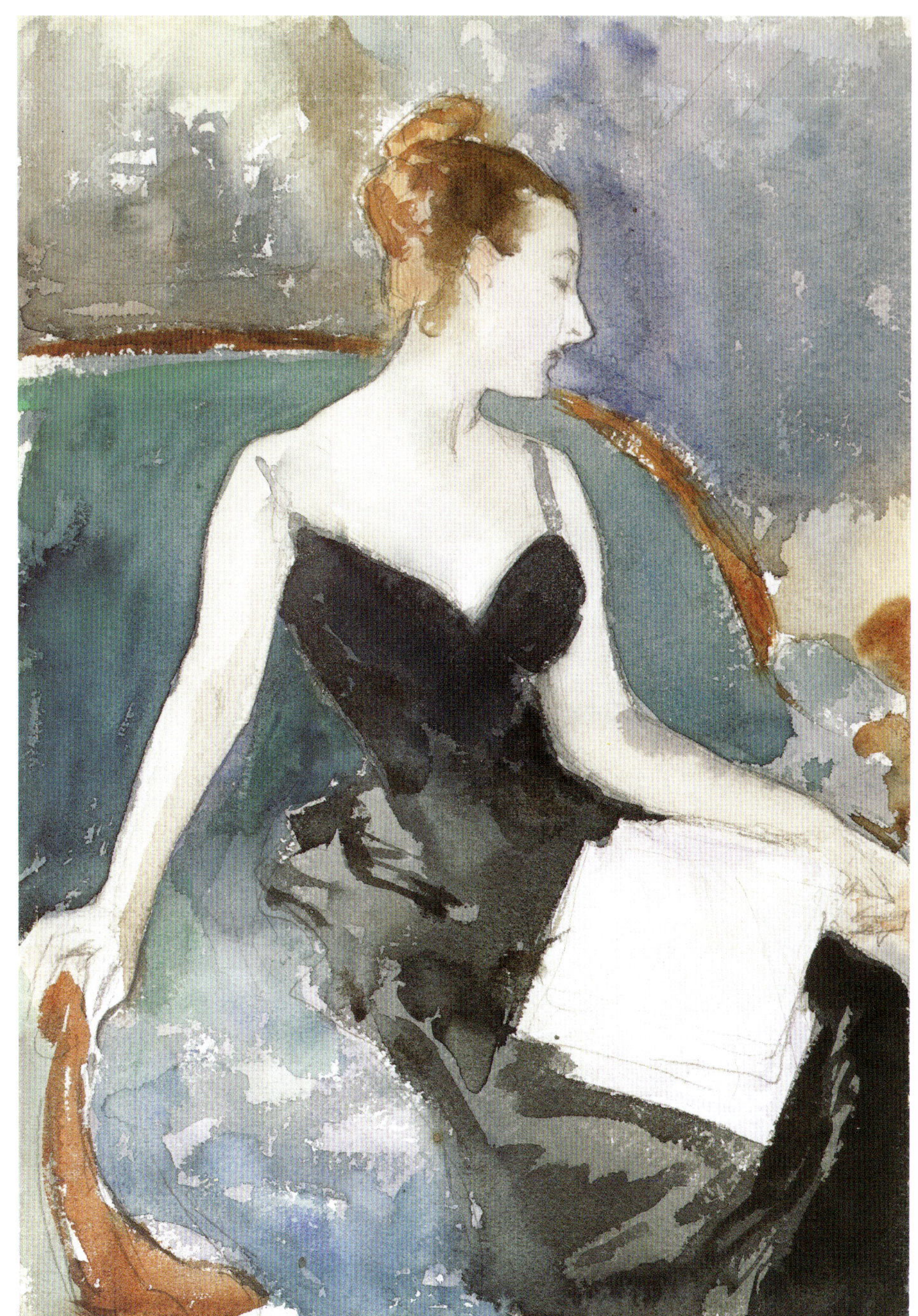

Portrait of Madame Gautreau c. 1883
Watercolor and graphite on white paper
14 x 9 15/16 in. (35.5 x 25.2 cm.)
Courtesy of the Fogg Art Museum,
Harvard University Art Museums,
Bequest of Grenville L. Winthrop
© President and Fellows of Harvard College,
Harvard University

Study for the Spanish Dancer 1882
Watercolor on paper
11 13/16 x 7 7/8 in. (30 x 20 cm.)
Dallas Museum of Art,
Foundation for the Arts Collection,
Gift of Margaret J. & George V. Chariton,
in Memory of Eugene McDermott

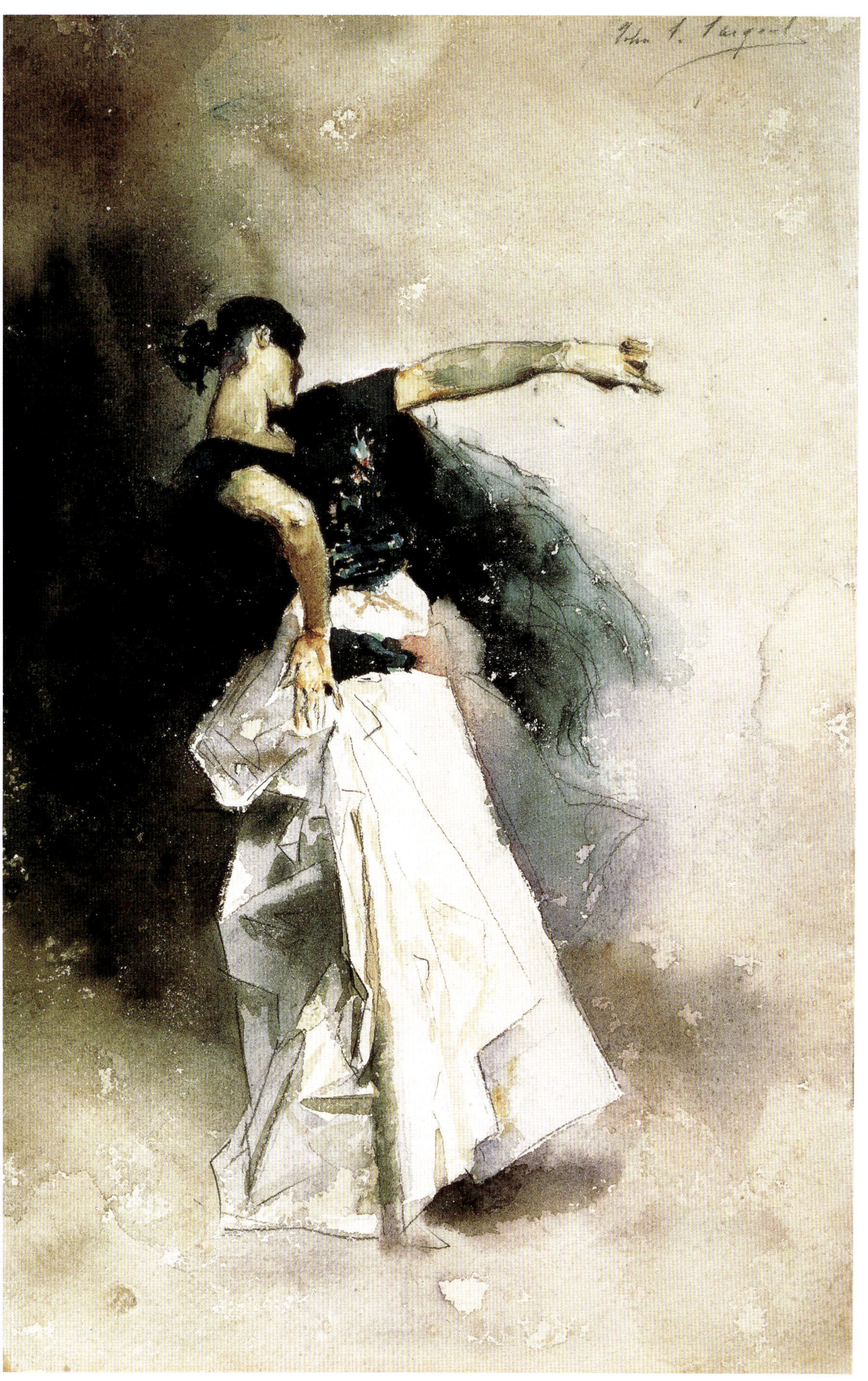

He painted, if such an expression may be allowed in this connection, straight from the shoulder. Both in his water-colours and oils he transposes beauty of fact into a key of his own, direct, emphatic and suggestive, often satisfying in design, and rich in colour and decorative value.

—Evan Charteris, 1927

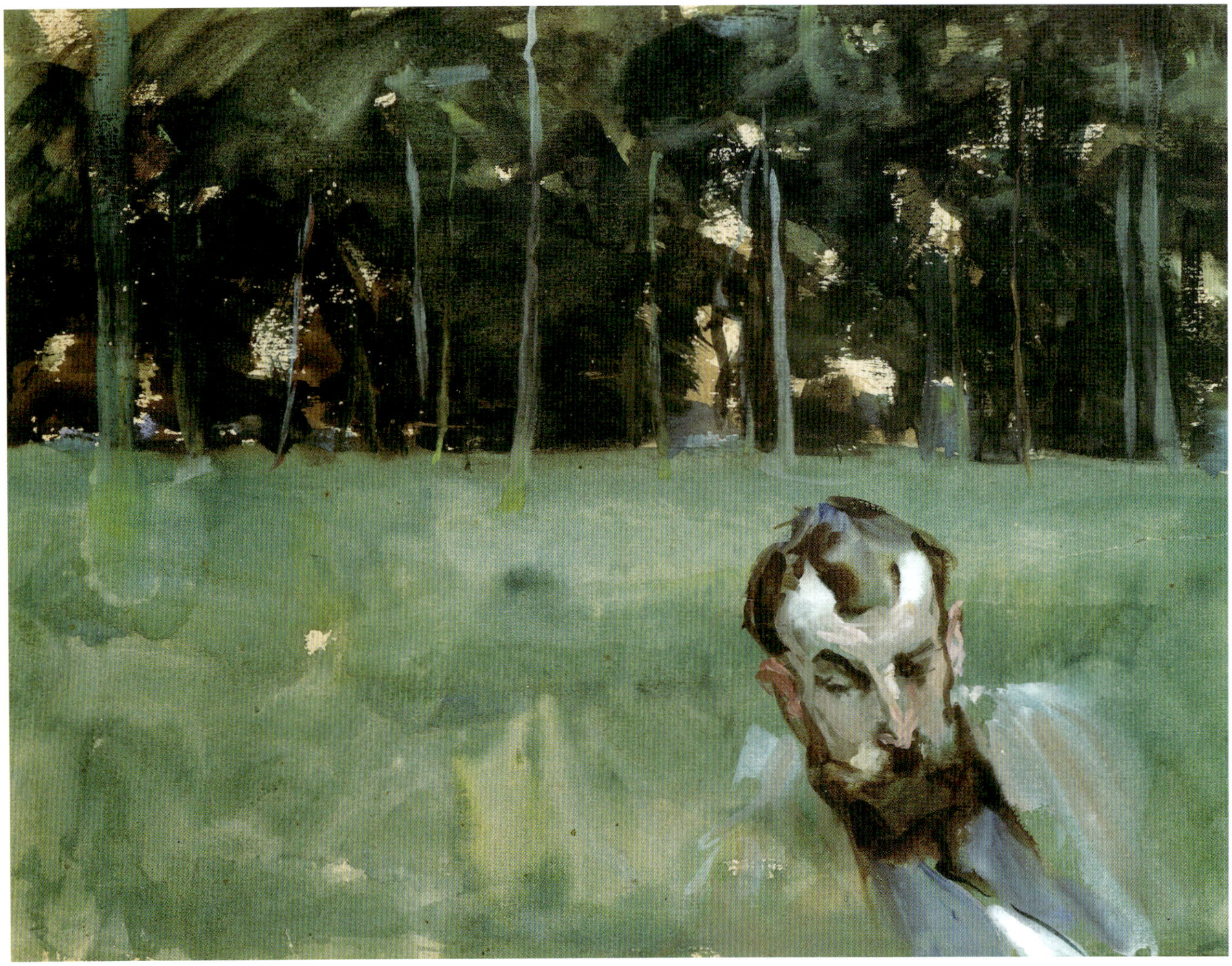

George Hitchcock c. 1880
Watercolor on paper
8 7/8 x 11 3/8 in. (22.5 x 28.9 cm.)
Private collection, New York
Courtesy Richard L. Feigen & Co., New York

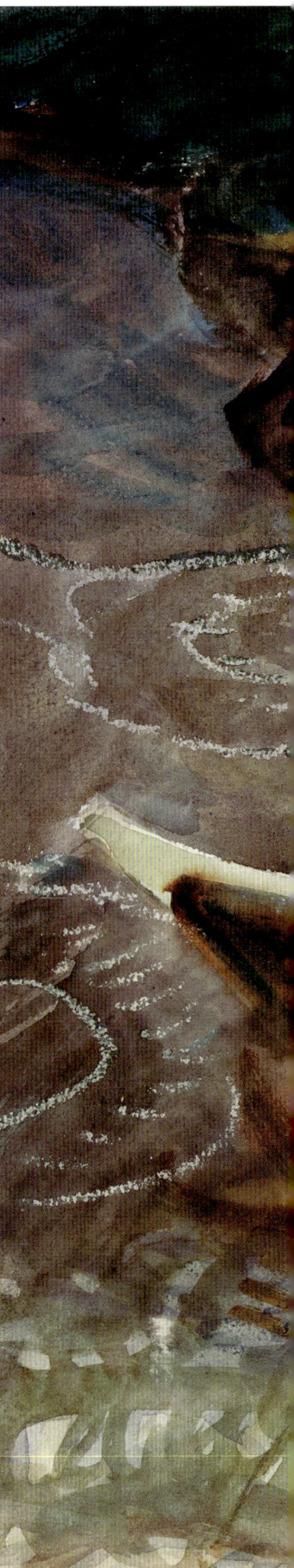

In the Generalife 1912
Watercolor, wax, and graphite on white wove paper
14 7/8 x 18 in. (37.8 x 45.7 cm.)
The Metropolitan Museum of Art,
Purchase, Joseph Pulitzer Bequest, 1915 (15.142.8)
Photograph © 1982 The Metropolitan Museum of Art

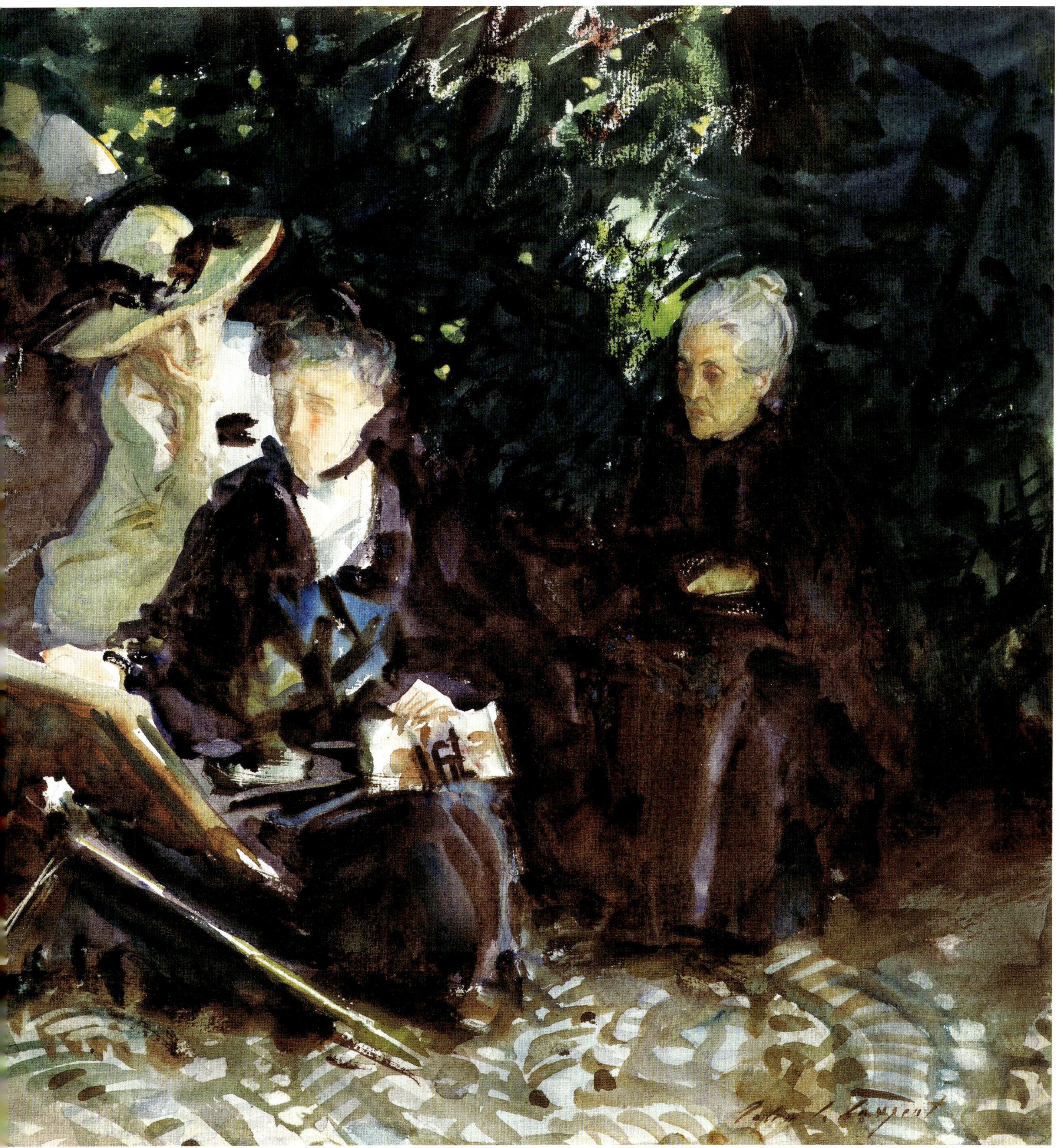

A Tramp c. 1900–08
Watercolor
20 x 14 in. (50.7 x 35.6 cm.)
The Brooklyn Museum of Art,
Purchased by special subscription,
(09.810)

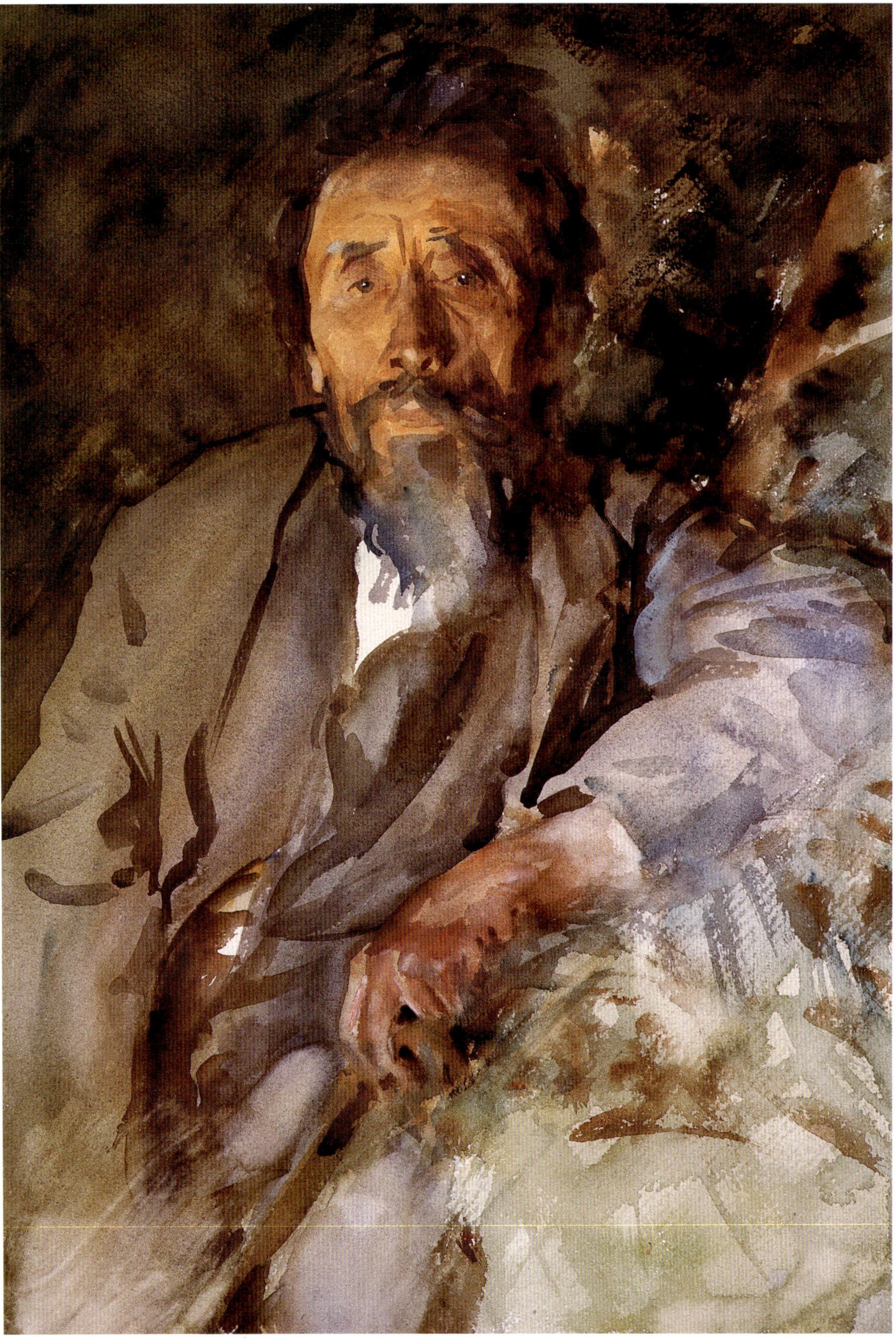

(opposite)

In a Hayloft c. 1904–07
Watercolor
16 x 12 in. (40.6 x 30.5 cm.)
The Brooklyn Museum of Art,
Purchased by special subscription,
(09.824)

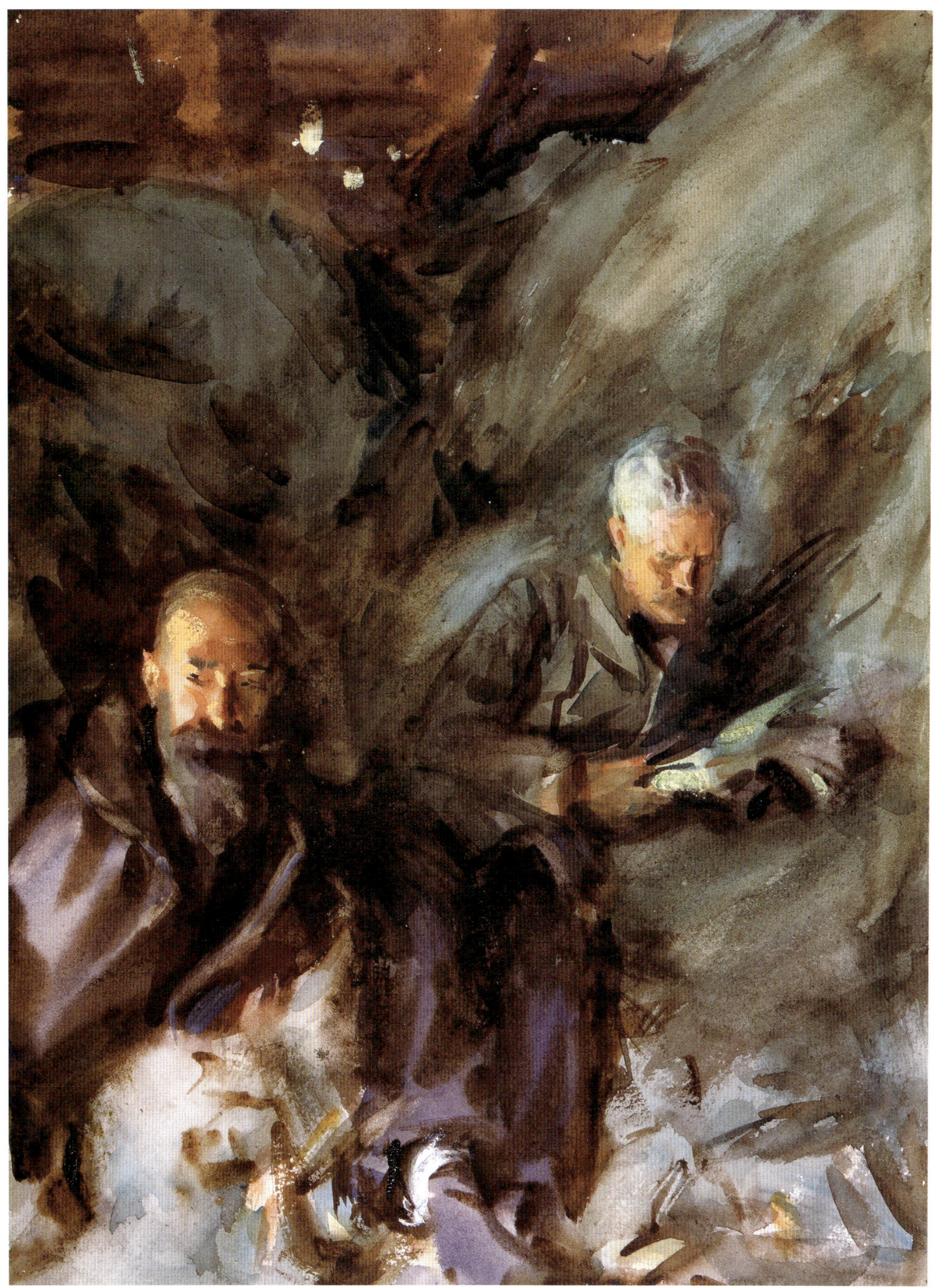

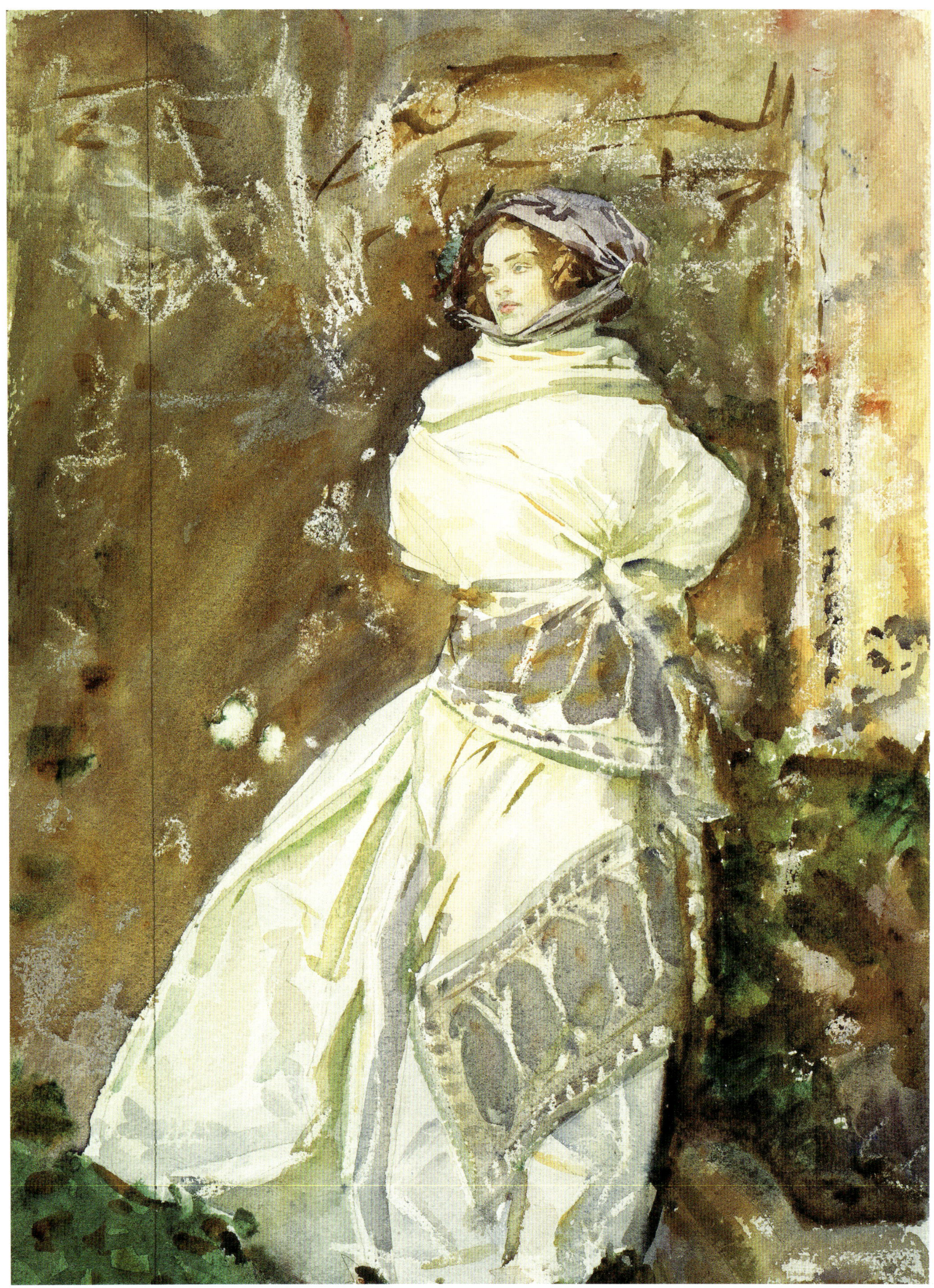

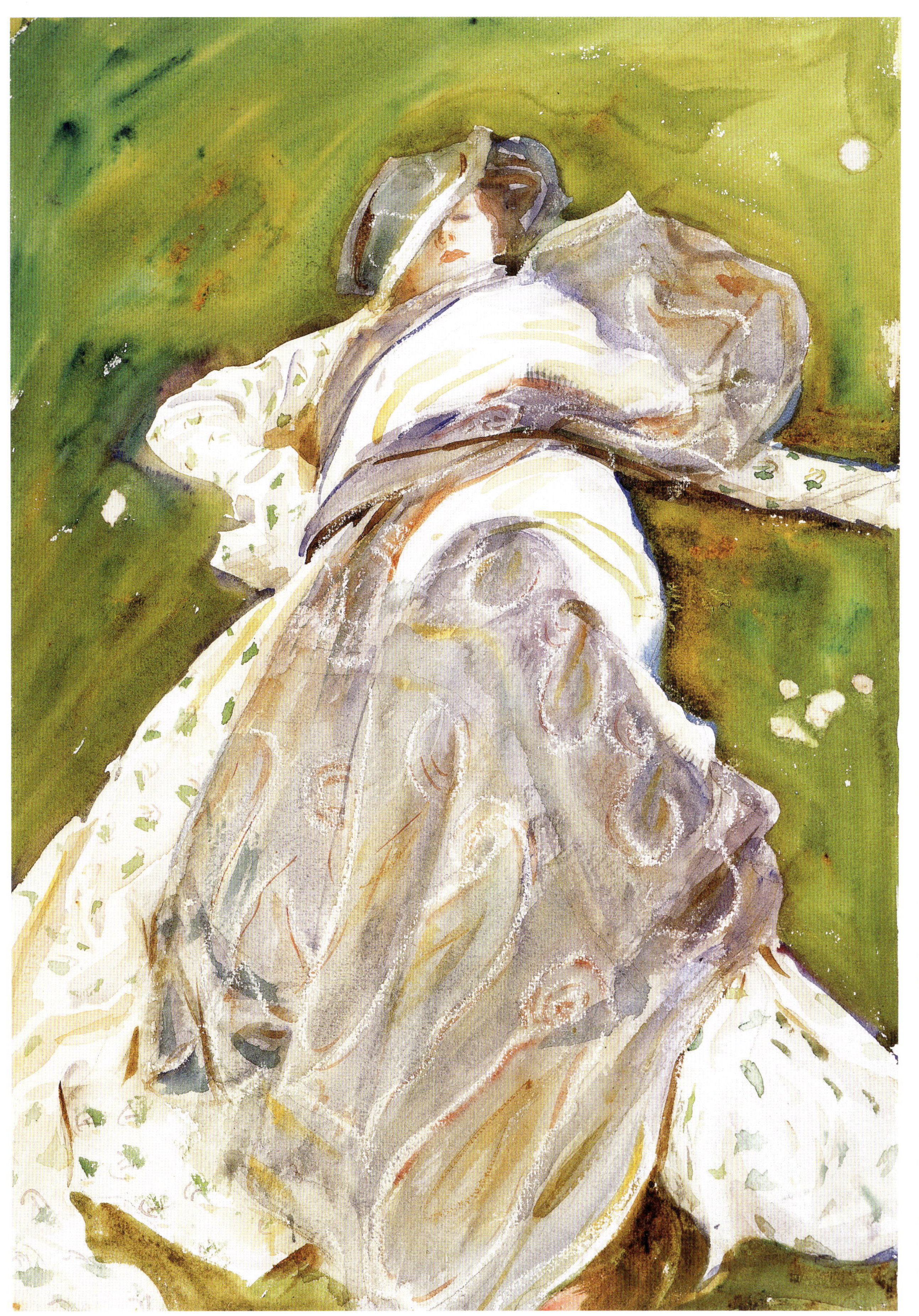

(opposite)

The Cashmere Shawl 1911
Watercolor
19 3/4 x 11 3/4 in.
(50.2 x 29.8 cm.)
Charles Henry Hayden Fund,
Courtesy, Museum of Fine Arts,
Boston

Woman Reclining c. 1908
Watercolor on paper
20 1/16 x 14 1/16 in.
(51 x 35.7 cm.)
Cincinnati Art Museum,
Bequest of Mary Hanna,
1956.101

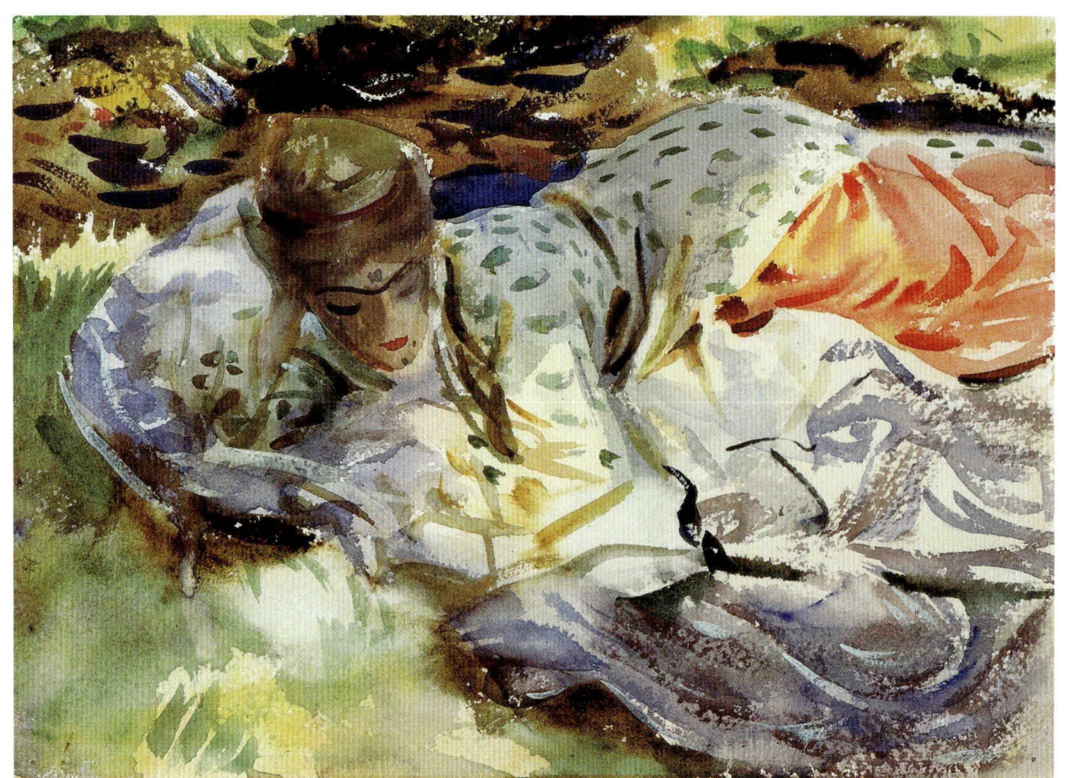

Zuleika c. 1908
Watercolor
10 x 14 in. (25.4 x 35.5 cm.)
The Brooklyn Museum of Art,
Purchased by special
subscription, (09.847)

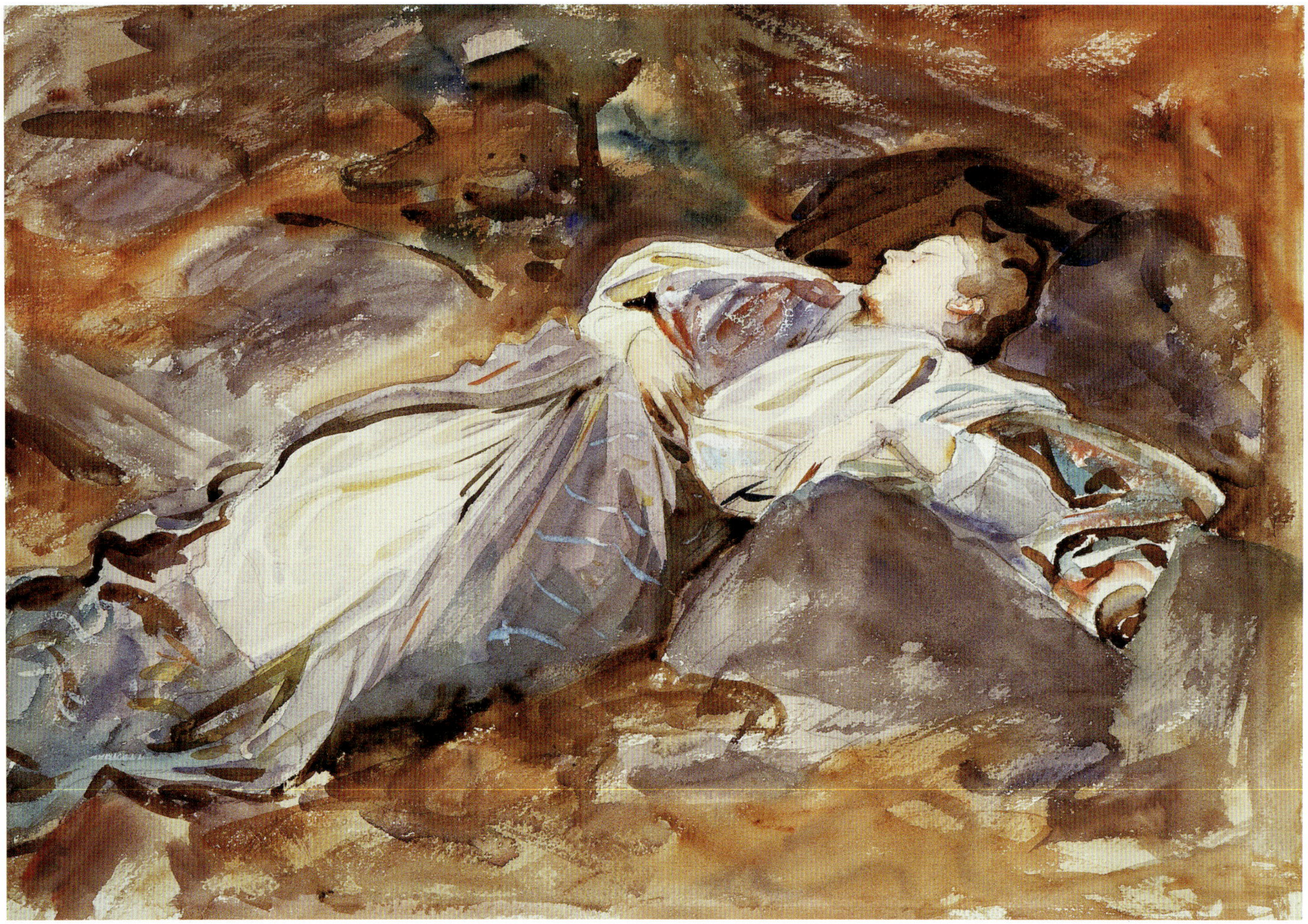

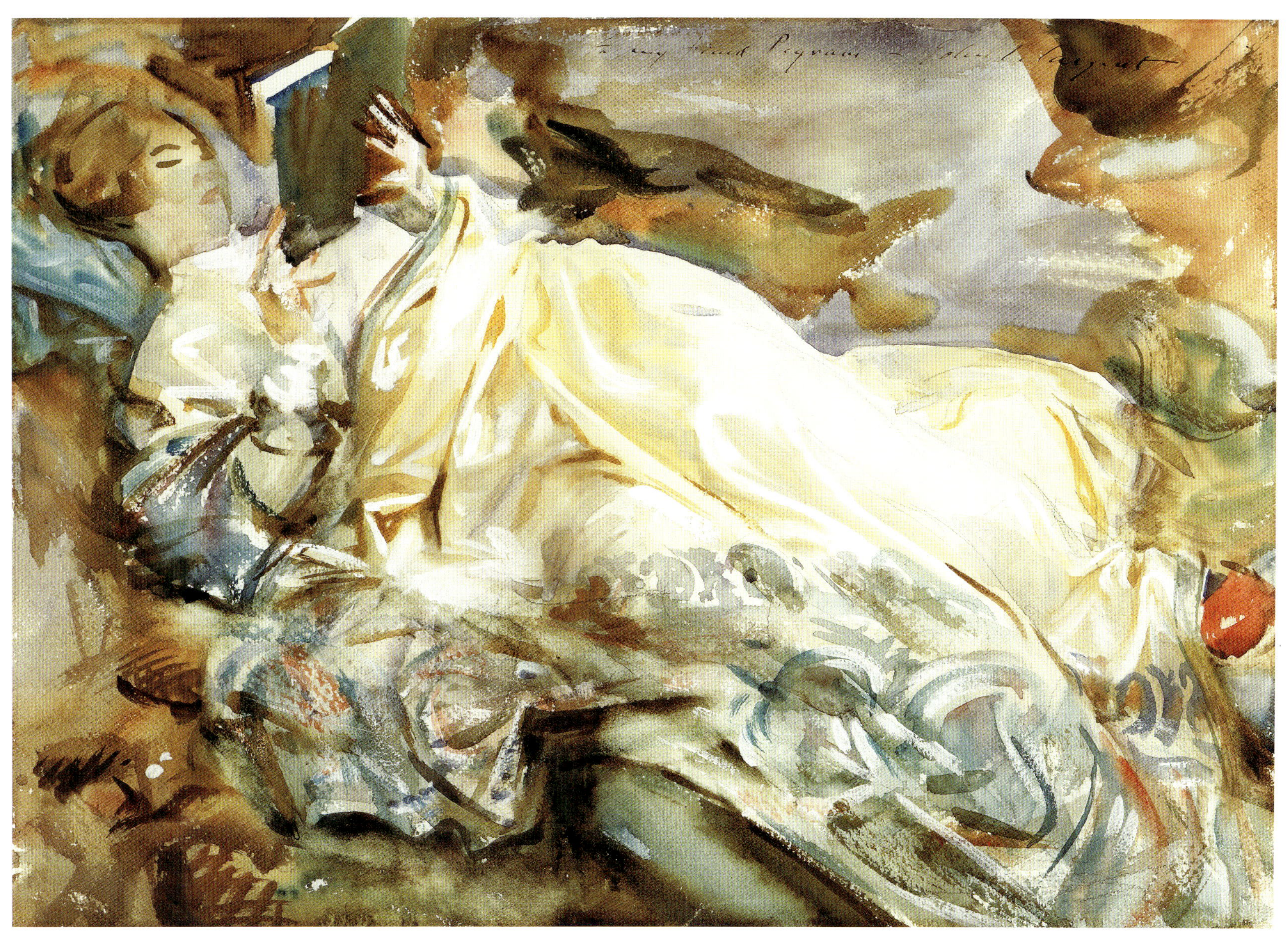

Violet Sleeping c. 1907–10
Watercolor and pencil on paperboard
14 11/16 x 21 5/16 in. (37.3 x 54.2 cm.)
The Brooklyn Museum of Art,
Gift of Mrs. Lawrence B. Dunham, (77.145)

Rose-Marie Ormond Reading in a Cashmere Shawl c. 1908–1912
Watercolor
12 1/2 x 19 1/2 in. (37.3 x 54.2 cm.)
Los Angeles County Museum of Art,
Gift of the Art Museum Council

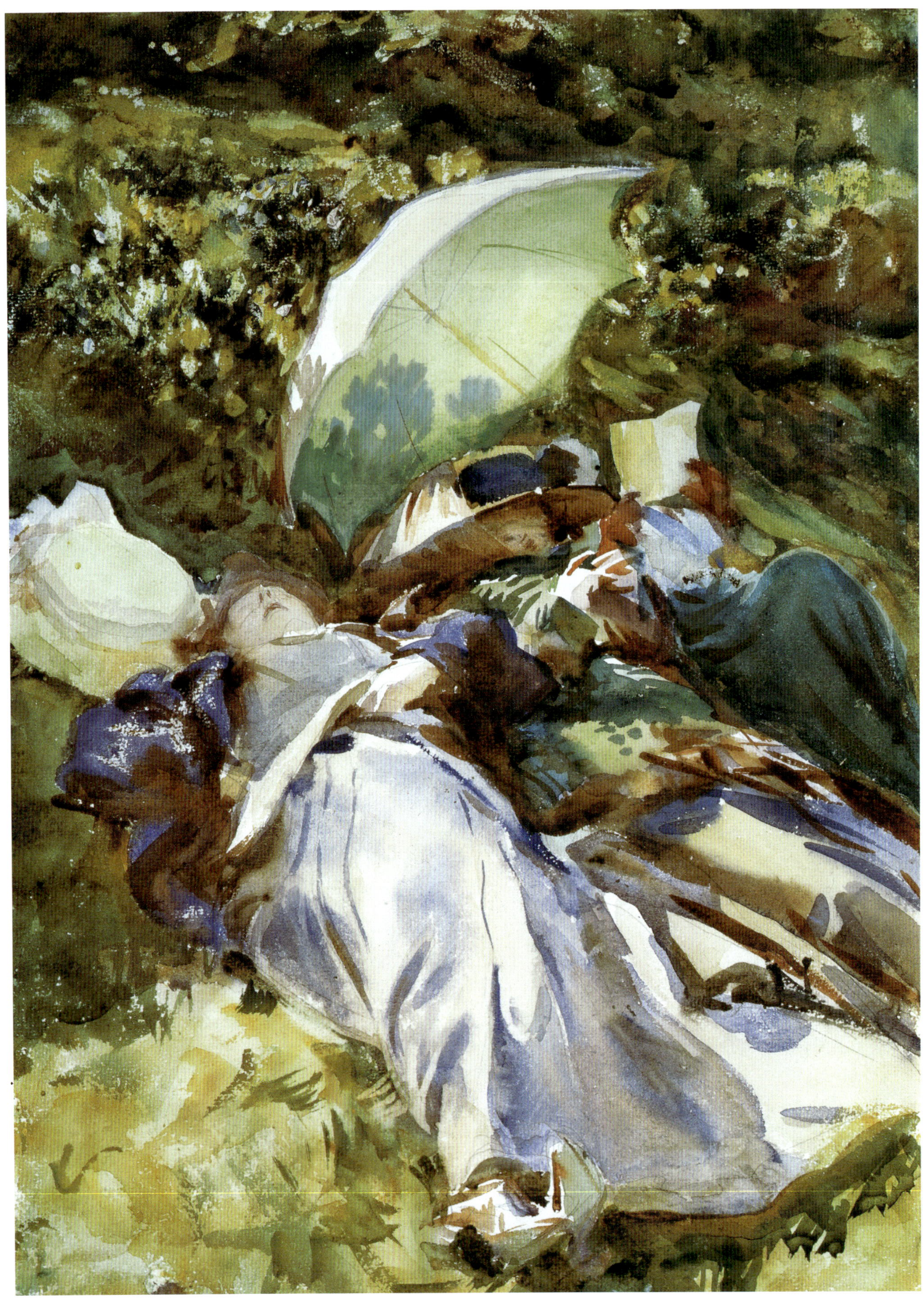

(opposite)

The Green Parasol c. 1910
Pencil, watercolor and bodycolor
18 1/4 x 13 3/4 in. (47.5 x 35 cm.)
Courtesy Christie's Images

Moreover, persuaded as I am that the individual temperament of every artist expresses itself with unconscious imperative far more in "how" he paints than in "what he chooses to be painting," I account by this for the way [Sargent] laid down his perfectly pure and sharply contrasted colours; above all, for the rushing lines and wilful but broadly generous angles, out of which the unerring speed of his hand and his eye built up the likeness of men and things.

—Vernon Lee, 1925

In Switzerland 1908
Watercolor and pencil
9 11/16 x 13 1/16 in. (24.6 x 33.2 cm.)
The Brooklyn Museum of Art,
Purchased by special subscription, (09.827)

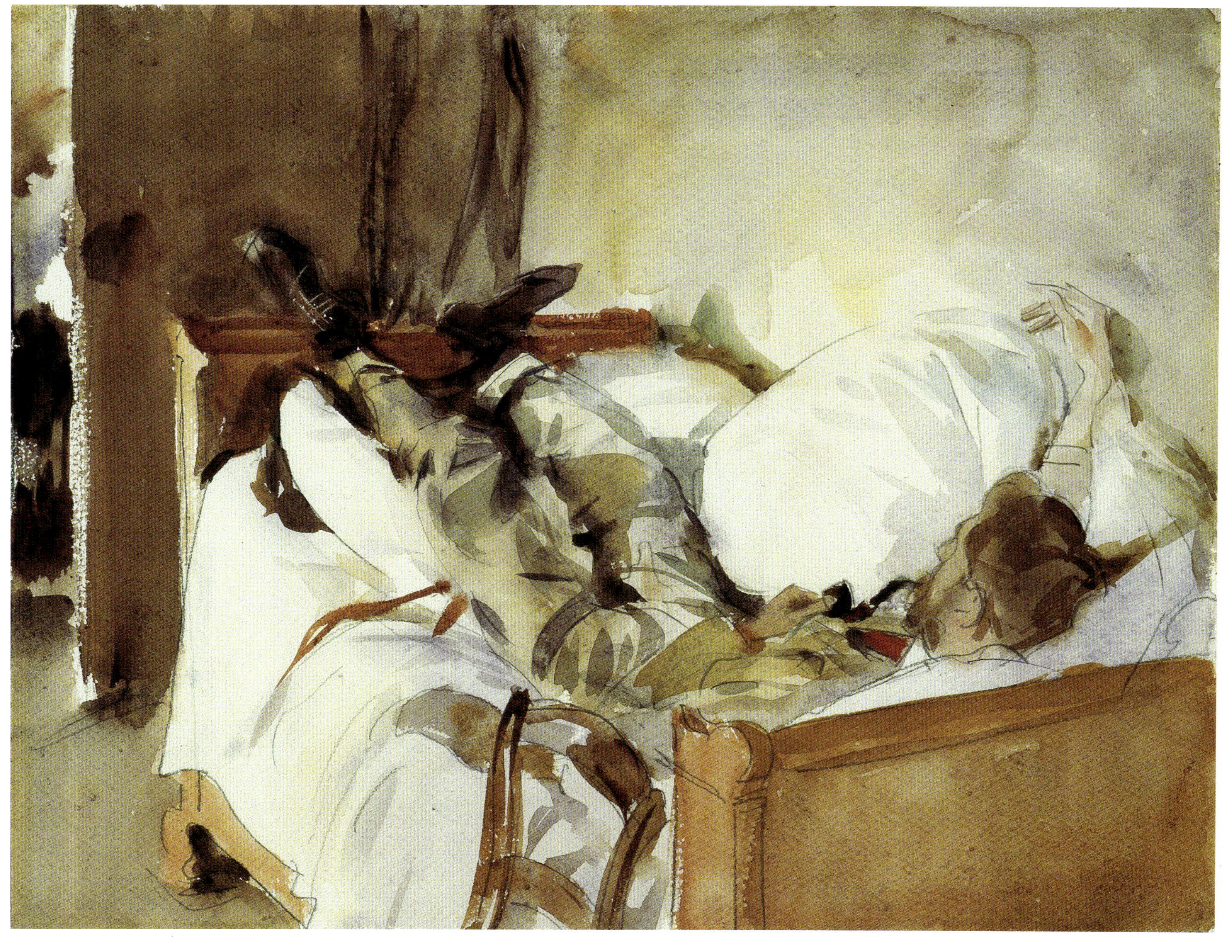

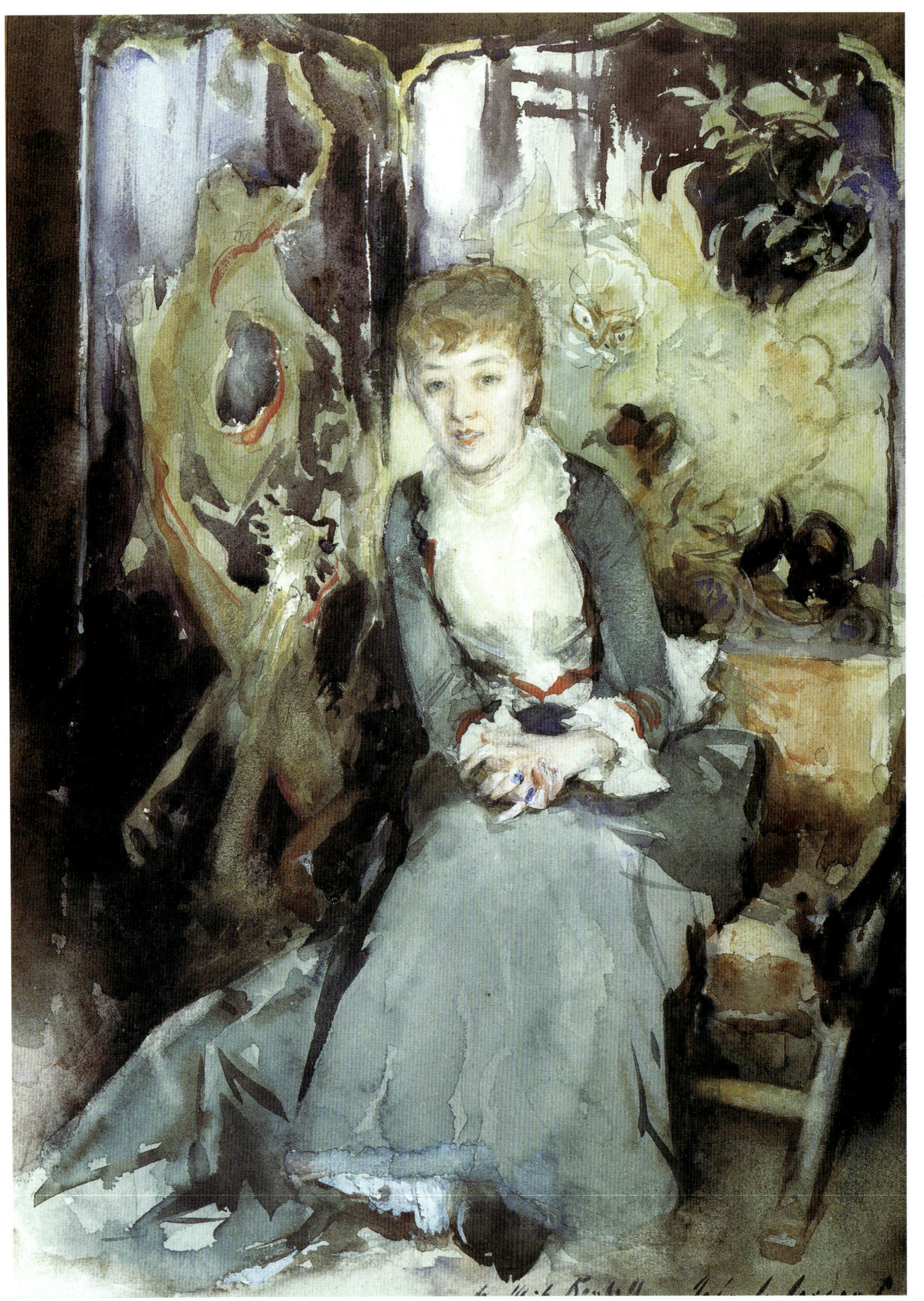

Miss Reubell in Front of a Screen n.d.
Watercolor and gouache
13 3/4 x 10 in. (34.9 x 25.4 cm.)
Private Collection
Photo courtesy of R. H. Love Galleries, Inc., Chicago

He [Sargent] showed how much could be expressed in painting the form of the brow, the cheek-bones, and the moving muscles around the eyes and mouth, where the character betrayed itself most readily; and under his hands, a head would be an amazing likeness long before he had so much as indicated the features themselves.

—Julie Heynemann

(opposite)

Mrs. Gardner in White 1922
Watercolor on paper
16 3/4 x 12 1/2 in. (43 x 32 cm.)
Isabella Stewart Gardner Museum, Boston

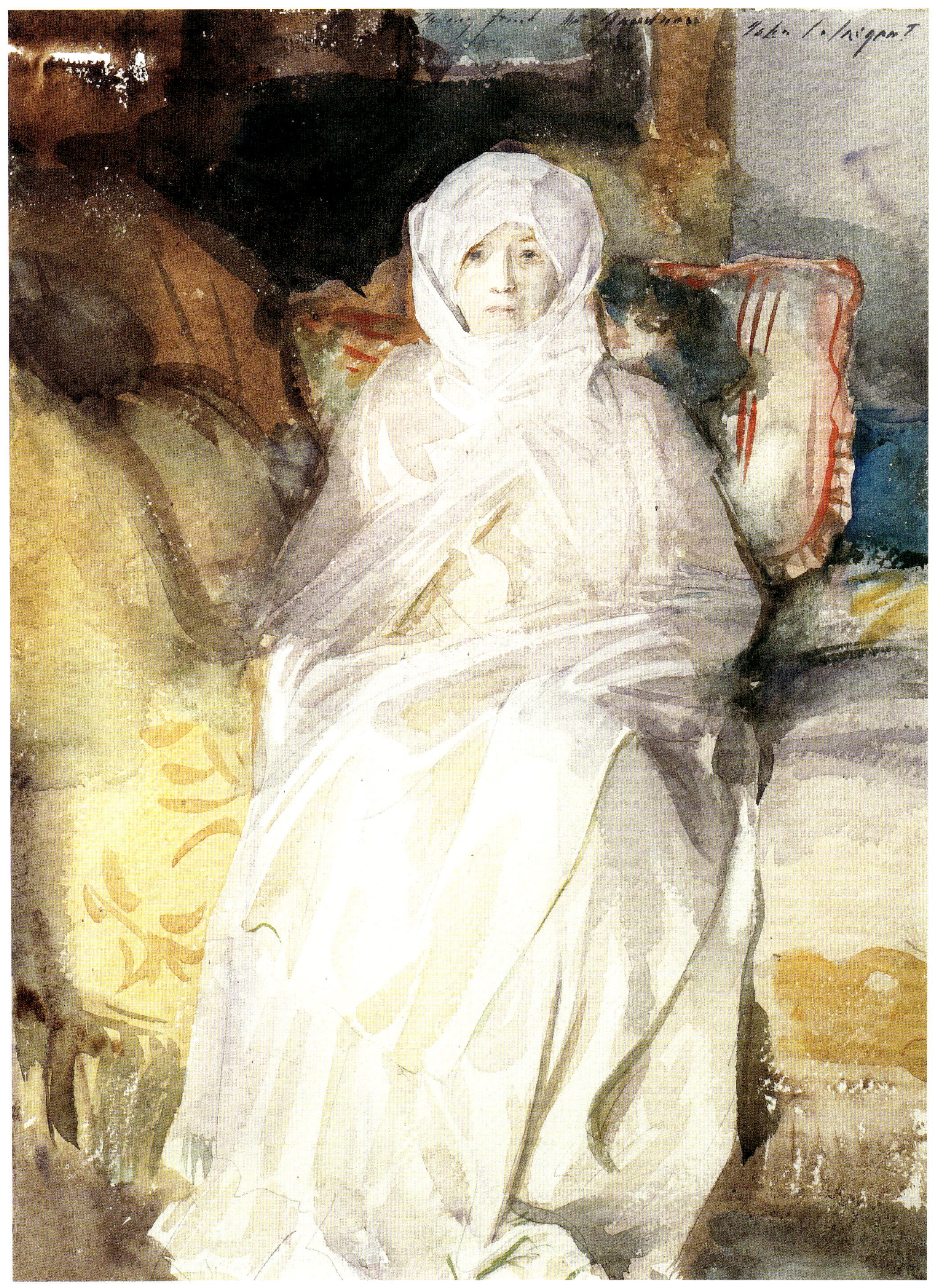

Venice

As an artist, Sargent began his love affair with Venice in the early 1880s. By the time of his final visits in the early 'teens, he had made hundreds of watercolors of the canals and waterfront. Trained to pick out the particulars of his surroundings from an early age, he created a wide-ranging visual representation of the shimmering city. The arching bridges that spanned the waterways, the gondolas with their singular shape (like an Arabian slipper) and plucky navigators—all proved irrestible to the watercolorist. His realistic eye remained true all the while, although the romance of Venice infuses some of his watercolors.

Sargent responded with special zeal to the architecture. Taken one day by the ornate balcony of a palazzo, the next by a church entrance, he created a personal inventory of the city's buildings. The watercolor medium seems perfectly suited to rendering these edifices that float upon the waters at the head of the Adriatic Sea.

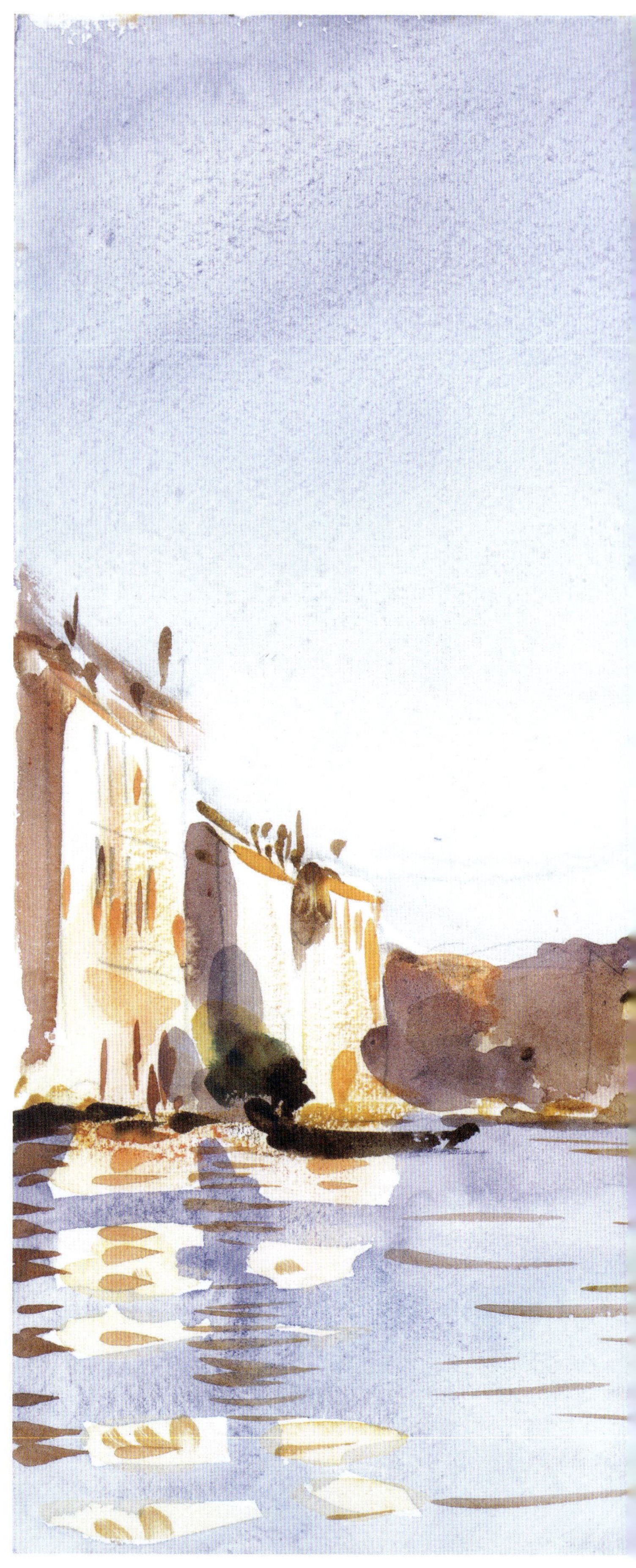

The Grand Canal, Venice c. 1902
Watercolor over graphite on white wove paper
9 13/16 x 13 7/8 in. (24.9 x 35.3 cm.)
Courtesy of the Fogg Art Museum,
Harvard University Art Museums,
Bequest of Grenville L. Winthrop
© President and Fellows of Harvard College,
Harvard University
Photo: Photographic Services

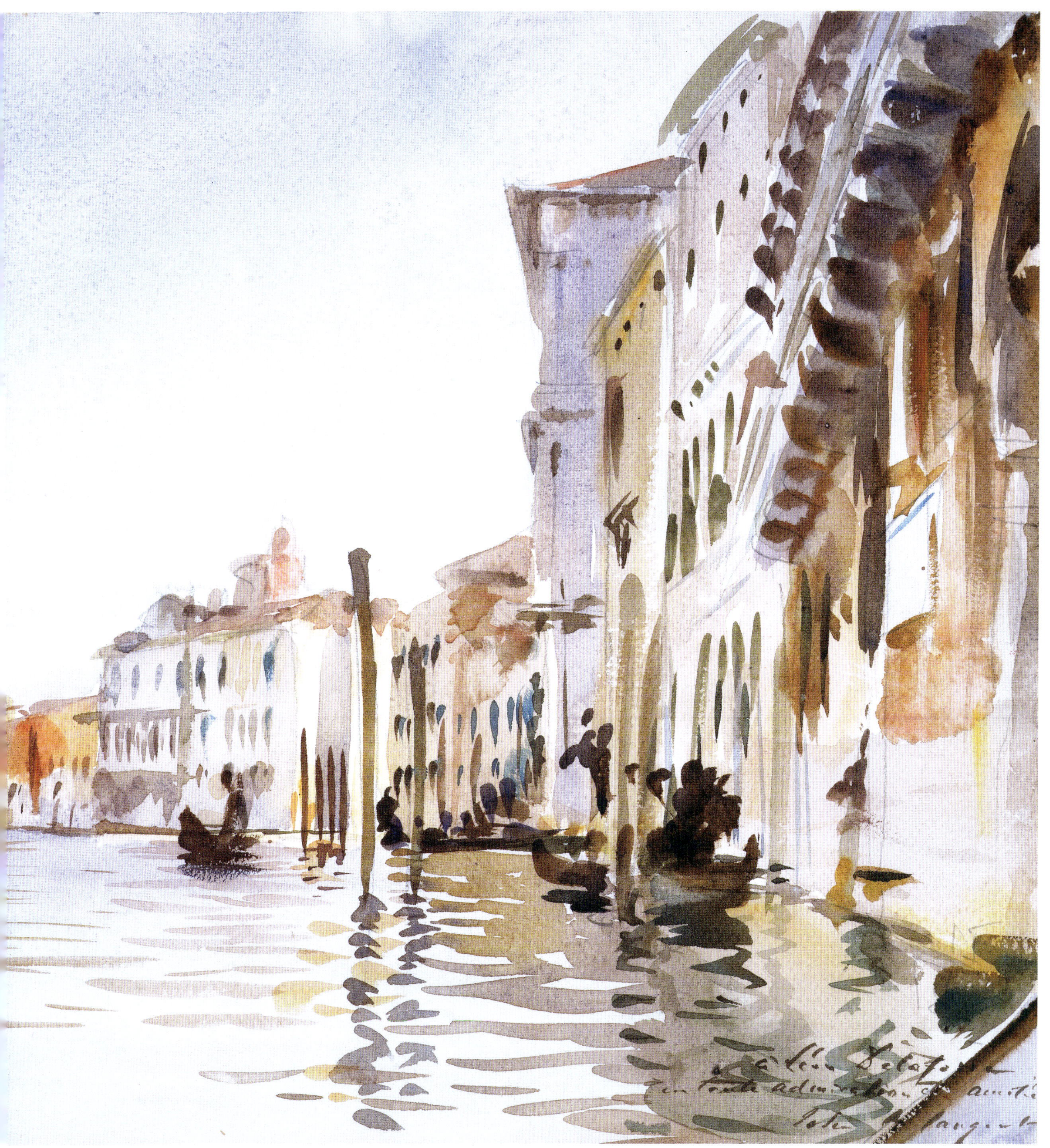

La Riva c. 1903–08
Watercolor
14 x 20 1/16 in. (35.6 x 50.9 cm.)
The Brooklyn Museum of Art,
Purchased by special subscription, (09.828)

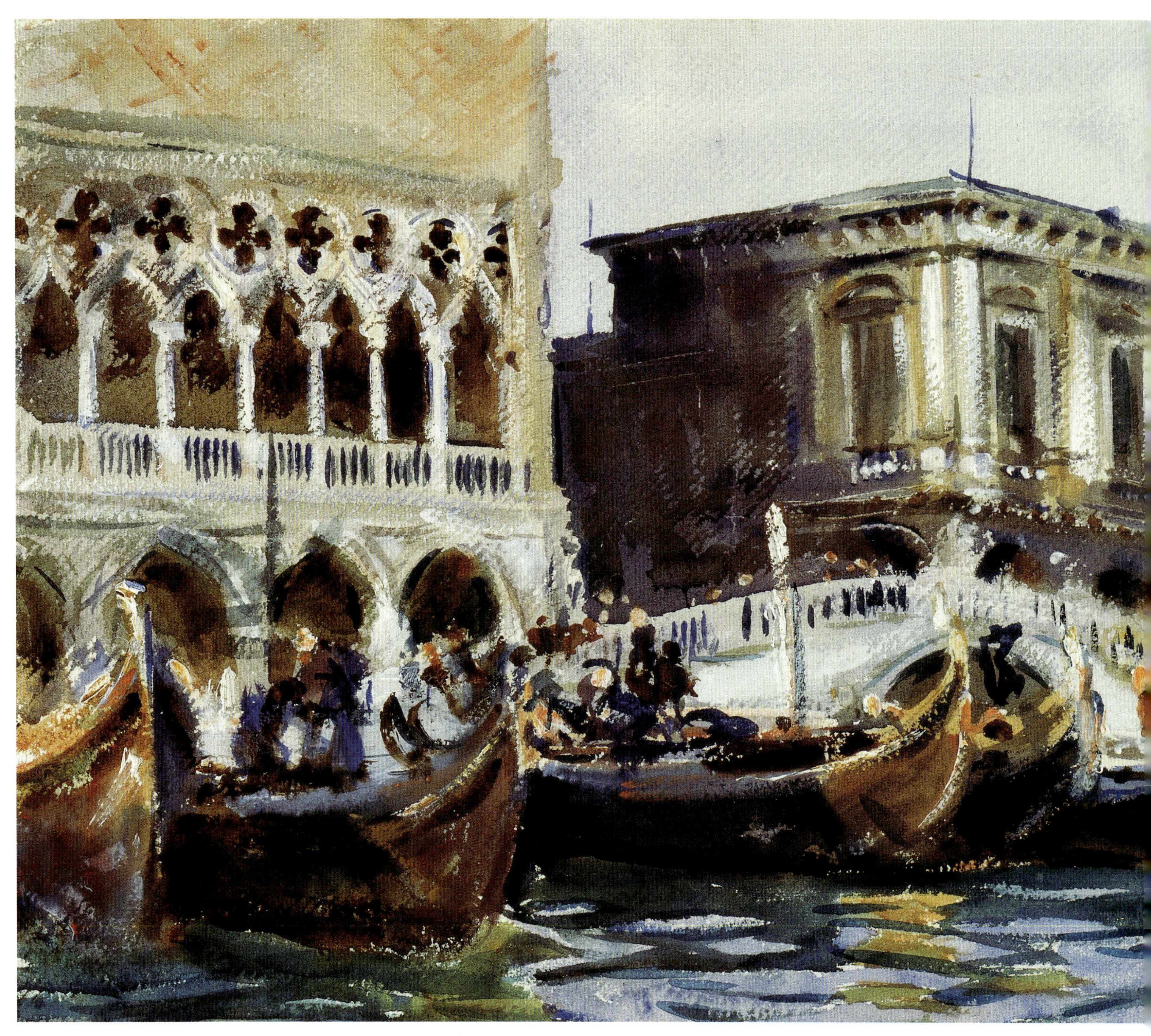

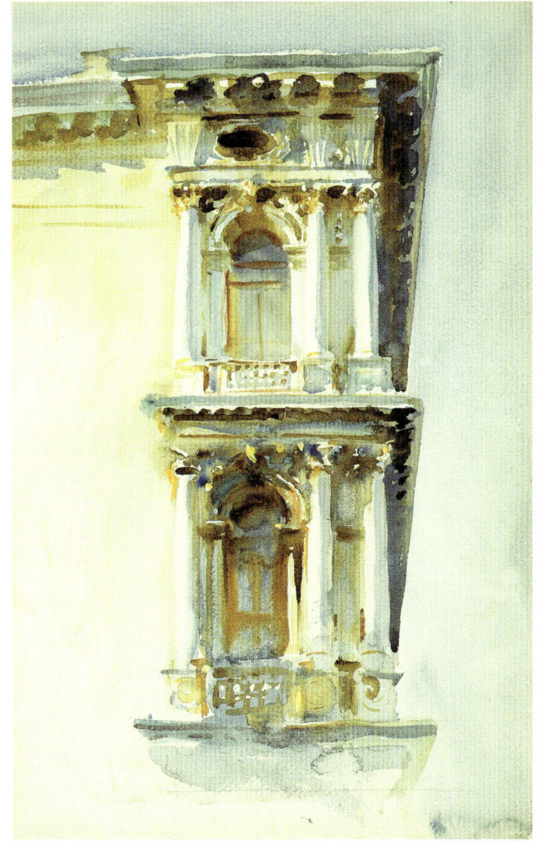

Venice: La Libreria n.d.
Watercolor on paper
20 x 12 3/4 in. (50.8 x 32.4 cm.)
Courtesy Christie's Images

The Piazzetta, Venice c. 1904
Watercolor
13 1/2 x 21 3/16 in. (34.3 x 53.7 cm.)
Tate Gallery, London
Art Resource, New York

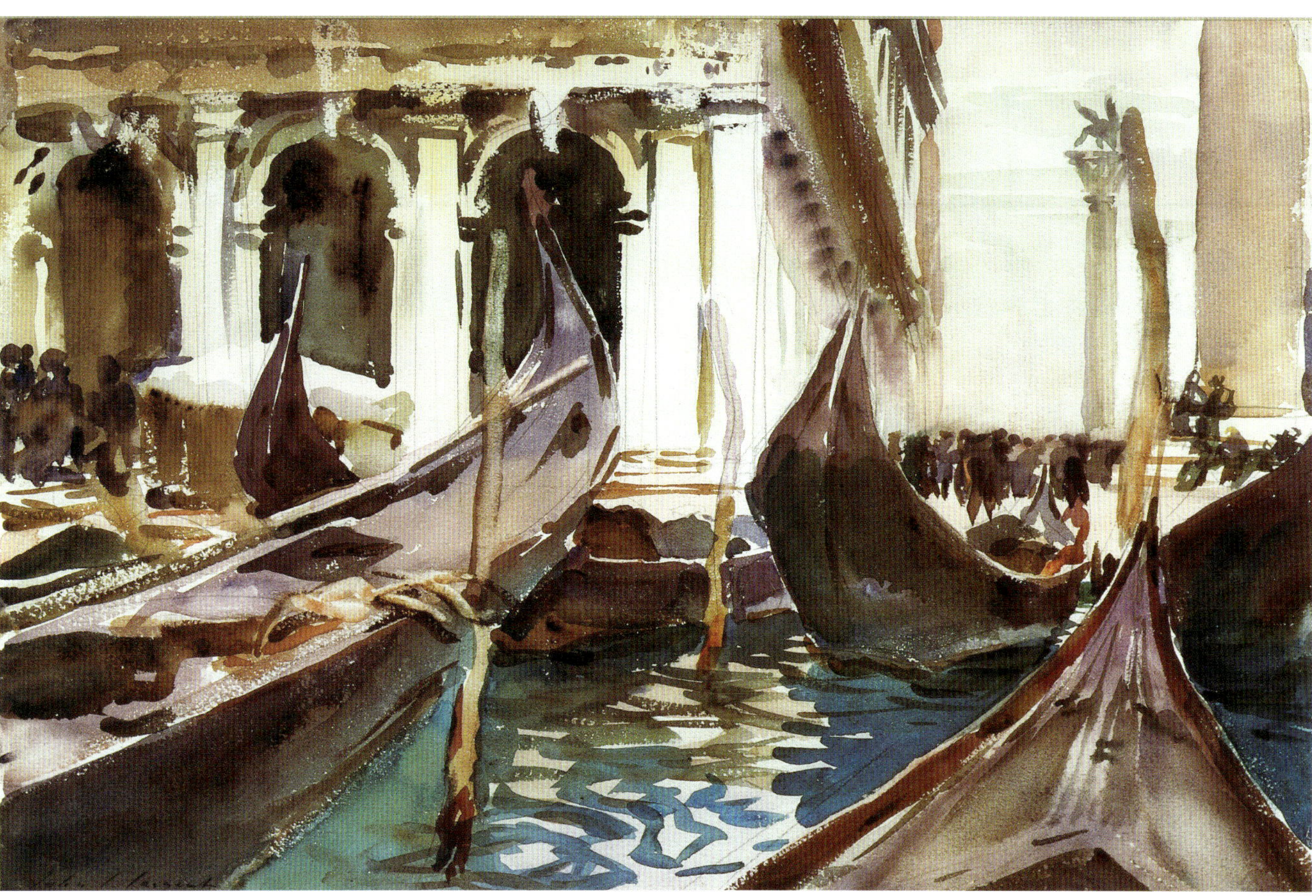

Base of a Palace N.D.
Watercolor on paper laid down on board
14 1/4 x 20 in. (36.3 x 51 cm.)
Courtesy Christie's Images

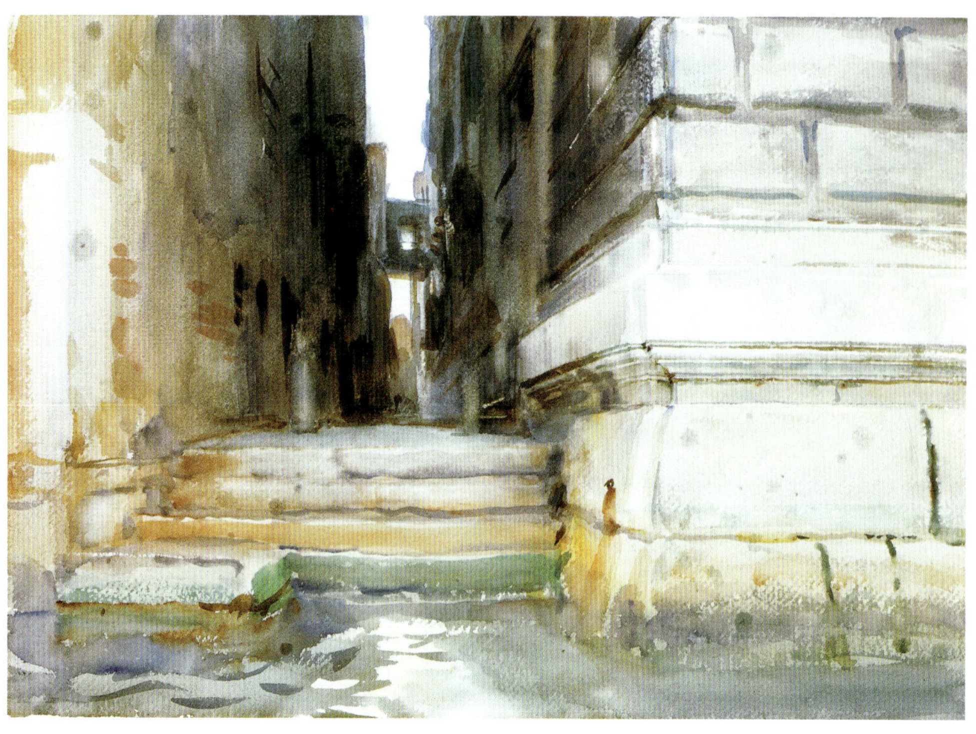

(opposite)

Venetian Fishing Boats c. 1904
Watercolor
19 1/4 x 13 3/4 in. (48.9 x34.9 cm.)
Tate Gallery, Liverpool, Great Britain
Art Resource, New York

Rio di San Salvatore, Venice c. 1903–04
Watercolor on paper
10 x 13 1/2 in. (25 x 34 cm.)
Isabella Stewart Gardner Museum, Boston

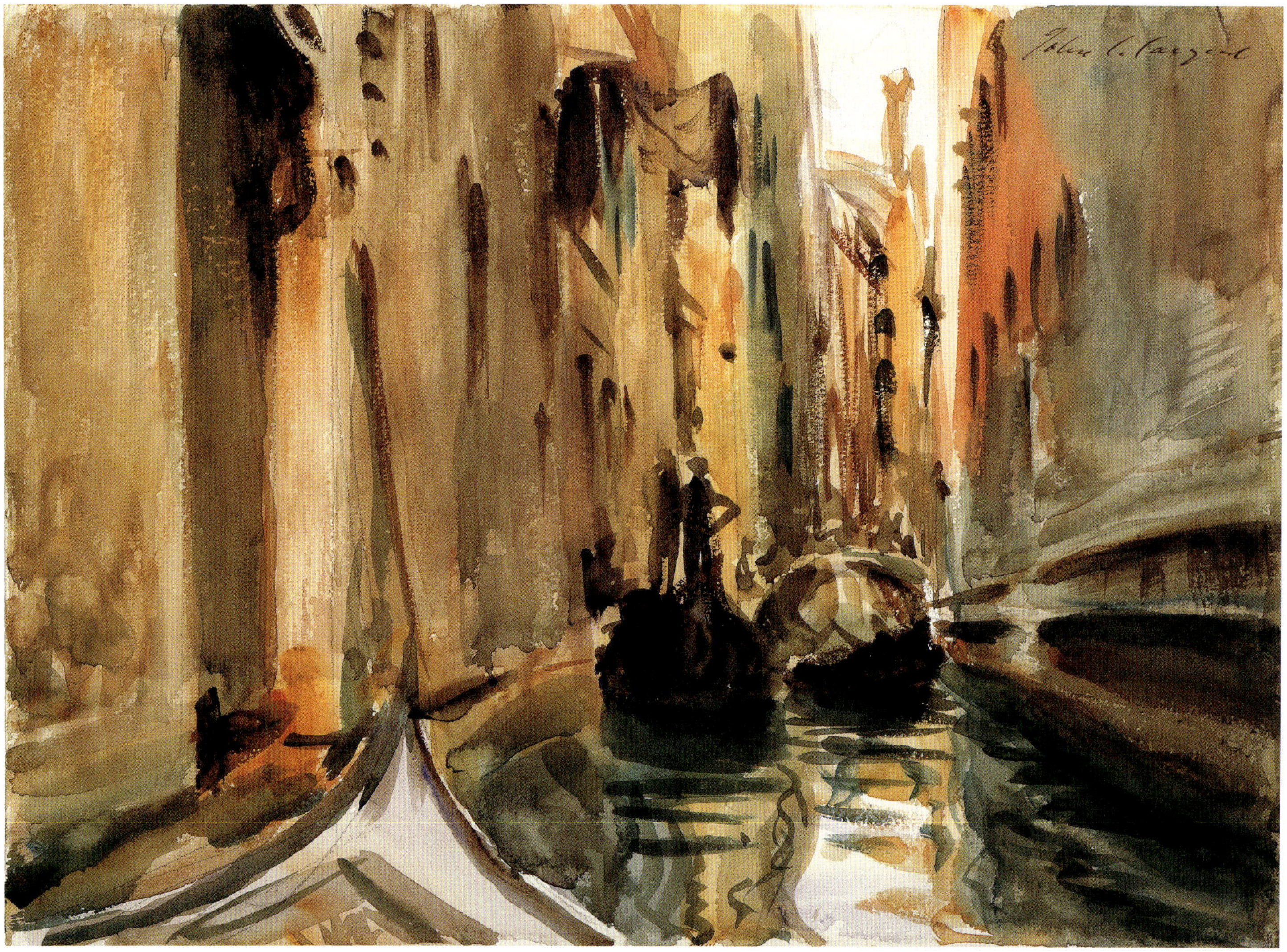

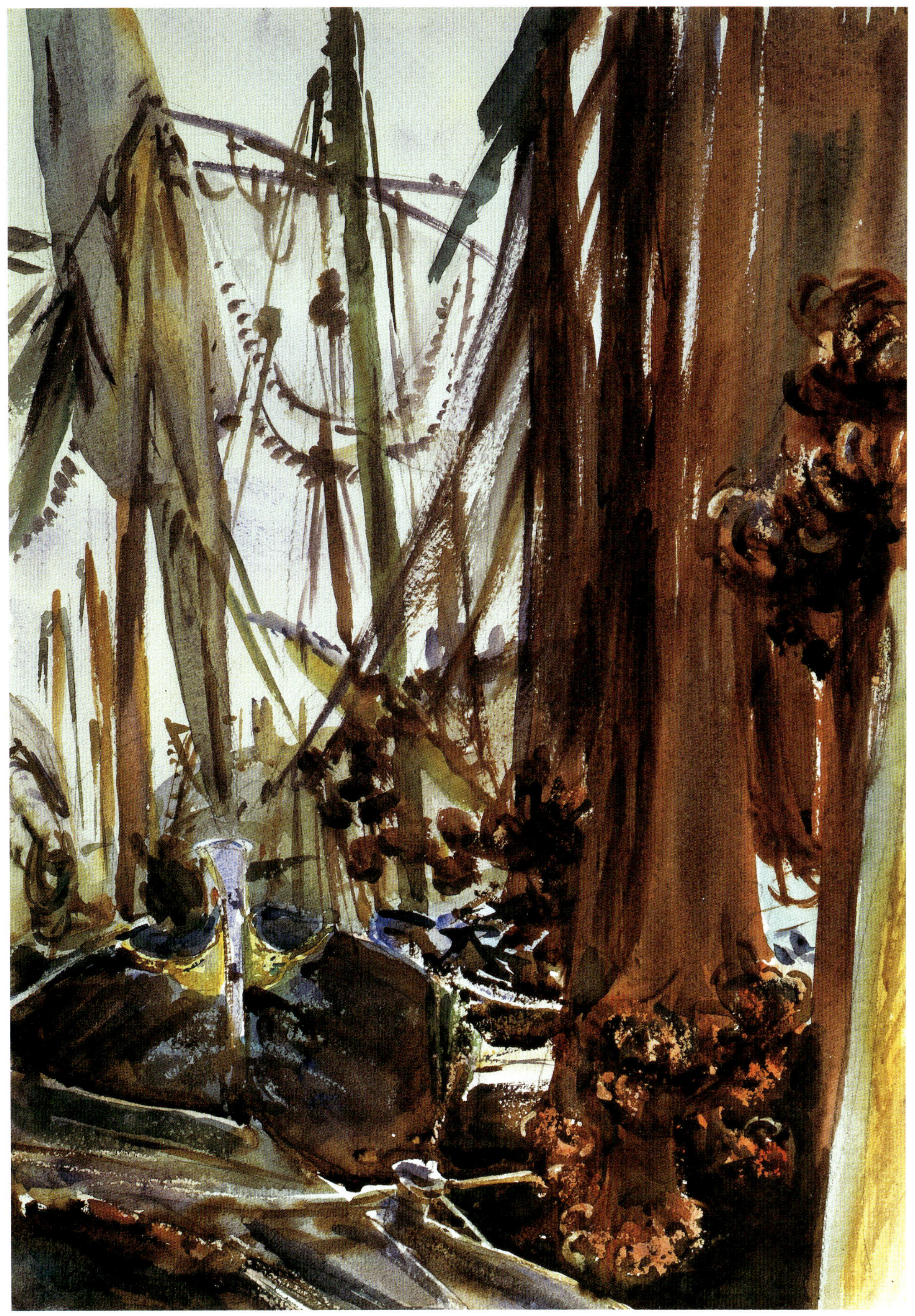

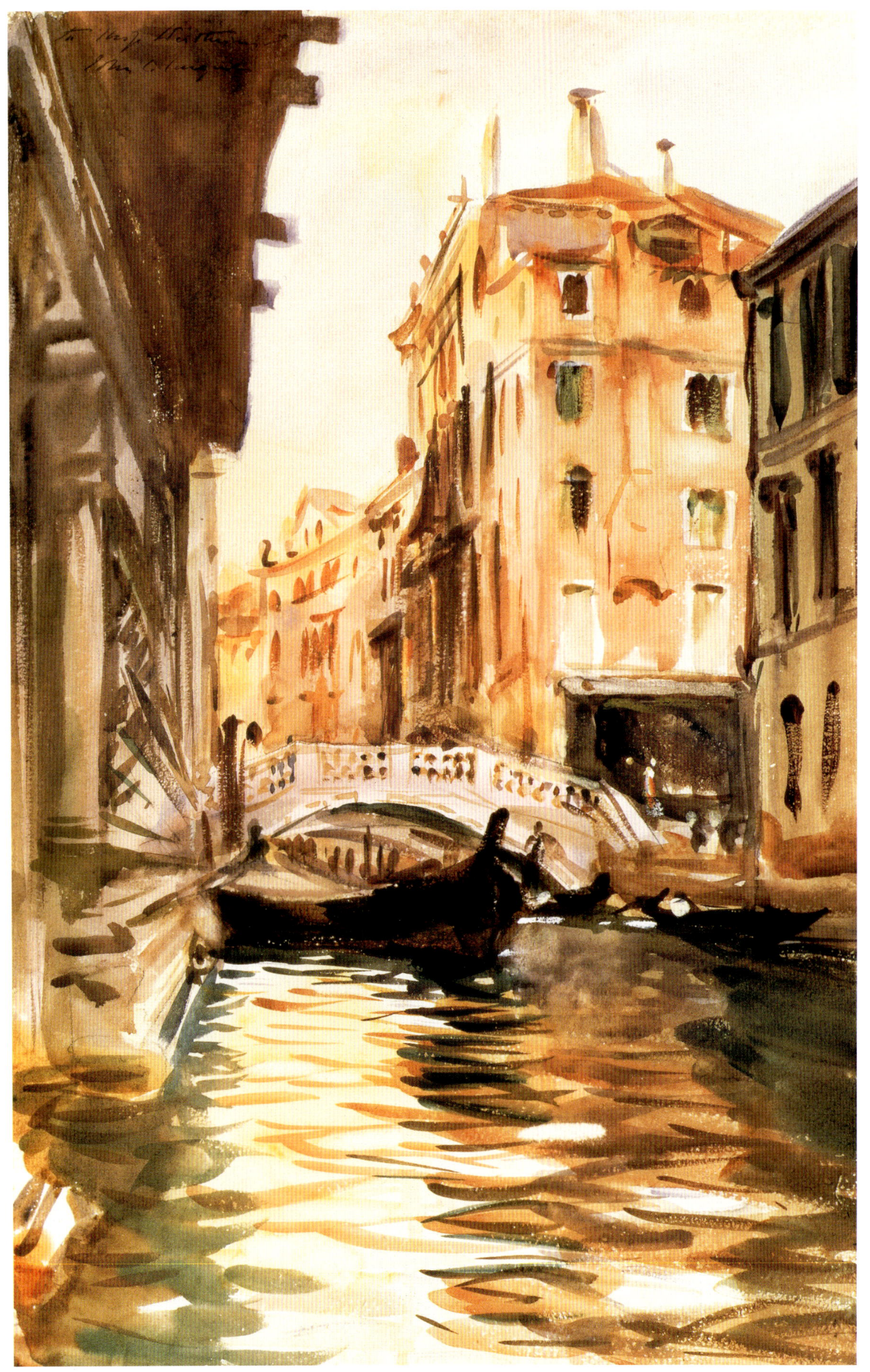

(opposite, above)

San Giuseppe di Castello, Venice c. 1903–04
Watercolor on paper
11 1/2 x 17 3/4 in. (29 x 45 cm.)
Isabella Stewart Gardner Museum, Boston

(opposite, below)

Rio di Santa Maria Formosa, Venice n.d.
Watercolor over pencil
13 13/16 x 19 3/8 in. (33.5 x 49.2 cm.)
Museum of Art,
Rhode Island School of Design,
Gift of Mrs. Murray S. Danforth
Photography by Del Bogart

Ponte della Canonica c. 1903–04
Watercolor on paper
17 1/2 x 11 1/2 in. (44 x 29 cm.)
Isabella Stewart Gardner Museum,
Boston

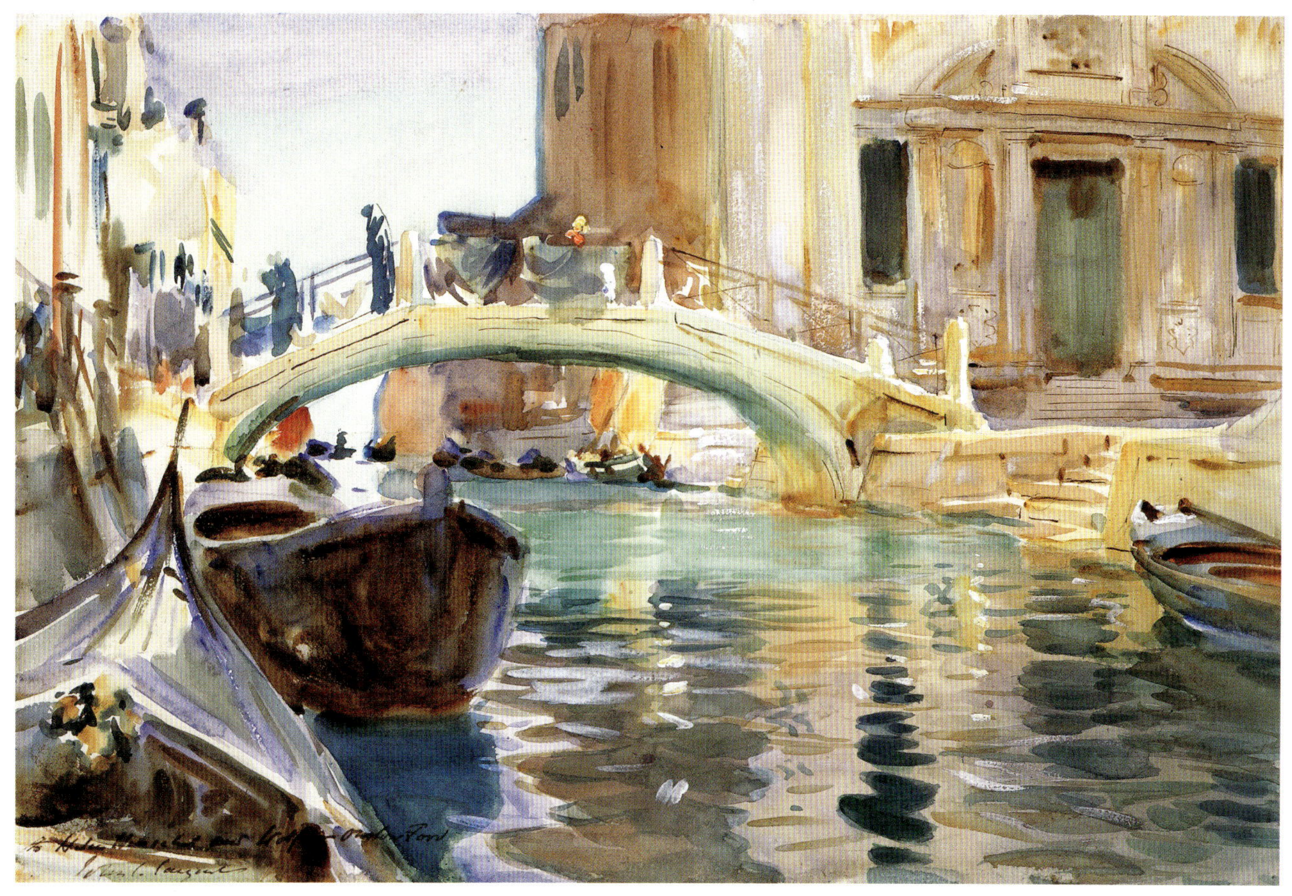

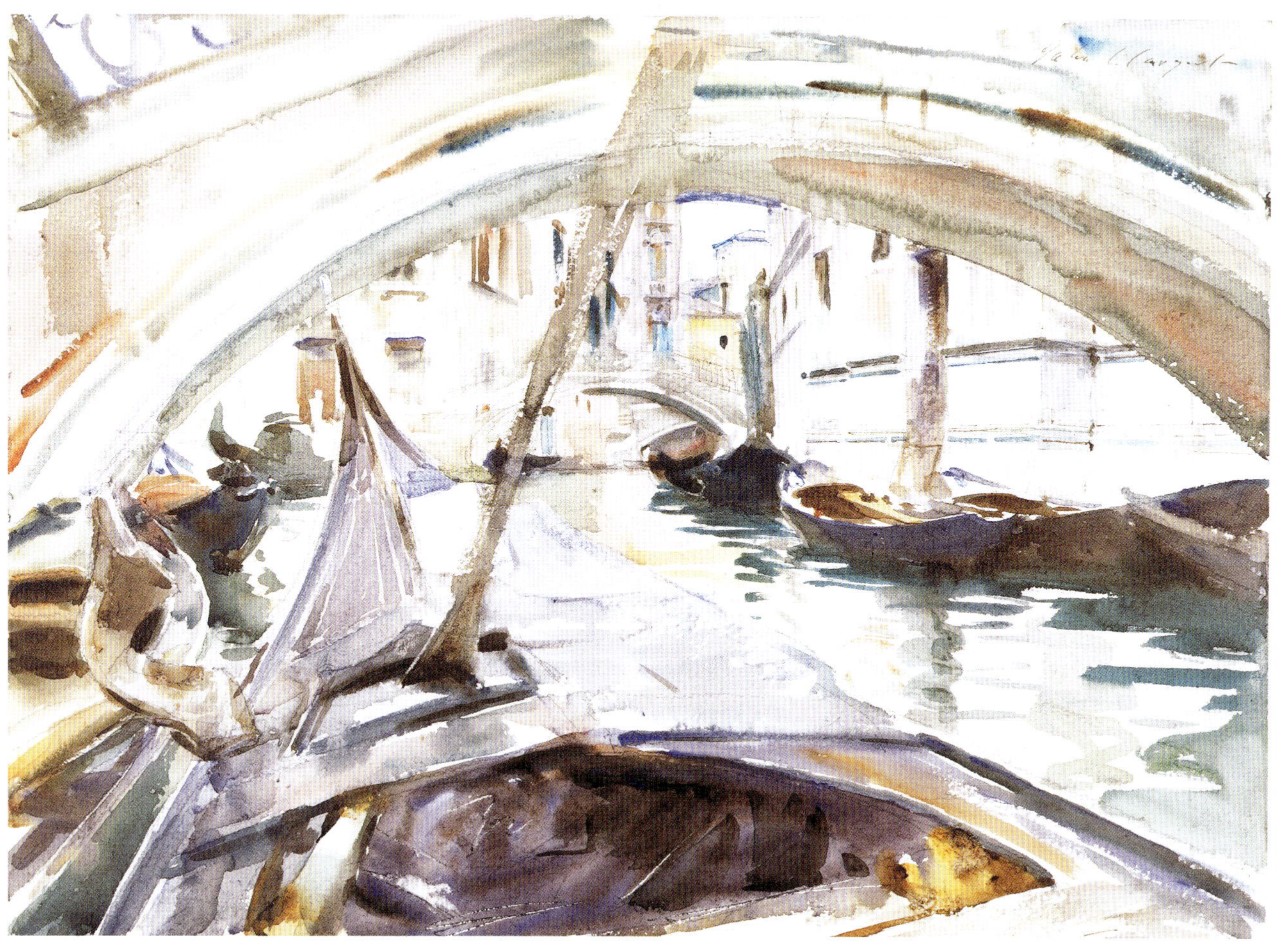

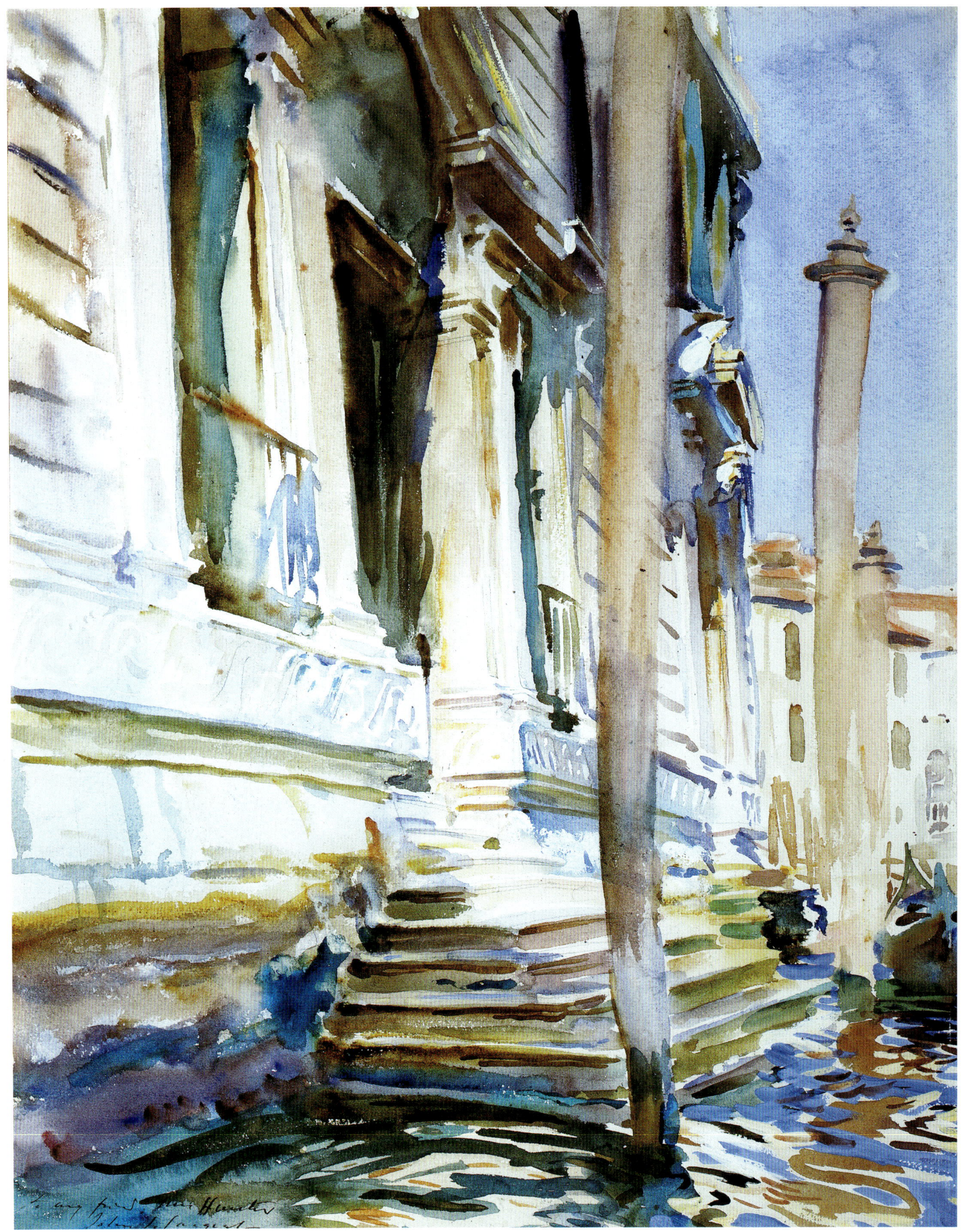

Doorway of a Venetian Palace c. 1901–10
Watercolor on paper
23 x 18 in. (58.4 x 45.7 cm.)
Collection of Westmoreland Museum of Art,
Greensburg, Pennsylvania,
Anonymous Gift #78.14

Grand Canal, Venice 1907
Watercolor over graphite
Approximate: 16 x 17 7/8 in. (40.6 x 45.5 cm.)
Ailsa Mellon Bruce Collection,
© 1998 Board of Trustees,
National Gallery of Art, Washington

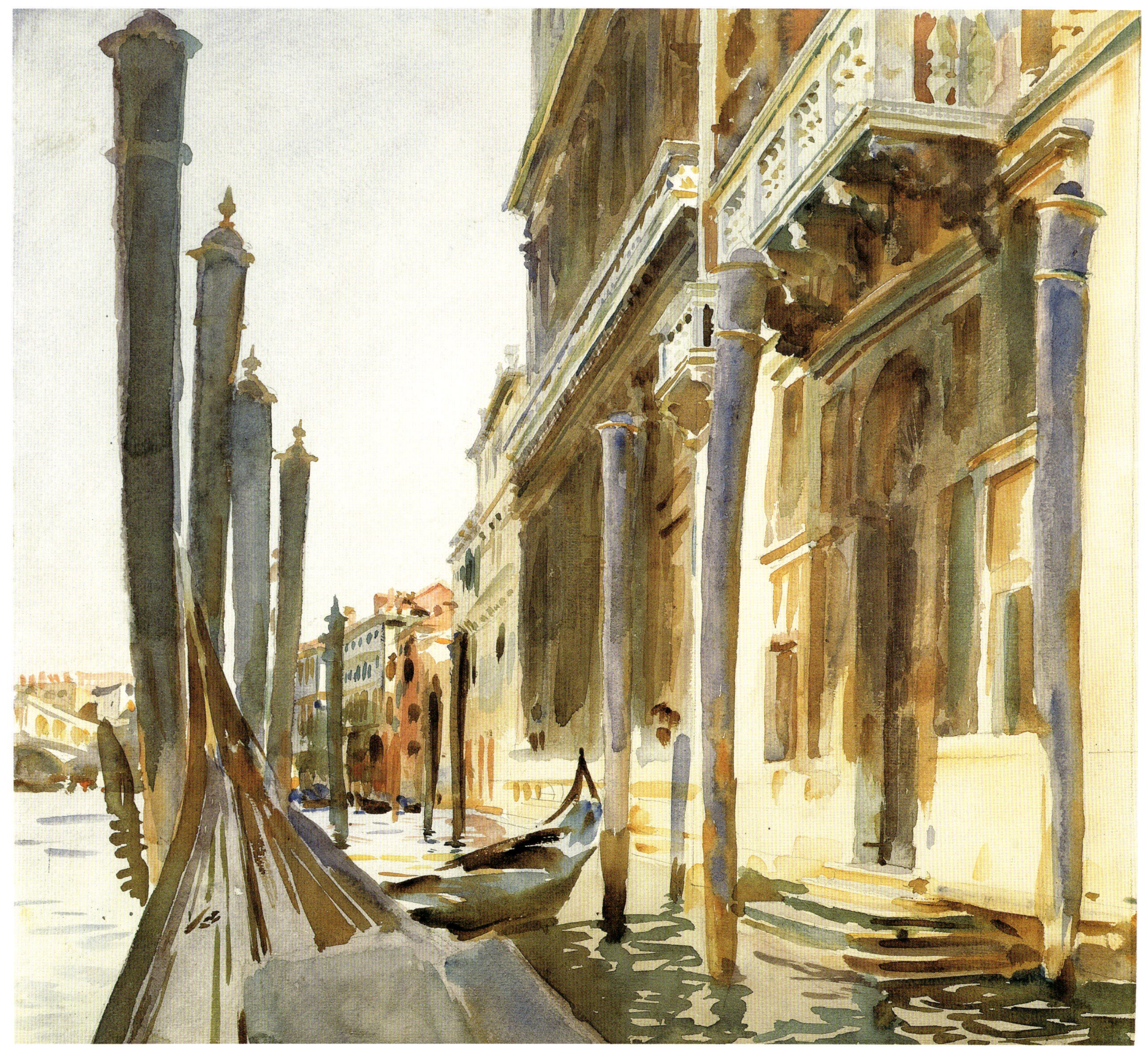

. . . Wonderfully light and fine is the touch by which the painter evokes the small Venetian realities . . . and keeps the whole thing free from the element of humbug which has ever attended most attempts to reproduce the idiosyncracies of Italy.

—Henry James

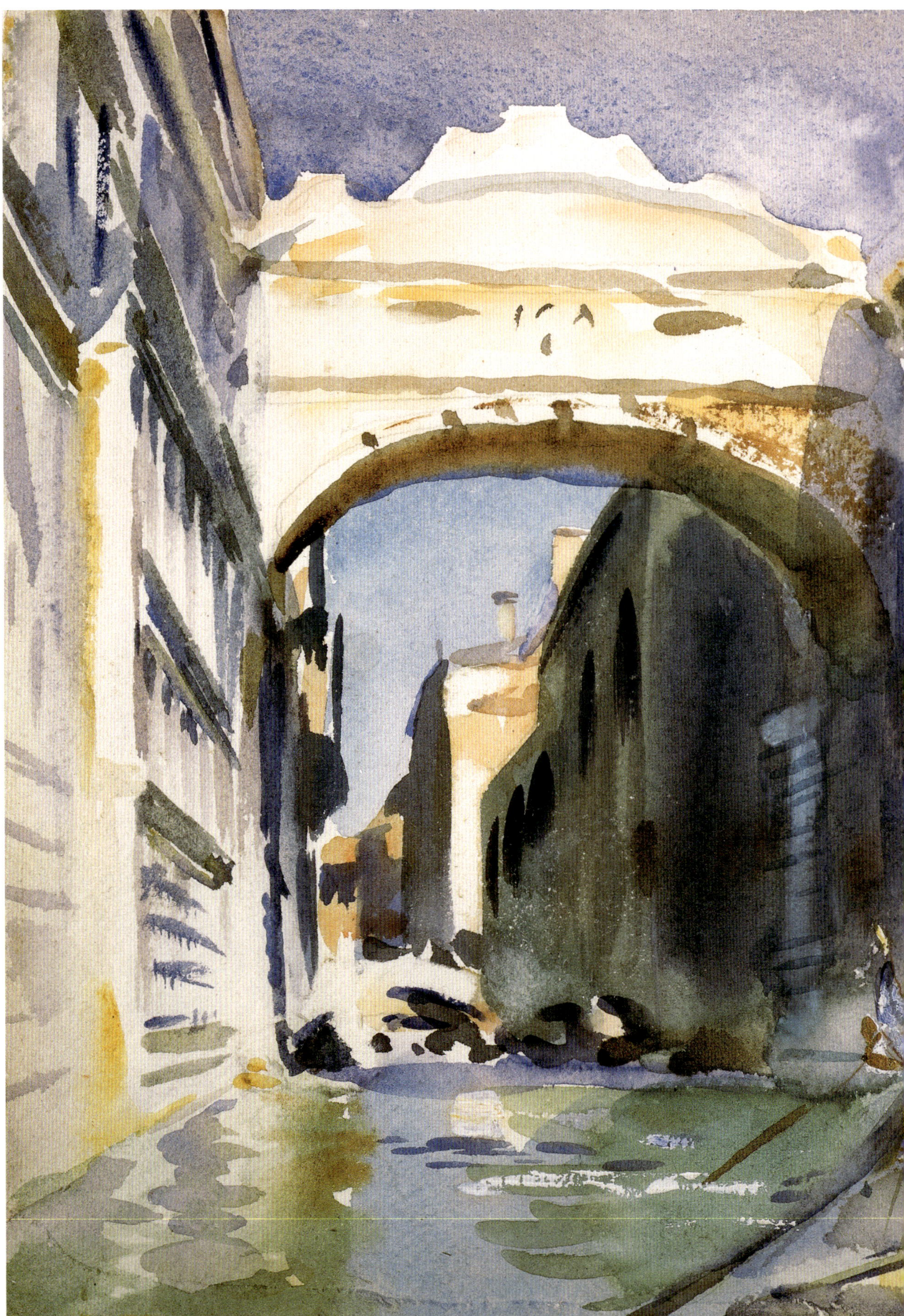

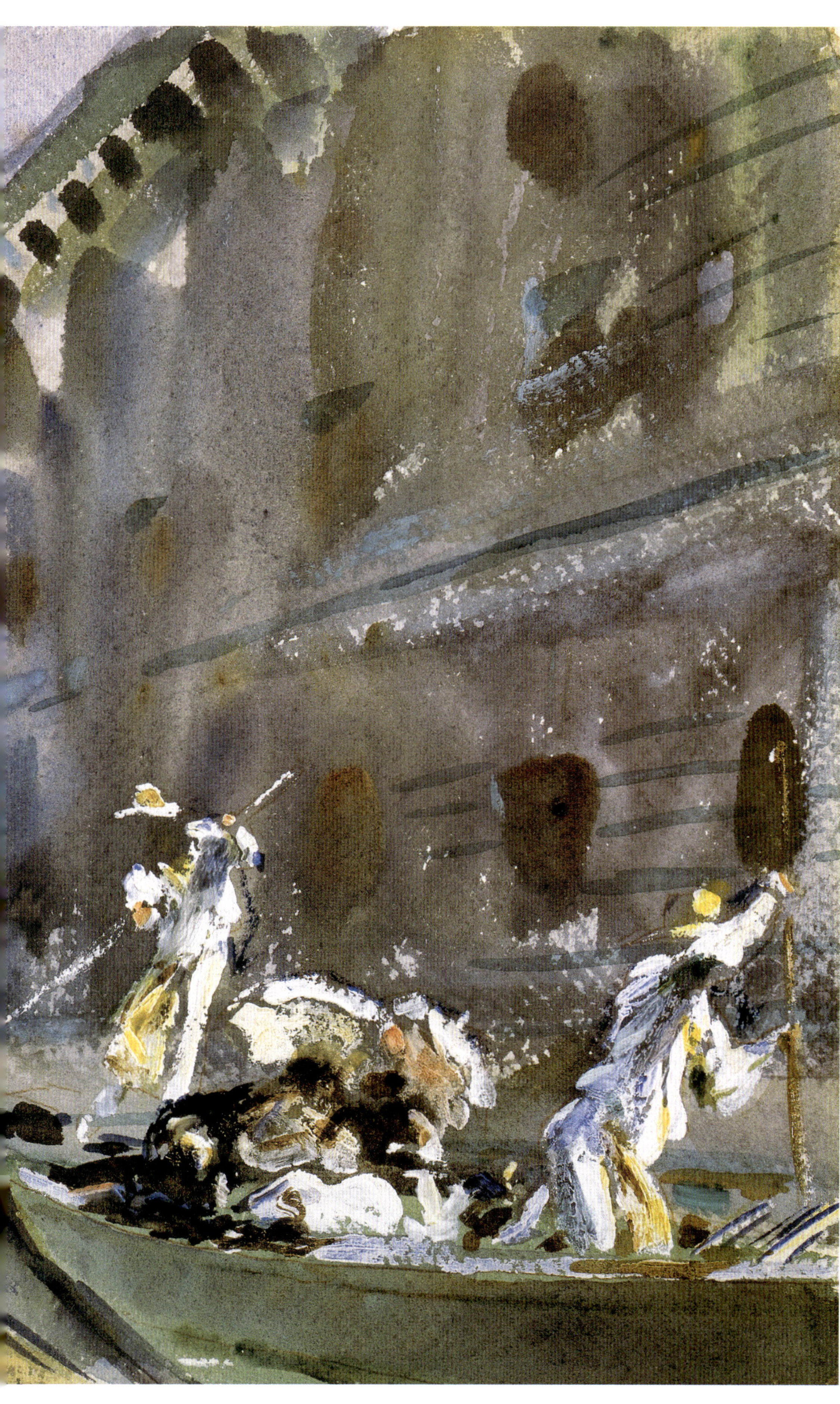

Bridge of Sighs c. 1905–08
Watercolor heightened with white
10 x 14 in. (25.3 x 35.5 cm.)
The Brooklyn Museum of Art,
Purchased by special subscription, (09.819)

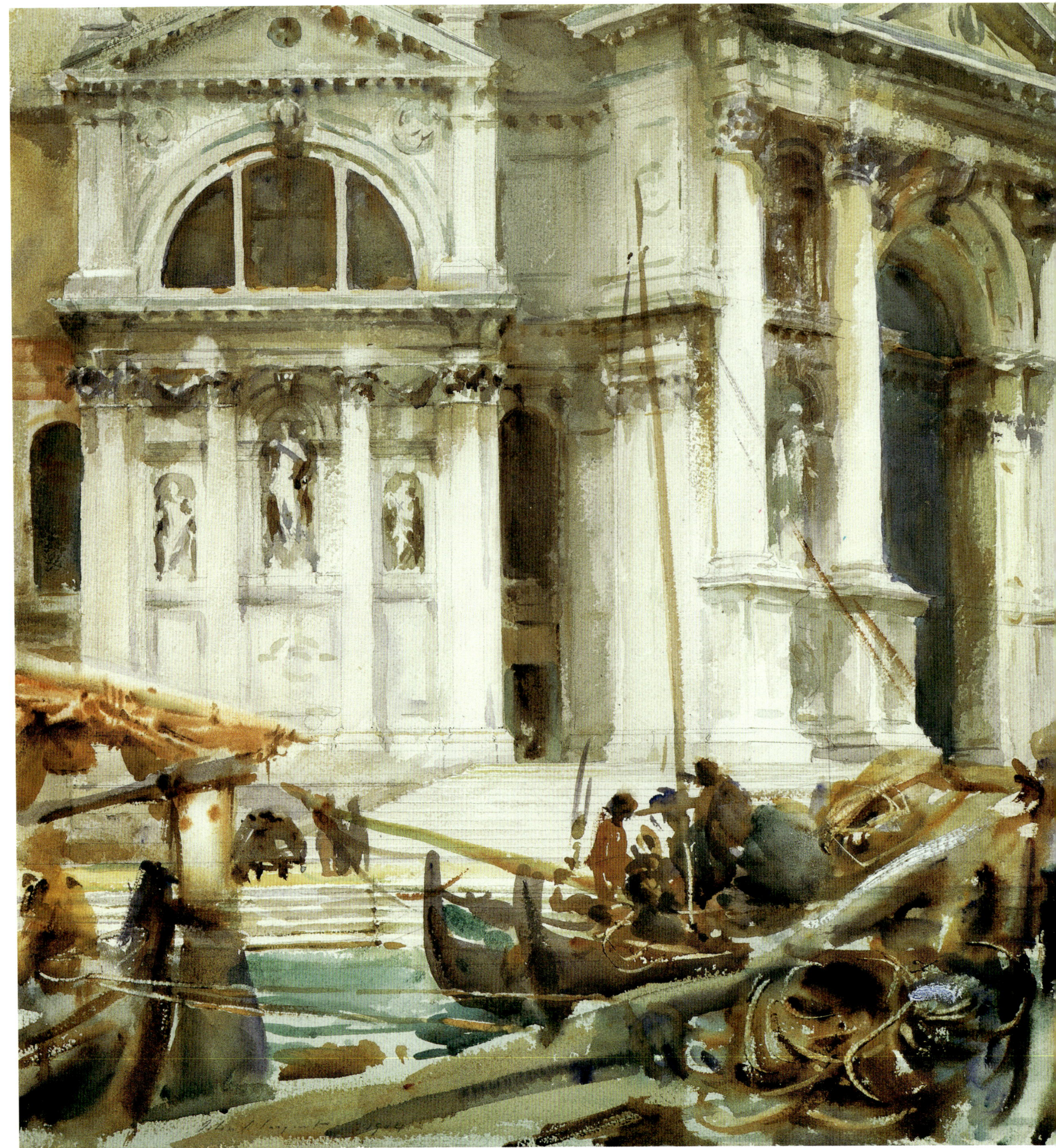

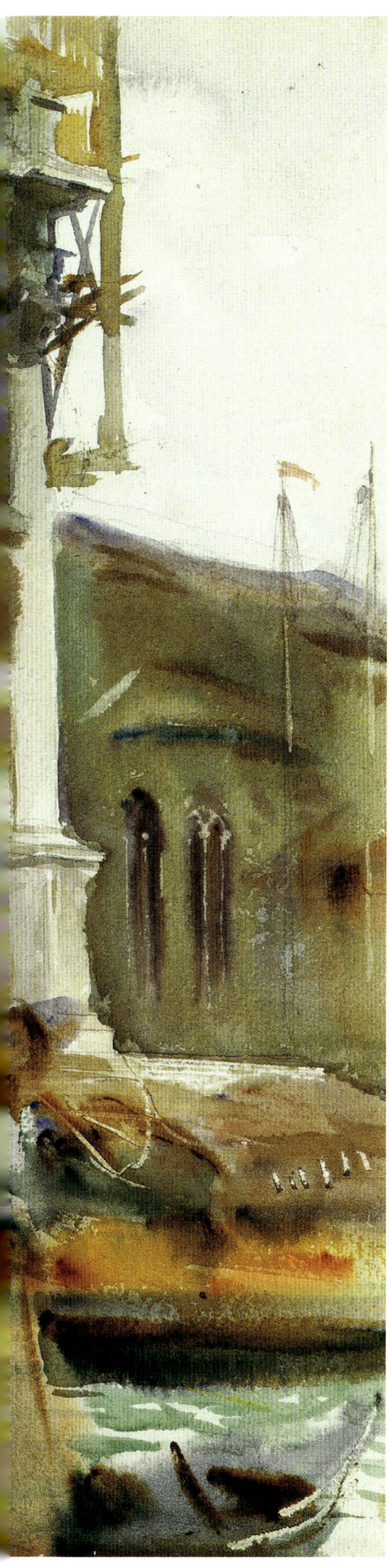

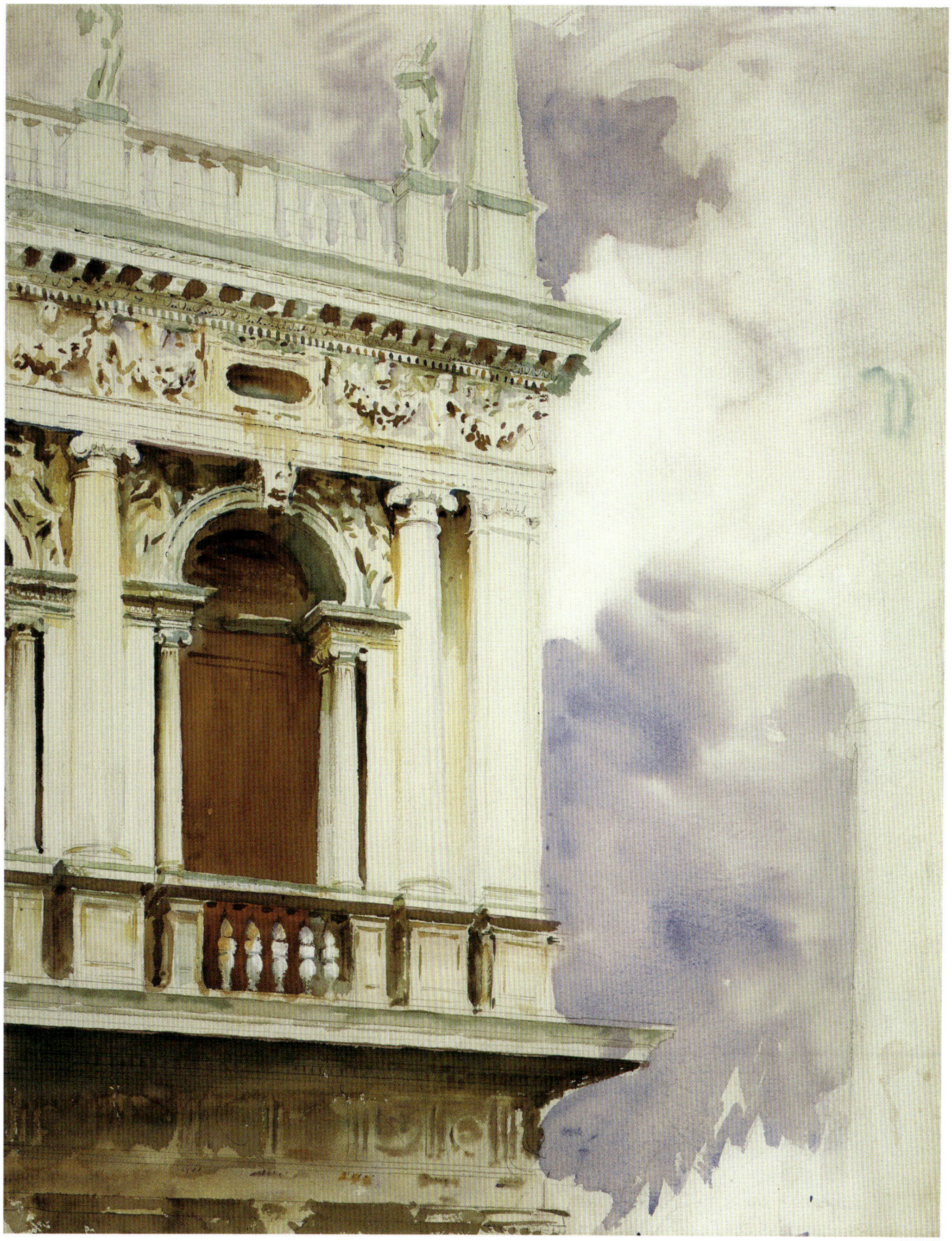

Santa Maria della Salute 1904
Watercolor and pencil heightened with white
18 3/16 x 22 15/16. (46.2 x 58.2 cm.)
The Brooklyn Museum of Art,
Purchased by special subscription, (09.838)

The Library in Venice 1904
Watercolor with white gouache over graphite
22 3/8 x 17 3/4 in. (56.8 x 45.1 cm.)
Ailsa Mellon Bruce Collection
© 1998 Board of Trustees,
National Gallery of Art, Washington

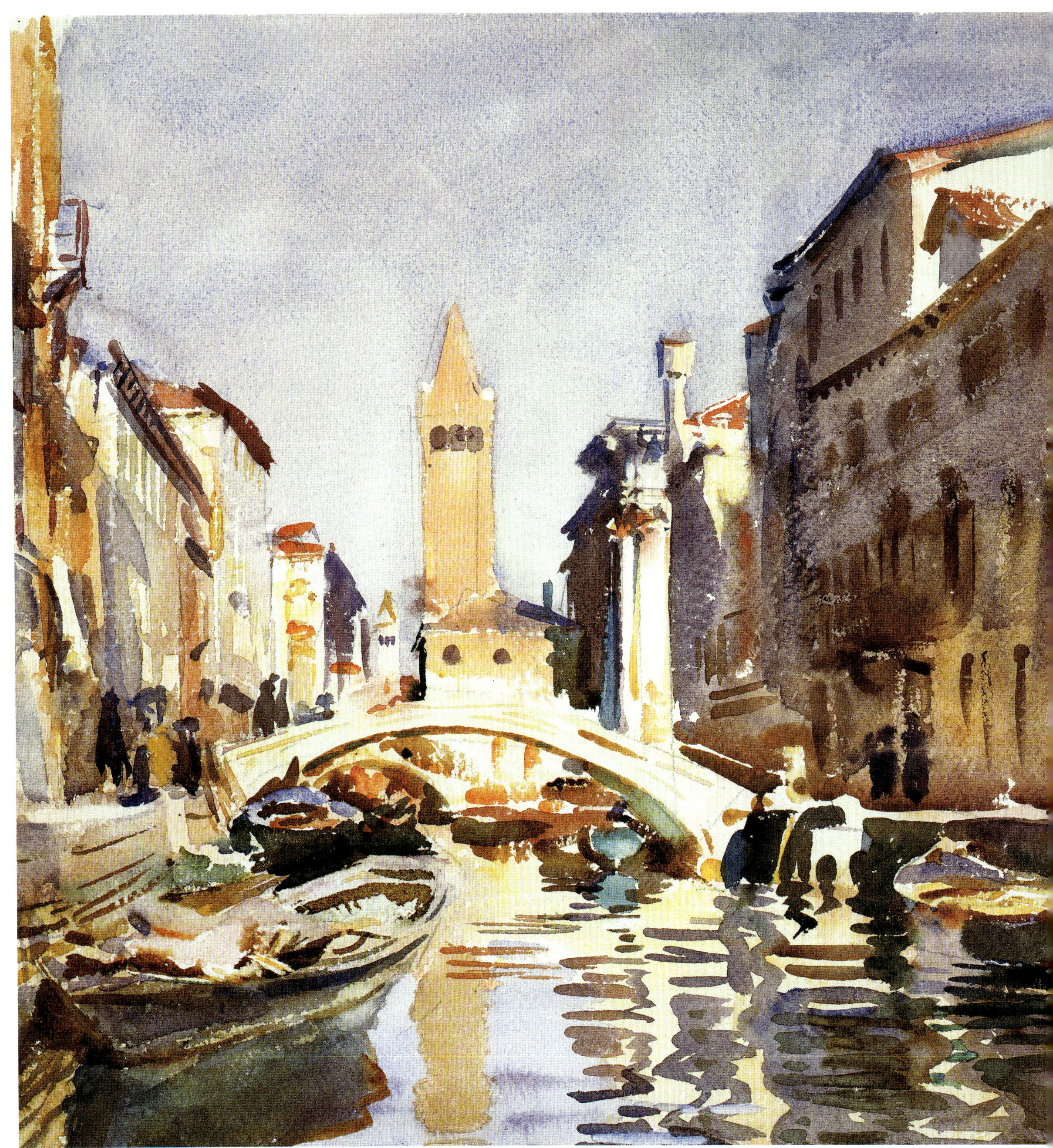

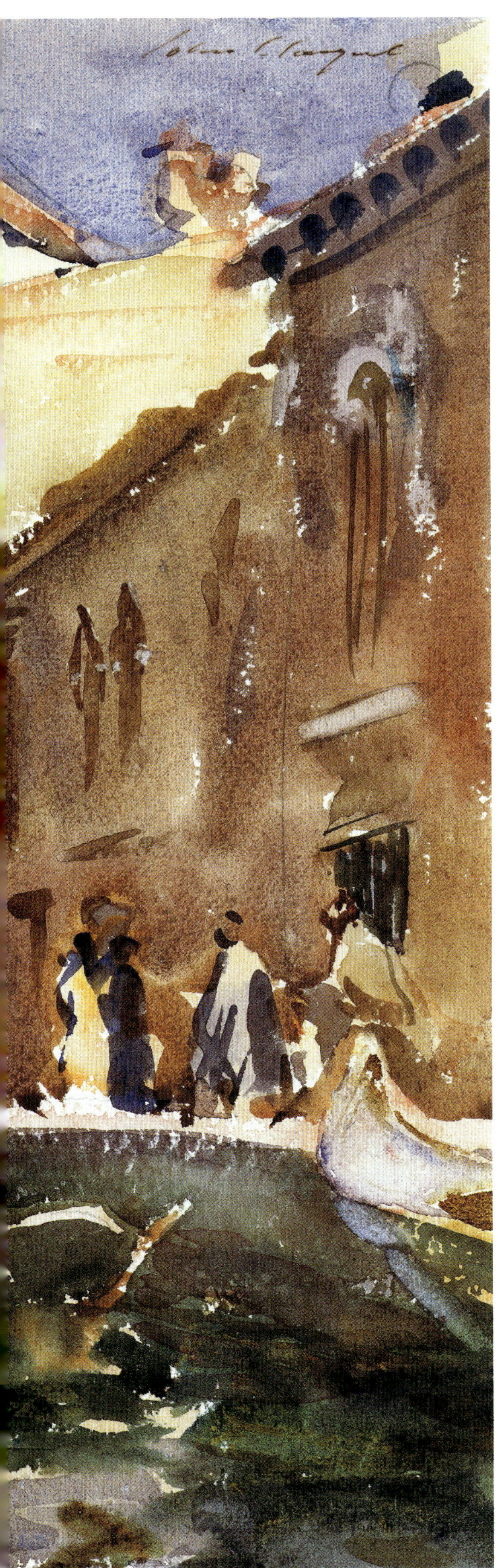

Venetian Canal N.D.
Watercolor and graphite underdrawing on white wove paper
15 3/4 x 21 in. (40 x 53.3 cm.)
The Metropolitan Museum of Art,
Purchase, Joseph Pulitzer Bequest, 1915 (15.142.10)
Photograph by Geoffrey Clements

Venice c. 1902
Watercolor over graphite on off-white wove paper
10 x 14 in. (25.2 x 35.4 cm.)
Worcester Art Museum, Worcester, Massachusetts
gift of Mr. and Mrs. Stuart Riley, Jr., 1974.332

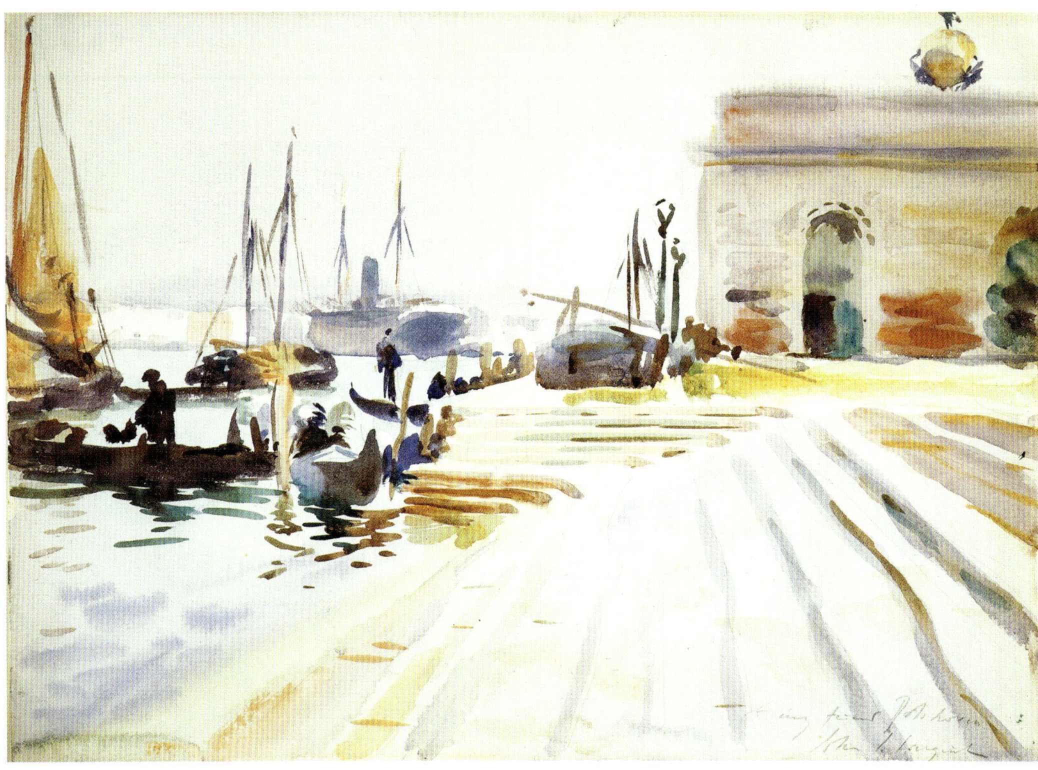

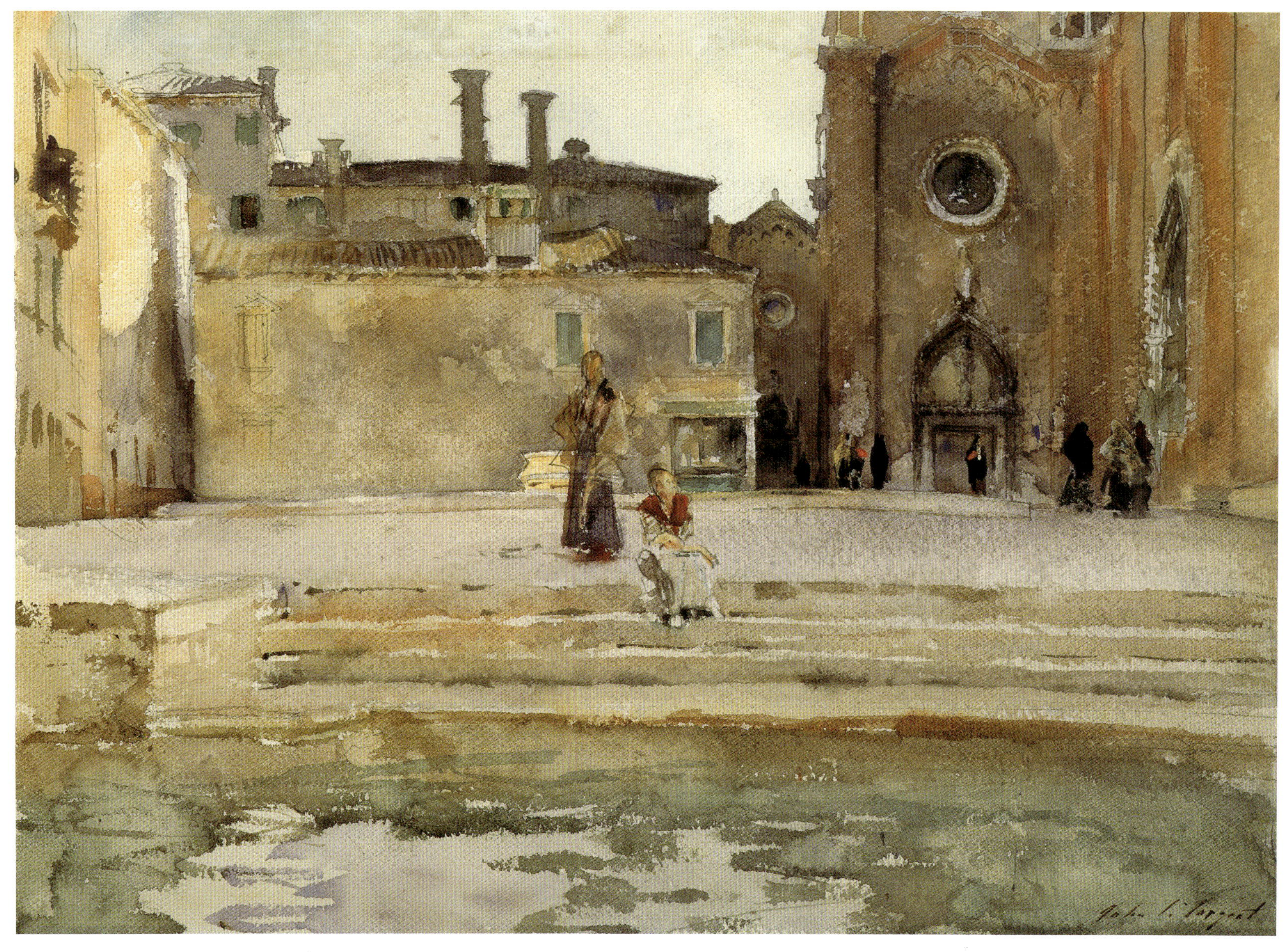

Campo dei Frari, Venice 1880

Watercolor over pencil with gouache on cream wove paper

9 7/8 x 14 in. (25.1 x 35.6 cm.)

In the Collection of The Corcoran Gallery of Art, Washington, DC

Gift of Mrs. Francis Ormond (Violet Sargent) and Miss Emily Sargent 52.10

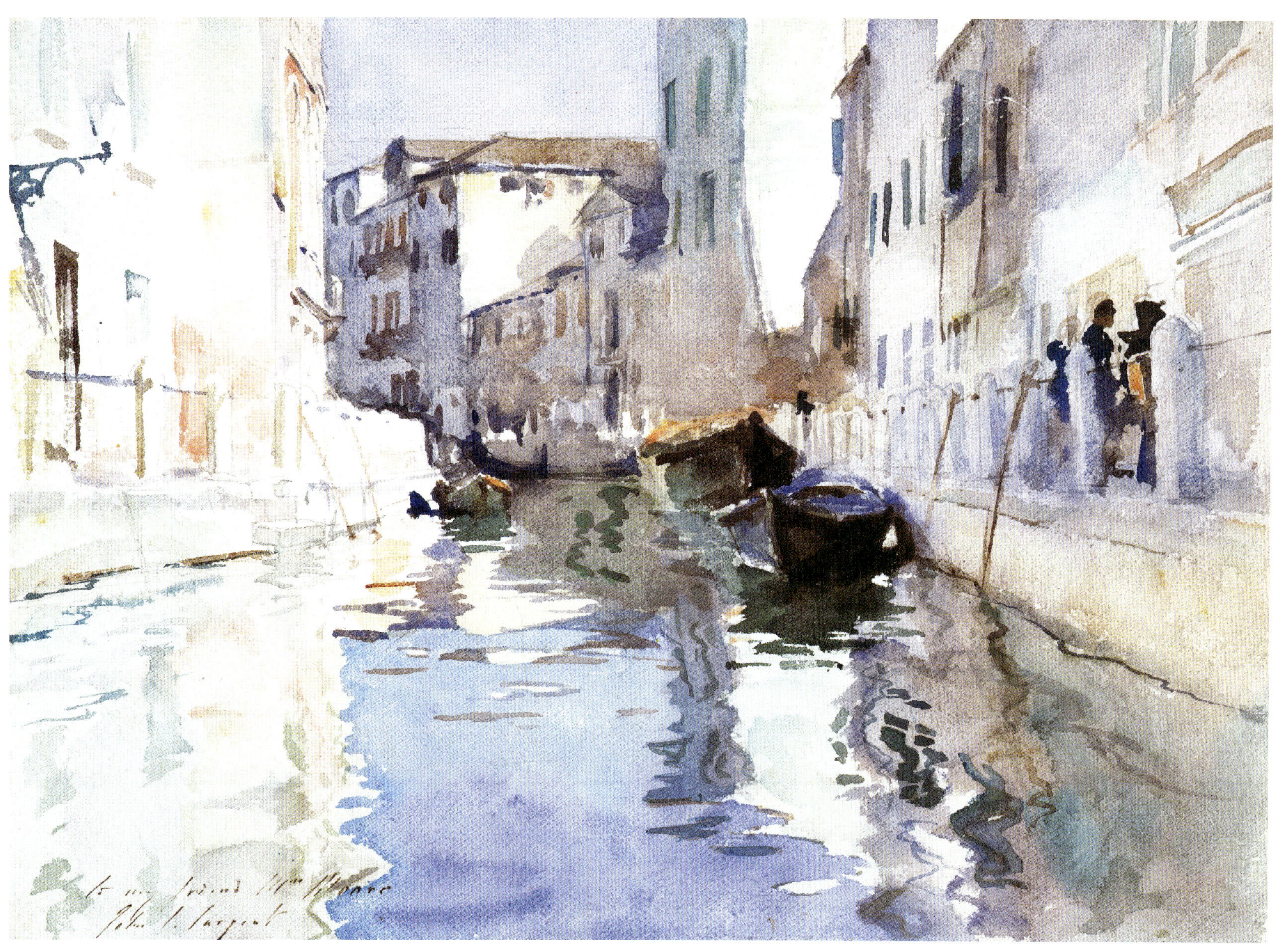

Zattere Rio Eremite, Venice 1904
Watercolor, gouache and pencil on paper
9 3/4 x 13 1/4 in. (24.8 x 34.9 cm.)
Private collection, New York
Courtesy Richard L. Feigen & Co., New York

The Middle East and North Africa

On trips to the Middle East and North Africa, Sargent was voracious in his appetite for visual data. He painted numerous studies of Bedouins, nomadic people whose way of life greatly intrigued this resident of proper London. In painting a dark-eyed desert wanderer he captured the fierceness of the man's comportment, but he could just as readily make a moving study of a mother and child standing in the shadows of a tent. His watercolors of the famous horses on which they rode show them in a line in open-air stables.

Whether on the plains of Galilee or in the desert, Sargent depicted men and women in their daily routines, mending sails, tilling the soil with a pair of oxen. These quick, loosely-painted renderings were sometimes translated into a painting or used as an *aide-memoire* when working on a section of the Boston Public Library murals. In the remarkable view of the desert from Jerusalem, Sargent seemed to seek the essential color harmonies of the scenery, the hot pinks and oranges of the dry country shimmering before his eyes.

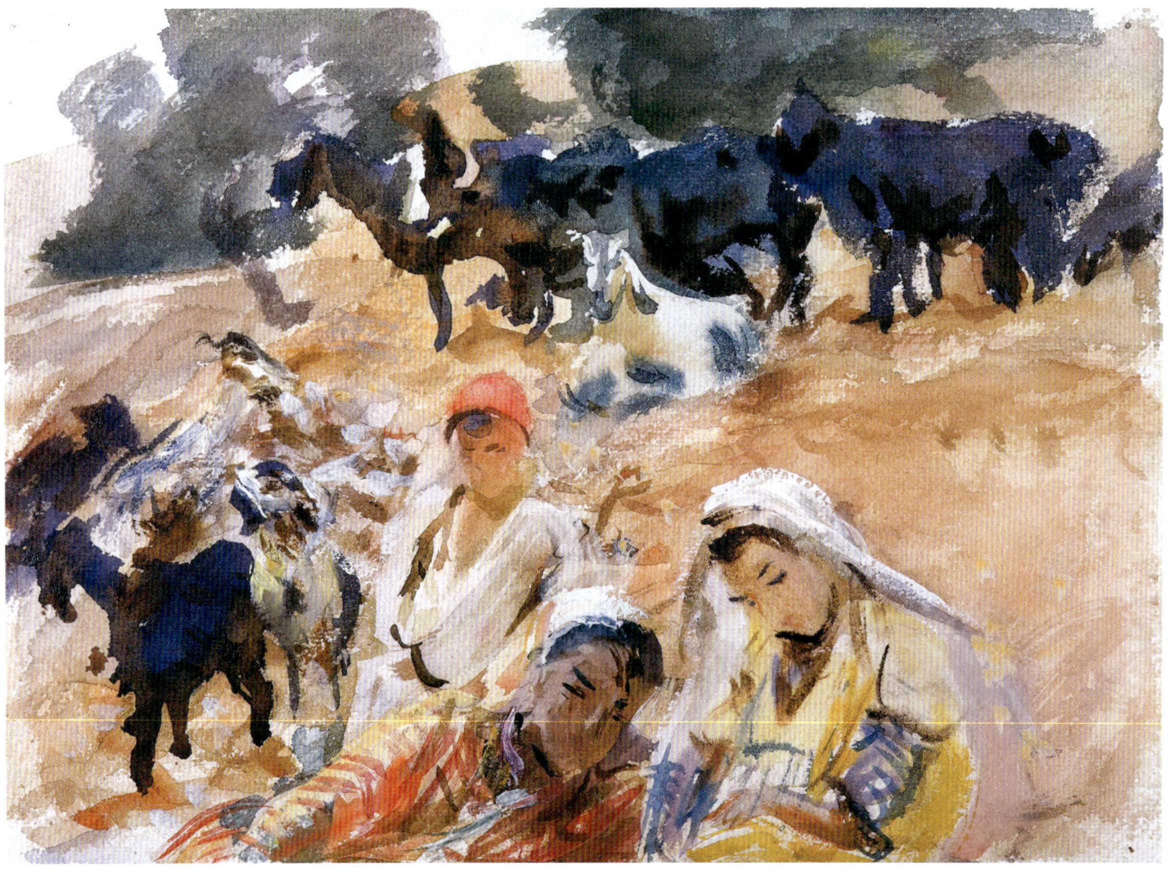

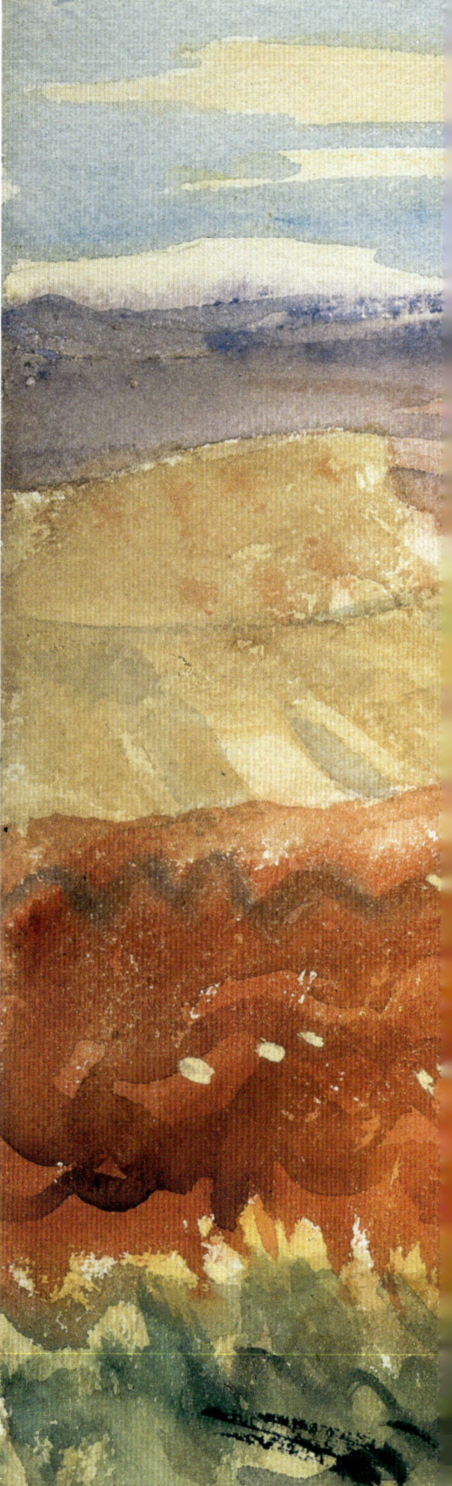

Goatherds c. 1905–06
Watercolor
10 x 14 in. (25.4 x 35.6 cm.)
The Brooklyn Museum of Art,
Purchased by special subscription, (09.821)

Hills of Galilee, c. 1905–06
Watercolor heightened with white
12 x 18 in. (30.5 x 45.7 cm.)
The Brooklyn Museum of Art,
Purchased by special subscription, (09.823)

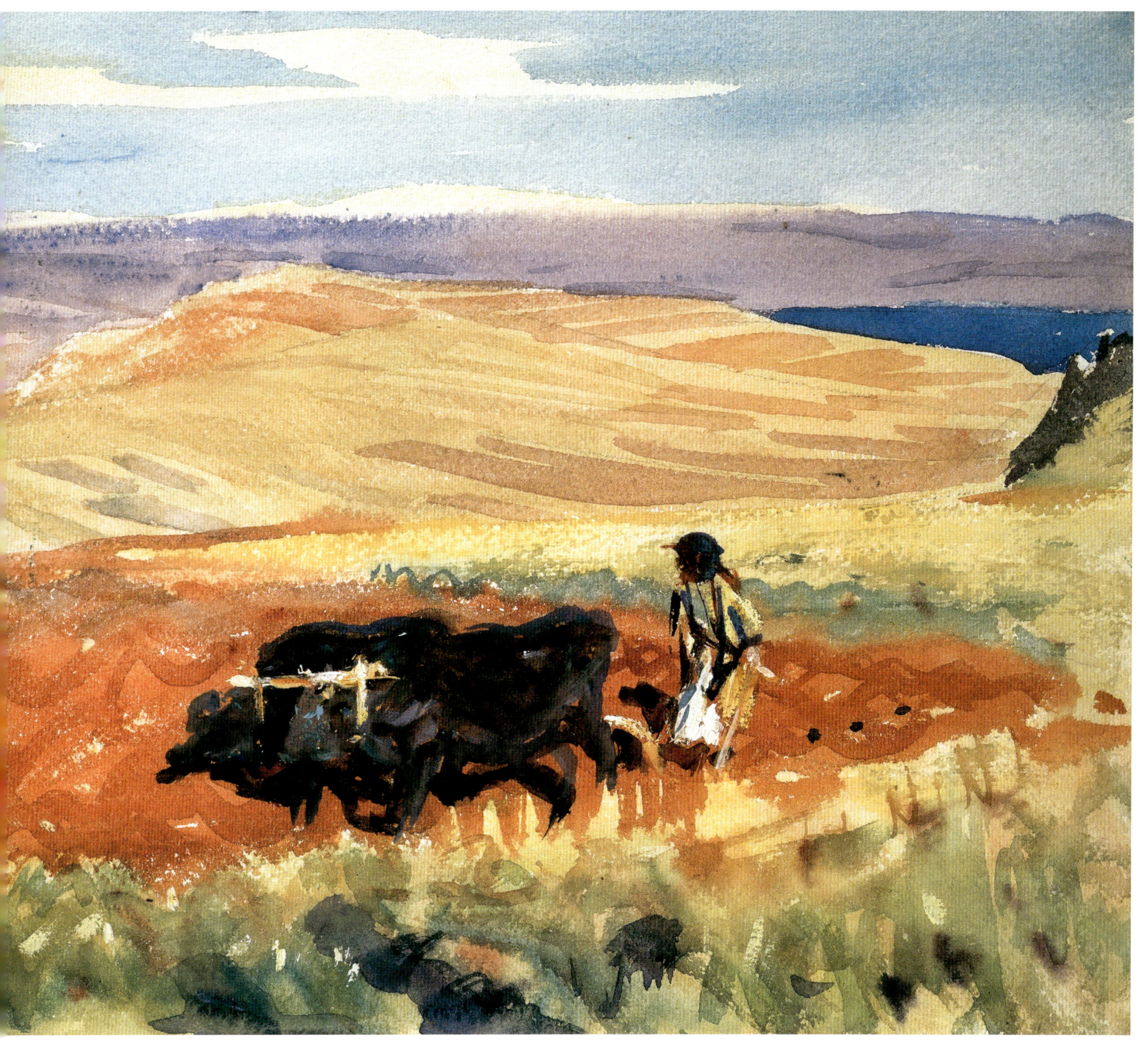

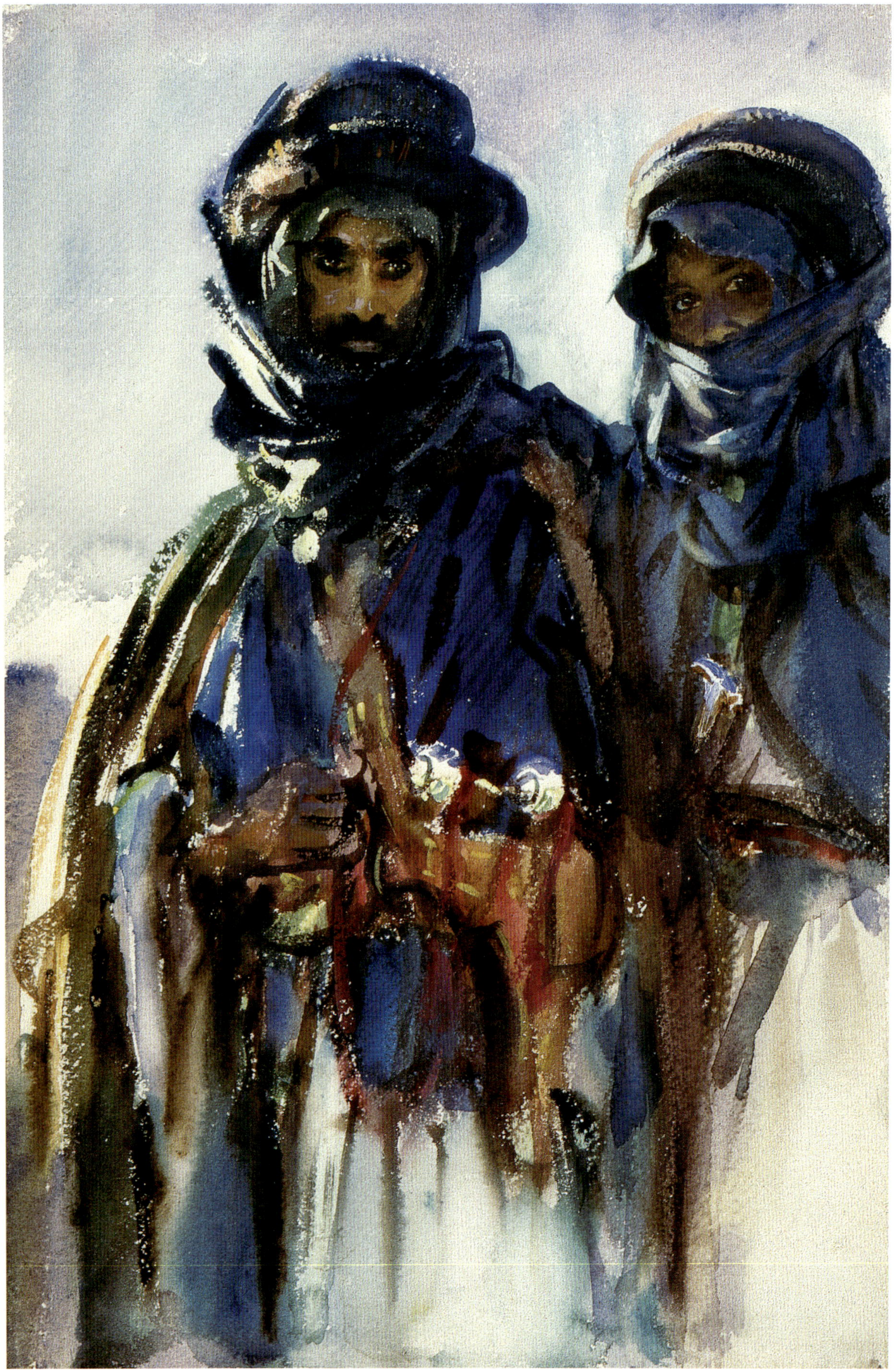

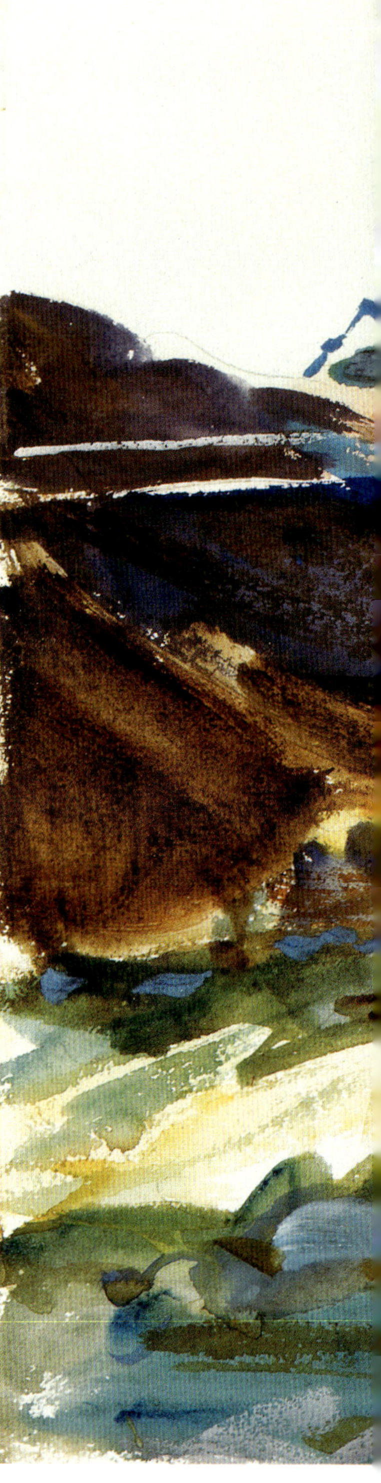

Bedouins c. 1905–06
Watercolor
18 x 12 in. (45.8 x 30.5 cm.)
The Brooklyn Museum of Art,
Purchased by special subscription, (09.814)

Bedouin Women c. 1905–06
Watercolor heightened with white
12 x 18 1/16 in. (30.5 x 45.9 cm.)
The Brooklyn Museum of Art,
Purchased by special subscription, (09.46)

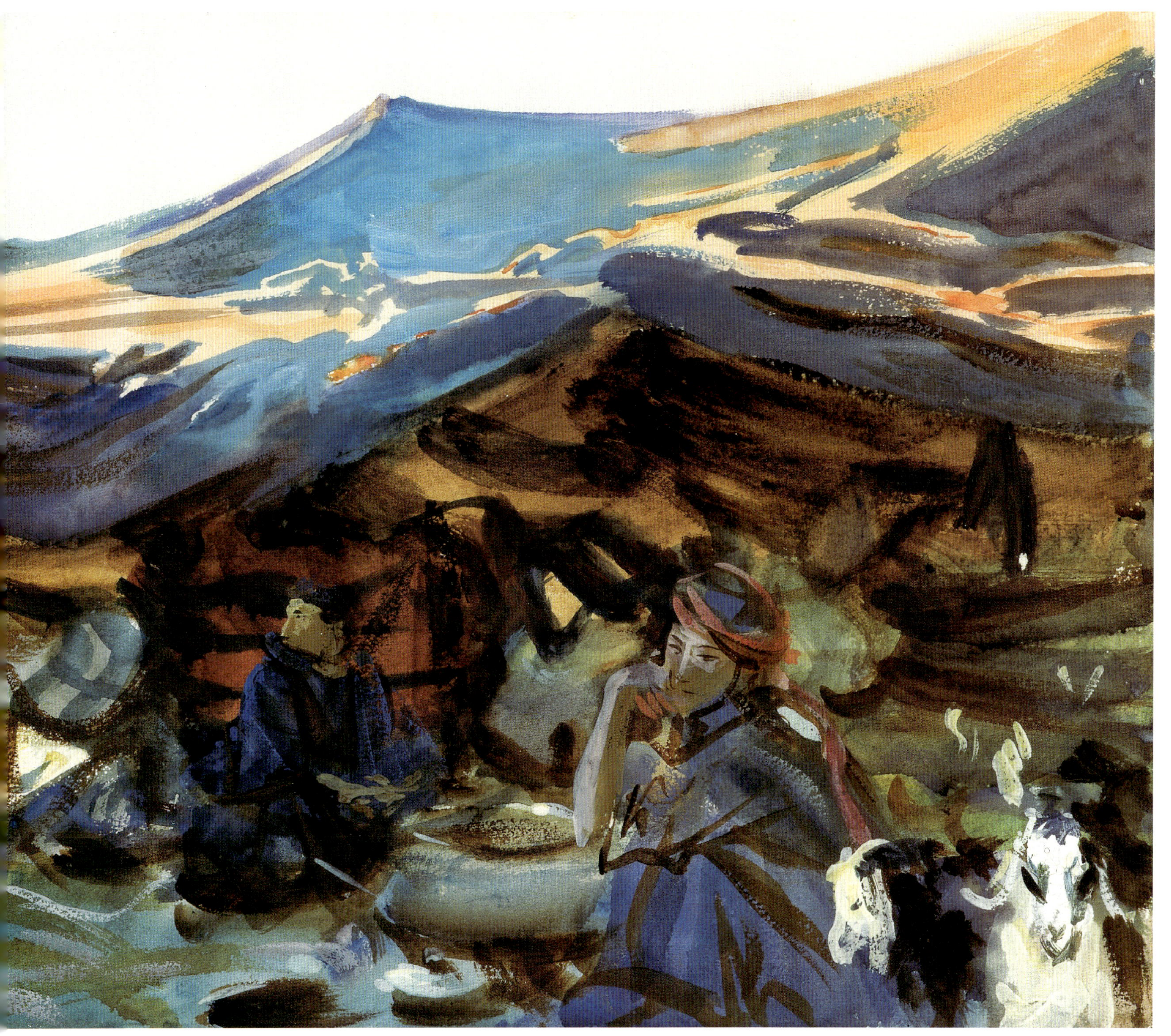

Black Tent c. 1905–06
Watercolor heightened with white
12 x 18 1/8 in. (30.5 x 46.0 cm.)
The Brooklyn Museum of Art,
Purchased by special subscription, (09.815)

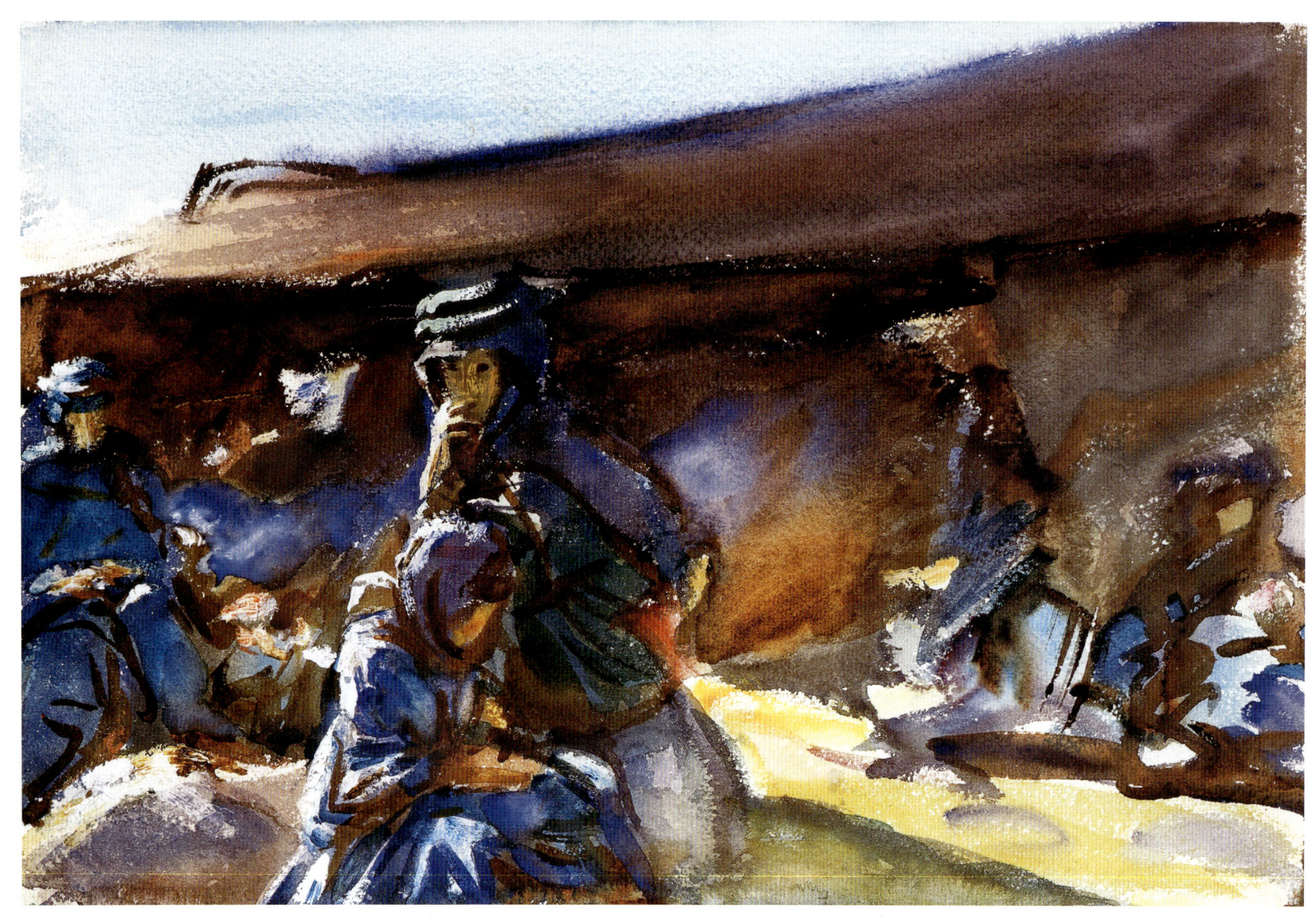

Arab Woman n.d.
Watercolor, gouache, on off-white wove paper
17 7/8 x 12 in. (45.4 x 30.5 cm.)
The Metropolitan Museum of Art,
Gift of Mrs. Francis Ormond, 1950 (50.130.43)

Bedouin Mother 1905
Watercolor
18 1/16 x 12 in. (45.9 x 30.5 cm.)
The Brooklyn Museum of Art,
Purchased by special subscription, (09.812)

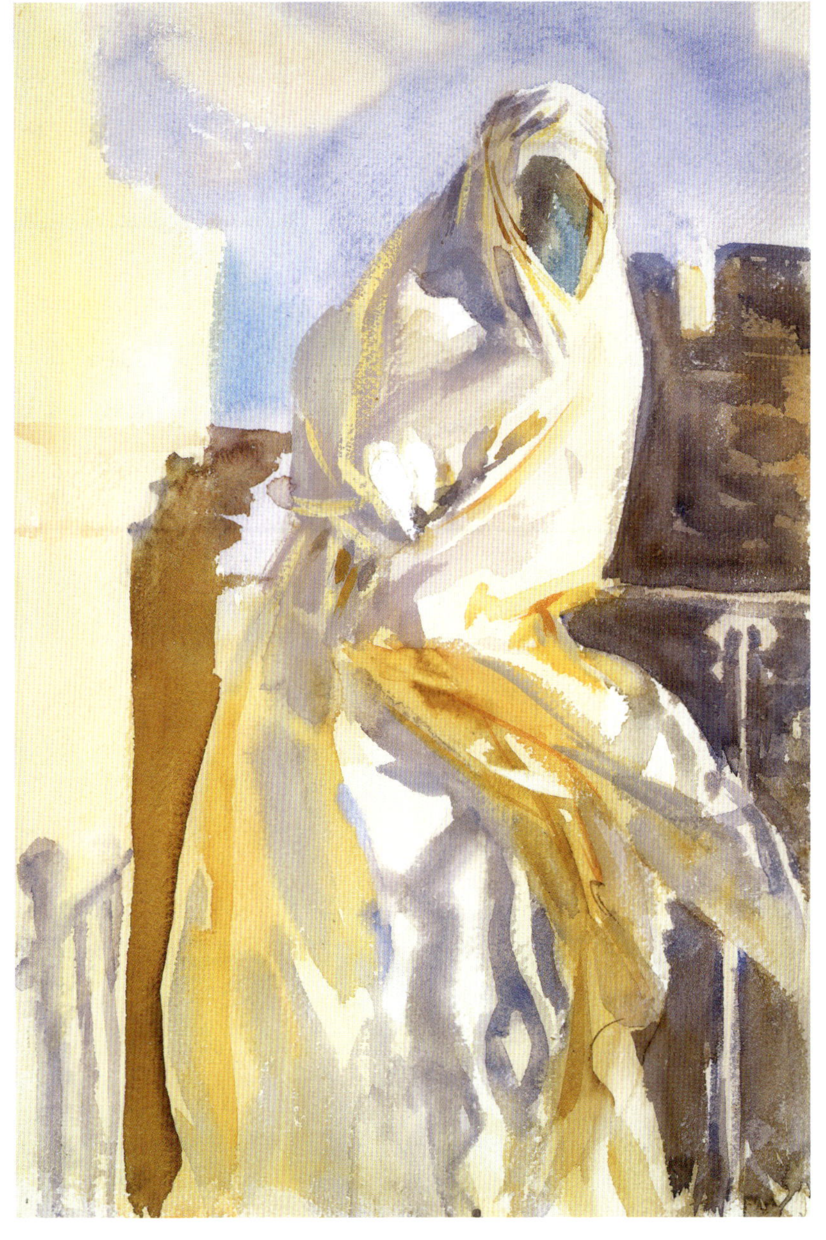

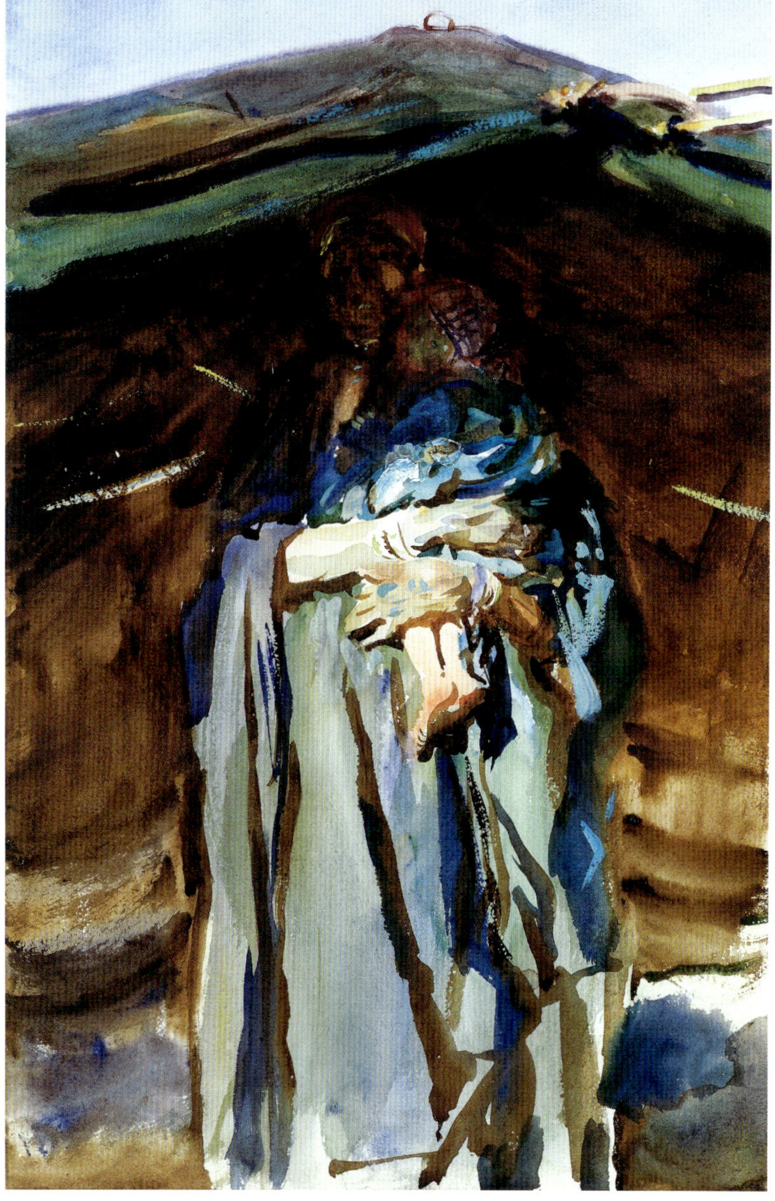

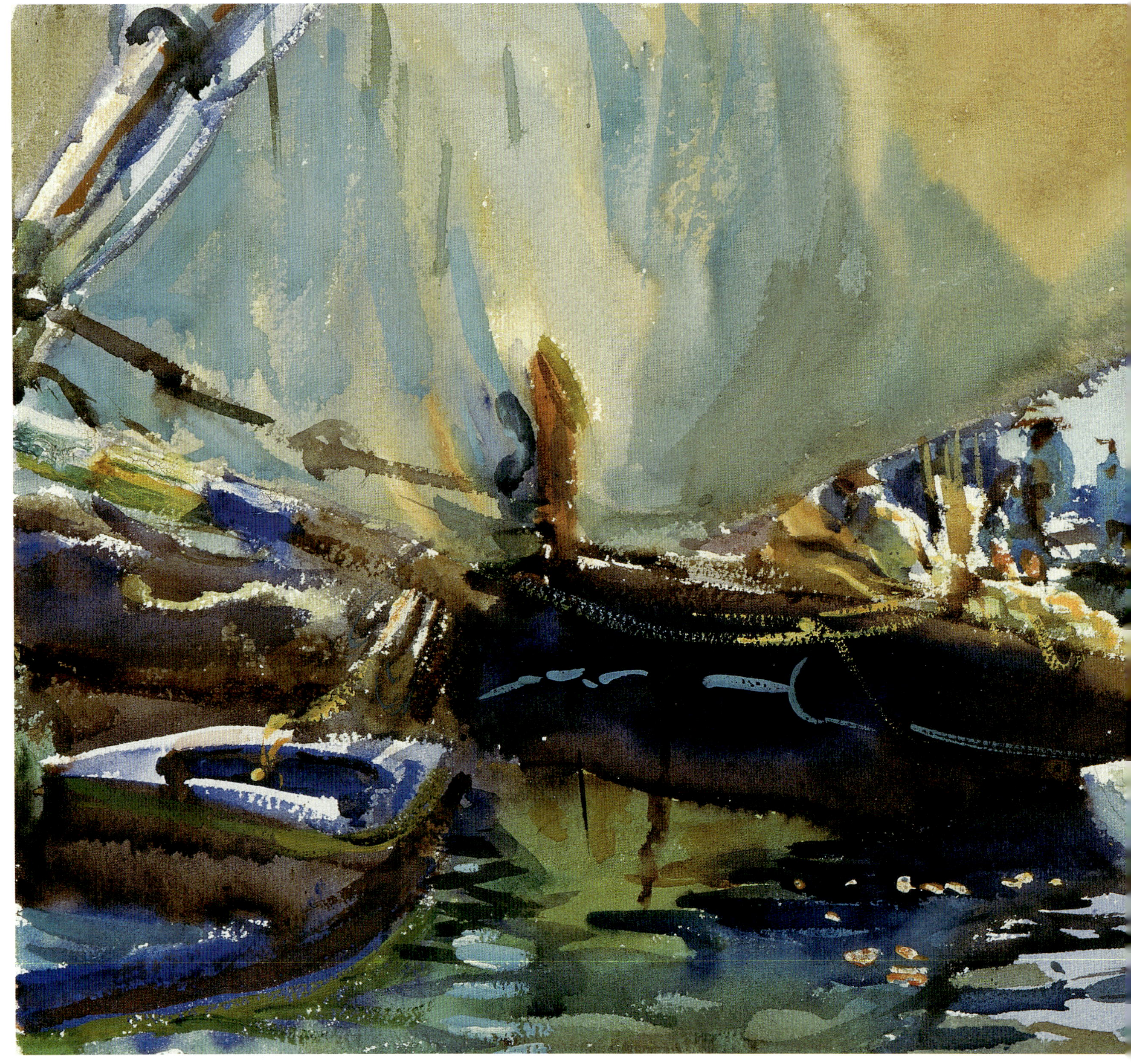

. . . Whatever he [Sargent] painted, water-colour in his hands seemed to lose something of its limitation and become a more powerful medium, giving the substances represented a solidity and volume more associated with oil-colour.

—Evan Charteris, 1927

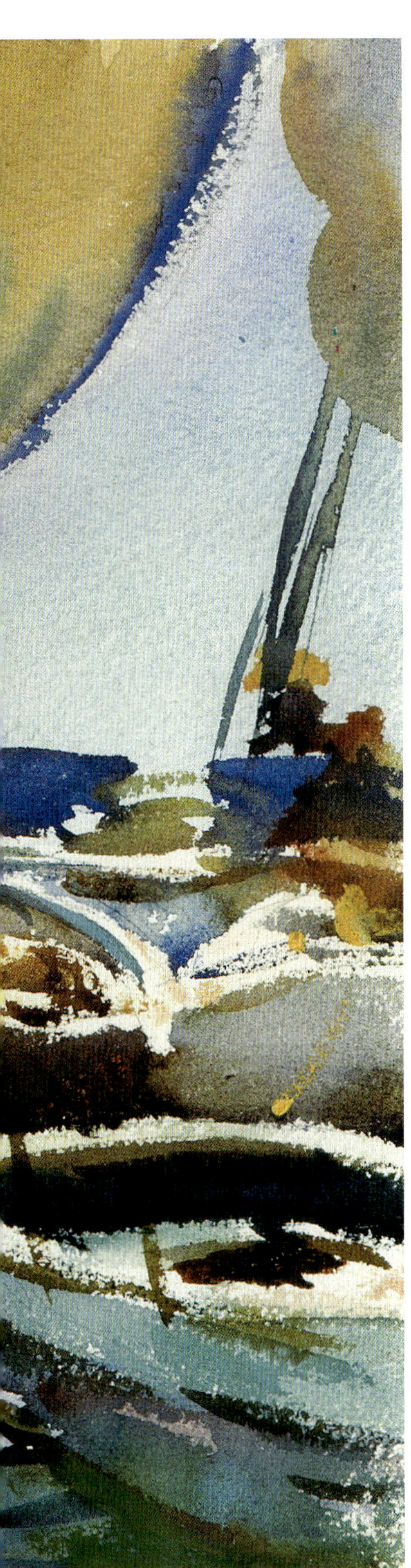

Melon Boats c. 1905
Watercolor
14 x 19 15/16 in. (35.6 x 50.7 cm.)
The Brooklyn Museum of Art,
Purchased by special subscription, (09.829)

Mending a Sail c. 1905–06
Watercolor over pencil
10 1/16 x 14 in. (25.6 x 35.5 cm.)
The Brooklyn Museum of Art,
Purchased by special subscription, (09.830)

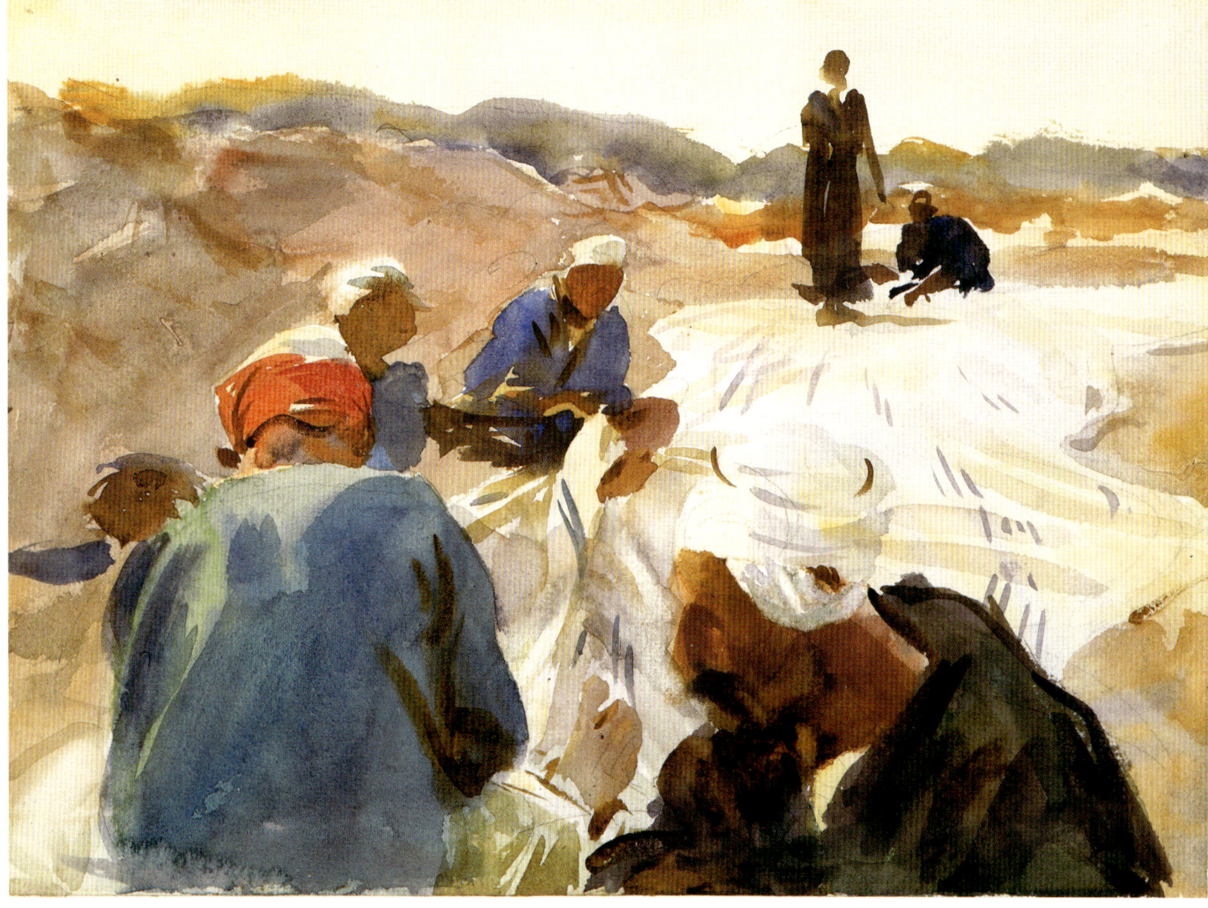

To see one of Sargent's water colours in the making always reminded me of the first chapter of Genesis, when the evening and the morning were the first day, order developed from chaos, and one thing after another was created of its kind.

—Mary Newbold Patterson Hale, 1927

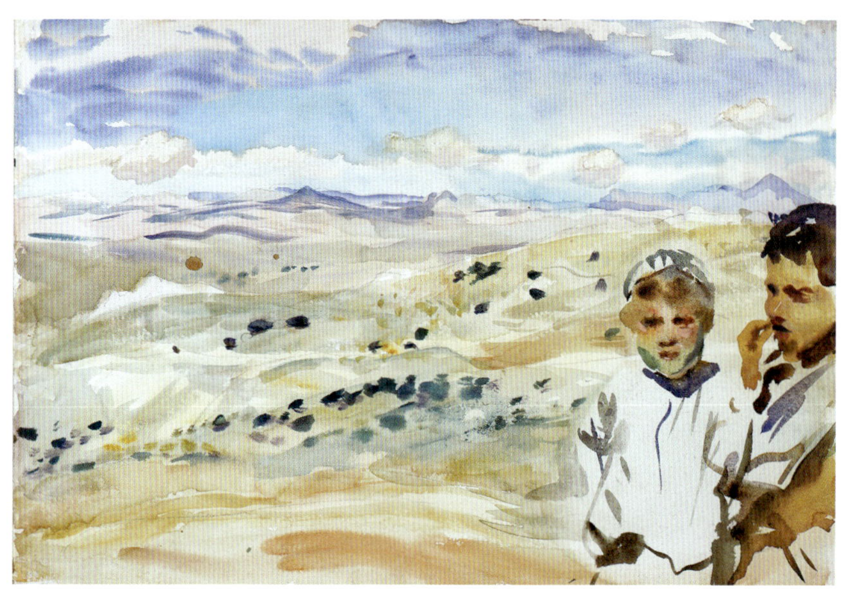

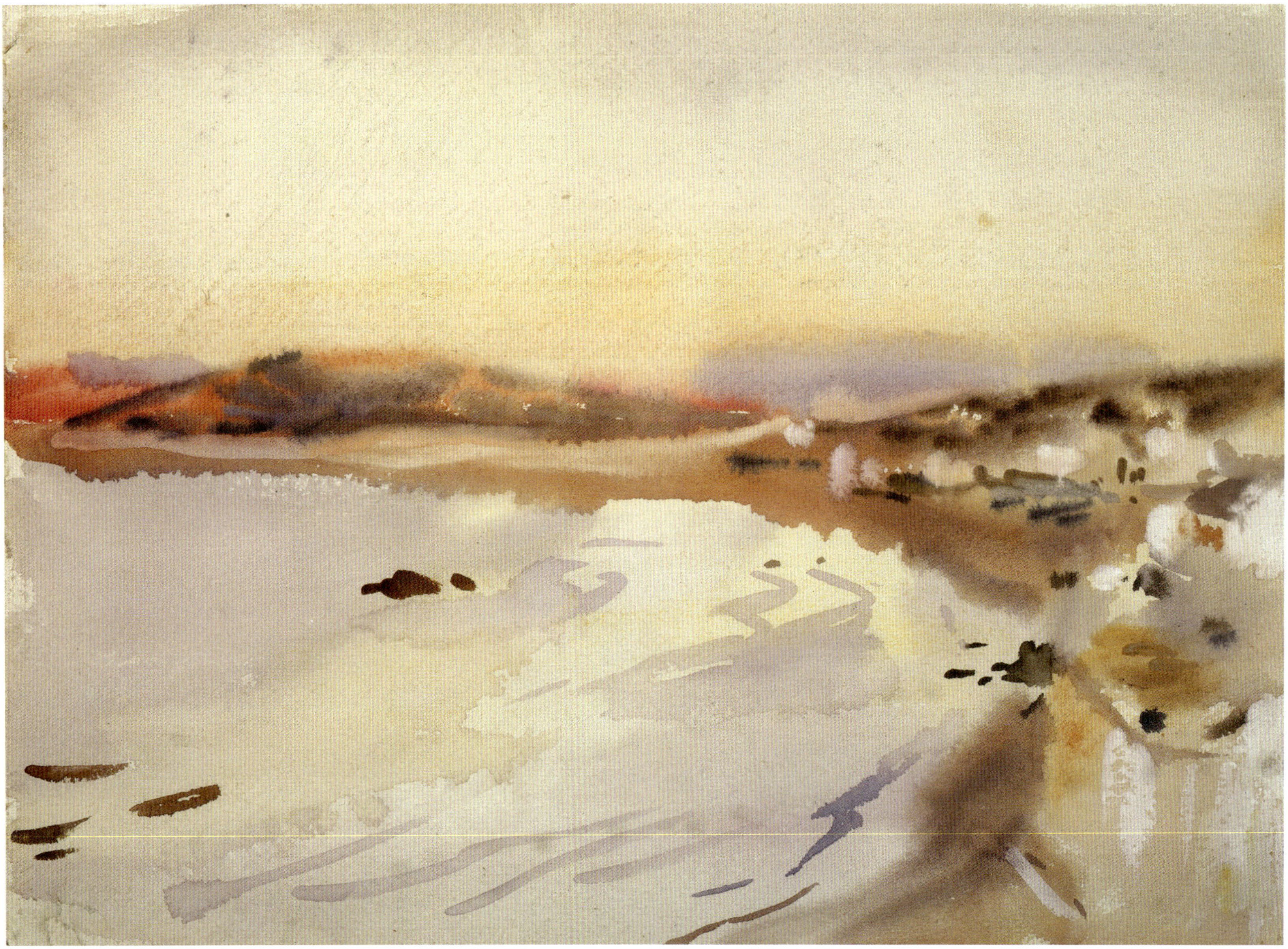

(opposite, above)

Girgenti c. 1901
Watercolor on paper
12 x 18 in. (30.5 x 45.7 cm.)
Private collection

(opposite, below)

Tangier, c. 1905–06
Watercolor
10 x 14 in. (25.4 x 35.5 cm.)
The Brooklyn Museum of Art,
Purchased by special subscription, (09.841)

The Desert from Jerusalem 1905
Gouache on paper
10 7/16 x 14 3/8 in. (26.5 x 36.5 cm.)
The Nelson-Atkins Museum of Art, Kansas City, Missouri
(Gift of Stevenson Scott) © The Nelson Gallery Foundation

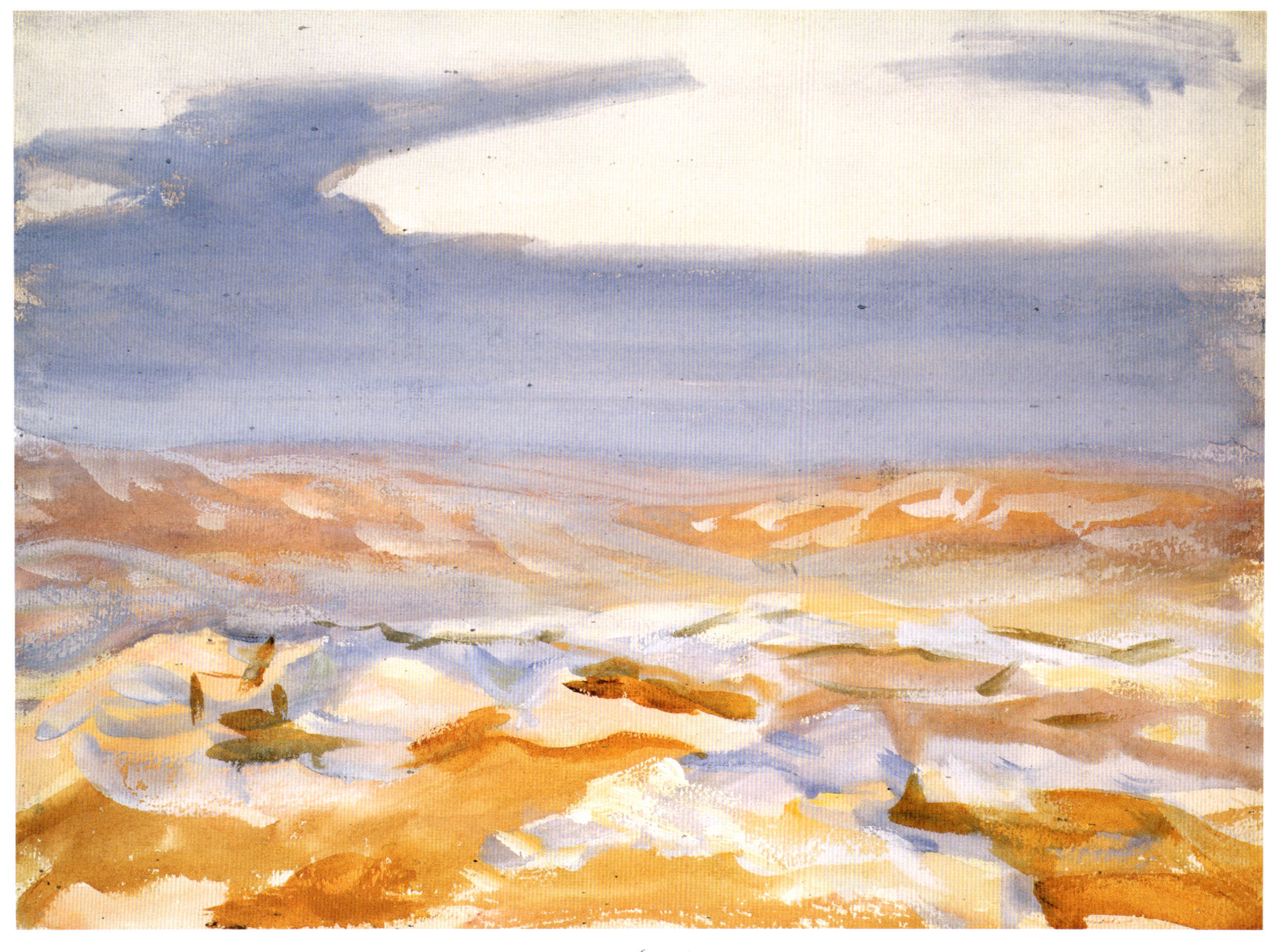

In water-colour, he [Sargent] found endless scope for his driving need of unhampered personal expression.

—MARTIN HARDIE, 1930

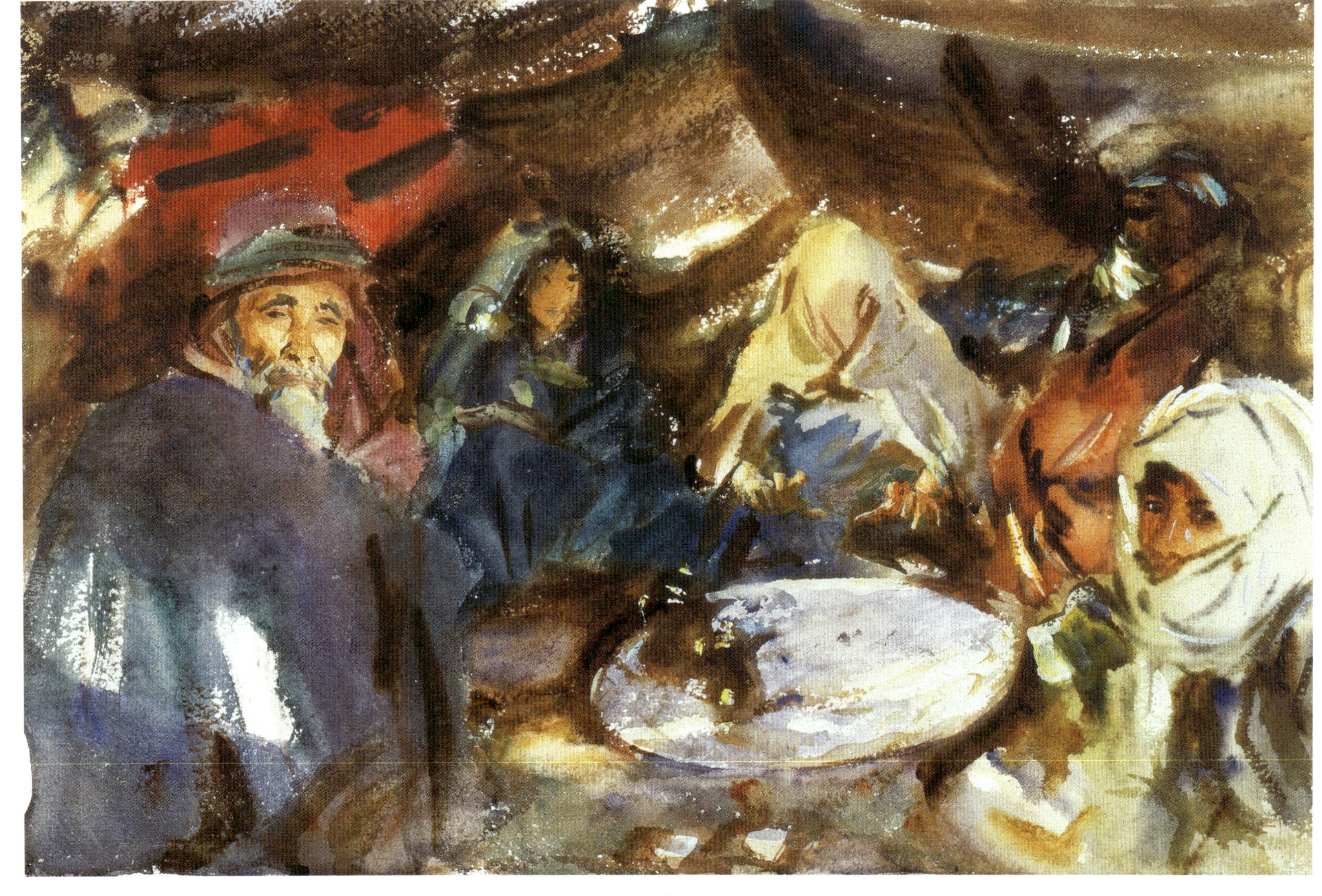

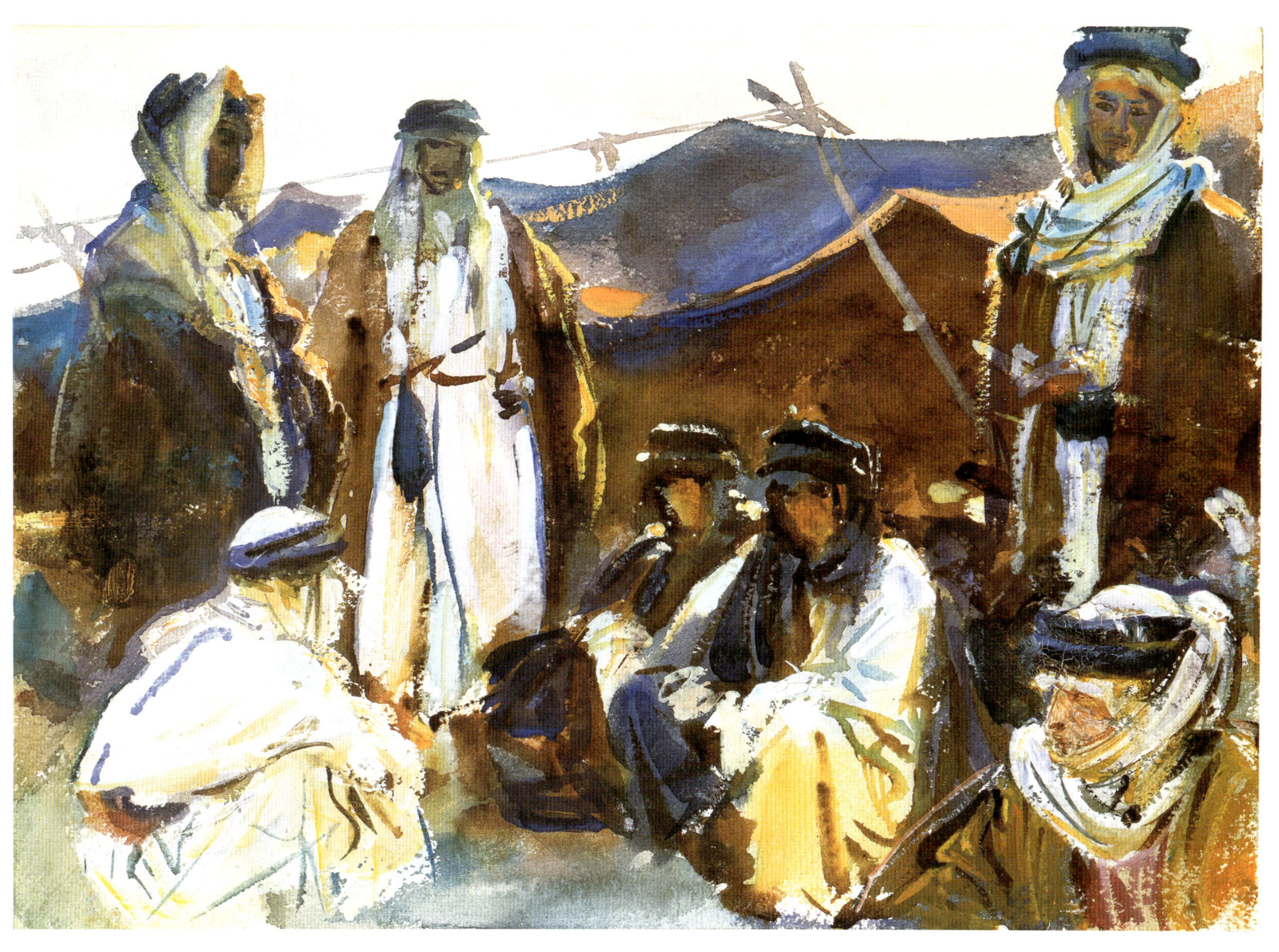

Arab Gypsies in a Tent c. 1905–06
Watercolor
10 7/16 x 14 3/8 in. (26.5 x 36.6 cm.)
The Brooklyn Museum of Art,
Purchased by special subscription, (09.808)

Bedouin Camp c. 1905–06
Watercolor
10 x 14 1/16 in. (25.4 x 35.7 cm.)
The Brooklyn Museum of Art,
Purchased by special subscription, (09.811)

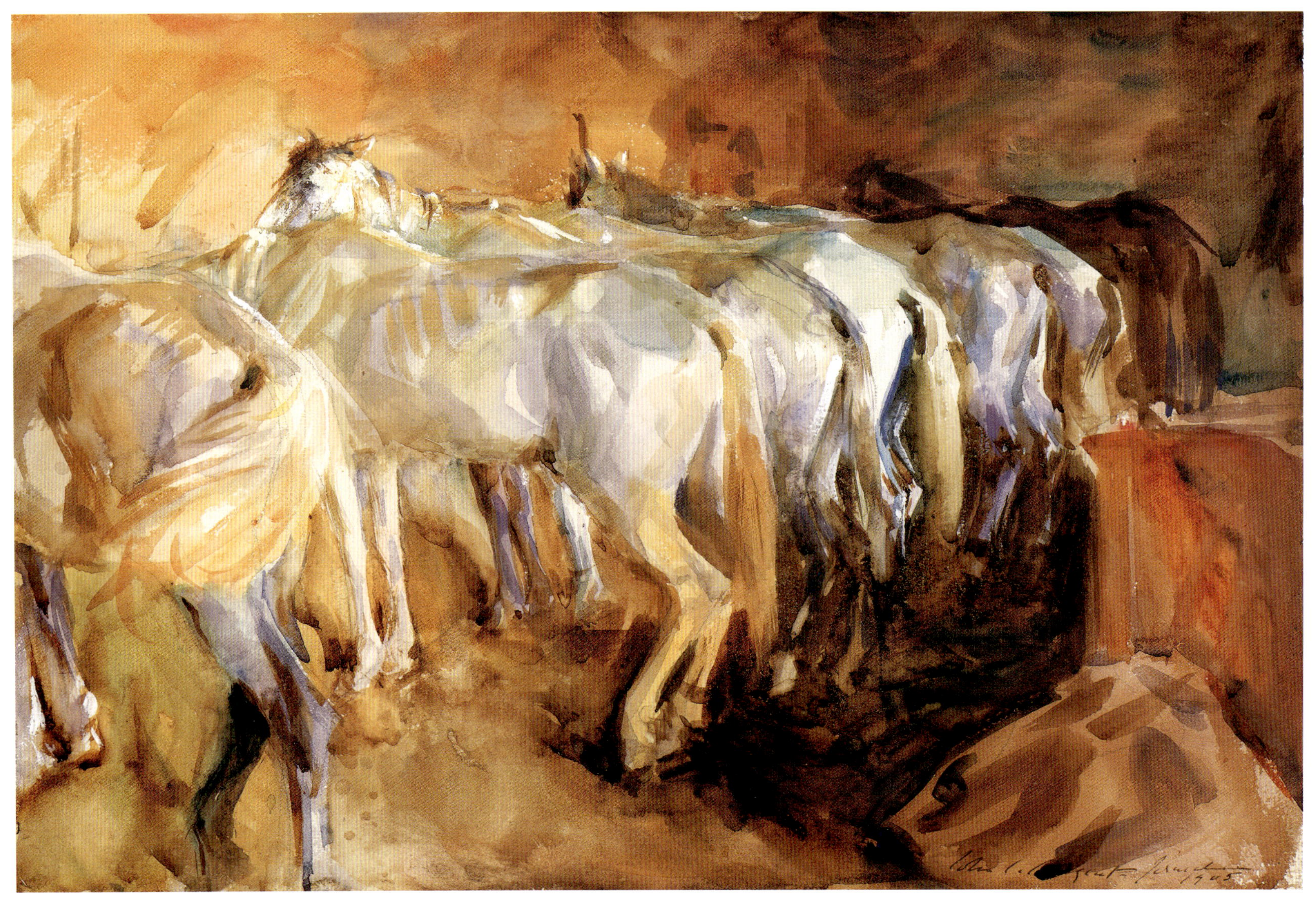

It is very kind of you to have written to me of the comfortableness of the horses in their new abode—I feel that to be worthy of this promotion they ought to have had blue ribands plaited into their tails and manes, like Herod's horses in Flaubert's beautiful Herodiade. You know your sketch was done in Jerusalem, but the stalls were not Herod's but Thomas Cook's who has succeeded him in Palestine.

—John Singer Sargent, letter to Isabella Stewart Gardner, January 7, 1907

Bus Horses in Jerusalem 1905
Watercolor on paper
11 3/4 x 17 3/4 (30 x 45 cm.)
Isabella Stewart Gardner Museum, Boston

Arab Stable c. 1905–06
Watercolor
10 7/16 x 14 3/8 in. (26.5 x 36.6 cm.)
The Brooklyn Museum of Art,
Purchased by special subscription, (09.808)

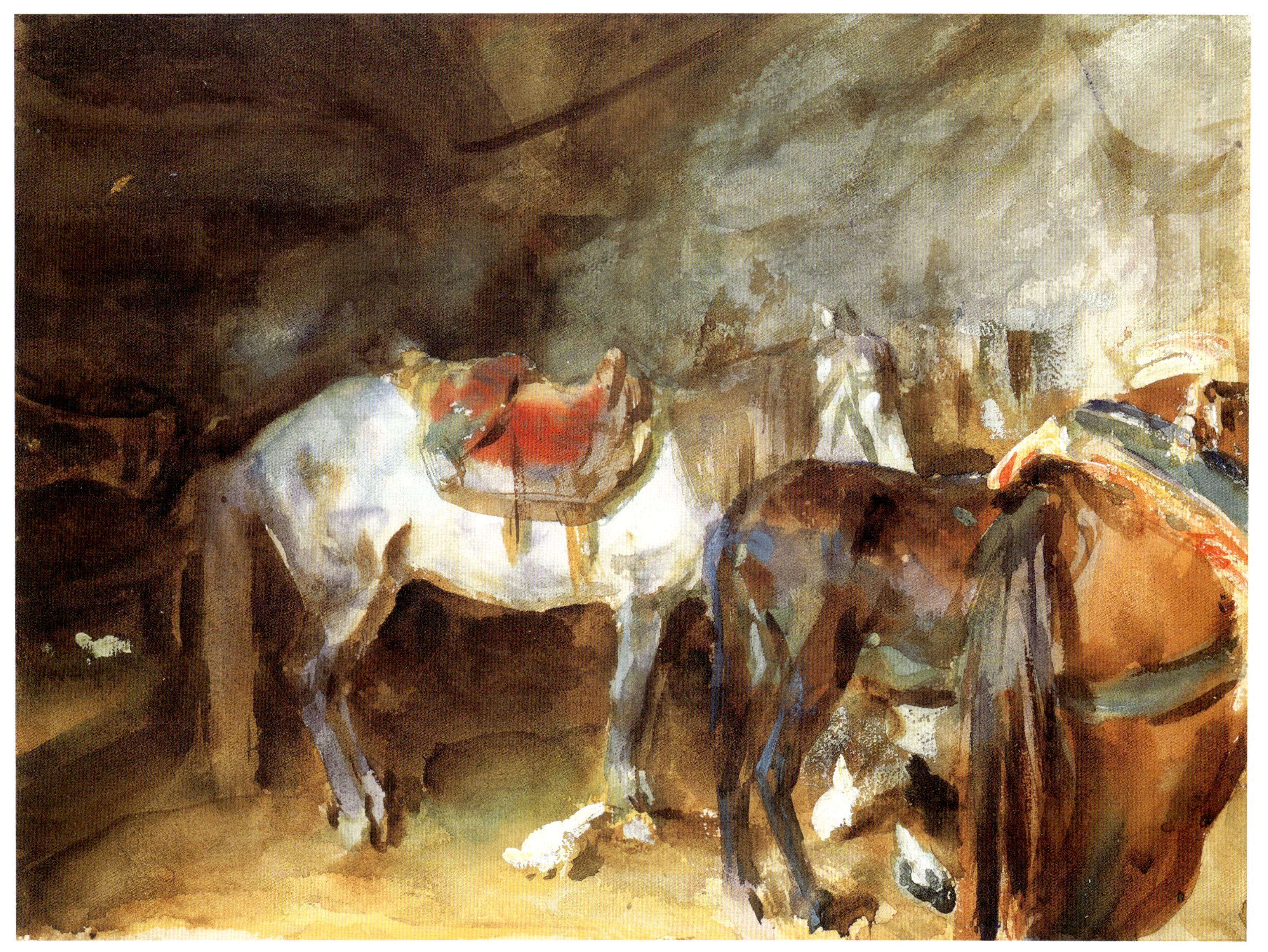

In the Mountains

In the course of annual excursions into the Alps, Sargent maintained his rigorous habits of painting. Even when the initial rumblings of the First World War were being heard, and he and his traveling companions experienced difficulties crossing borders, the artist never stopped working; indeed, he is known to have barely acknowledged the situation.

Sargent frequently included one or more figures in his mountain landscapes. At the same time, he turned out some of the purest vistas of his artistic career. He was something of a geologist in his choice of subjects, which included an avalanche track and crags in the Simplon Pass and great blocks of marble in the Carrara quarries. Glacial brooks and streams that cut their way down the precipitous slopes cast a special spell on the artist and led to numerous watercolors.

The painter who had captured the lines of a Baroque church in Venice and the sumptuous gardens of European aristocracy could also find visual pleasure in the roughhewn structure of a mountain hut with geese waddling across the foreground.

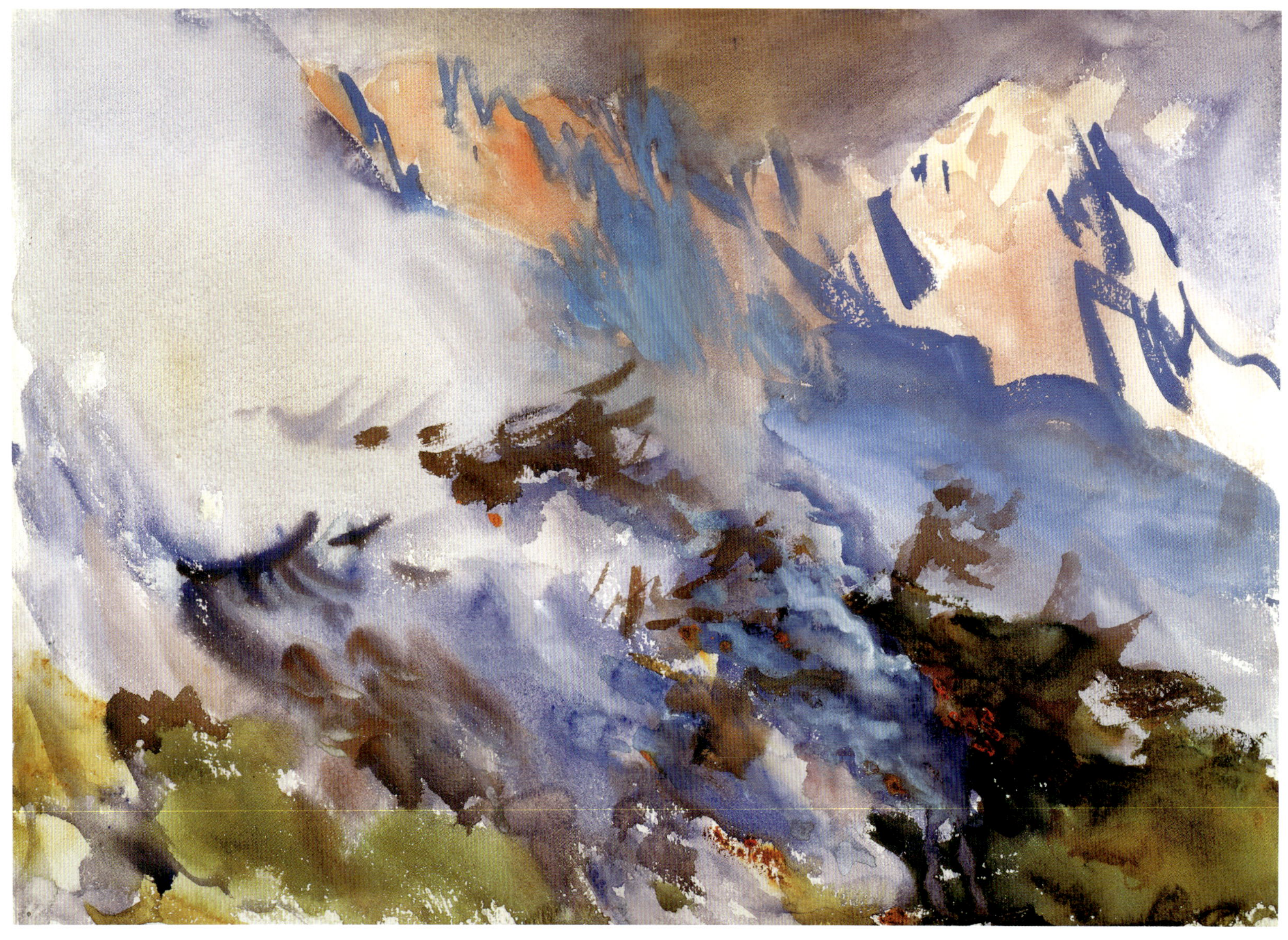

The Simplon N.D.
Watercolor, 11 3/4 x 17 1/2 in. (29.8 x 44.5 cm.)
Museum of Art, Rhode Island School of Design,
Gift of Mrs. Gustav Radeke

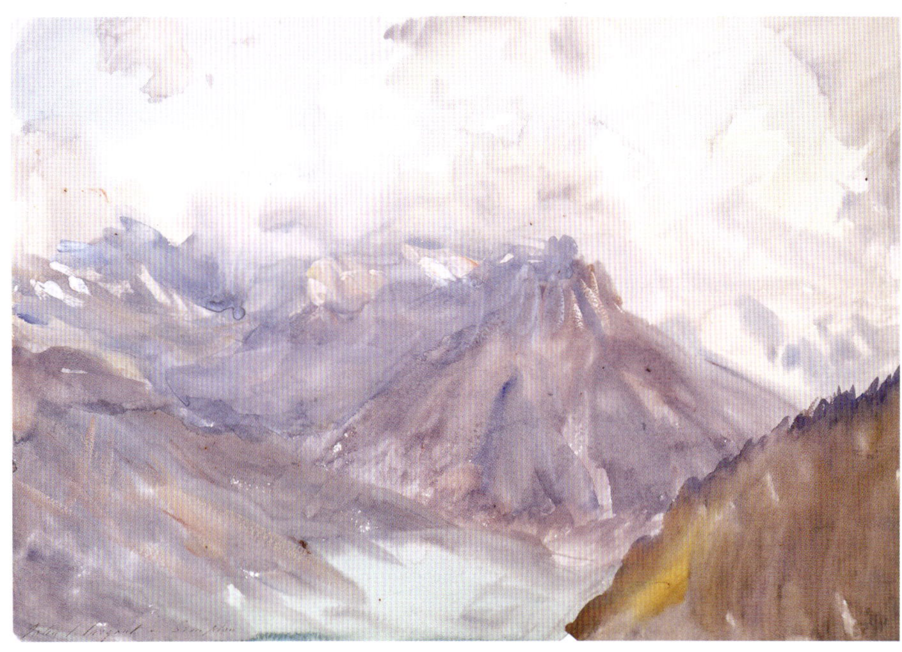

(opposite)
Mountain Fire c. 1903-08
Watercolor, 14 x 20 in. (35.5 x 50.8 cm.)
The Brooklyn Museum of Art,
Purchased by special subscription, (09.831)

The Simplon c. 1910
Watercolor and pencil on paper
13 7/8 x 20 in. (37 x 50.8 cm.)
Courtesy Christie's Images

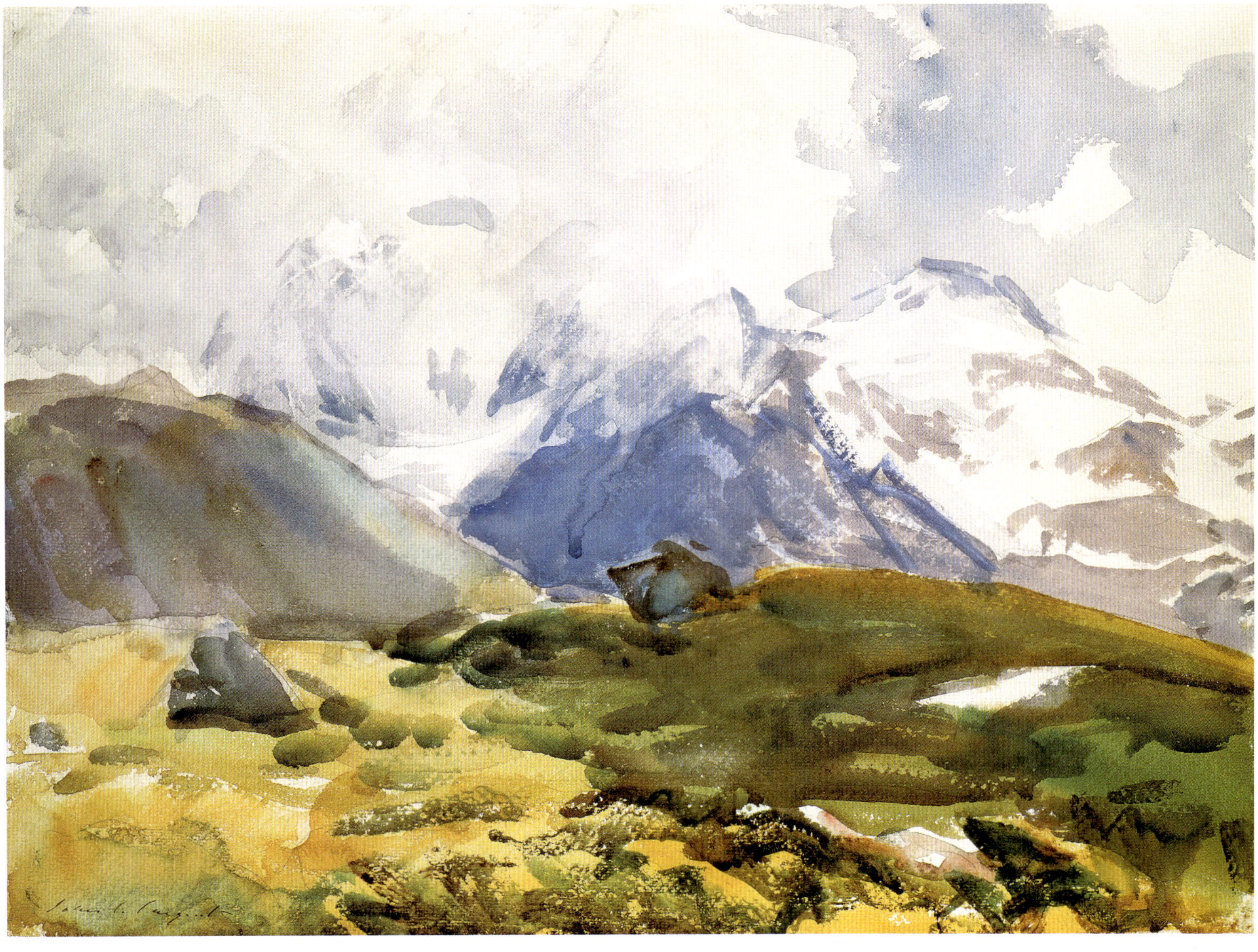

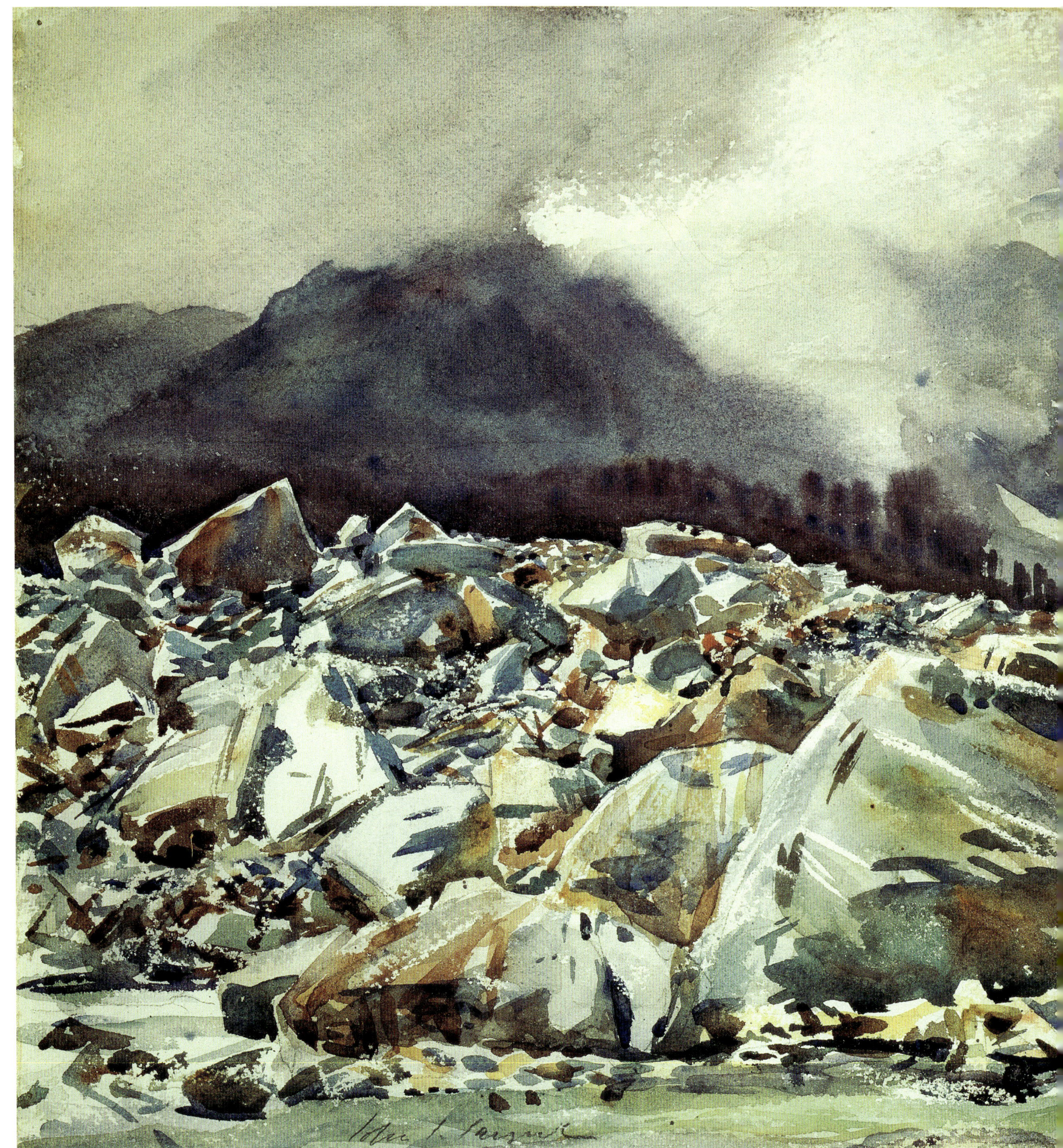

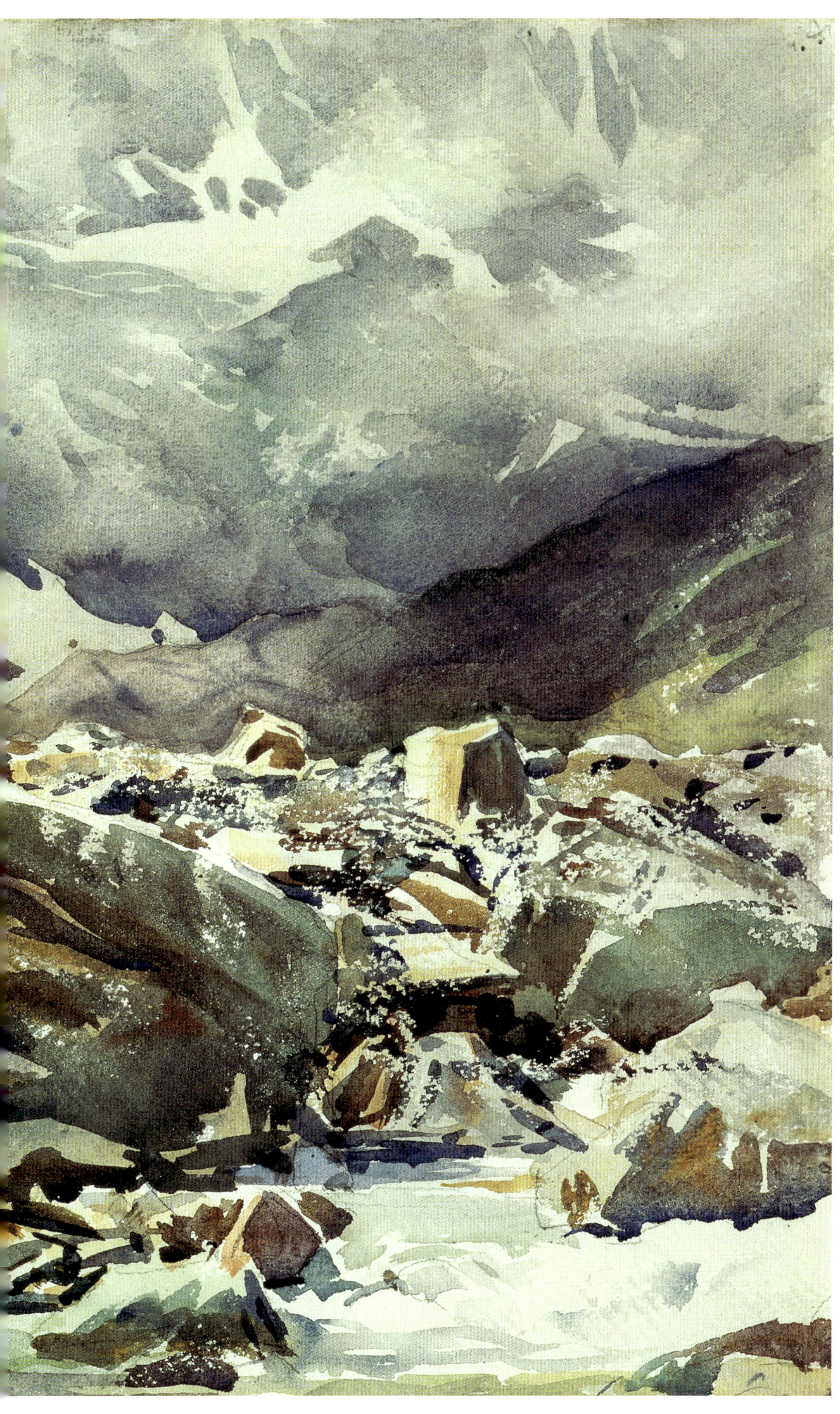

At one pole of his self-expression stand the splendid notes of travel and holiday, in which, with an authority quite unequaled in his formal canvases, he [Sargent] has resolved the complicated appearances of an outdoor scene into a coherent design.

—New York Times, 1925

Simplon Pass: Avalanche Track n.d.
Watercolor on paper
13 x 20 1/2 in. (33 x 52 cm.)
Charles Henry Hayden Fund,
Courtesy, Museum of Fine Arts, Boston

Simplon Pass: Crags 1911
Watercolor
13 11/16 x 19 in. (34.8 x 48.2 cm.)
Hayden Collection,
Courtesy, Museum of Fine Arts, Boston

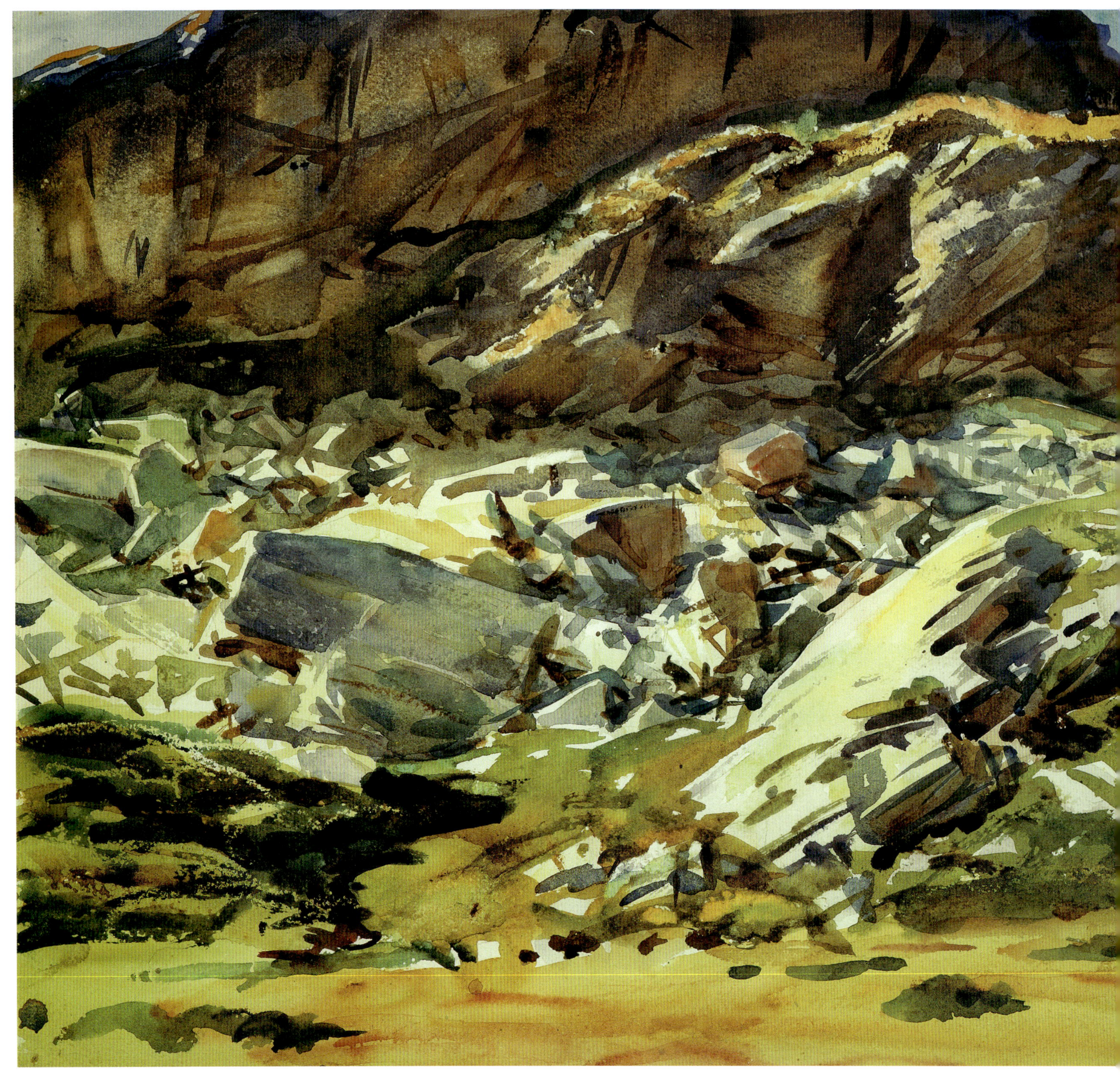

(top)

The Shallows N.D.
Watercolor
15 3/4 x 20 1/2 in. (40 x 52.1 cm.)
Hayden Collection, Charles Henry Hayden Fund,
Courtesy, Museum of Fine Arts, Boston

(bottom)

Brook among Rocks C. 1907
Watercolor
9 1/2 x 19 1/8 in. (24.1 x 48.5 cm.)
Bequest of Elise Faye Loeffler,
Courtesy, Museum of Fine Arts, Boston

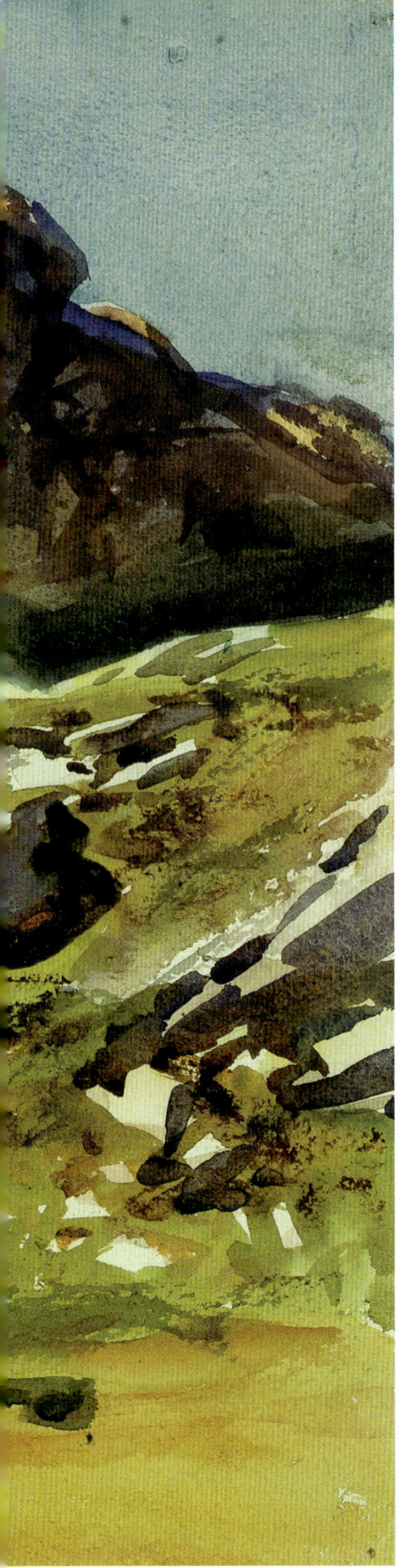

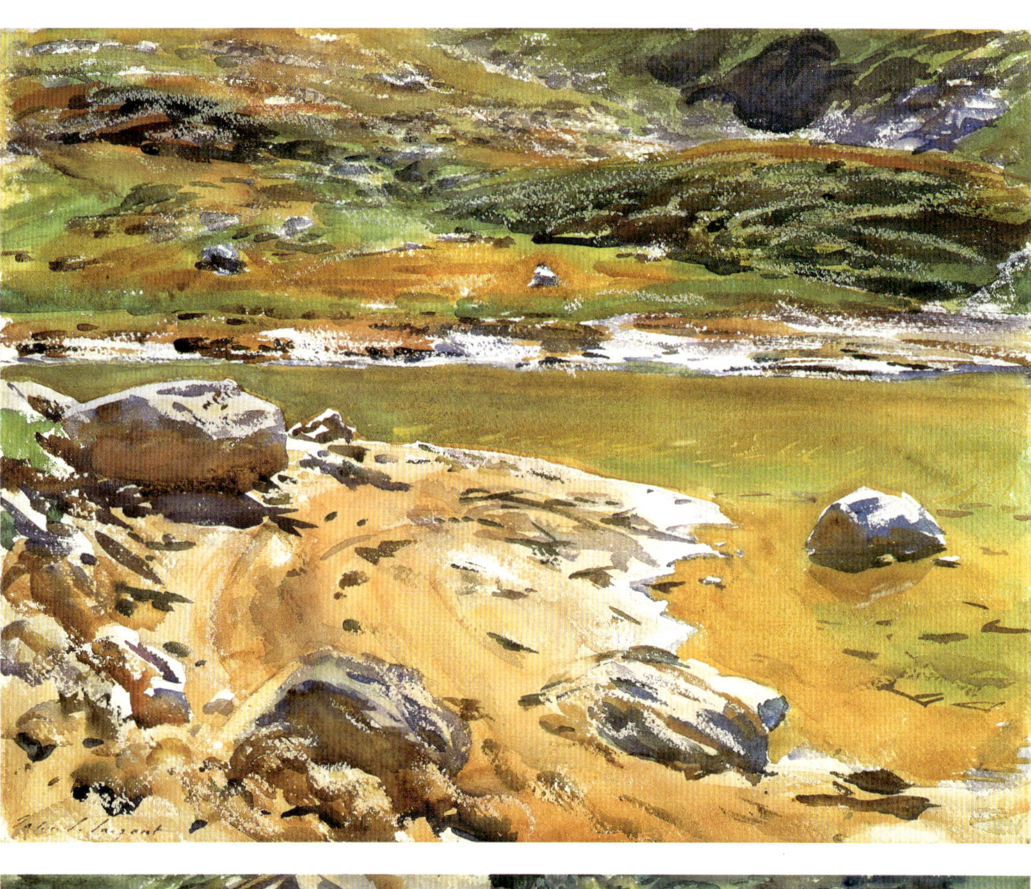

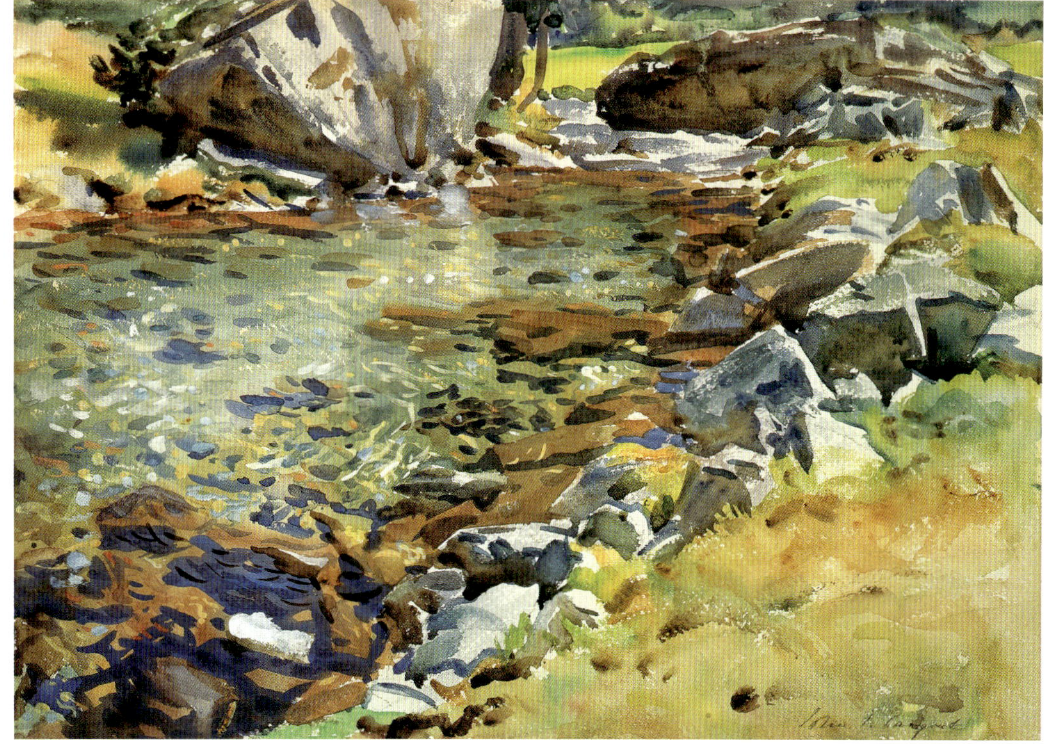

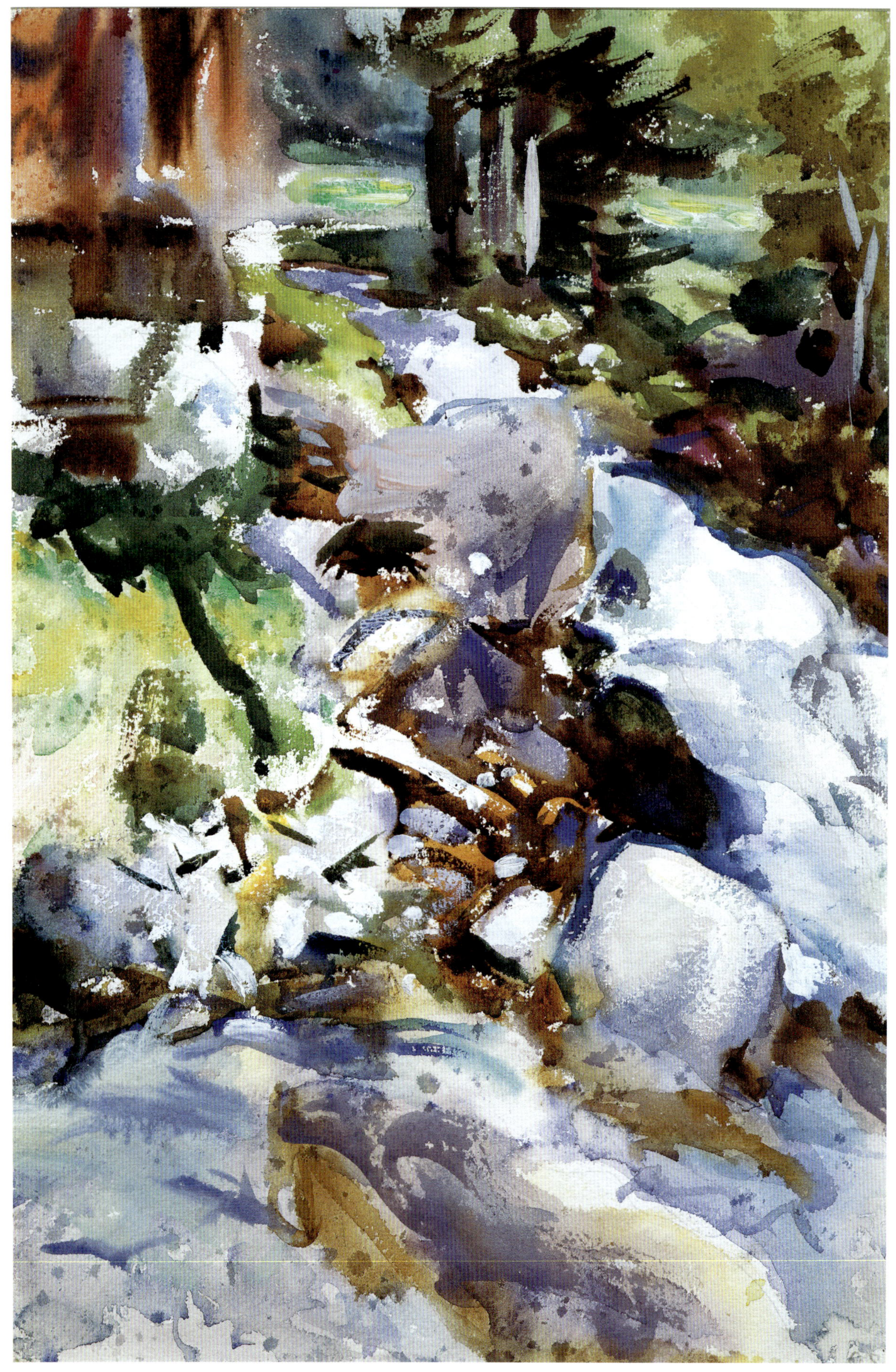

He [Sargent] followed his own pleasure; every [watercolor] picture is the offspring of exultation in his facility; their spontaneity is pronounced, they flow from his hand with the turbulence of water from a mill race.

—Evan Charteris, 1927

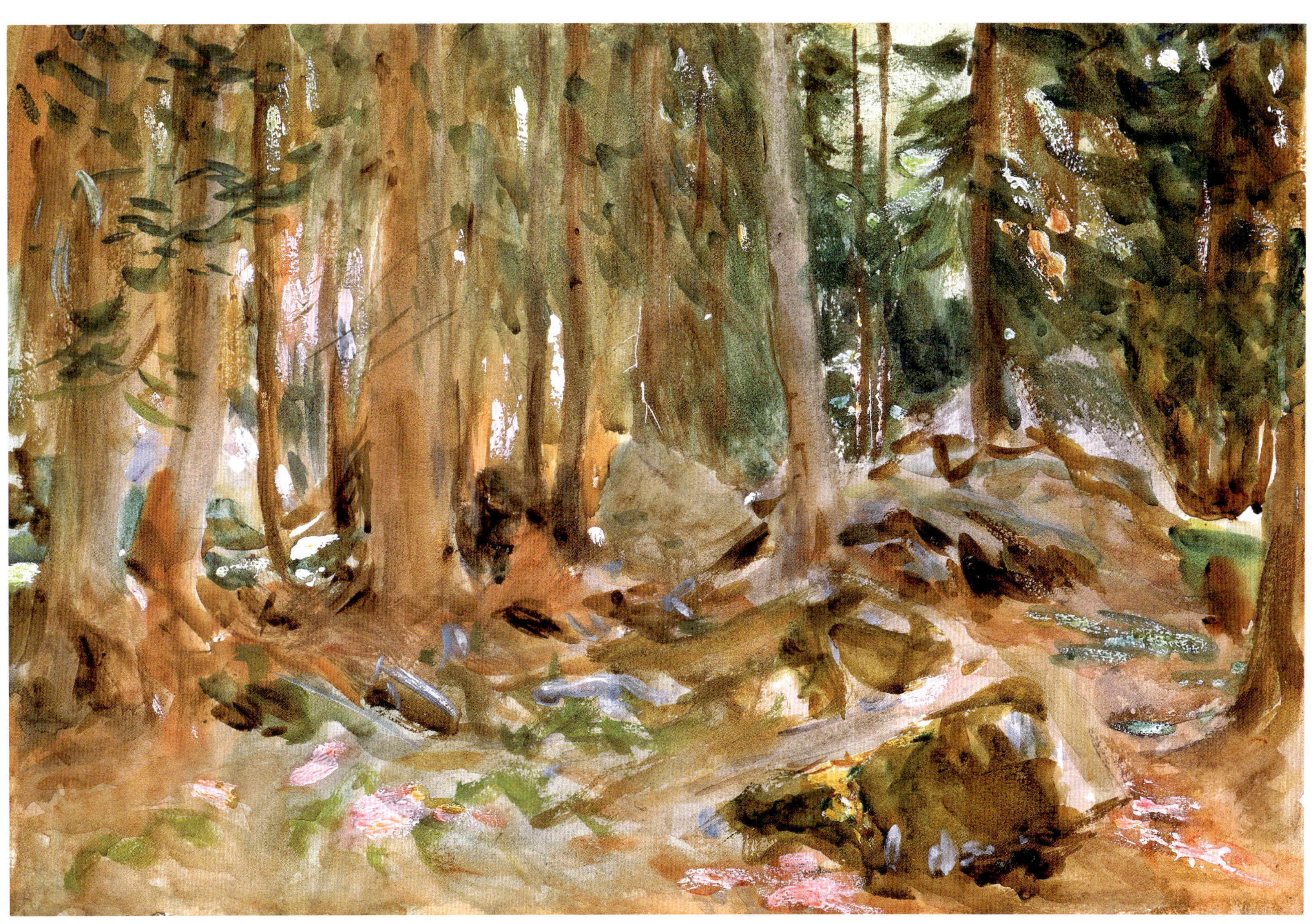

Rushing Brook n.d.
Watercolor, gouache, and graphite underdrawing on off-white wove paper
18 3/8 x 12 3/8 in. (46.7 x 31.4 cm.)
The Metropolitan Museum of Art,
Gift of Mrs. Francis Ormond, 1950 (50.130.801)
Photograph by Geoffrey Clements

Pine Forest c. 1907–8
Watercolor and gouache on paper laid down on board
12 x 18 in. (30.5 x 45.7 cm.)
Courtesy Christie's Images

Artist in the Simplon c. 1910–11
Watercolor over graphite on white wove paper
15 13/16 x 20 13/16 in. (40.2 x 52.9 cm.)
Courtesy of the Fogg Art Museum,
Harvard University Art Museums,
Gift of Grenville L. Winthrop

Photo: Photographic Services

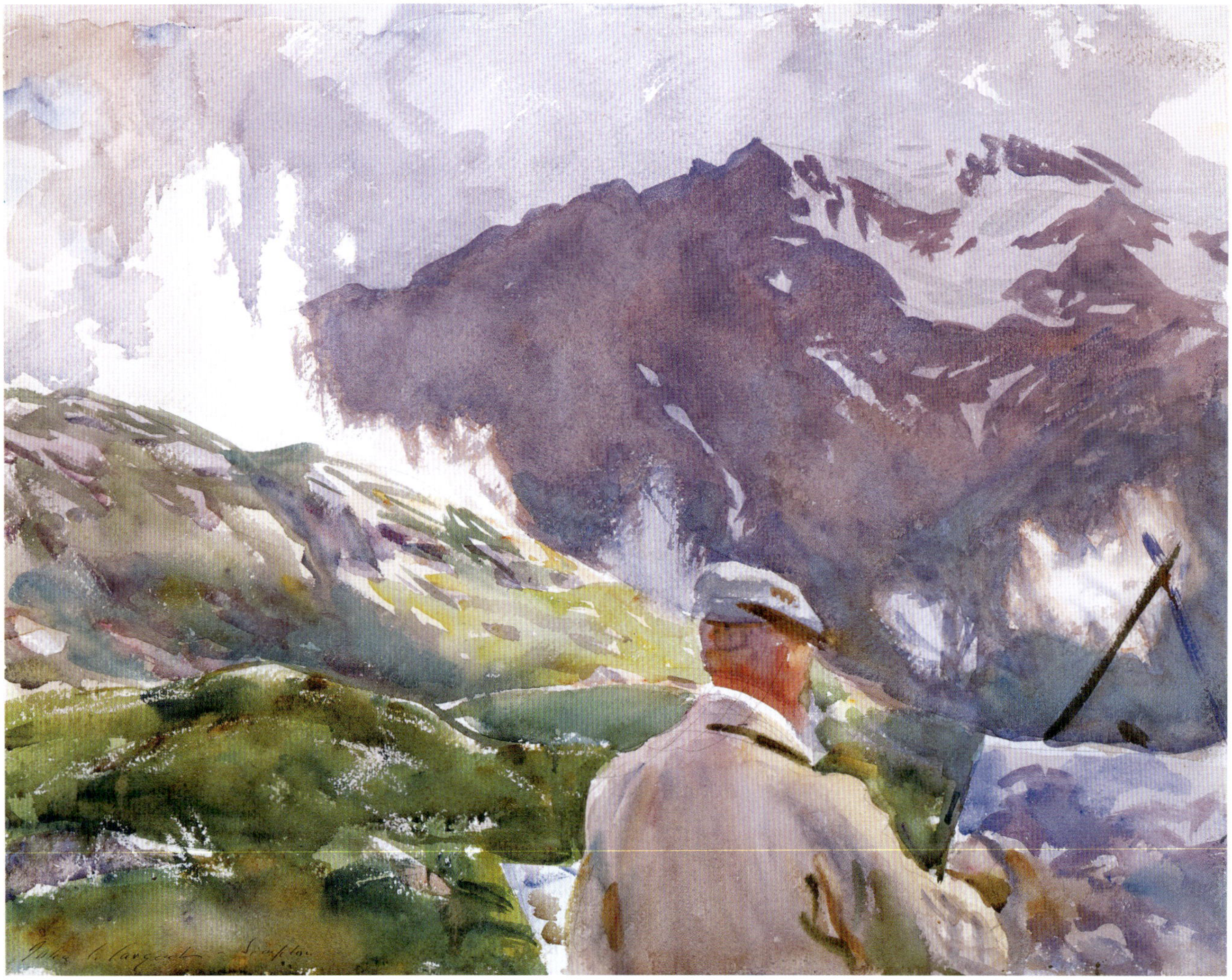

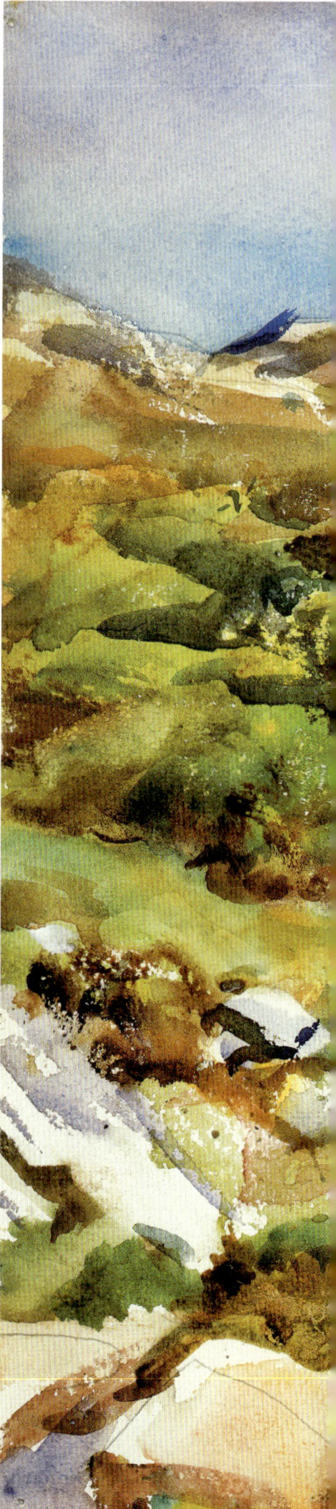

Simplon Pass: Mountain Brook N.D.
Watercolor
14 x 20 1/16 in. (35.5 x 51 cm.)
Charles Henry Hayden Fund,
Courtesy, Museum of Fine Arts, Boston

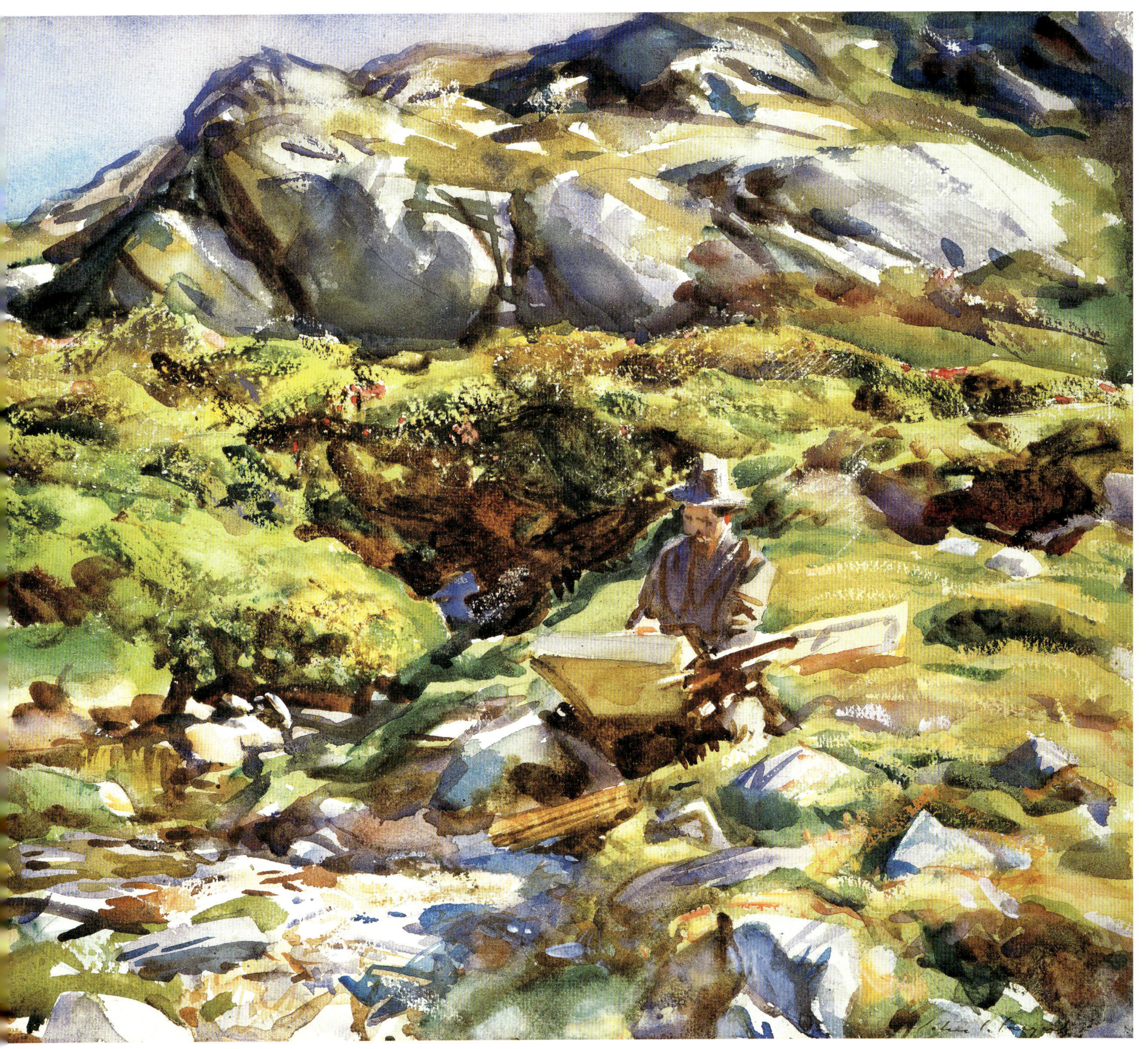

This group of landscapes with figures, in which the doings of the two or three ladies who were his traveling companions among the Alps are recorded in that wonderful stenographic style of his, leaves little to be desired in the way of breadth, suggestiveness, or the expression of life, light and color.

—William Howe Downes, 1925

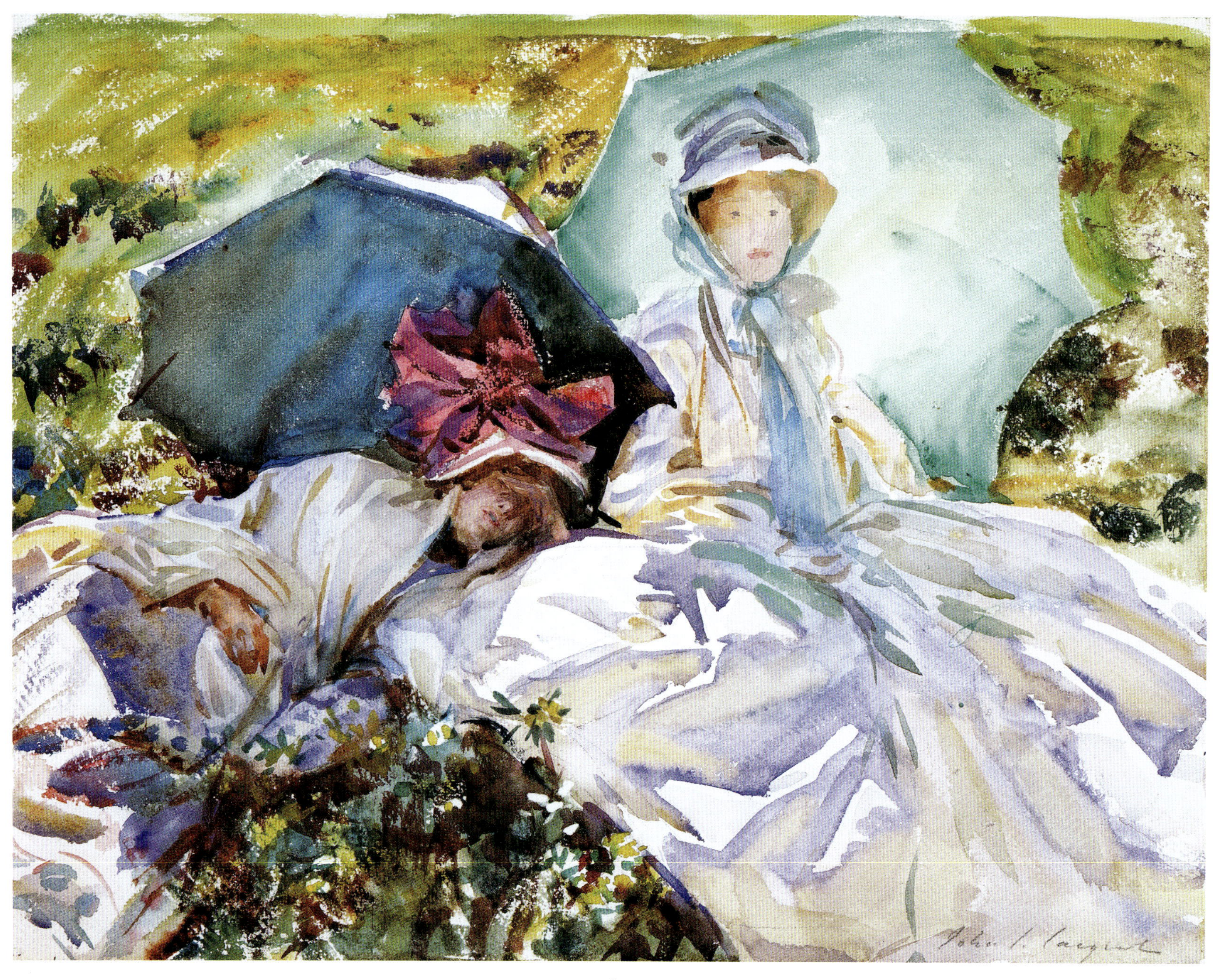

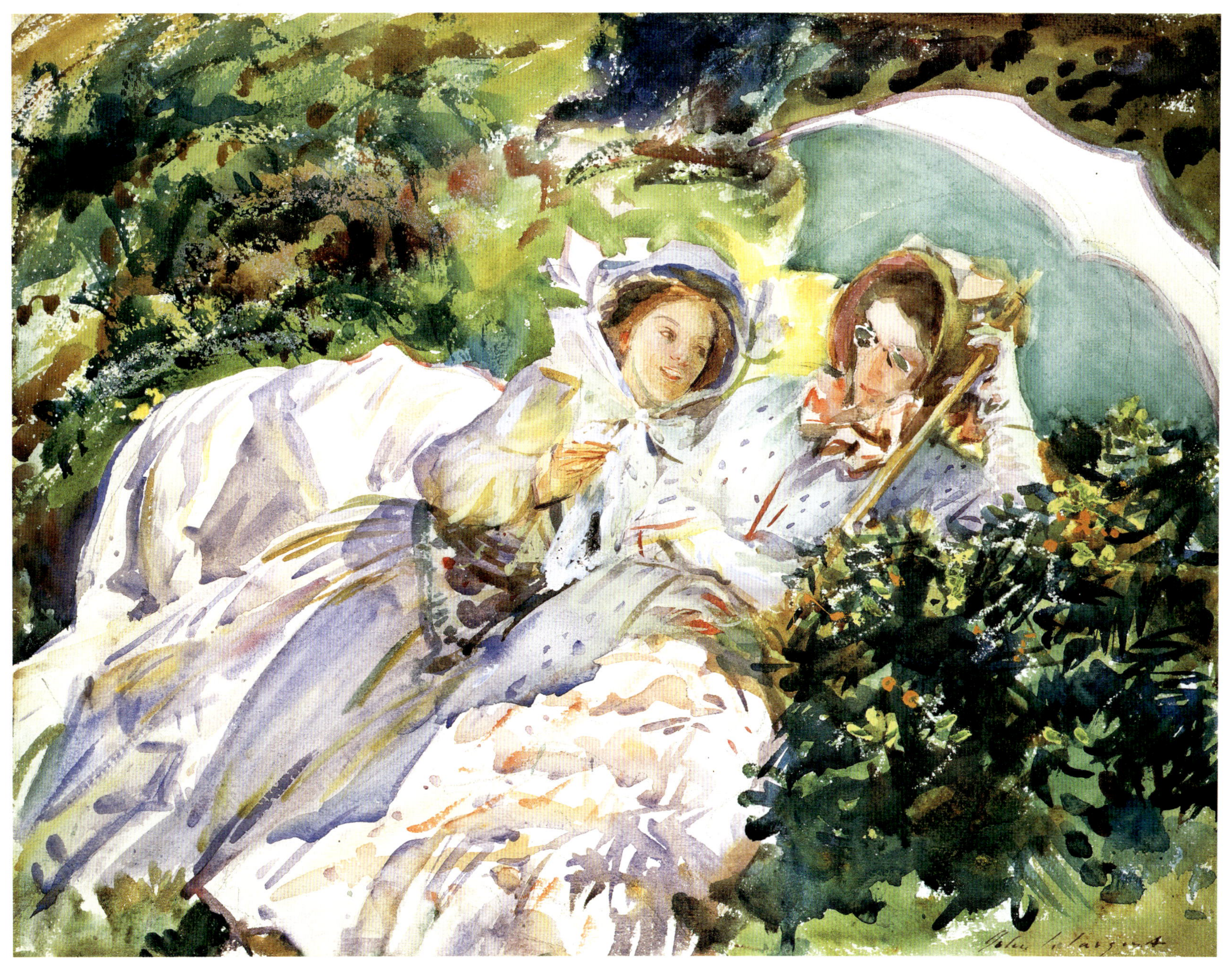

Simplon Pass: The Green Parasol 1911
Watercolor on paper
15 3/4 x 20 1/2 (40 x 52 cm.)
Hayden Collection,
Courtesy, Museum of Fine Arts, Boston

Simplon Pass: The Tease 1911
Watercolor over graphite on paper
15 3/4 x 20 5/8 in. (40 x 52.4 cm.)
Hayden Collection, Charles Henry Hayden Fund,
Courtesy, Museum of Fine Arts, Boston

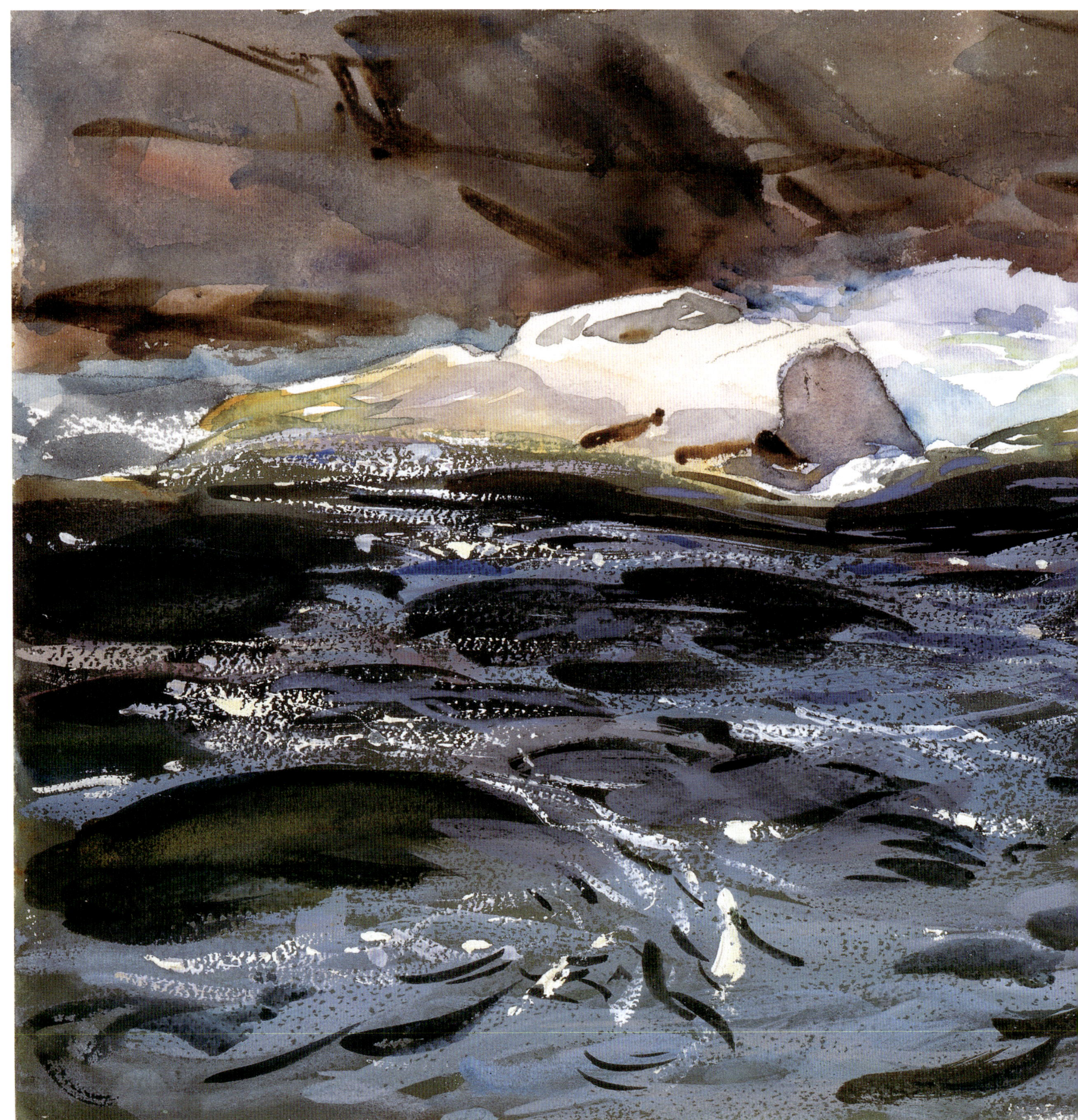

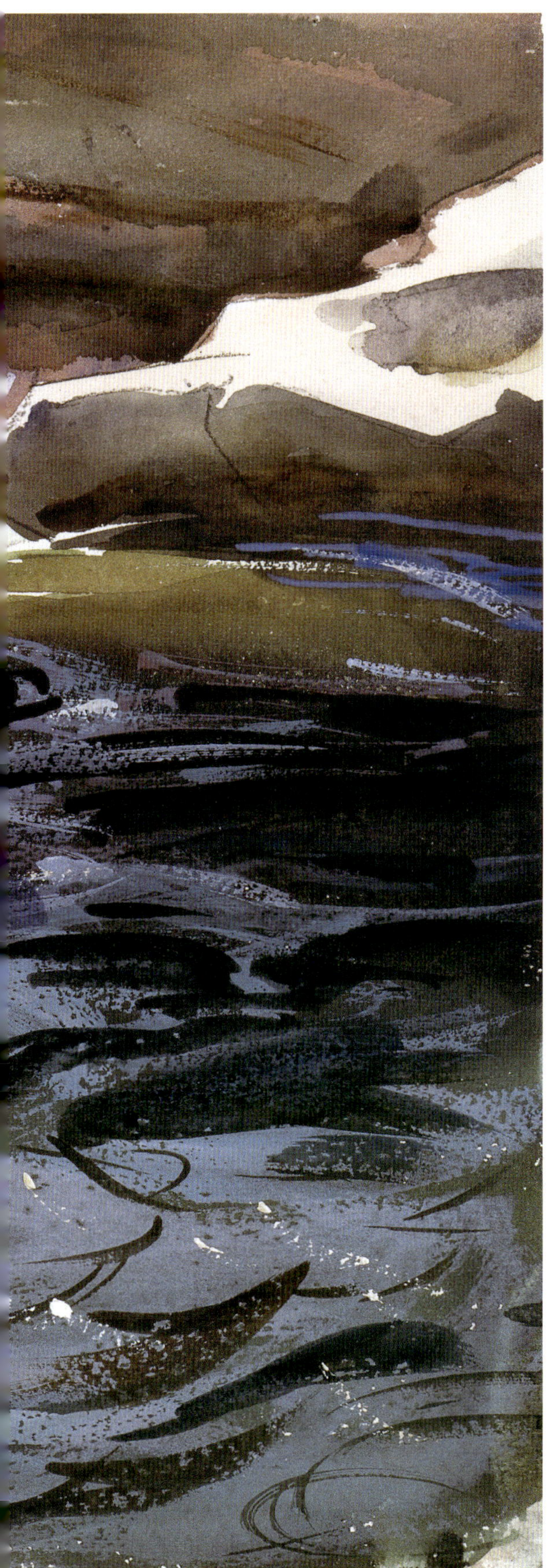

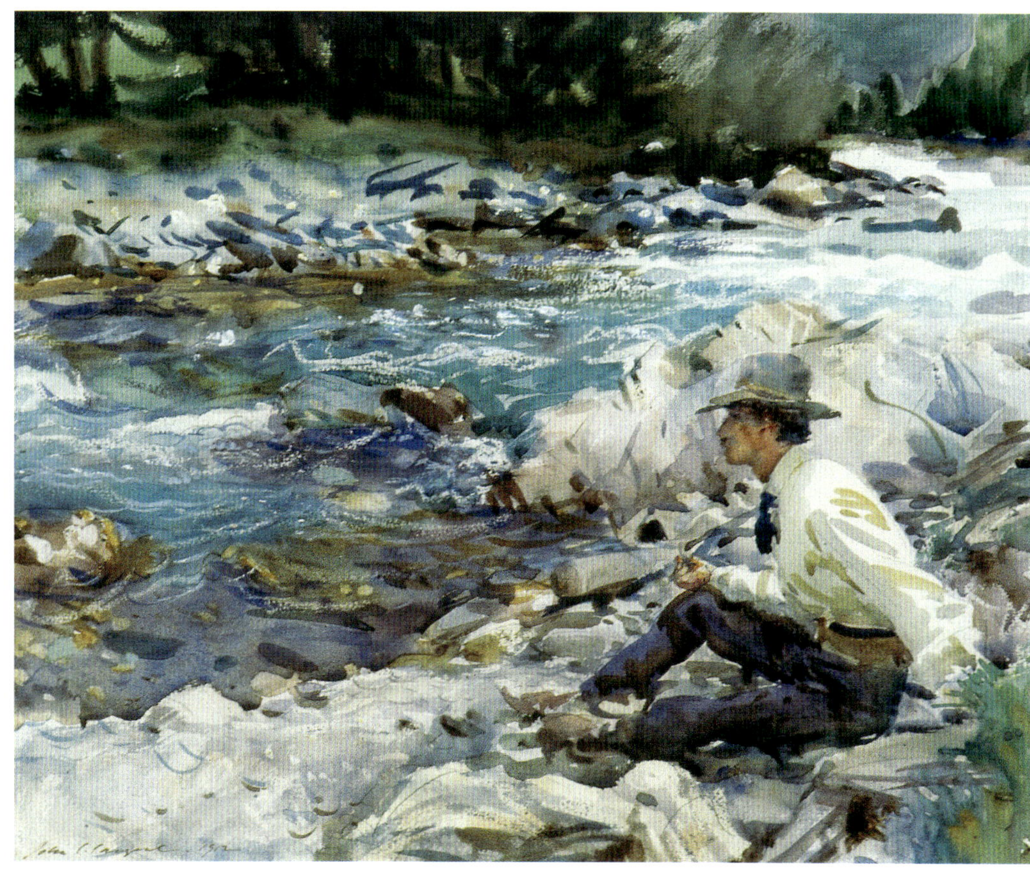

Trout Stream Tyrol 1912
Watercolor on paper
15 x 18 in. (38.1 x 45.7 cm.)
Private collection

Salmon River c. 1901
Watercolor
9 15/16 x 13 15/16 in. (25.3 x 35.4 cm.)
The Brooklyn Museum of Art,
Purchased by special subscription, (19.837)

All was rendered, or suggested, with the utmost fidelity. Parts were loaded, parts were painted clear and smooth, every touch was individual and conveyed a quick unerring message from the brain. It was—if you will—a kind of shorthand, but it was magical!

—Adrian Stokes, 1925

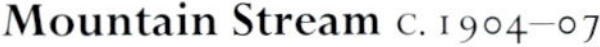

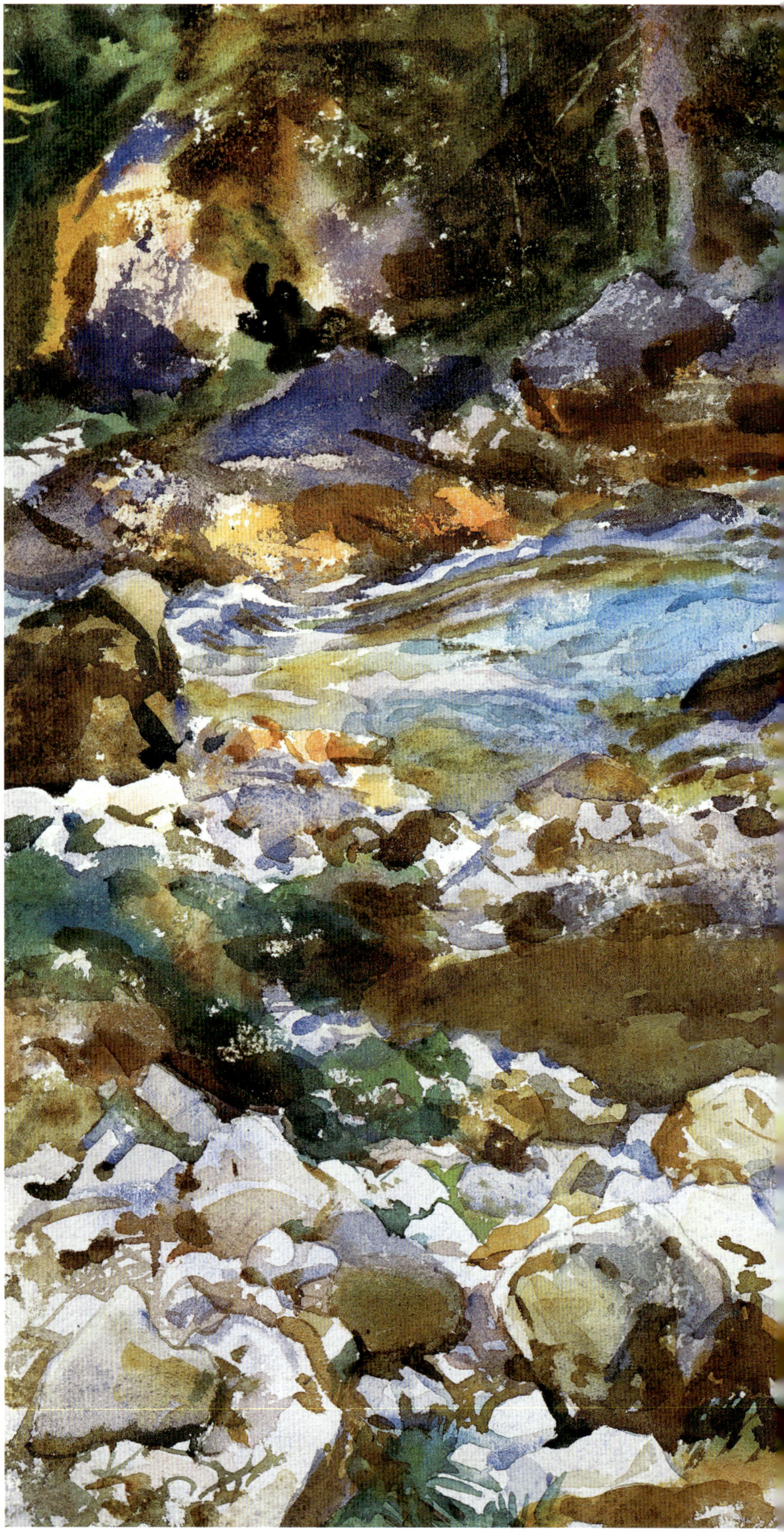

Mountain Stream c. 1904–07
Watercolor, wax, and graphite on white wove paper
13 3/4 x 21 in. (34.9 x 53.3 cm.)
The Metropolitan Museum of Art,
Purchase, Joseph Pulitzer Bequest, 1915 (15.142.2)
Photograph © 1989 The Metropolitan Museum of Art

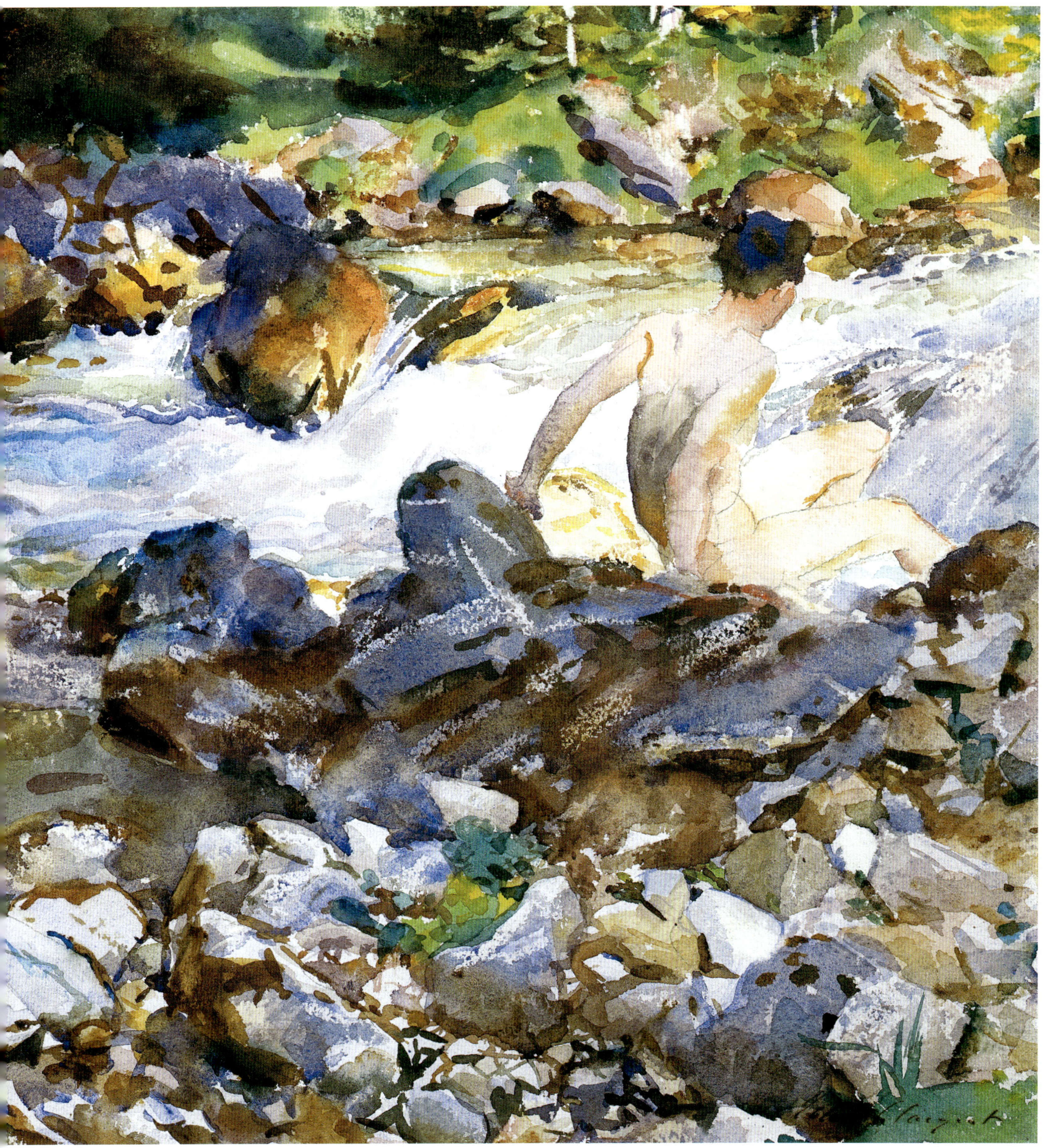

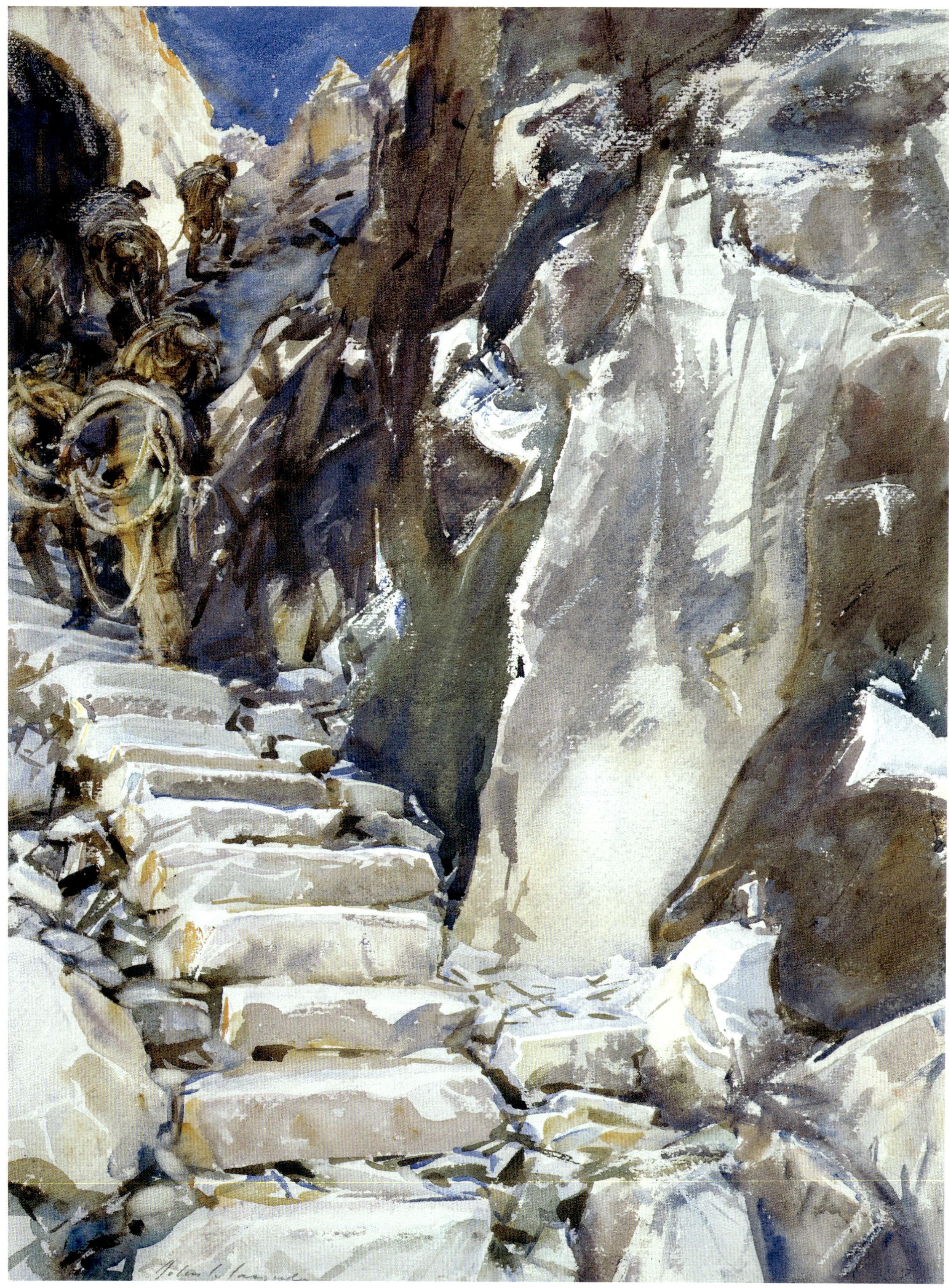

Lizzatori I 1911
Watercolor
20 3/4 x 16 in. (52.7 x 40.6 cm.)
Charles Henry Hayden Fund,
Courtesy, Museum of Fine Arts, Boston

Workmen at Carrara c. 1911
Watercolor over graphite heightened with white gouache on ivory wove paper
16 3/8 x 20 5/8 in. (40.3 x 53.4 cm.)
The Art Institute of Chicago
Olivia Shaler Swan Memorial Collection, 1933.507

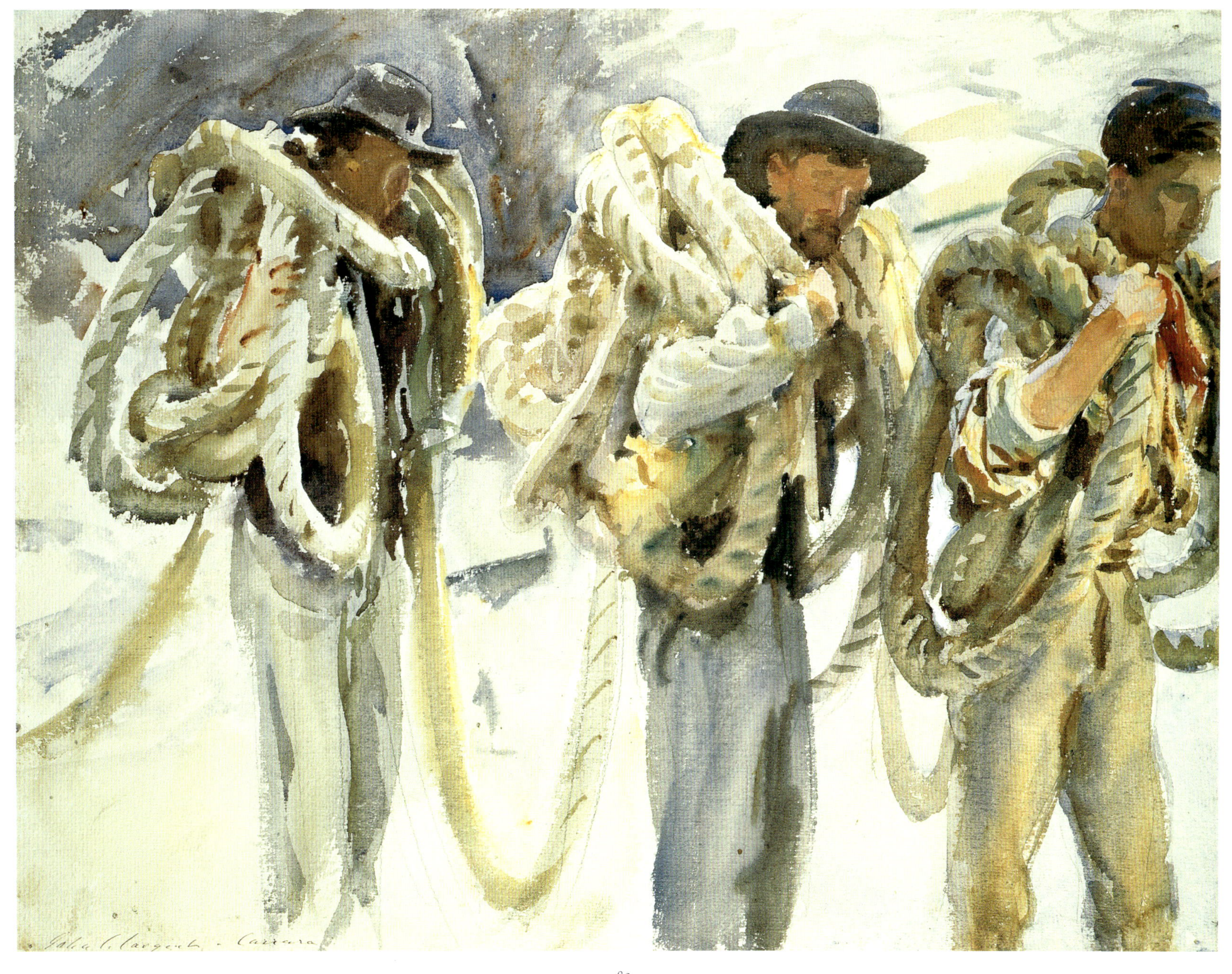

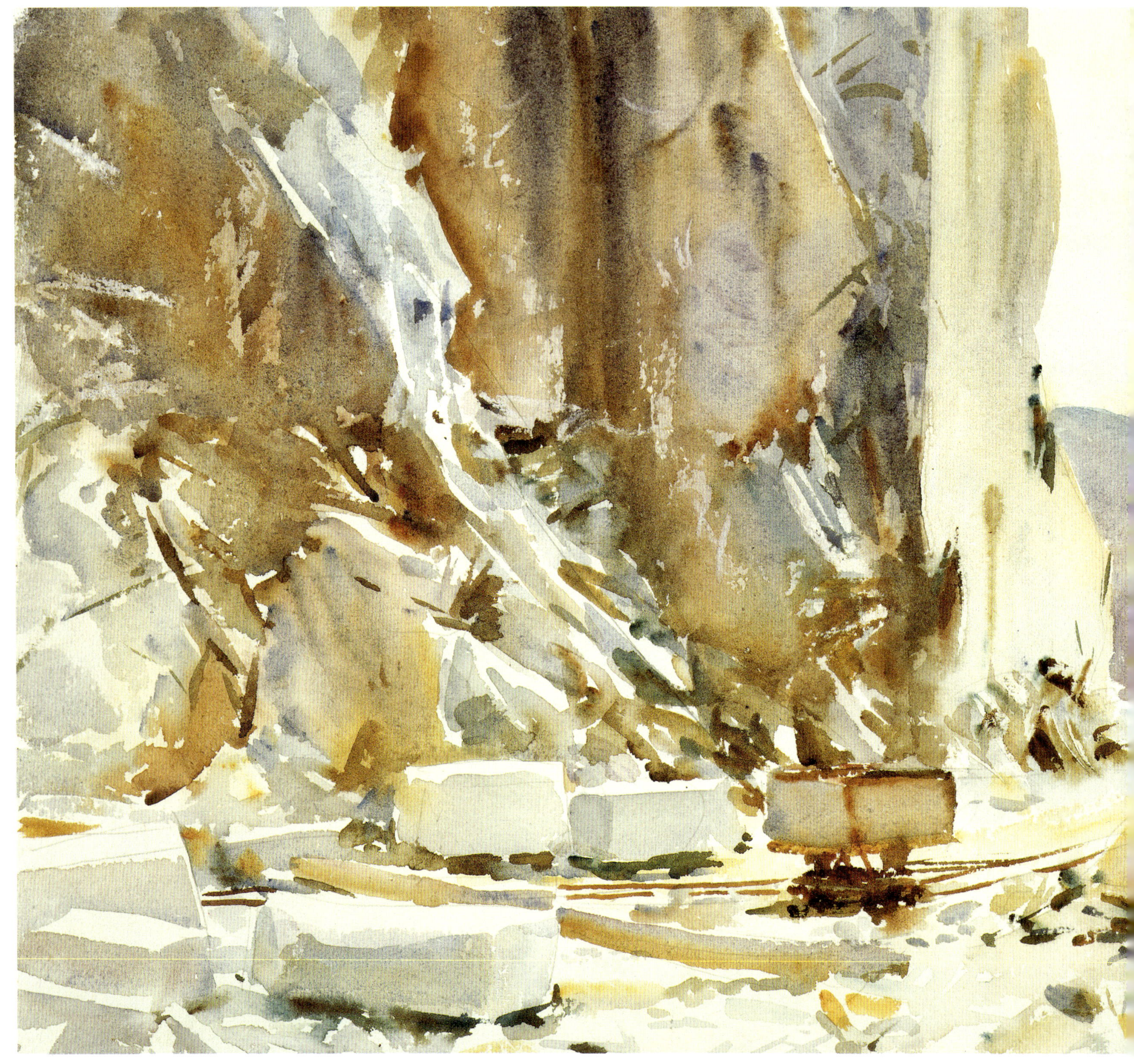

In rendering the tangible fact he [Sargent] was magnificiently proficient, adding to his record of the fact a beguiling note of style. He never in his life deliberately romanticized a theme, but he was too much of an artist ever to leave it exactly as he found it. The truth painted by Sargent was always truth raised to a higher power, made more interesting through the beauty of his art.

—New York Herald-Tribune, 1925

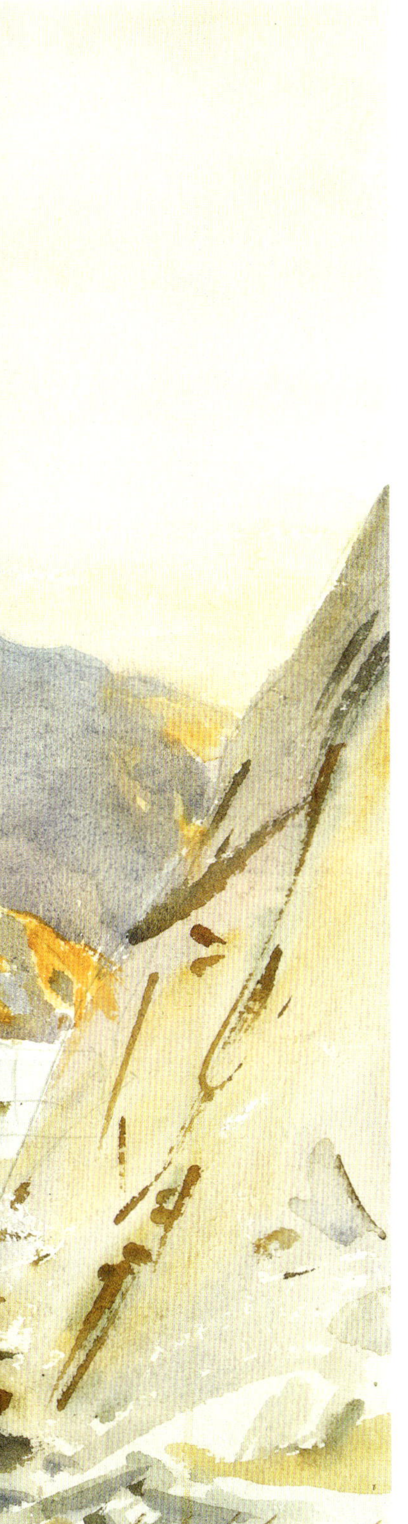

Carrara: Quarry II 1911
Watercolor
14 x 20 in. (25.4 x 52.1 cm.)
Hayden Collection,
Courtesy, Museum of Fine Arts, Boston

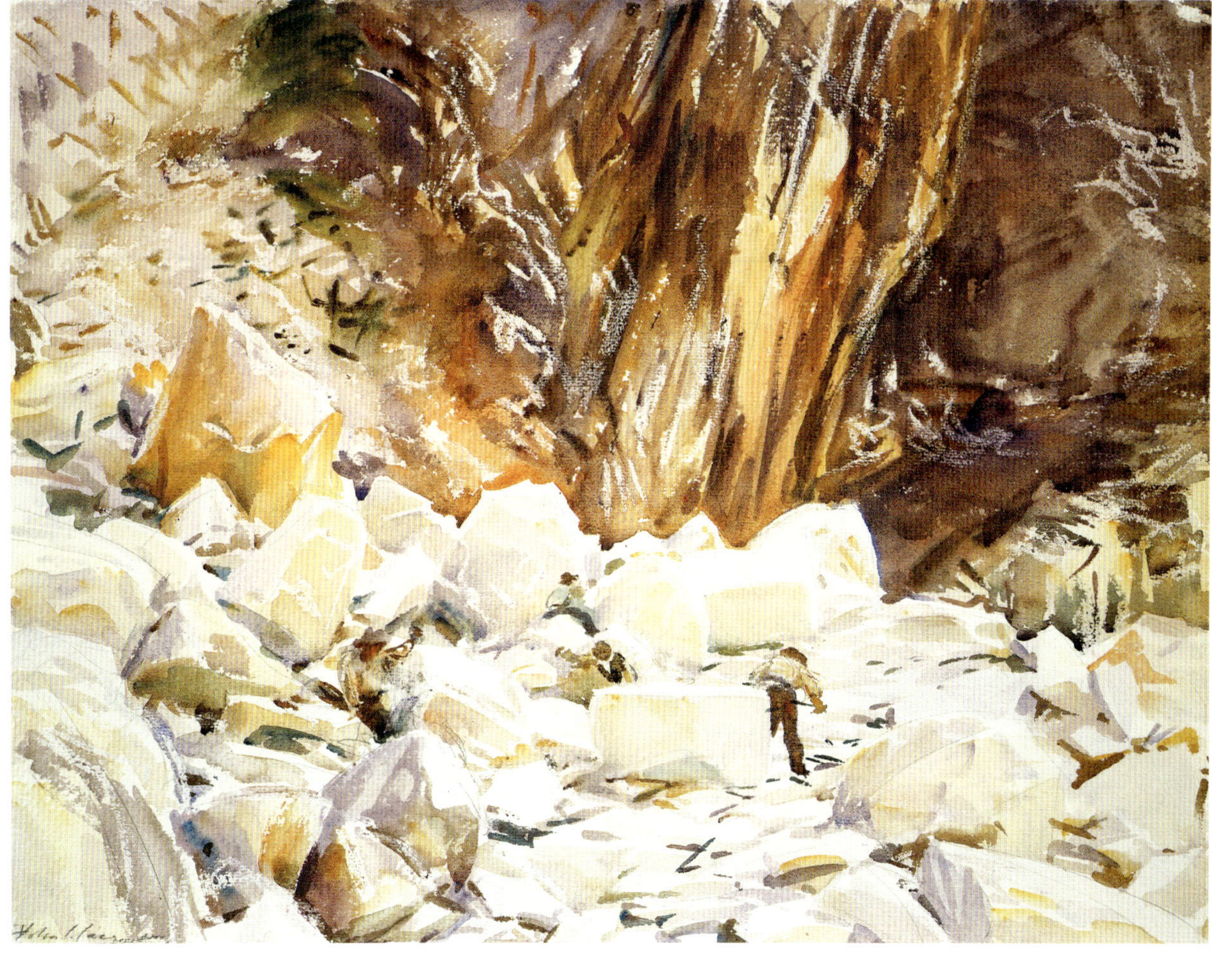

Carrara: Trajan's Quarry n.d.
Watercolor
16 x 20 3/4 in. (41 x 53 cm.)
Charles Henry Hayden Fund,
Courtesy, Museum of Fine Arts, Boston

Woodsheds, Tyrol 1914

Watercolor over touches of graphite on ivory wove paper

15 3/4 x 21 1/16 in. (40 x 53.5 cm.)

The Art Institute of Chicago

Olivia Shaler Swan Memorial Collection, 1933.506

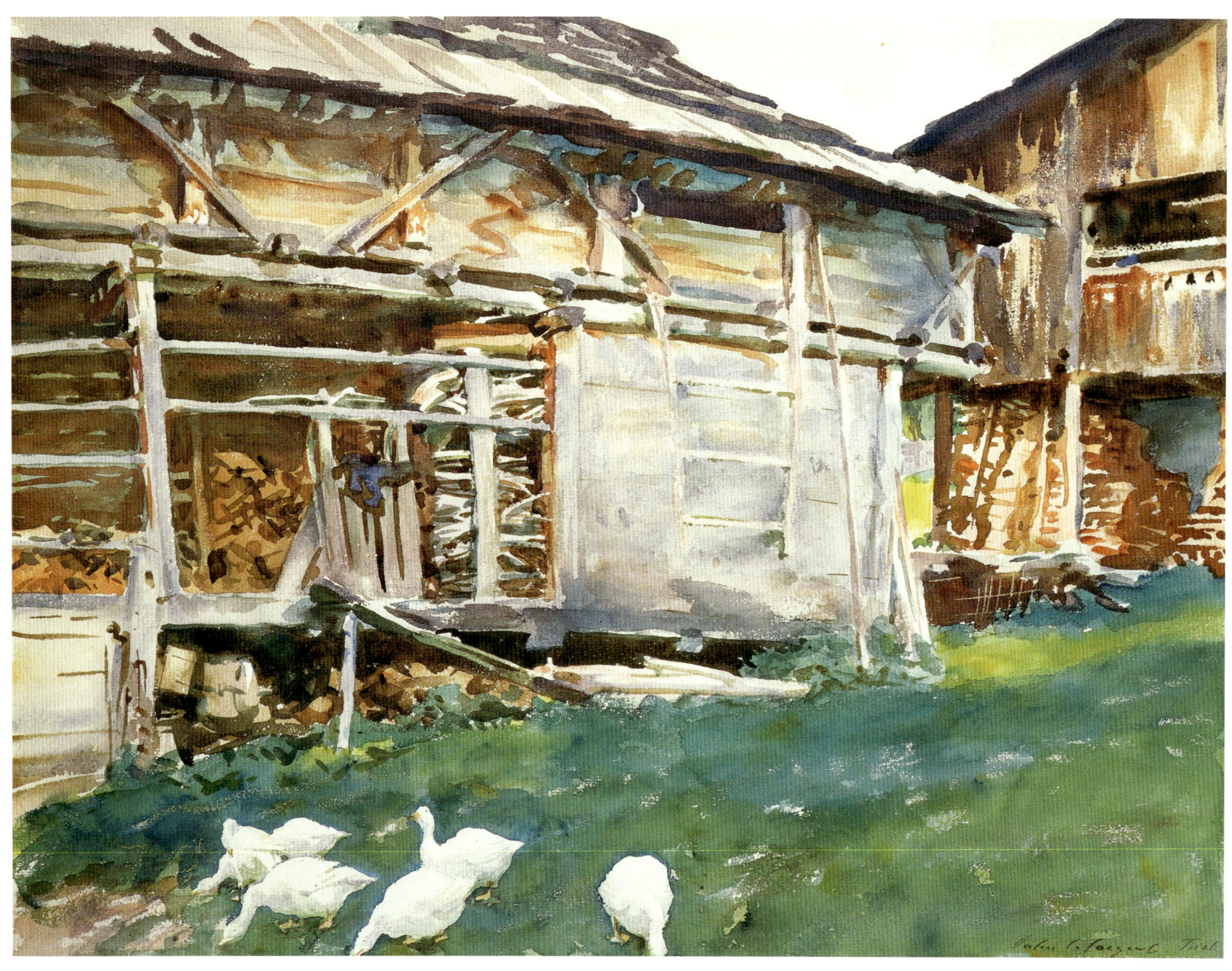

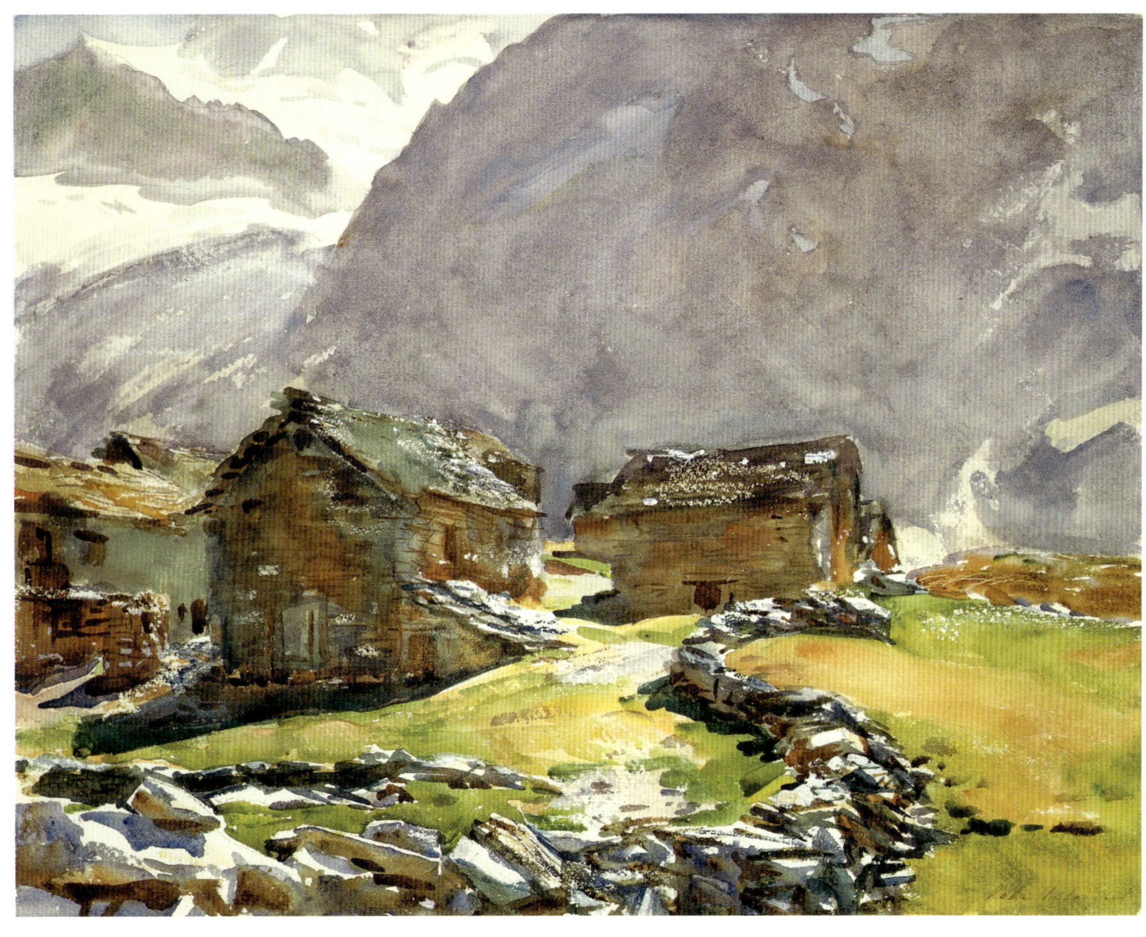

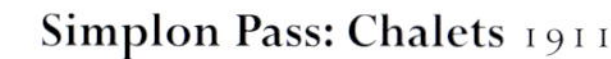

Simplon Pass: Chalets 1911

Watercolor on paper

15 3/4 x 20 1/2 in. (24.1 x 48.5 cm.)

Hayden Collection, Charles Henry Hayden Fund,

Courtesy, Museum of Fine Arts, Boston

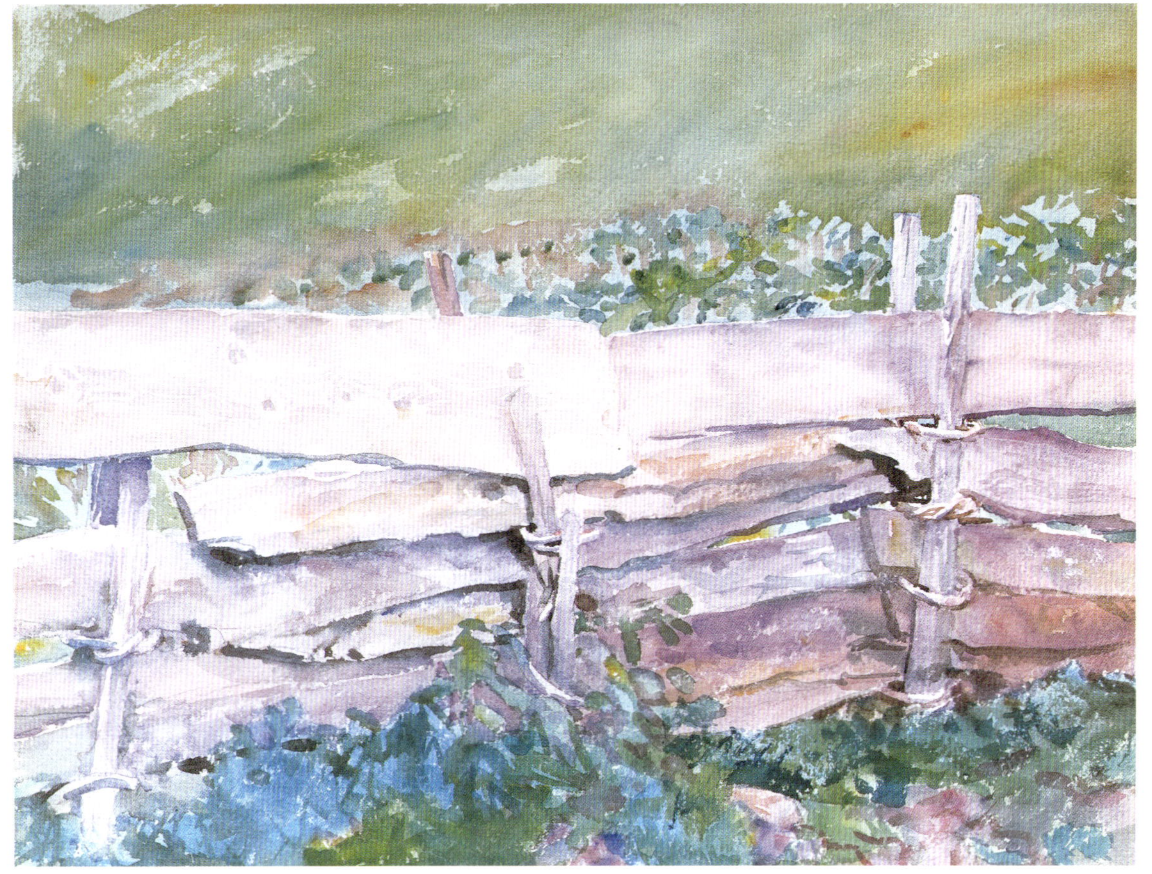

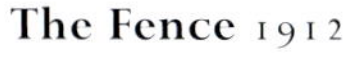

The Fence 1912

Watercolor

15 3/8 x 20 5/8 in. (39.1 x 52.4 cm.)

Collection of Tacoma Art Museum,

Gift of Mrs. L. T. Murray and friends of Mr. and Mrs. Charles Morey

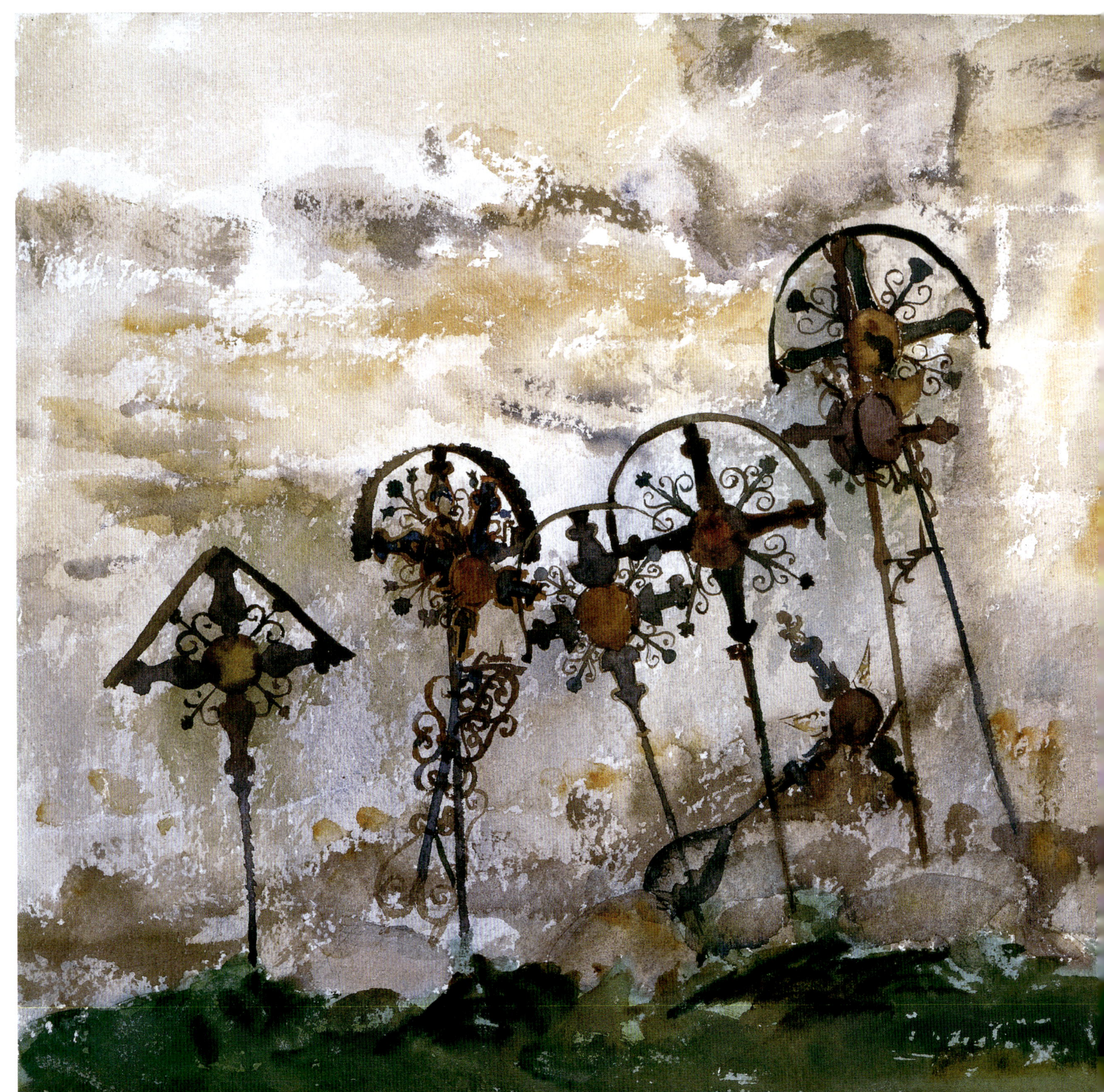

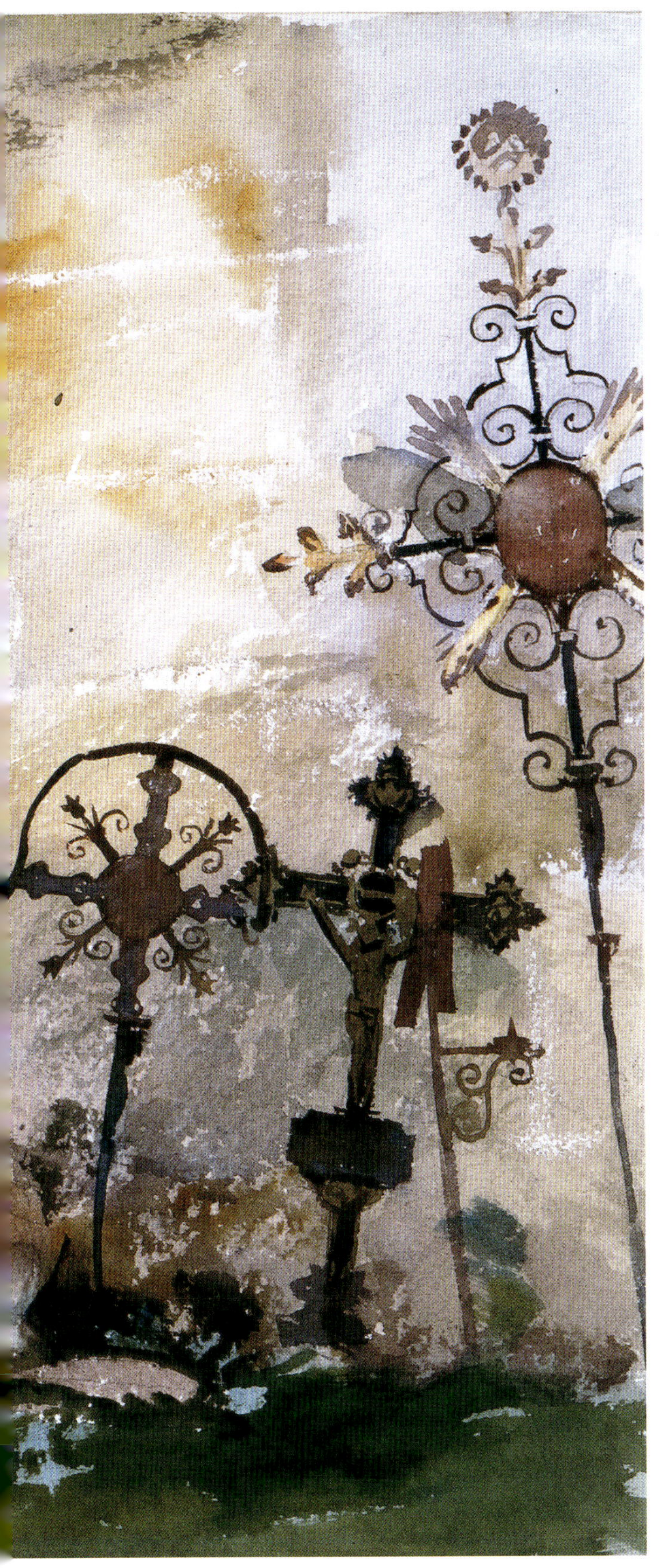

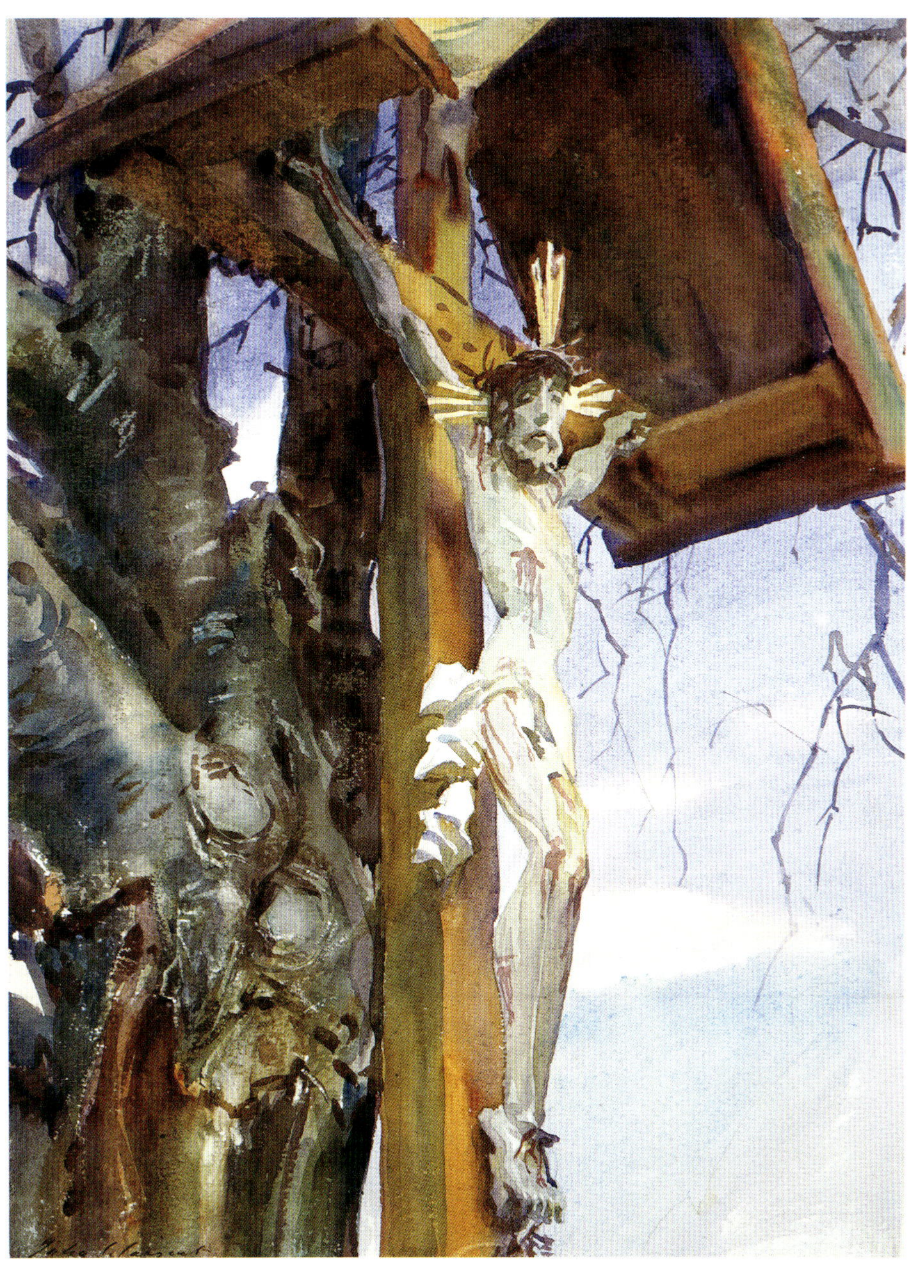

Tyrolese Crucifix c. 1914

Watercolor, wax, and graphite on white wove paper

21 x 15 11/16 in. (53.3 x 39.8 cm.)

The Metropolitan Museum of Art,

Purchase, Joseph Pulitzer Bequest, 1915 (15.142.7)

Photograph by Geoffrey Clements

Graveyard in the Tyrol 1914

Watercolor on paper, 13 9/8 x 20 7/8 in. (34.5 x 53.1 cm.)

Trustees of the British Museum, London

Gardens, Fountains and Statuary

Mrs. Sargent dragged the children from church to museum, from palace to garden, and back again; she looked, she pointed, she stared, she talked, she sketched. It was perpetual motion, and it was a manifestation of boundless curiosity.

—Stanley Olson

Sargent never lost this sense of exploration; his eye was forever wandering over the elements of his environs wherever he might find himself. As with his watercolor portraits, his renderings of fountains and statues tend to be informal yet readily identifiable even in their sketchiest manifestations. His fascination for objects raked by sun brings to mind Edward Hopper's love of the "clean glare" of American light.

Among his favorite haunts were the Boboli Gardens in Florence and the Villa di Marlia in Lucca, but Sargent also sought places of repose in Spain and Greece. Be it the interior of the cathedral in Toledo or a terrace on Corfu, each place has its own atmosphere. The watercolors capture the ambience of these locales, the shadowy niches, the flowing fountains, the statuary and stonework that stand out against the background of rich foliage. They invite the viewer to enter the scene and partake of the visual pleasures.

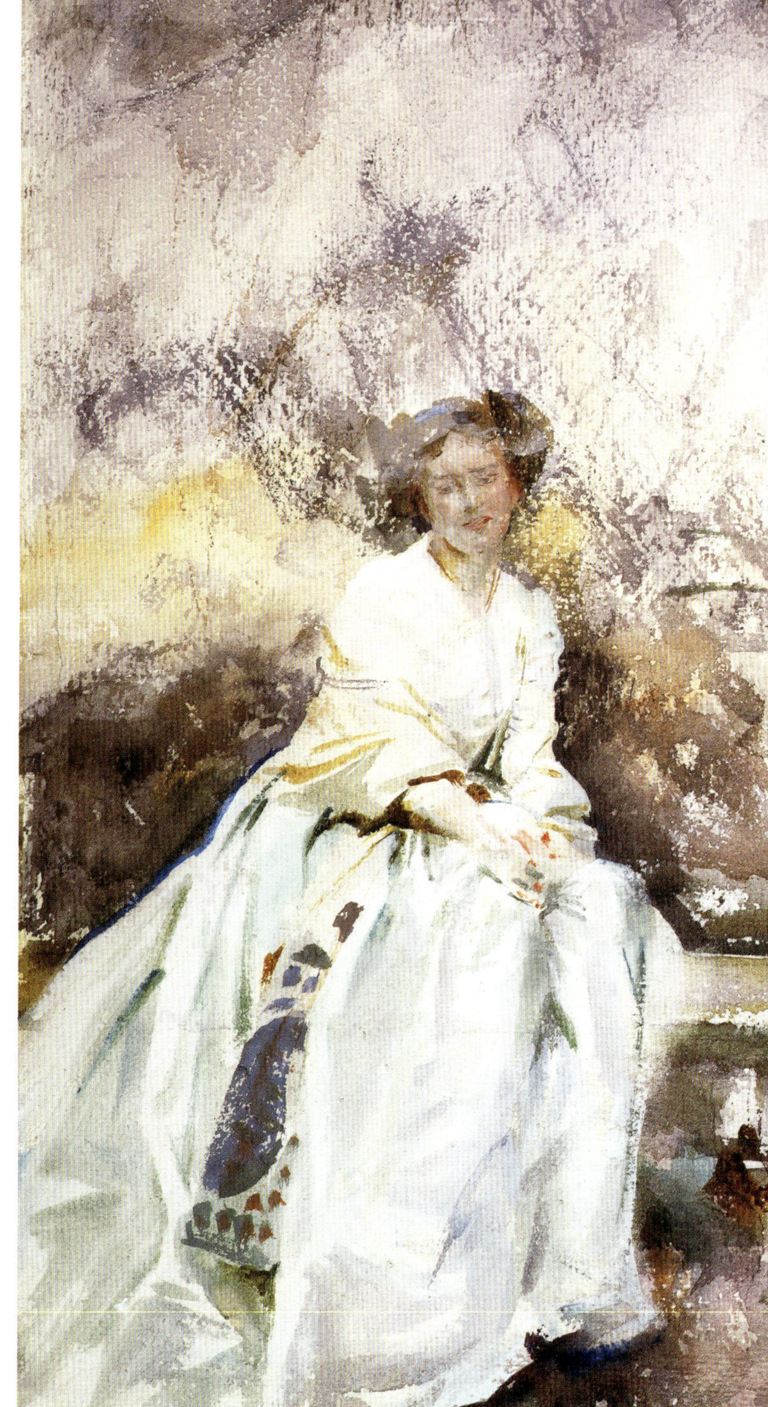

The Garden Wall 1910
Watercolor over graphite on paper
15 3/4 x 20 3/4 in. (40.3 x 53 cm.)
Hayden Collection, Charles Henry Hayden Fund,
Courtesy, Museum of Fine Arts, Boston

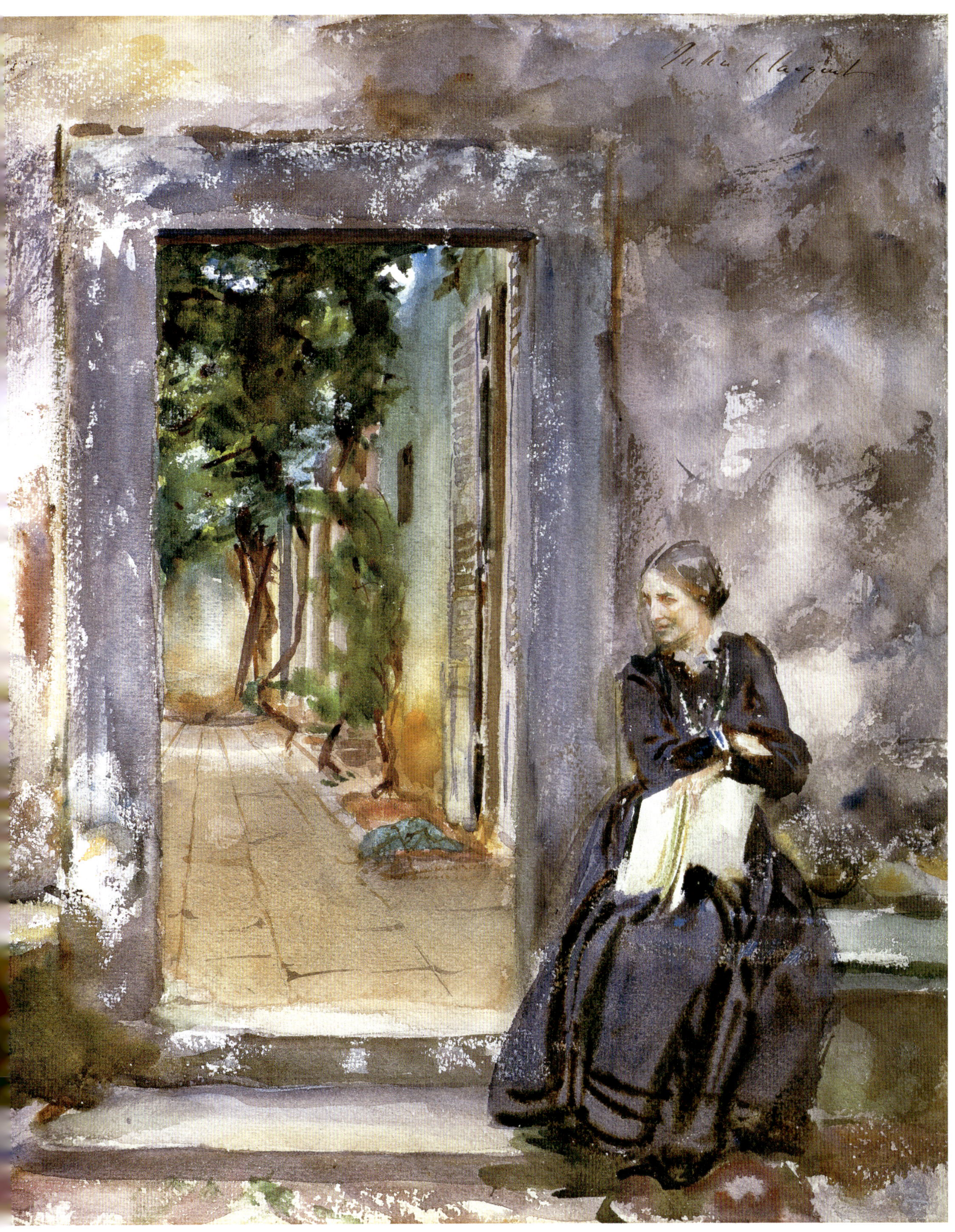

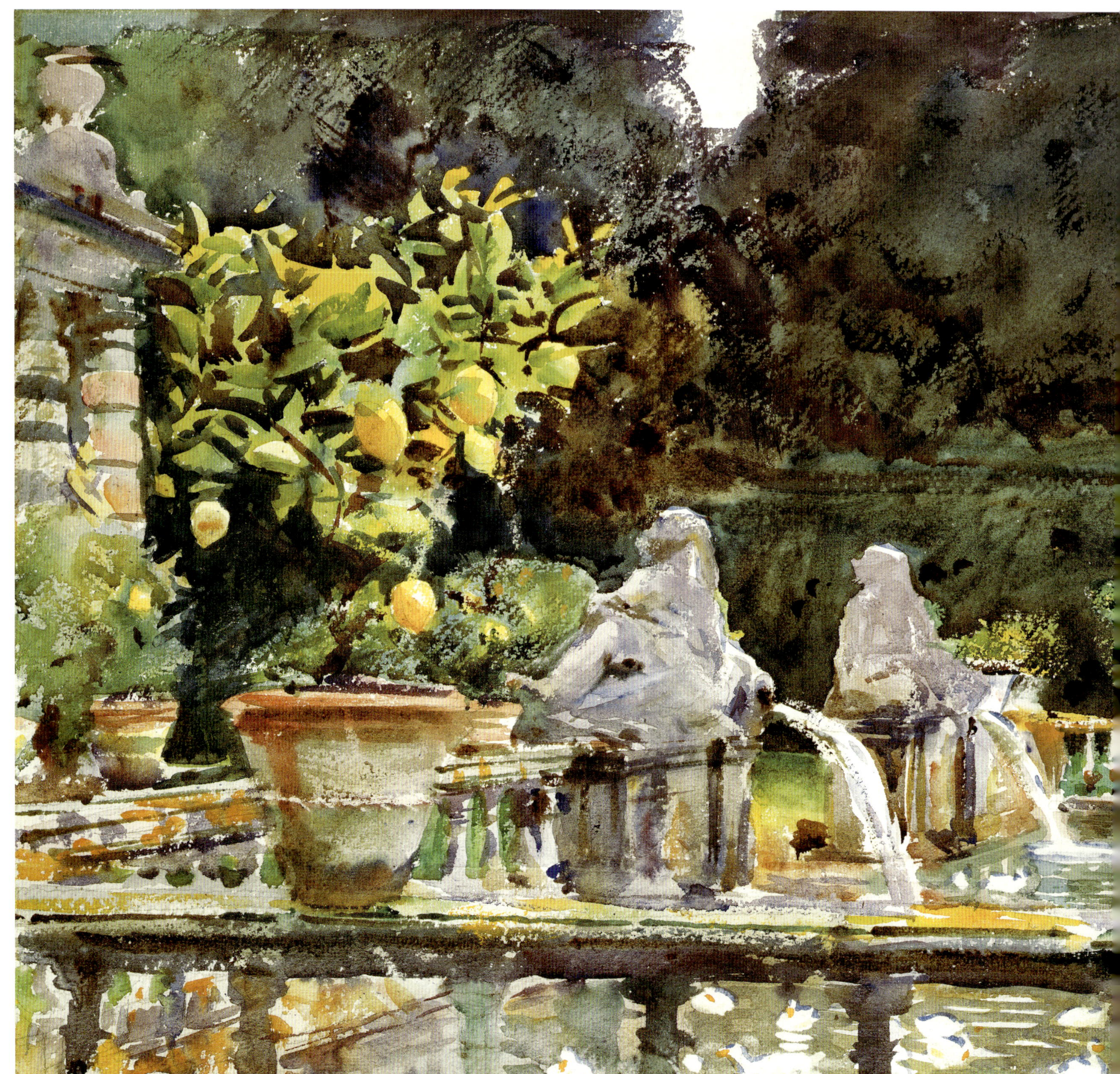

Villa di Marlia: A Fountain 1910
Watercolor on paper
16 x 20 3/4 in. (40.6 x 52.7 cm.)
Hayden Collection,
Courtesy, Museum of Fine Arts, Boston

Villa Torlonia, Frascati 1907
Watercolor with traces of pencil on paper
19 1/2 x 13 1/2 in. (49.5 x 34.5 cm.)
Courtesy Christie's Images

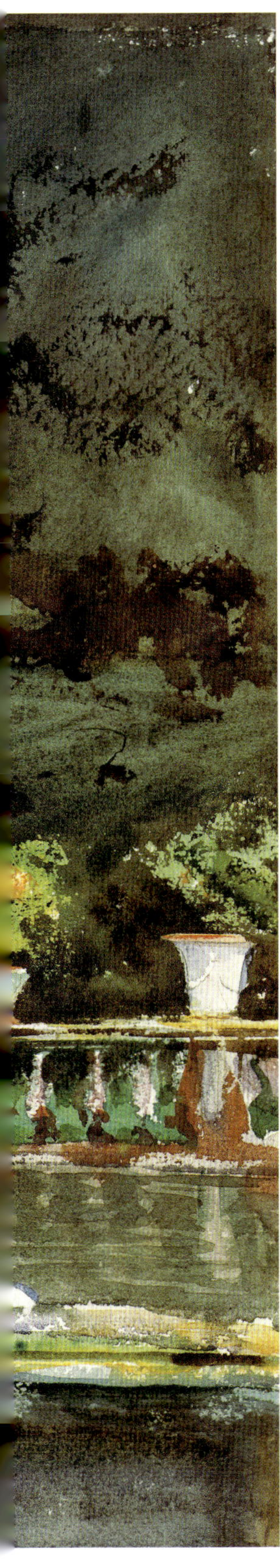

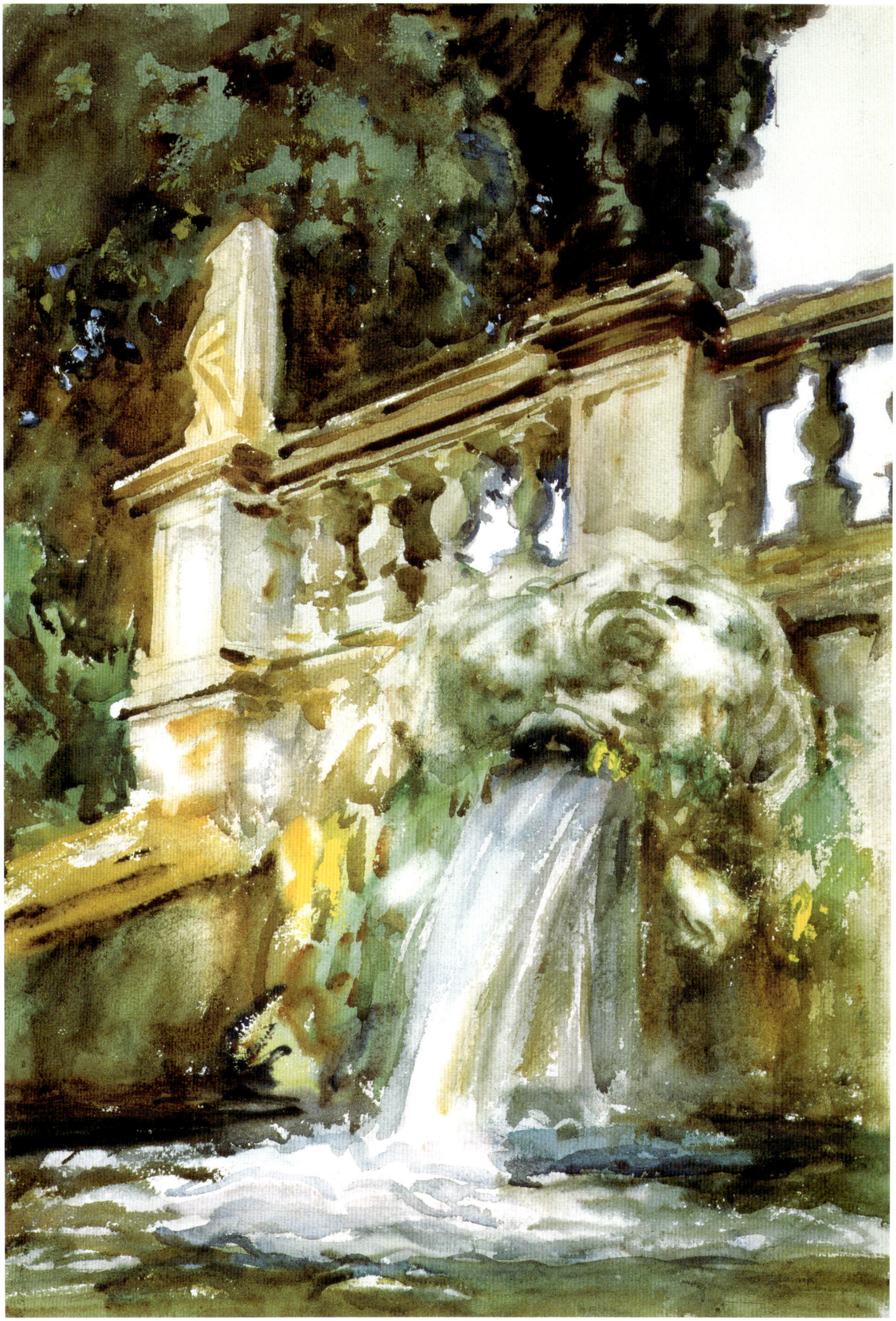

Corfu: The Terrace 1909
Watercolor on paper
20 3/4 x 15 3/4 in. (52.7 x 40 cm.)
Charles Henry Hayden Fund,
Courtesy, Museum of Fine Arts, Boston

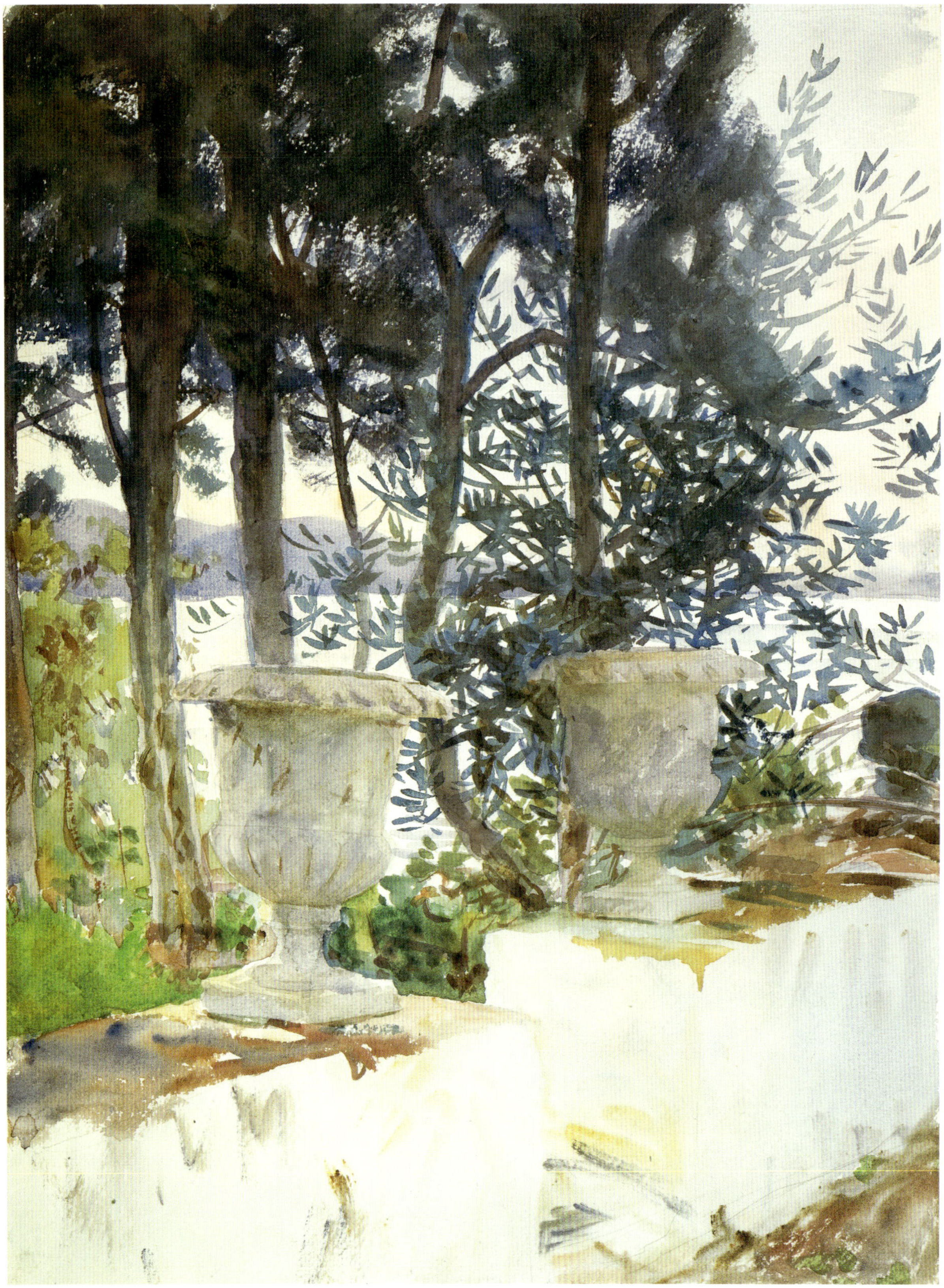

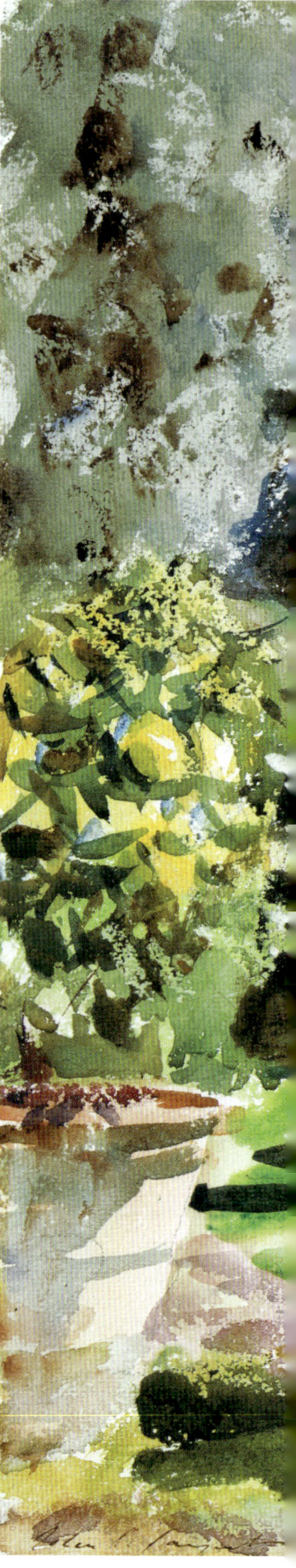

"Villa di Marlia, Lucca," done in 1910, has the kind of purely coloristic life absent from [Sargent's] oil landscapes, and that monumentality which arises—again and again, in the work of Cézanne—from sheer veracity of seeing.

—John Updike, 1989

Villa di Marlia, Lucca c. 1910
Watercolor
15 3/4 x 20 3/4 in. (40 x 54 cm.)
Charles Henry Hayden Fund,
Courtesy, Museum of Fine Arts, Boston

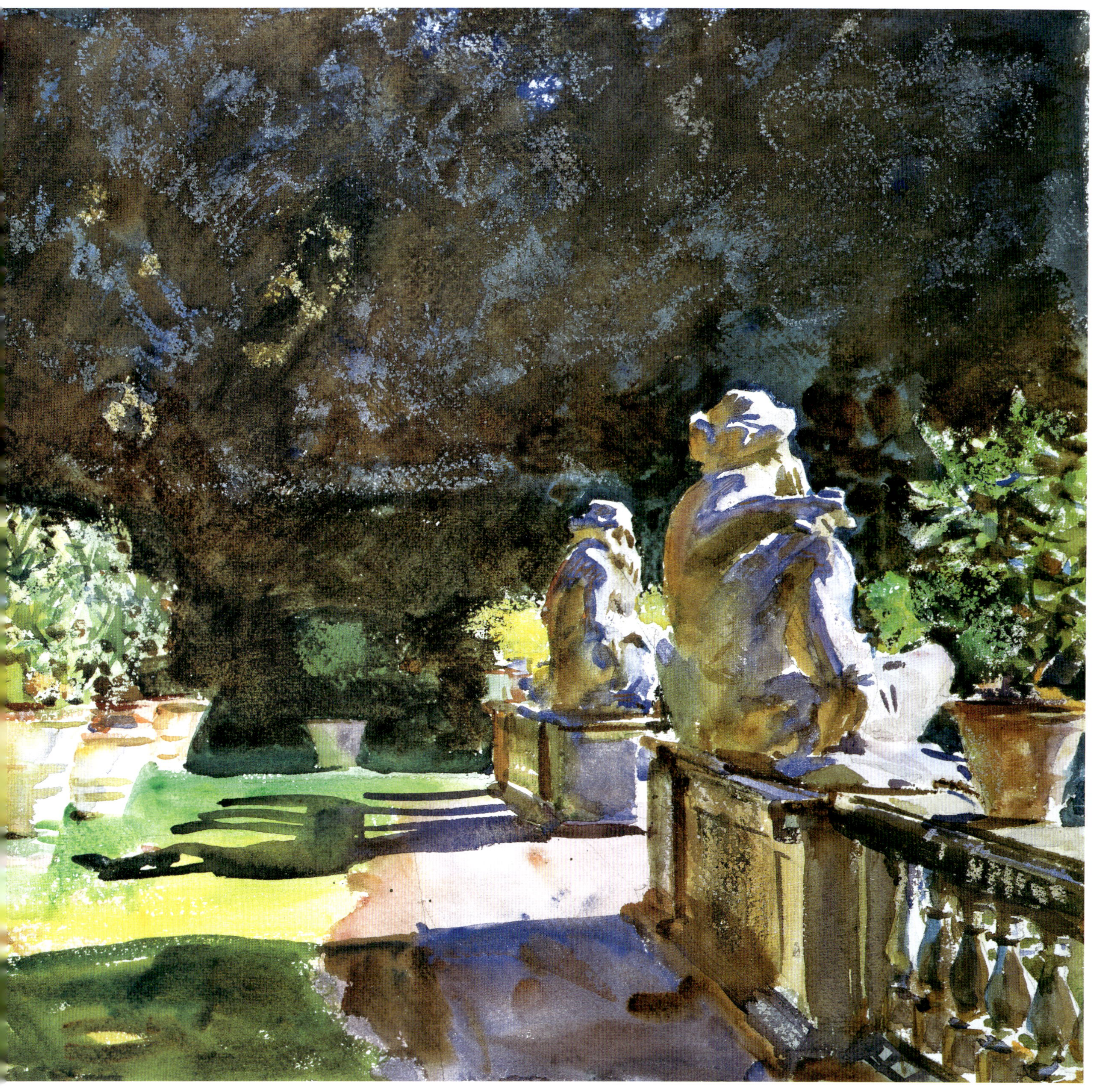

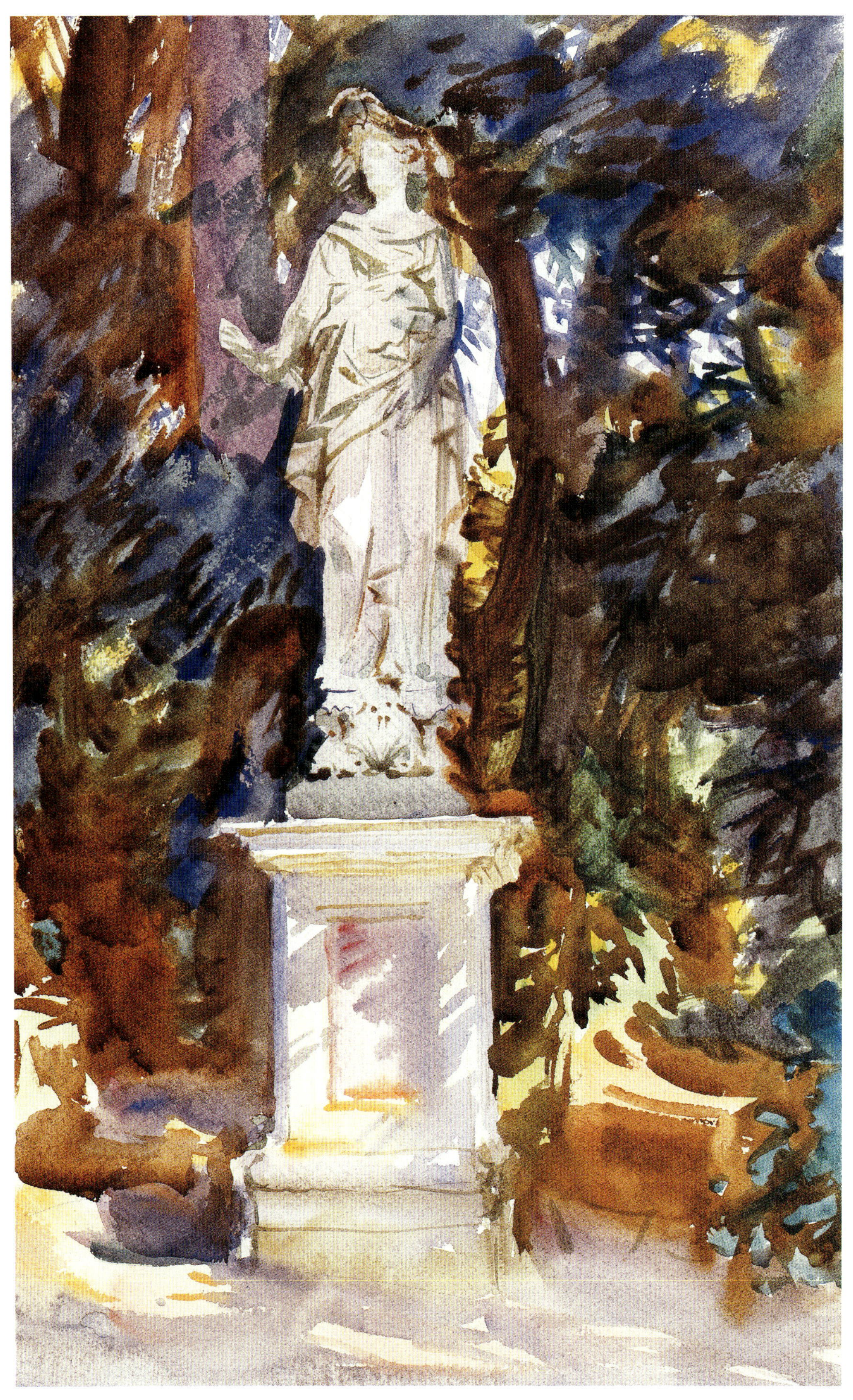

If the modern painter of water-colours aims at slightness, and today shorthand is preferred to definition, that was not the aim of Sargent. He never ran the risk of emptiness. He cultivated in his compositions full measure, pressed down and running over.

—Evan Charteris, 1927

Boboli 1907
Watercolor
18 1/8 x 11 7/16 in. (46.0 x 29.0 cm.)
The Brooklyn Museum of Art,
Purchased by special subscription,
(09.817)

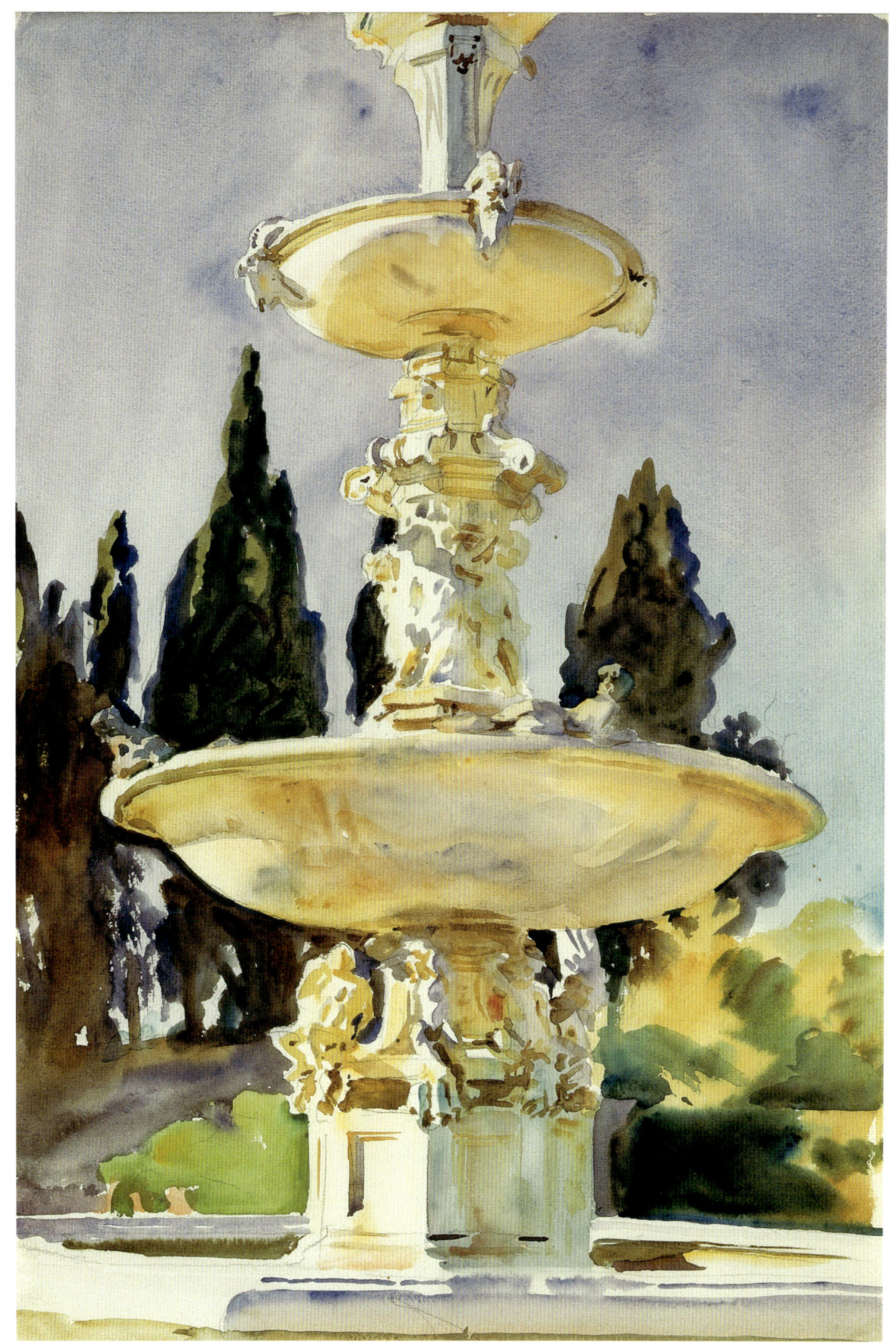

In a Medici Villa c. 1907
Watercolor and pencil
21 3/16 x 14 3/8 in. (53.8 x 36.6 cm.)
The Brooklyn Museum of Art,
Purchased by special subscription,
(09.826)

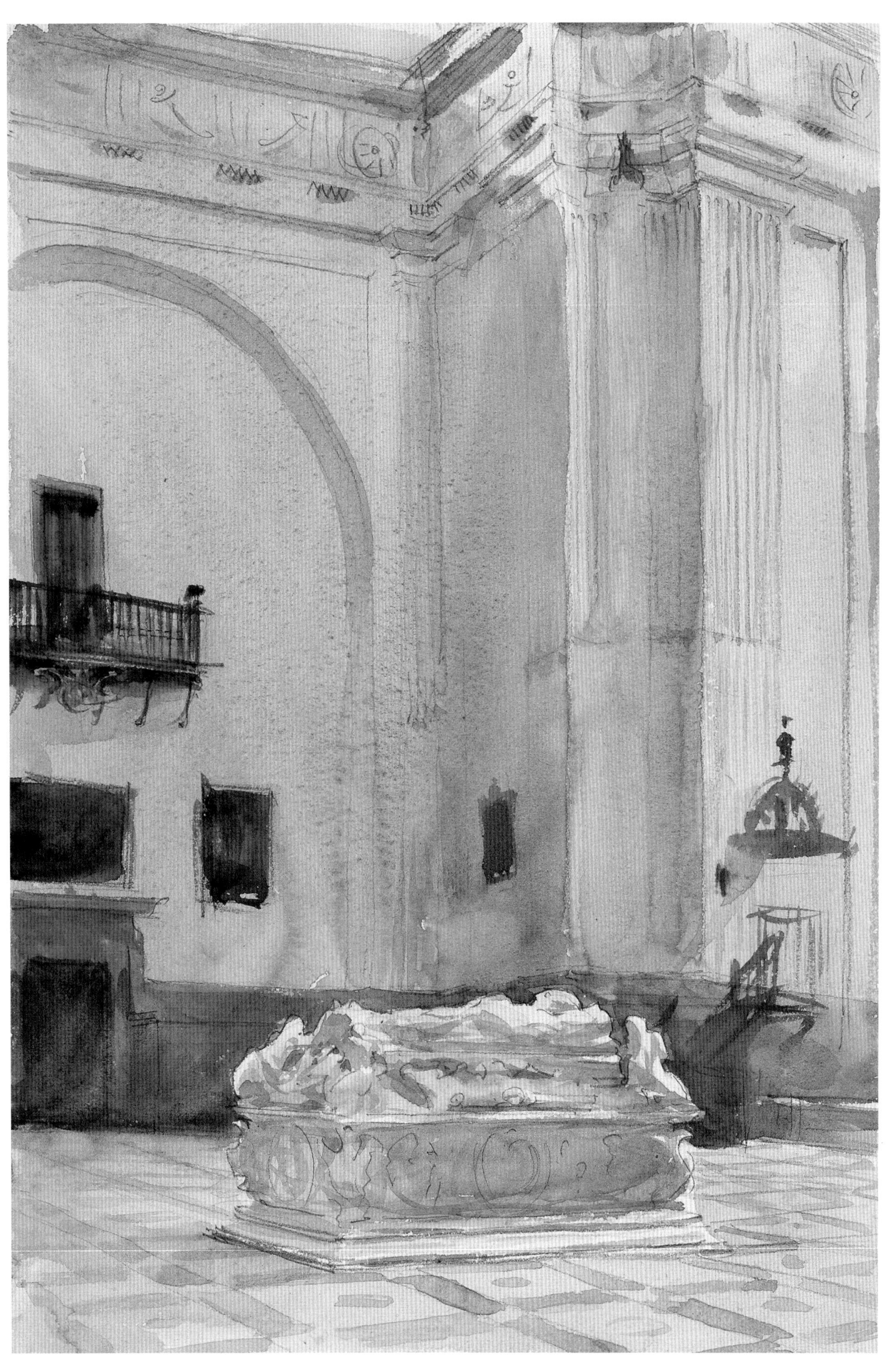

All [the watercolors] are wonderful in the power of summary expression of architecture and other forms with a few dashes of the brush. It is not the work of a brooder or dreamer; it is more like an athletic exercise with shape and space and light.

—D.S. MacColl,
Saturday Review, April 1, 1905

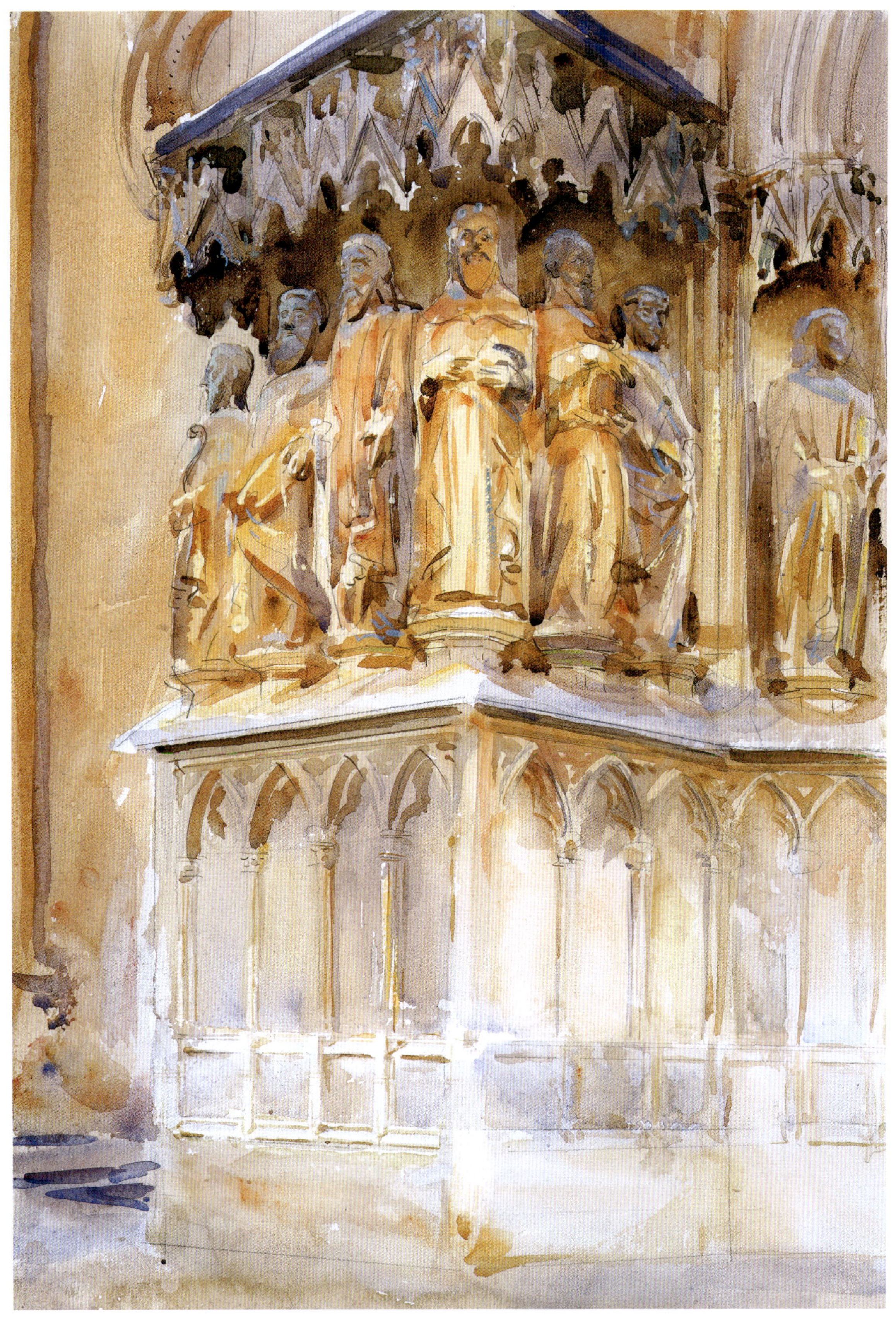

(opposite)

Tomb, Toledo n.d.
Watercolor
14 5/8 x 11 in. (37.1 x 27.9 cm.)
Museum of Art, Rhode Island School of Design, Anonymous Gift
Photography by Cathy Carver

Tarragona 1908
(Tarragona Cathedral)
Watercolor, gouache, and graphite on paper affixed to board
19 1/2 x 13 7/8 in. (49.5 x 35.2 cm.)
New Britain Museum of American Art, Connecticut, Grace Judd Landers Fund

The Terrace at La Granja c. 1903–04 or 1912
Watercolor on paper
11 3/4 x 17 3/4 in. (30 x 45 cm.)
Isabella Stewart Gardner Museum, Boston

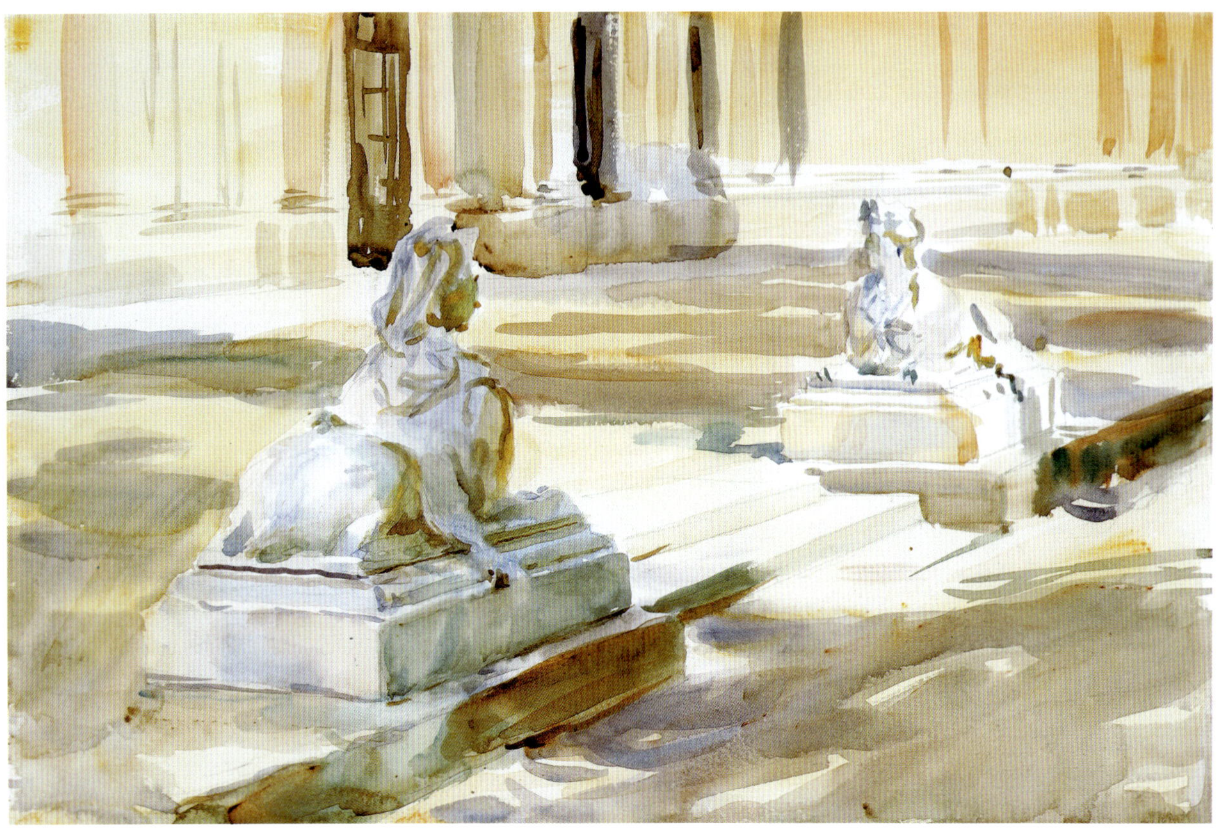

Gardens at Florence 1910
Watercolor over graphite on off-white paper
14 1/4 x 20 7/8 in. (36.2 x 53 cm.)
Courtesy of the Fogg Art Museum, Harvard University Art Museums,
Gift of Grenville L. Winthrop
© President and Fellows of Harvard College, Harvard University,
Photo: Photographic Services

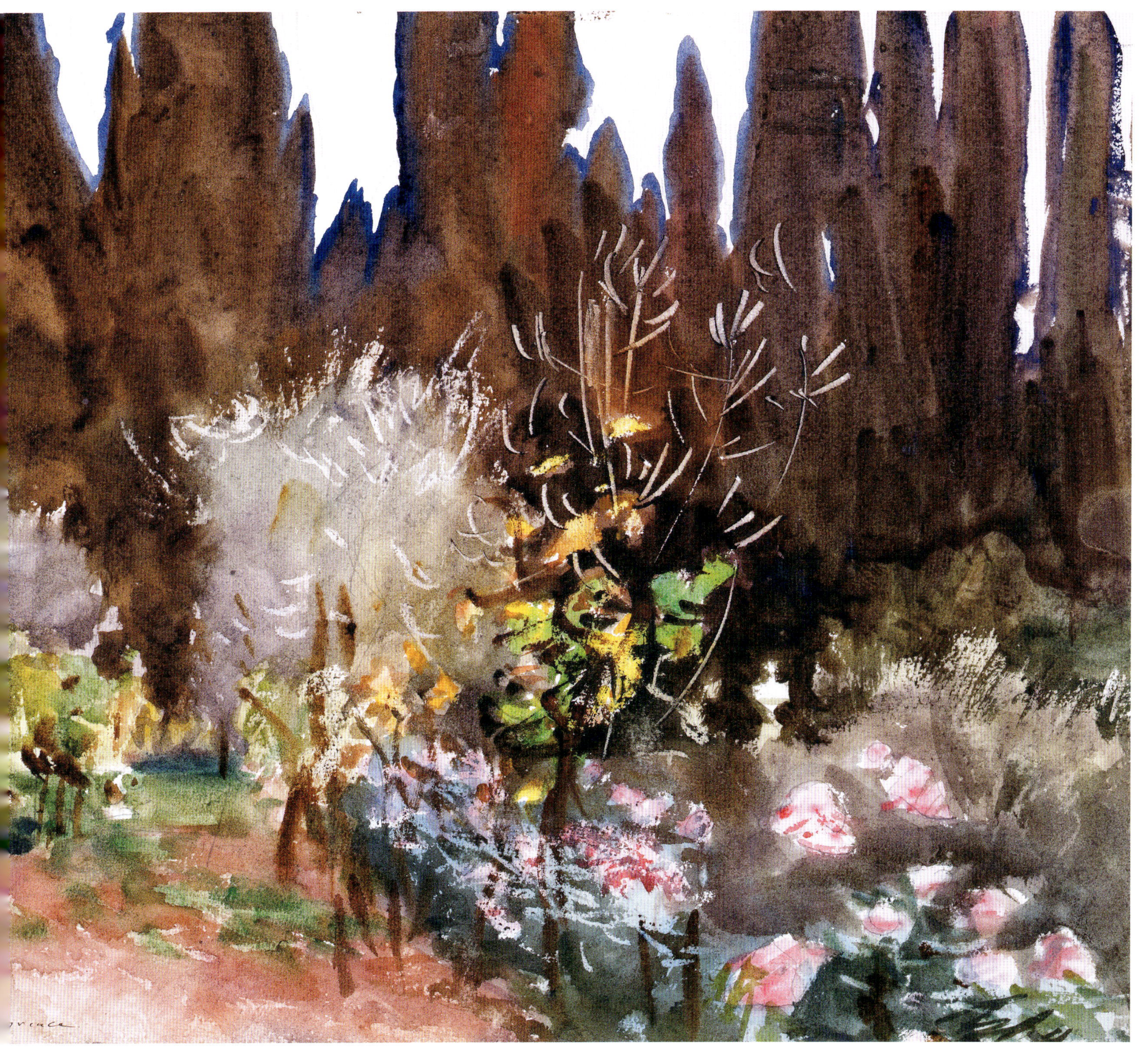

[The watercolours] have a happy air of impromptu, of the artist having come upon a scene at a particular moment and there and then translated it into paint. He set his face against anything like "picture-making"; his water-colours are fragmentary—pieces of the visible world broken off because they appealed to his eye. . . .

—Evan Charteris, 1927

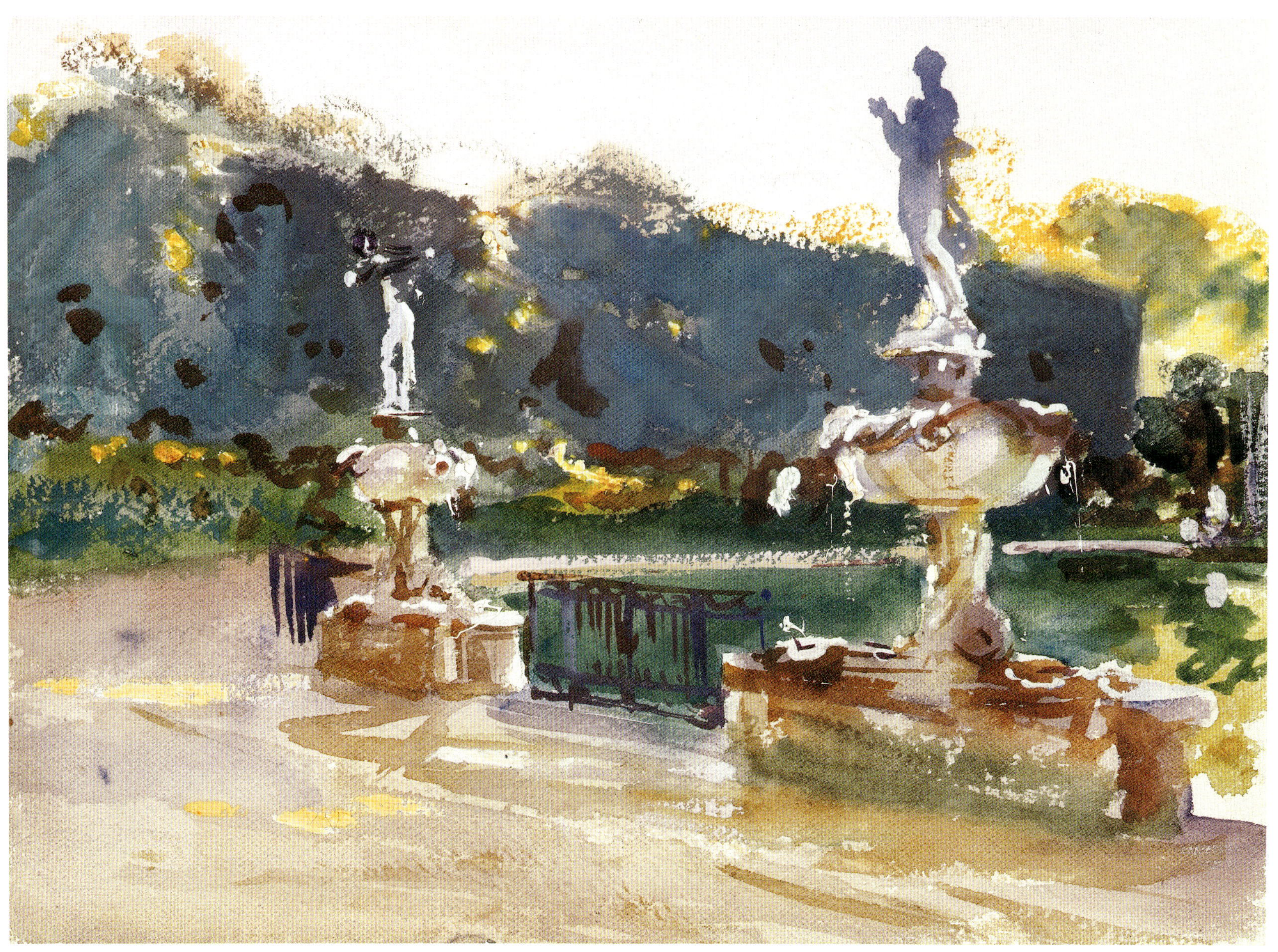

Boboli Gardens 1907
Watercolor
10 x 14 in. (25.4 x 35.6 cm.)
The Brooklyn Museum of Art,
Purchased by special subscription, (09.818)

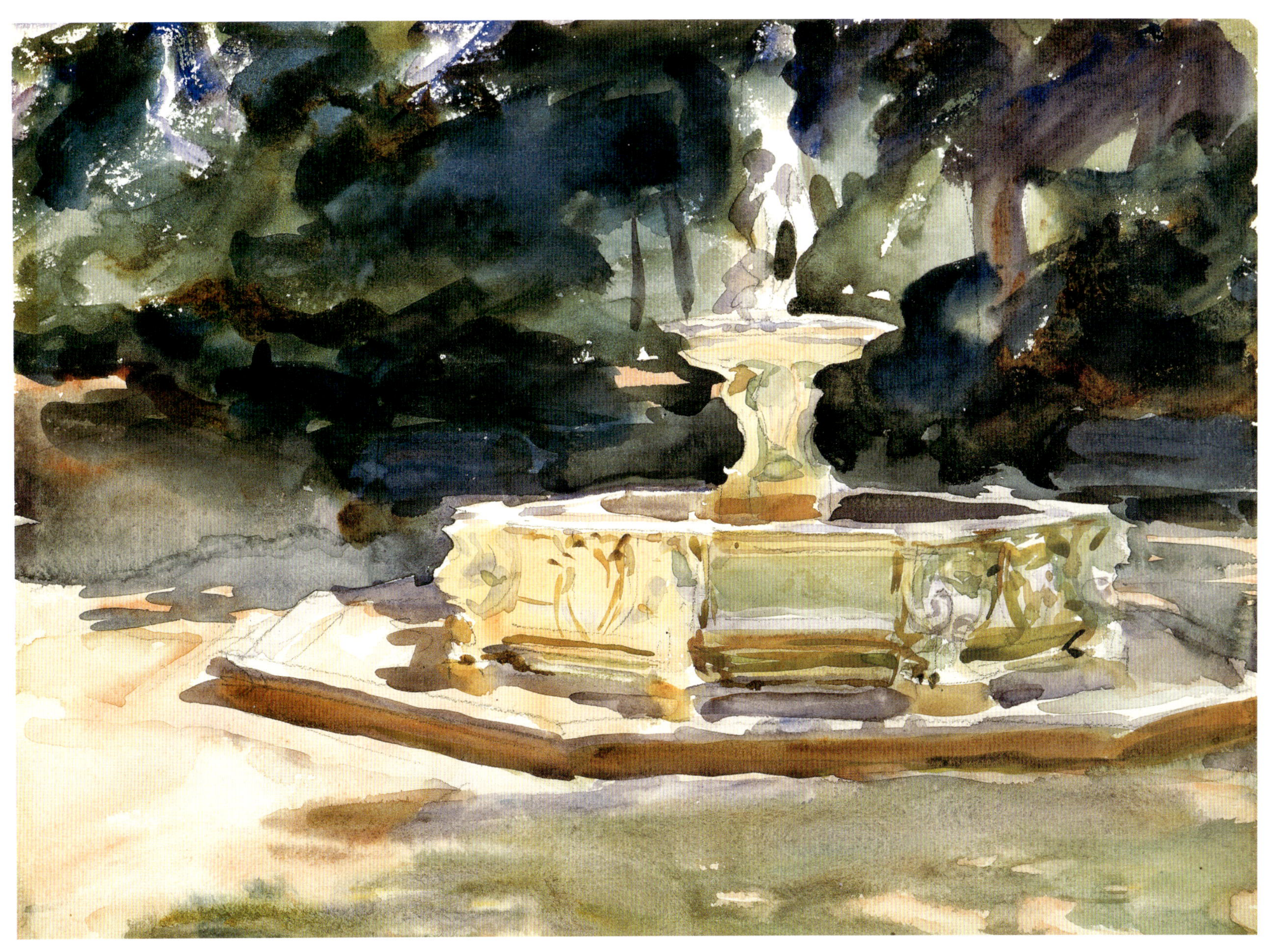

Aranjuez c. 1902–03
Watercolor over pencil
10 x 14 1/16 in. (25.5 x 35.7 cm.)
The Brooklyn Museum of Art,
Purchased by special subscription, (09.809)

Italy, Spain, Greece and Great Britain

From early childhood, Sargent took advantage of the portable nature of watercolor. He maintained this habit, carrying his paints wherever he went, including the Cotswolds in England and a loch in Scotland.

After 1900, Sargent would spend nearly every summer in extended holidays across Europe. The famous artist found visual sustenance on the shores of Lake Garda, on the islands of Corfu and Majorca, and in various retreats around the Mediterranean.

Sargent maintained a constant interest in old world architecture; the interior of the cathedral in Cordova and a courtyard in Florence testify to his fascination with the grandeur of past centuries and civilizations. At the same time, he could paint a humble house on Majorca, bringing to it all the skill he had at his command to render the sun-blanched walls.

The unruly qualities of the scenery also captured his fancy. The wild shapes of cypresses, that tree that had intrigued van Gogh, appealed to him, as did the olive trees on Corfu. His watercolor method followed the dictates of the particular subject: trunks and branches might be loosely sketched in while foliage might require broad washes. True to the motif and to his instincts, Sargent painted watercolor with a brio unsurpassed in his time.

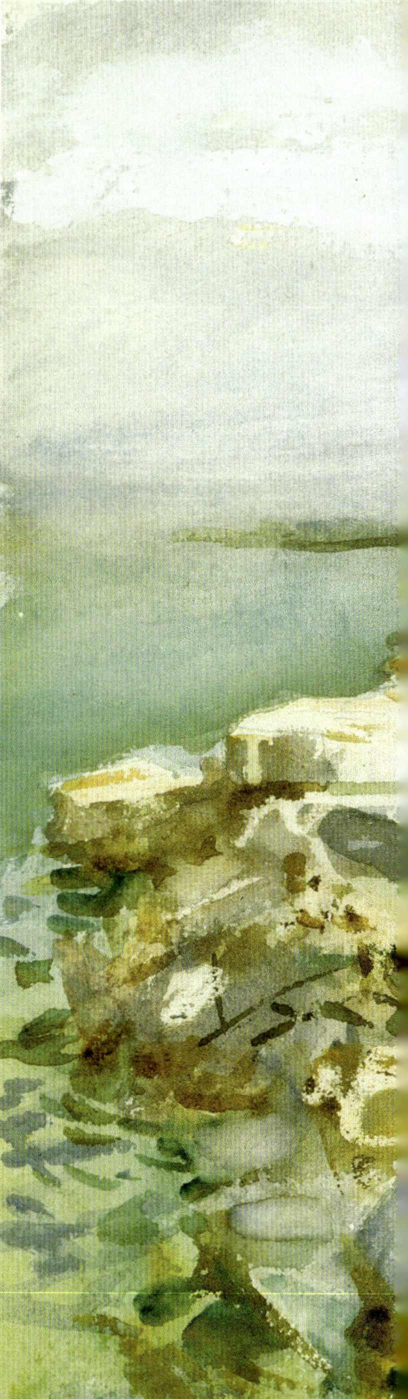

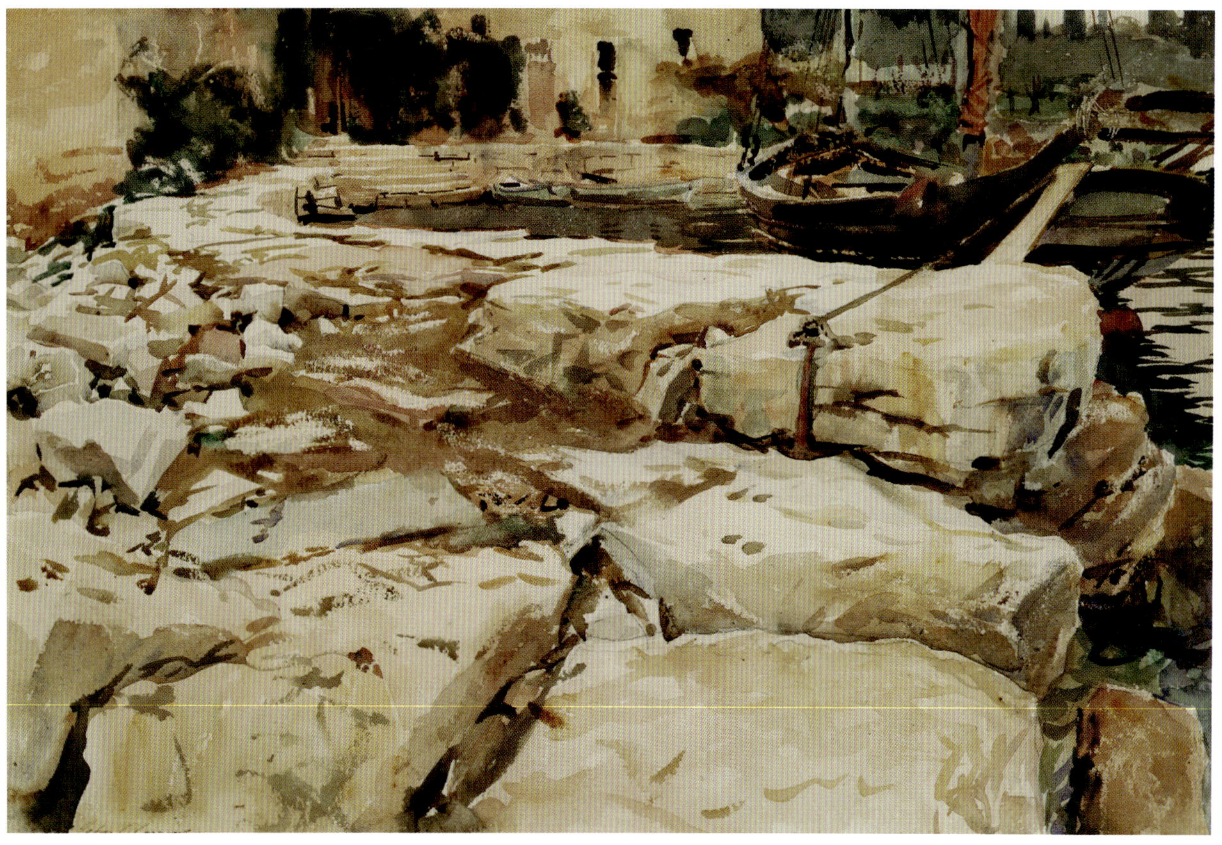

The Jetty at San Vigilio 1913
Watercolor and pencil on paper.
13 3/4 x 21 1/8 in. (34.8 x 53.7 cm.)
Courtesy Christie's Images

Above Lake Garda (at San Vigilio) 1913
Watercolor and gouache on paper
13 3/4 x 21 in. (34.9 x 53.4 cm.)
Courtesy Christie's Images

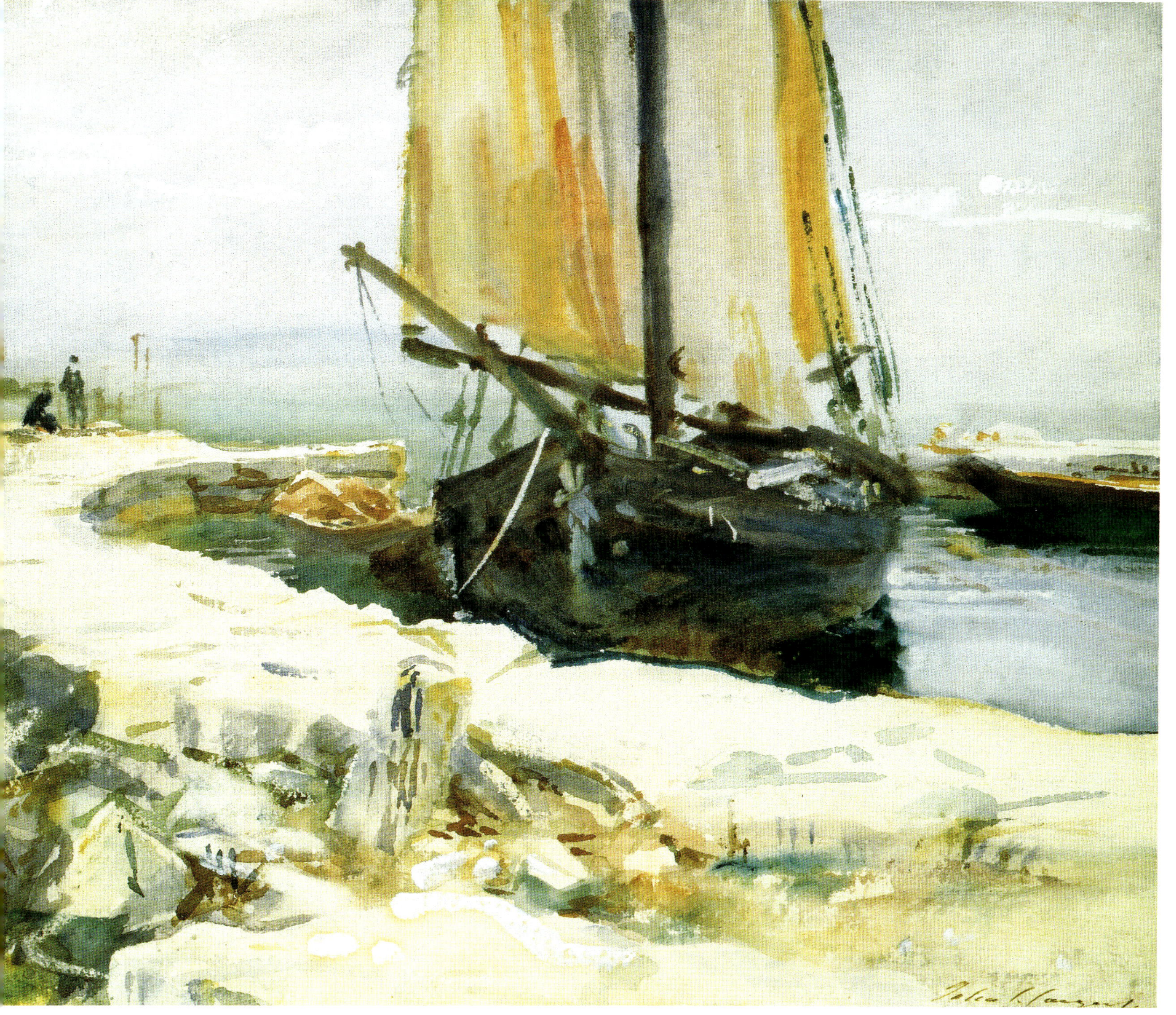

...Sargent is a supreme stylist, though the style is that of a speaker to whom, through long habit in the selection of words that convey just the right shade of meaning, as well as of images that nicely express his thought, it has become impossible to say anything other than beautifully and well.

—Lee Woodward Zeigler, 1924

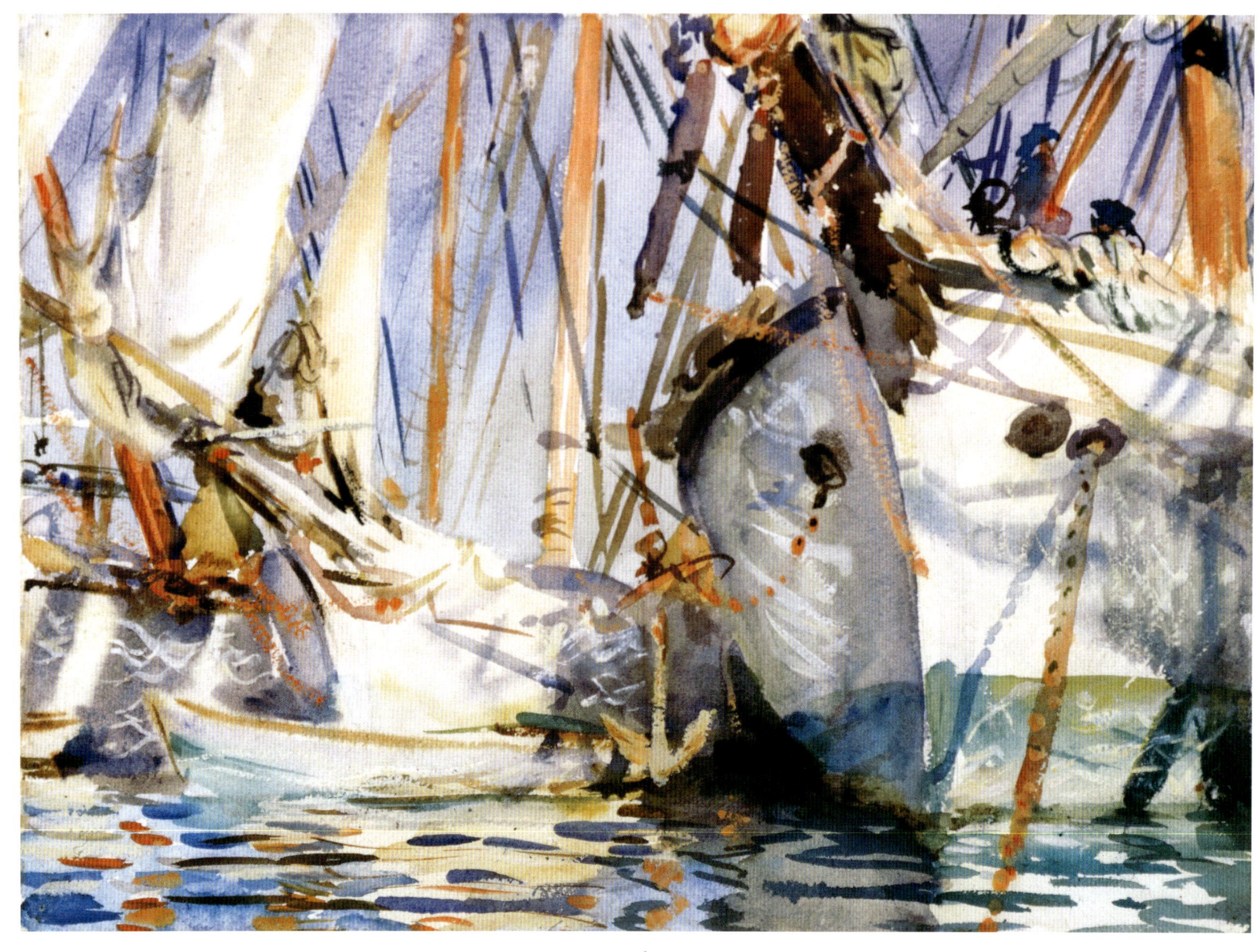

White Ships 1908
Watercolor and pencil
13 7/8 x 19 3/8 in. (35.2 x 49.2 cm.)
The Brooklyn Museum of Art,
Purchased by special subscription, (09.846)

Flotsam and Jetsam n.d.
Watercolor, gouache and pencil on paper
13 3/16 x 18 13/16 in. (33.5 x 46.2 cm.)
The Joan Whitney Payson Collection
at the Portland Museum of Art, Portland, Maine.
Lent by John Whitney Payson (7.1991.6)
Photo by Melville McLean

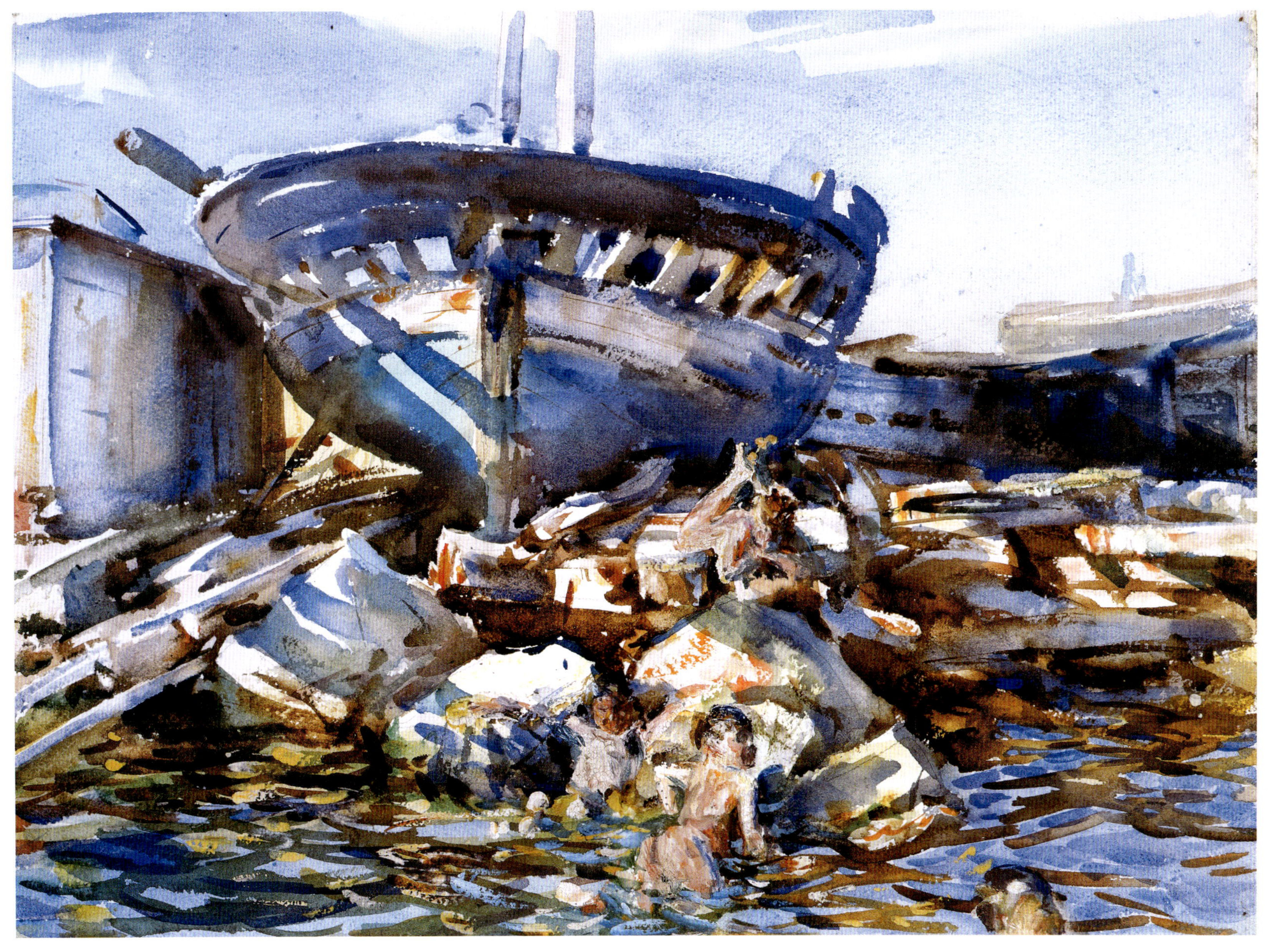

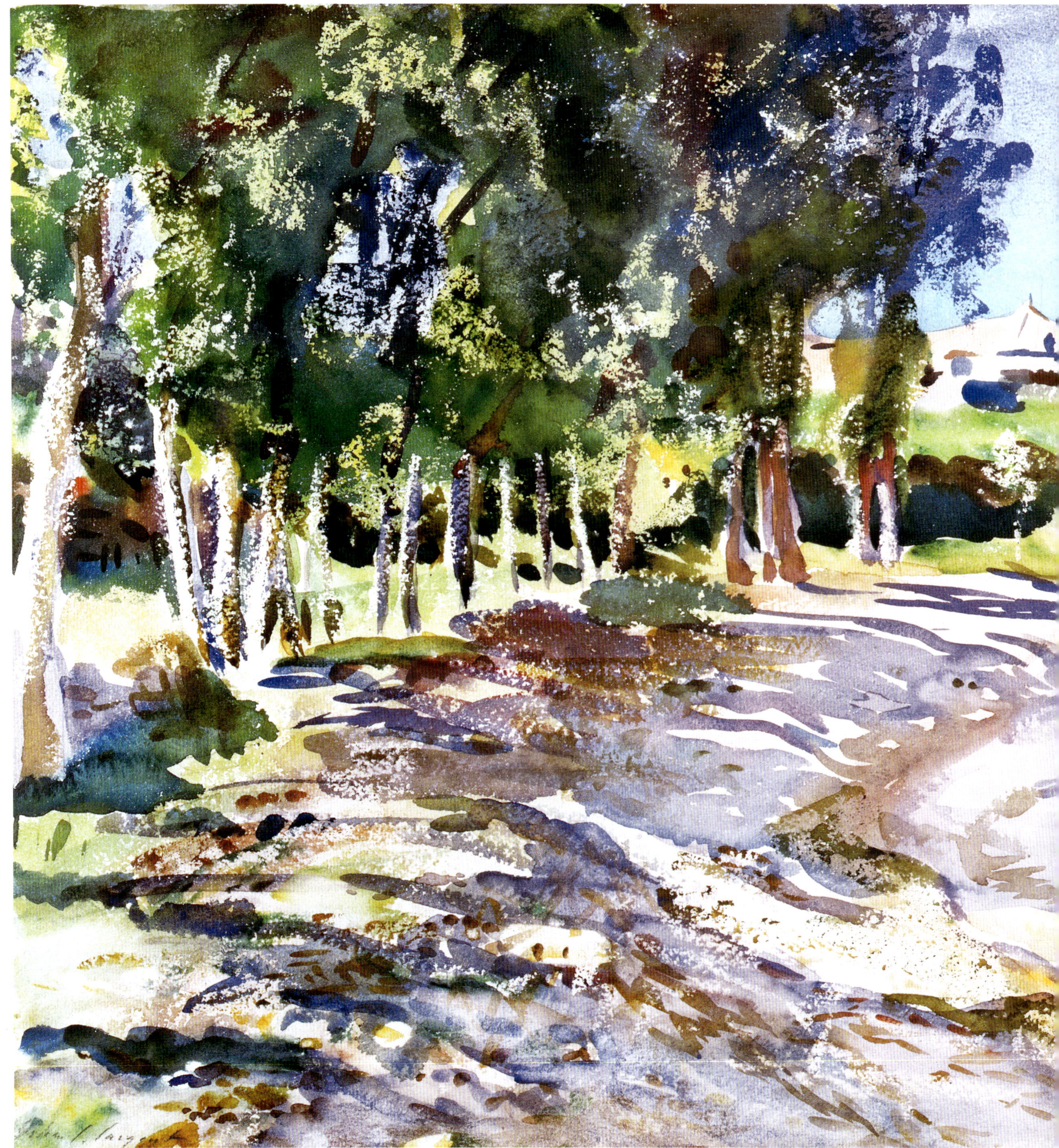

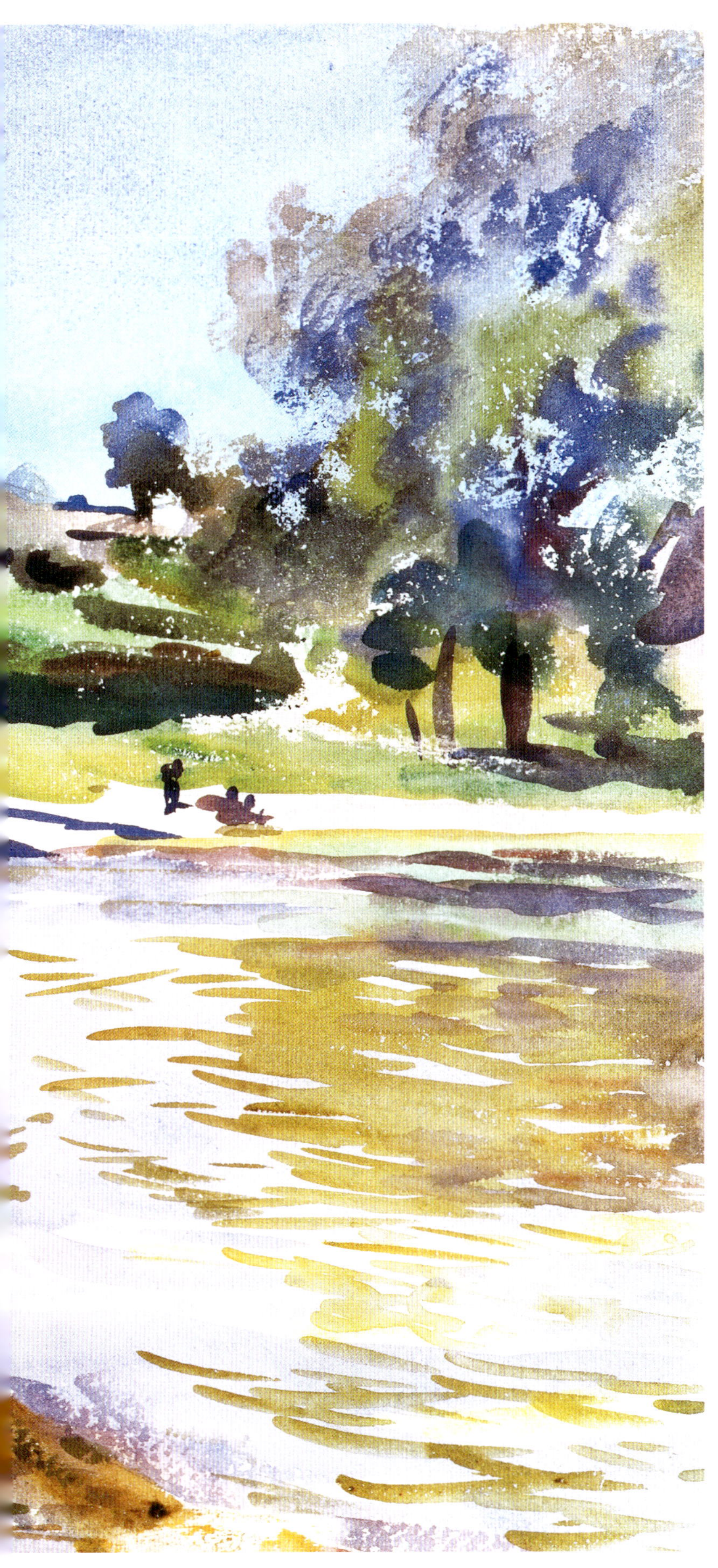

But it was away from his portraits, on the canals of Venice or the plains of Palestine, in the passes of the high Alps or among the dancers of Spain, or the fountains and cypresses of Italy and the gardens of Sicily, or, again, at Capri or Corfu, or on any one of the countless journeys that he made with friends, that his spirit was most at ease and serene—anywhere, in fact, where he could "make the best of an emergency" as he called painting a water-colour. And an emergency was seldom wanting.

—Evan Charteris, 1927

San Vigilio, Lago di Garda c. 1913
Watercolor
14 1/4 x 21 in. (36.2 x 53.3 cm.)
Tate Gallery, Liverpool, Great Britain
Art Resource, New York

To live with Sargent's water-colours is to live with sunshine captured and held, with the lustre of a bright and legible world, "the refluent shade" and "the ambient ardours of the noon."

—Evan Charteris, 1927

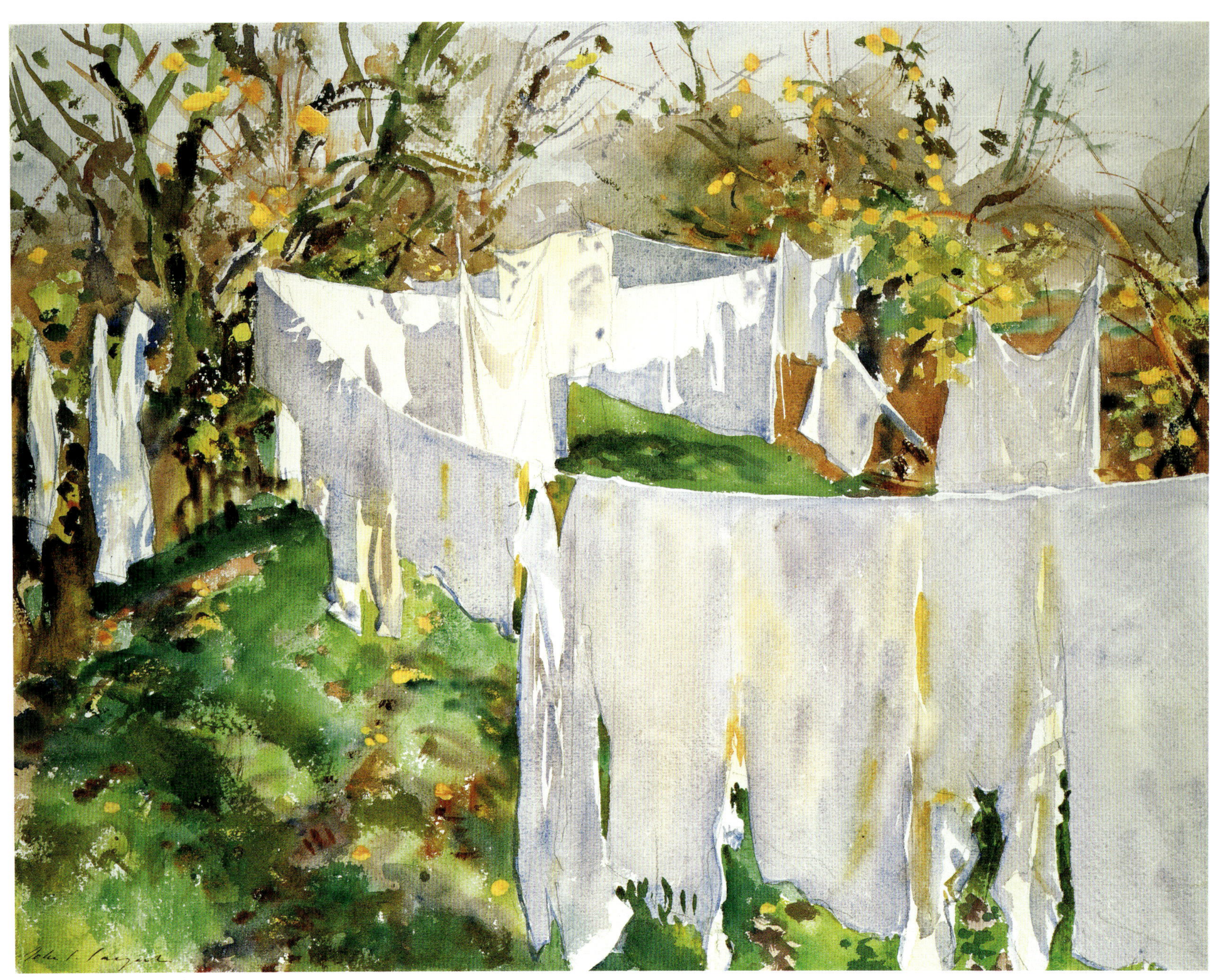

La Biancheria 1910
Watercolor
16 x 20 3/4 in. (41 x 53 cm.)
Hayden Collection,
Courtesy, Museum of Fine Arts, Boston

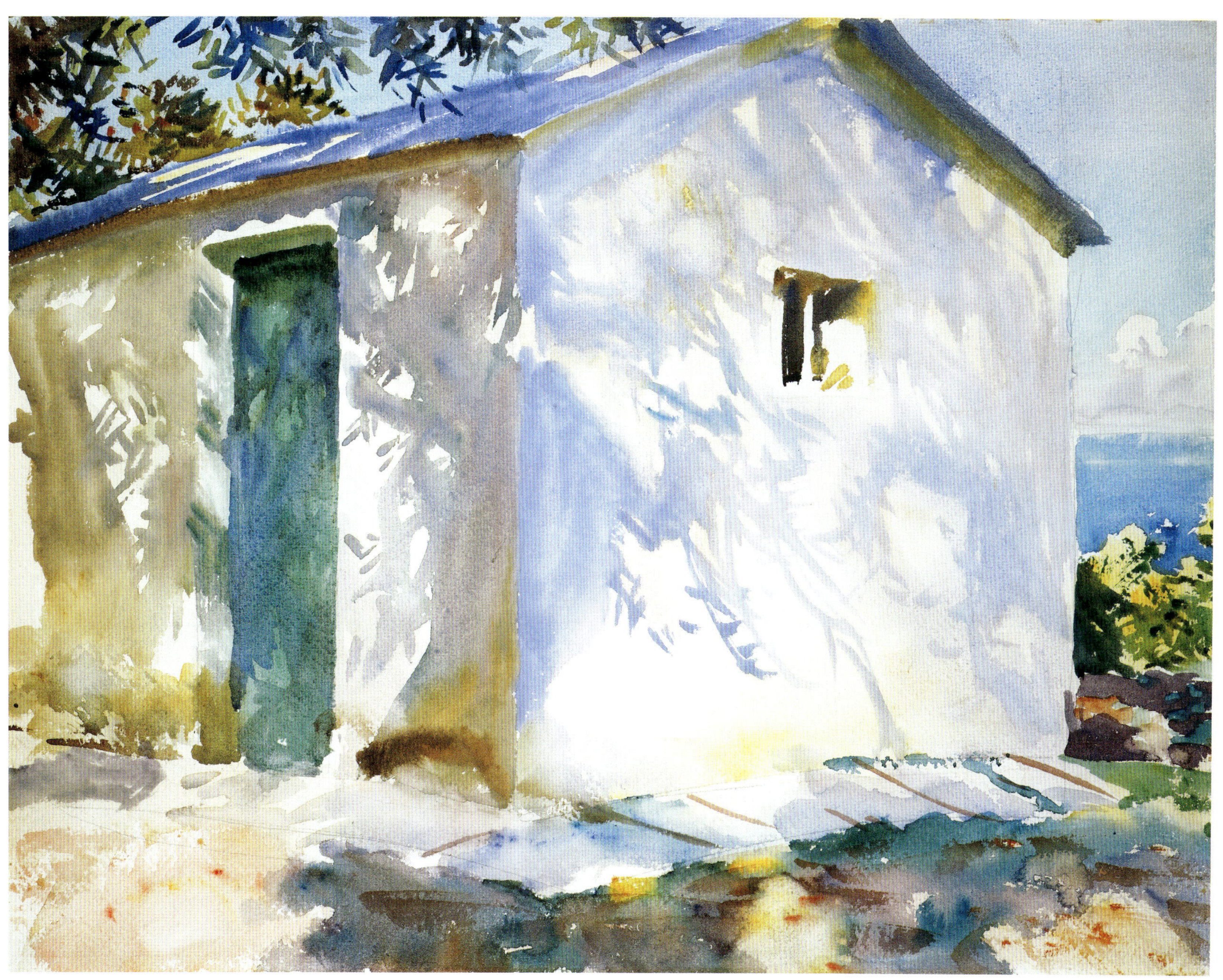

Corfu: Lights and Shadow 1909
Watercolor
15 3/4 x 20 1/2 in. (40 x 52.1 cm.)
Charles Henry Hayden Fund,
Courtesy, Museum of Fine Arts, Boston

Olive Trees, Corfu N.D.

Watercolor

14 x 20 in. (35.6 x 50.8 cm.)

The Art Institute of Chicago

Olivia Shaler Swan Memorial Collection, 1933.505

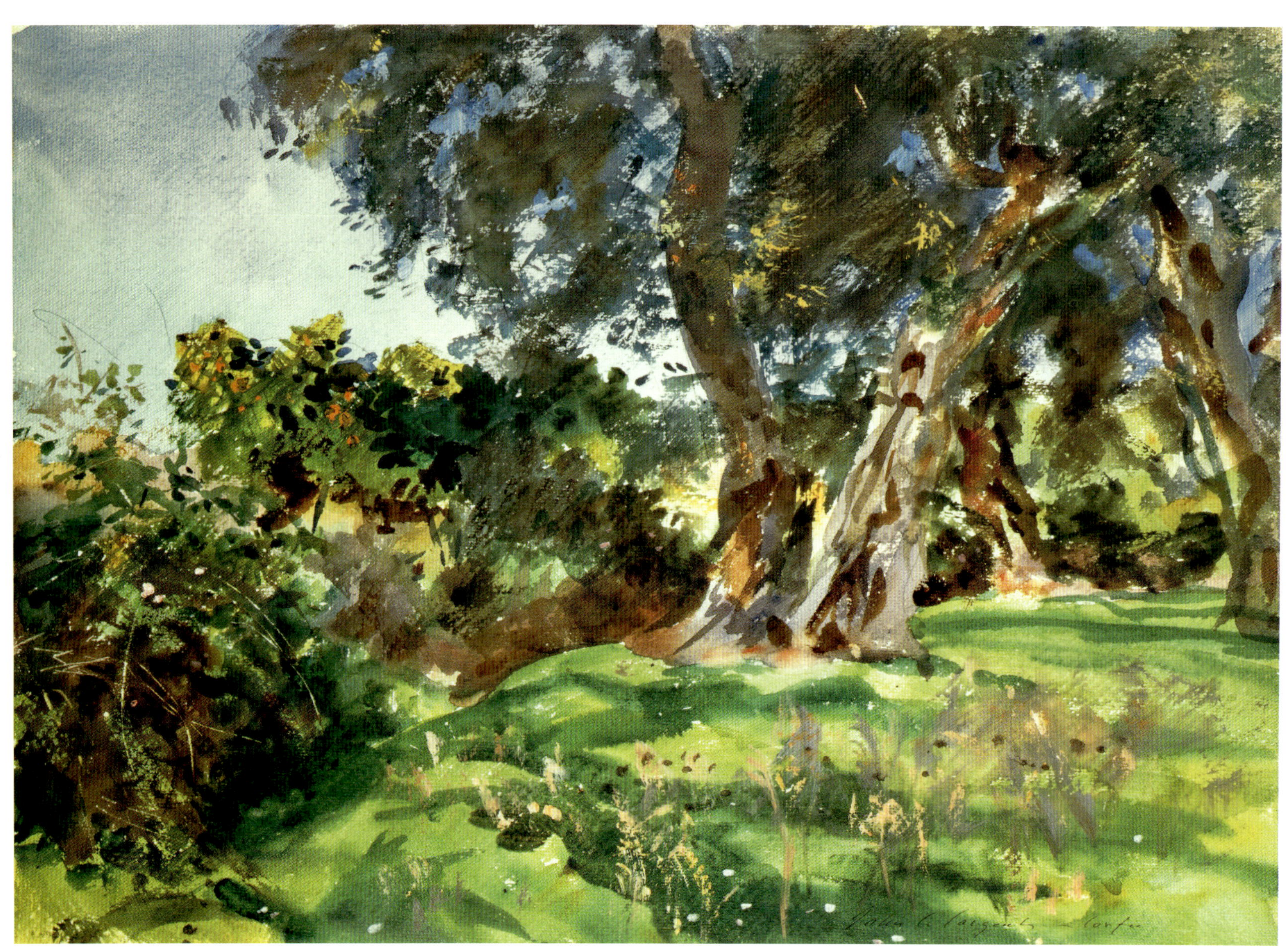

Olive Trees, Corfu 1909

Watercolor over graphite on white wove paper

14 x 20 in. (35.5 x 50.8 cm.)

Courtesy of the Fogg Art Museum,

Harvard University Art Museums,

Bequest of Grenville L. Winthrop

Photo: Photographic Services

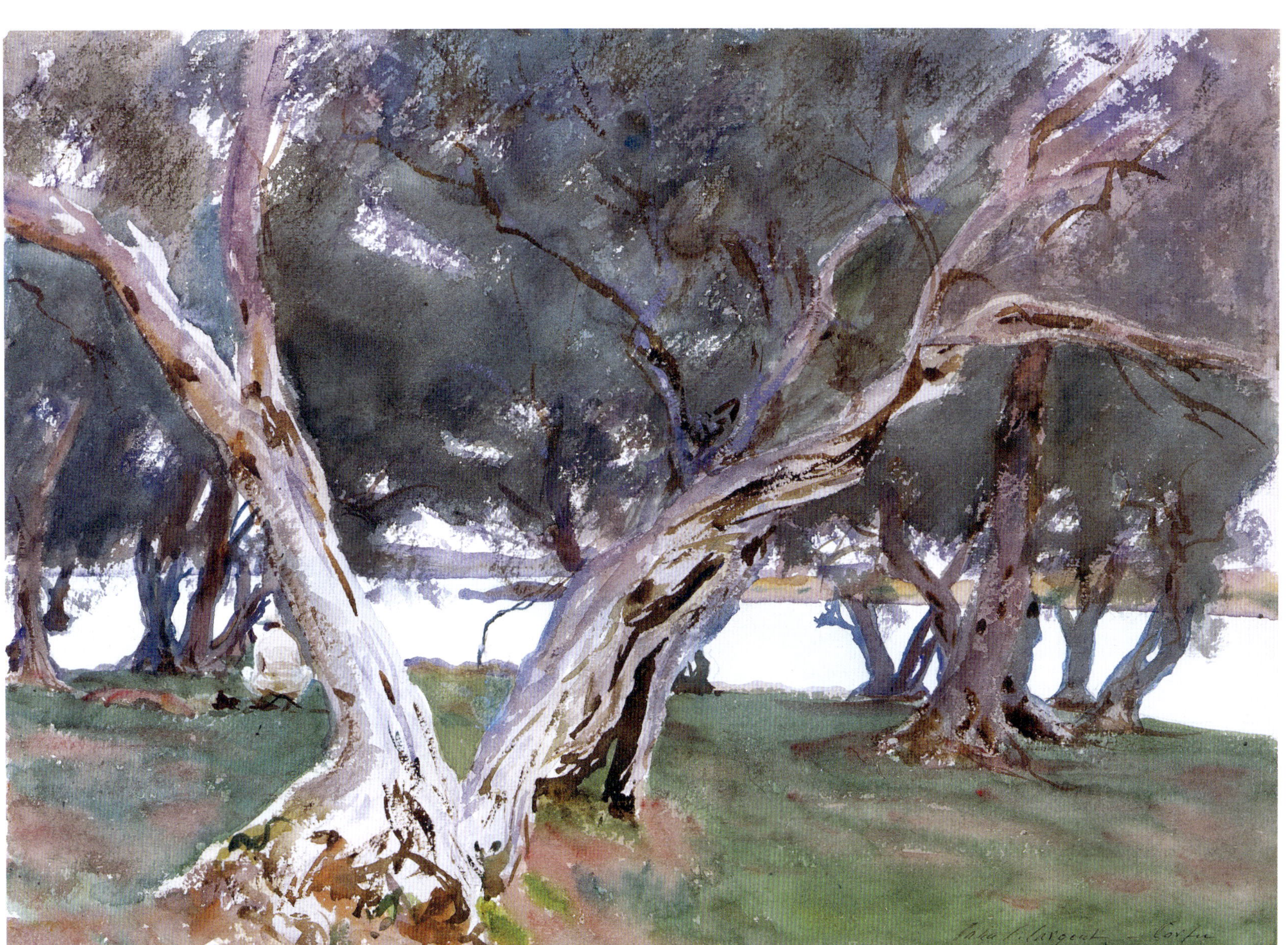

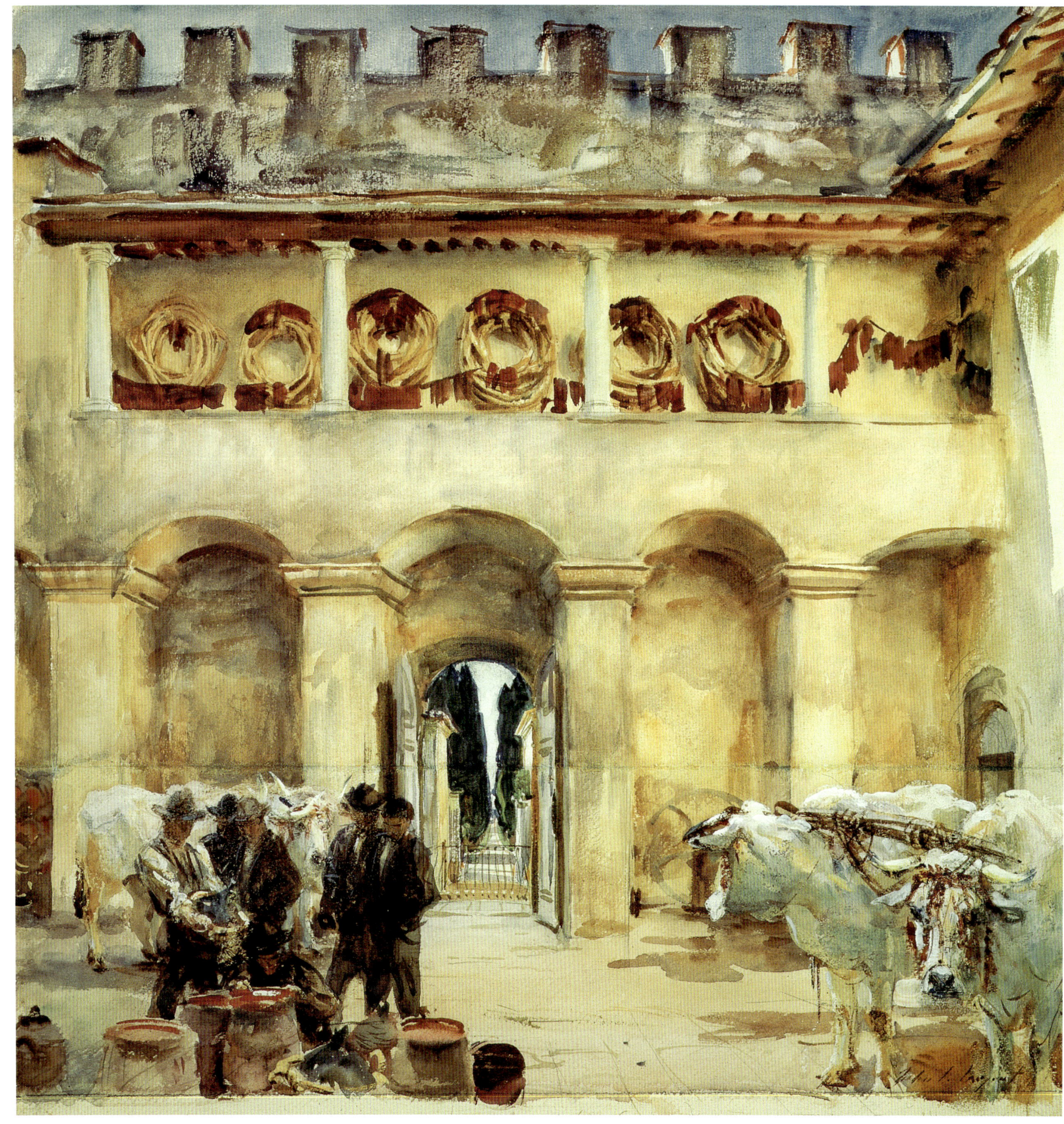

Spanish Soldiers c. 1902–03
Watercolor
18 1/16 x 12 1/16 in. (45.9 x 30.6 cm.)
The Brooklyn Museum of Art,
Purchased by special subscription, (09.840)

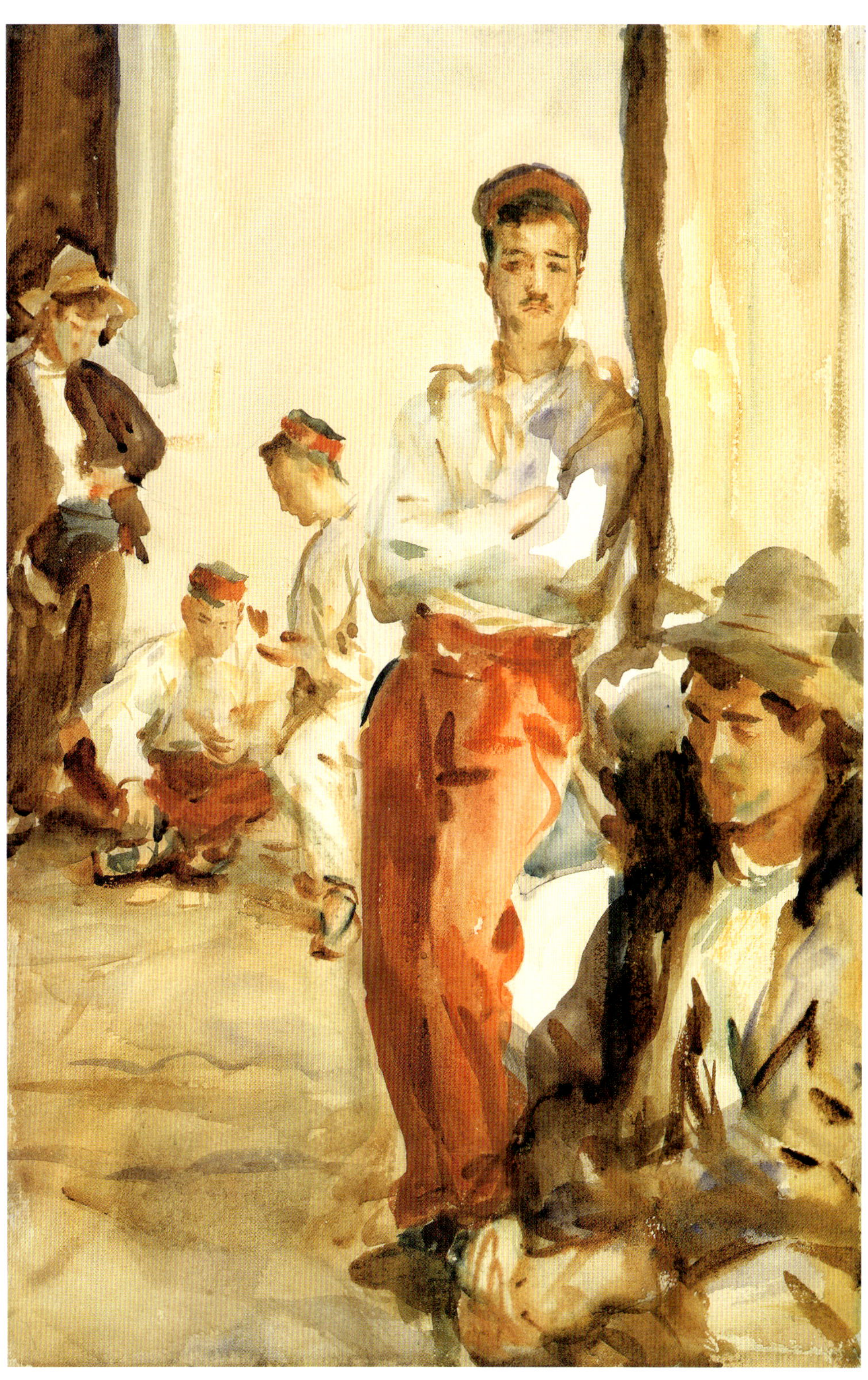

Florence: Torre Galle n.d.
Watercolor on paper
26 3/8 x 25 9/16 in. (67 x 65 cm.)
Charles Henry Hayden Fund,
Courtesy, Museum of Fine Arts, Boston

When he paints in Italy he does not paint fiction or romance... we shall look in vain in his cypress groves for the vision of a hamadryad or in his fountains for the glimpse of a naiad; all is rich and vivid and open to the day, painted with a fine sincerity of mind, the work of a painter who felt the immediate impression of the moment with an intensity that called for an instant response.

—Evan Charteris, 1927

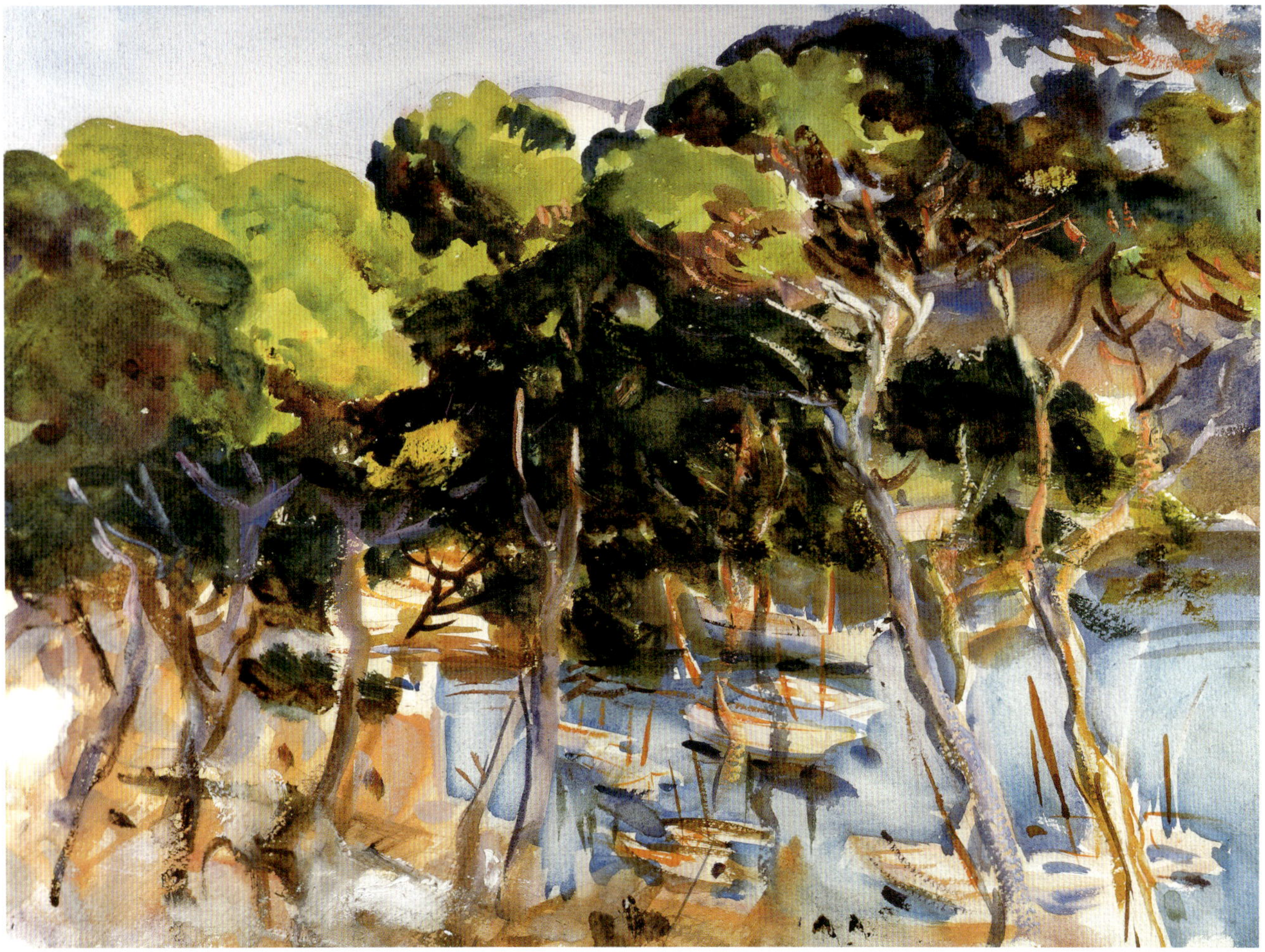

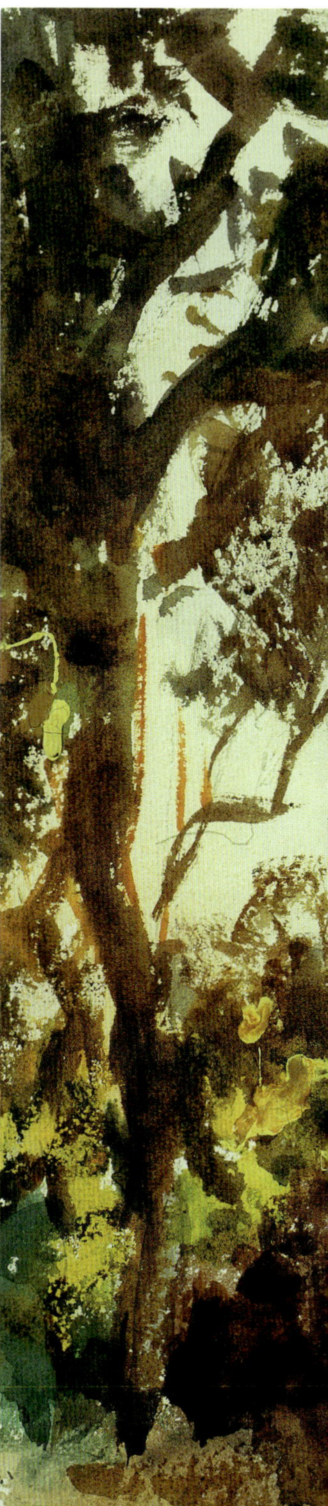

Port of Soller 1907–08
Watercolor
13 7/8 x 19 3/8 in. (35.3 x 49.2 cm.)
The Brooklyn Museum of Art,
Purchased by special subscription, (09.833)

Vines and Cypresses n.d.
Watercolor on paper
14 3/16 x 19 11/16 in. (36 x 50 cm.)
Charles Henry Hayden Fund,
Courtesy, Museum of Fine Arts, Boston

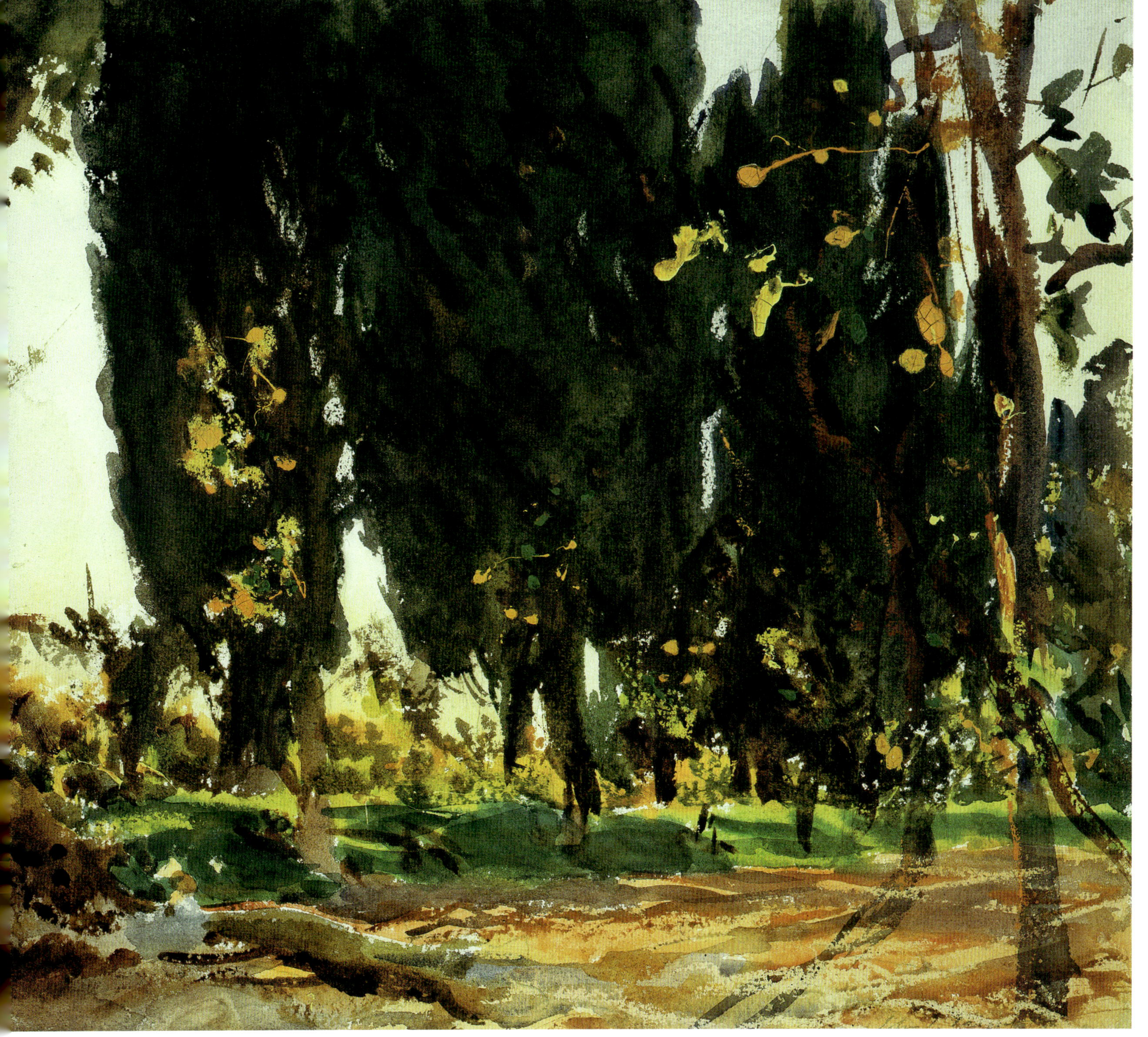

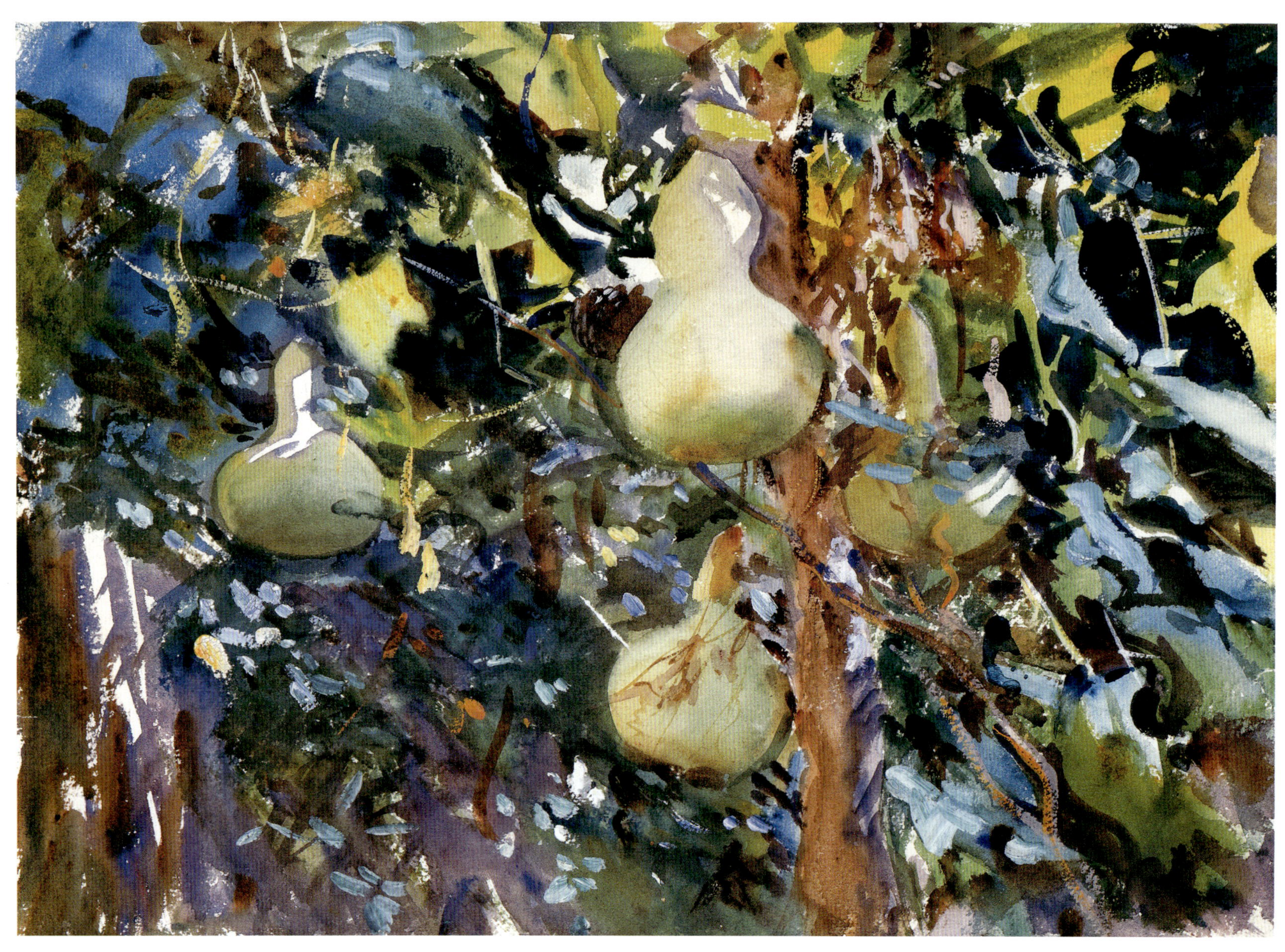

Gourds c. 1905–08
Watercolor
14 x 20 in. (35.5 x 50.7 cm.)
The Brooklyn Museum of Art,
Purchased by special subscription, (09.822)

Pomegranates 1908
Watercolor over pencil
21 3/16 x 14 7/16 in. (53.8 x 36.6 cm.)
The Brooklyn Museum of Art,
Purchased by special subscription, (09.832)

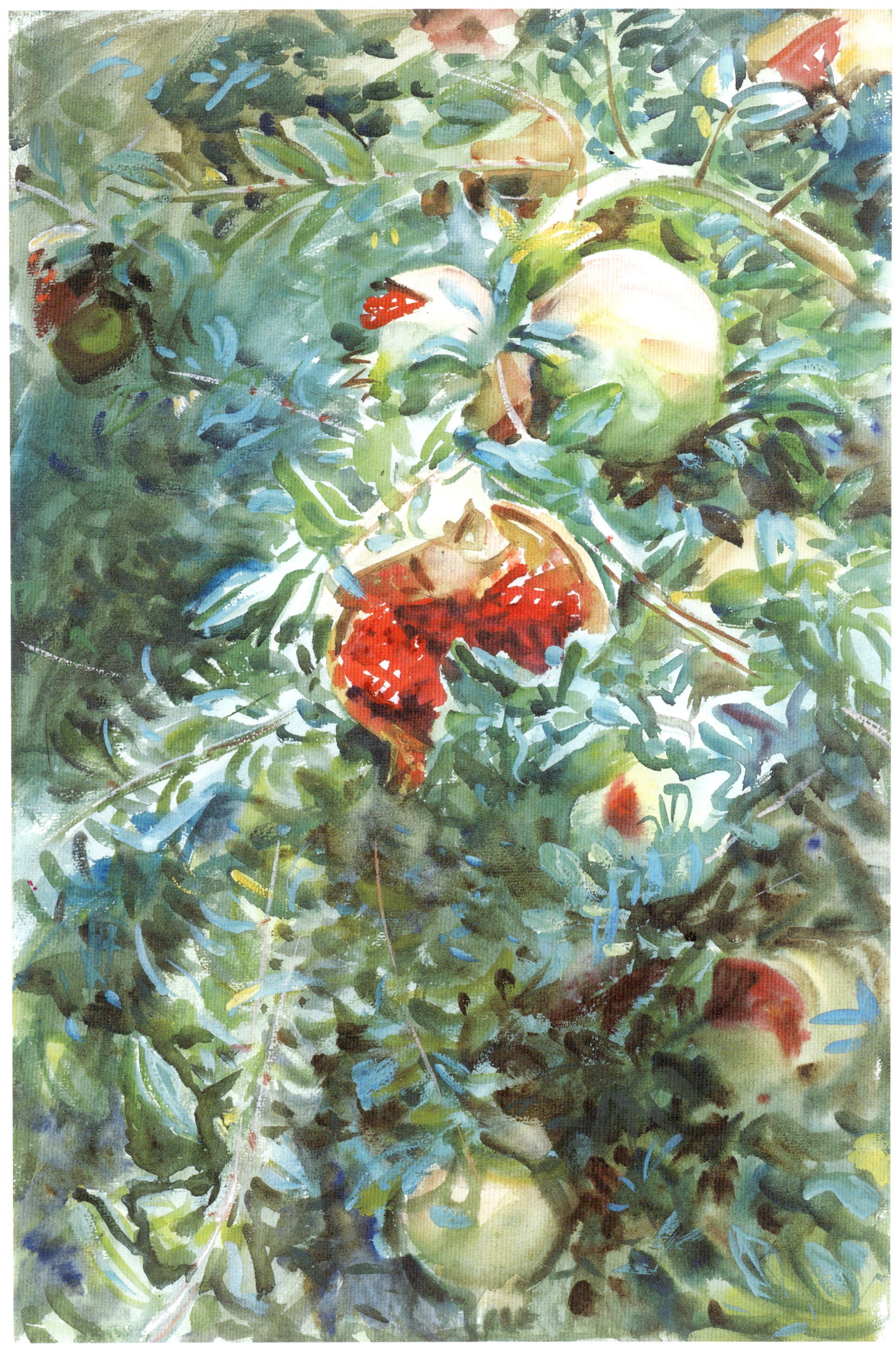

Loch Moidart, Inverness-shire 1896
Watercolor and Pencil
9 1/2 x 12 3/4 in. (24 x 32.5 cm.)
Courtesy Christie's Images

The Shadowed Stream c. 1884
Watercolor
13 1/2 x 9 1/2 in. (34.5 x 24 cm.)
Charles Henry Hayden Fund,
Courtesy, Museum of Fine Arts, Boston

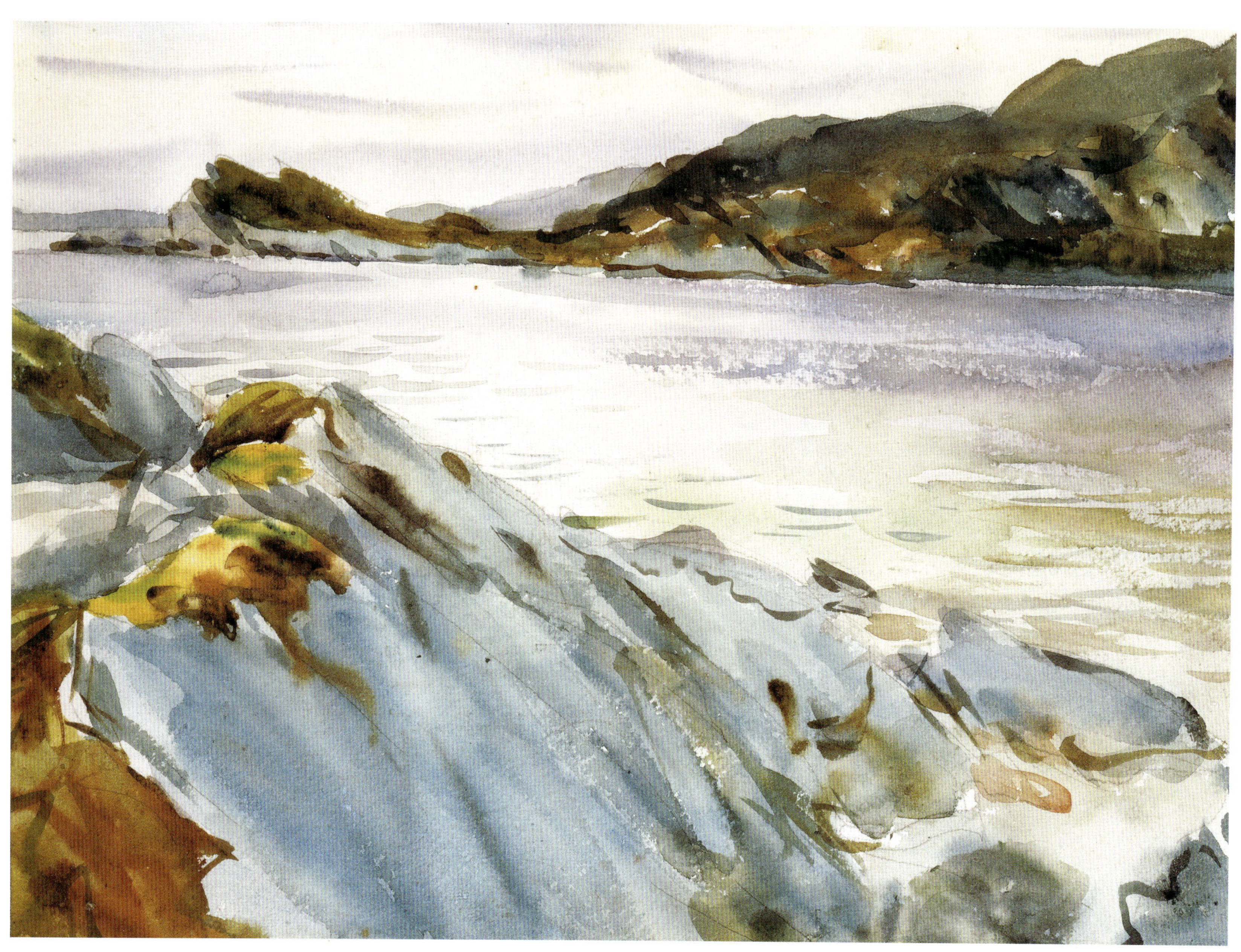

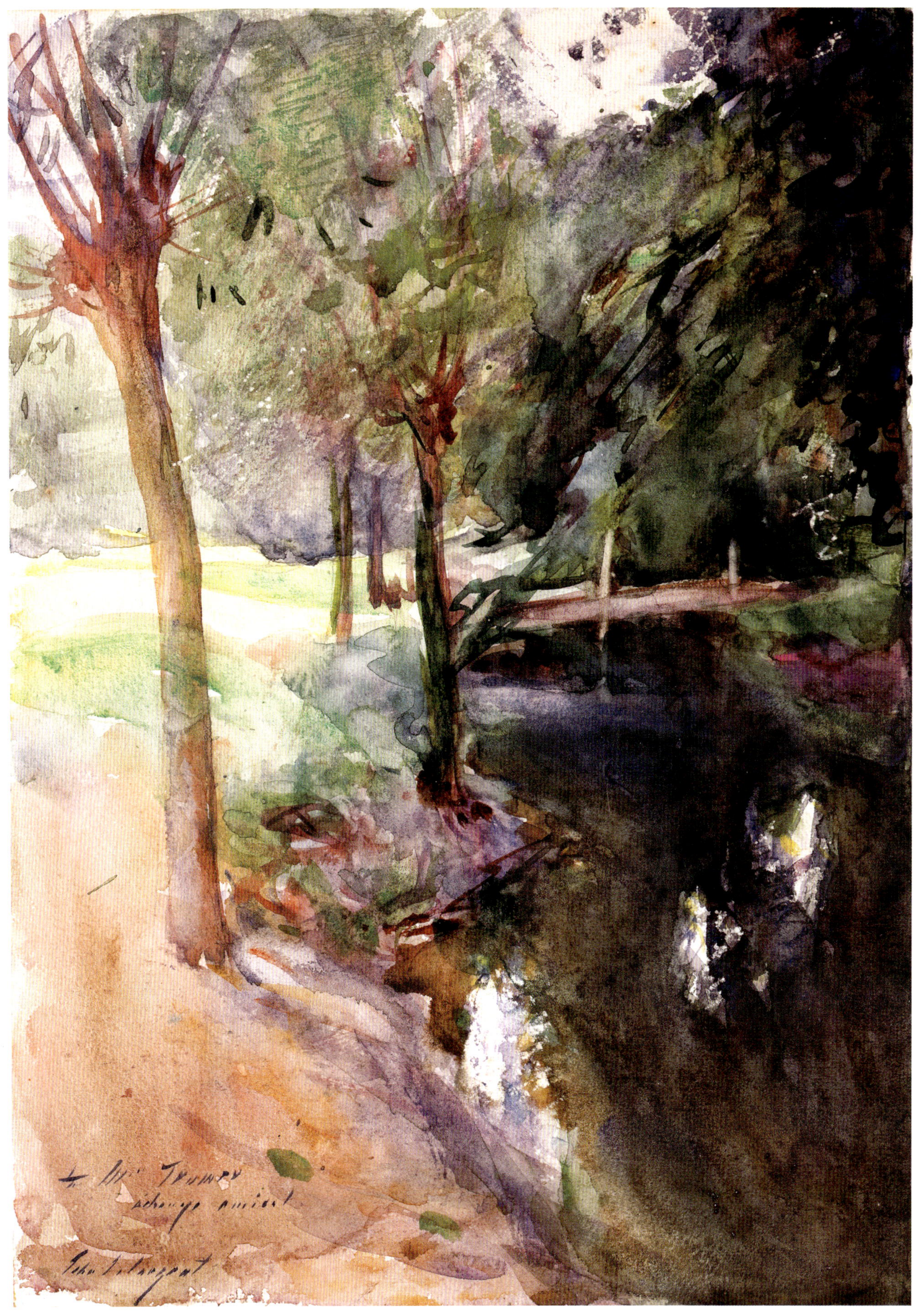

Cordova, Interior of a Cathedral c. 1903

Watercolor

10 x 13 3/4 in. (25.4 x 34.9 cm.)

Bequest of Elise Faye Loeffler,

Courtesy, Museum of Fine Arts, Boston

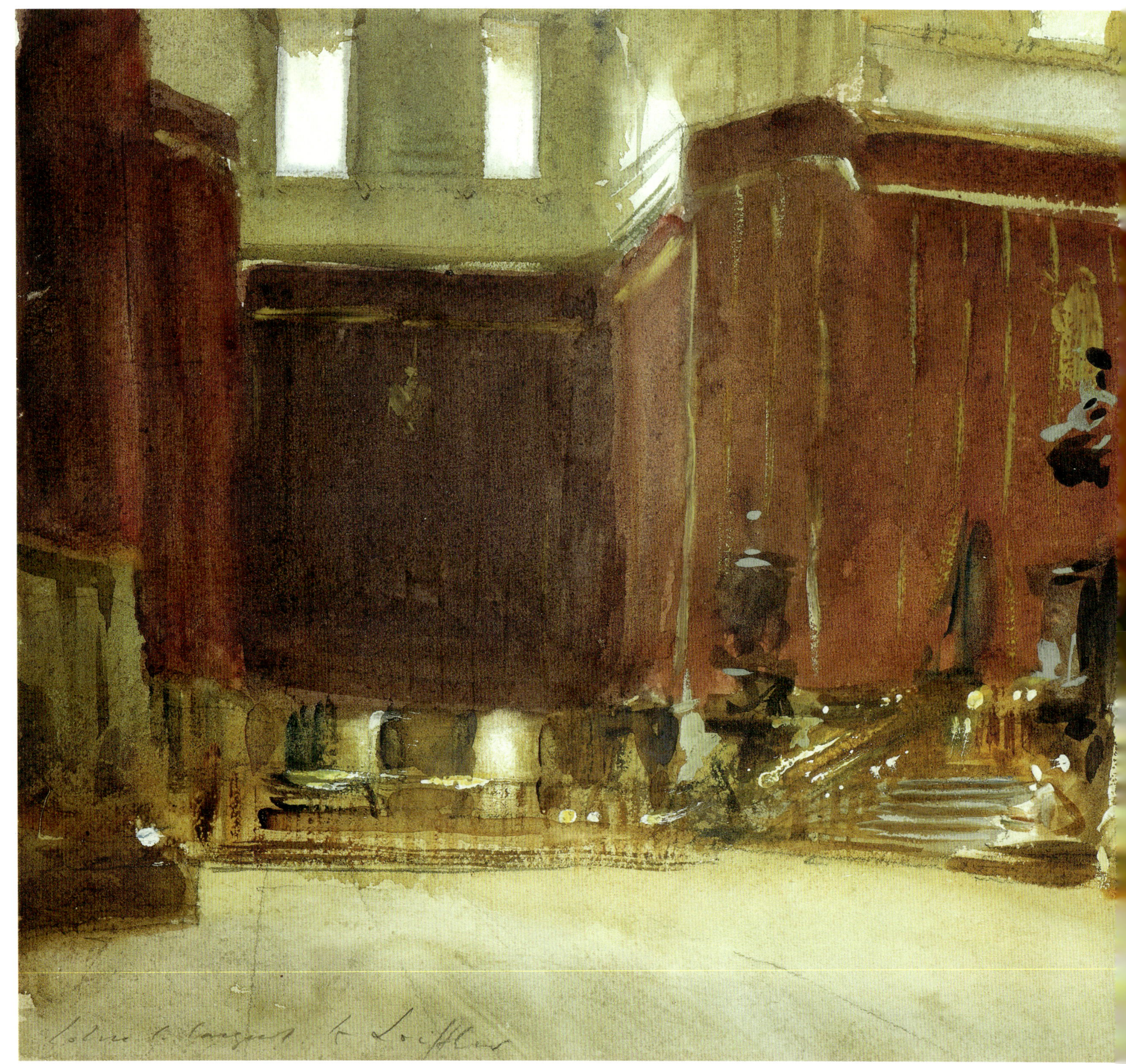

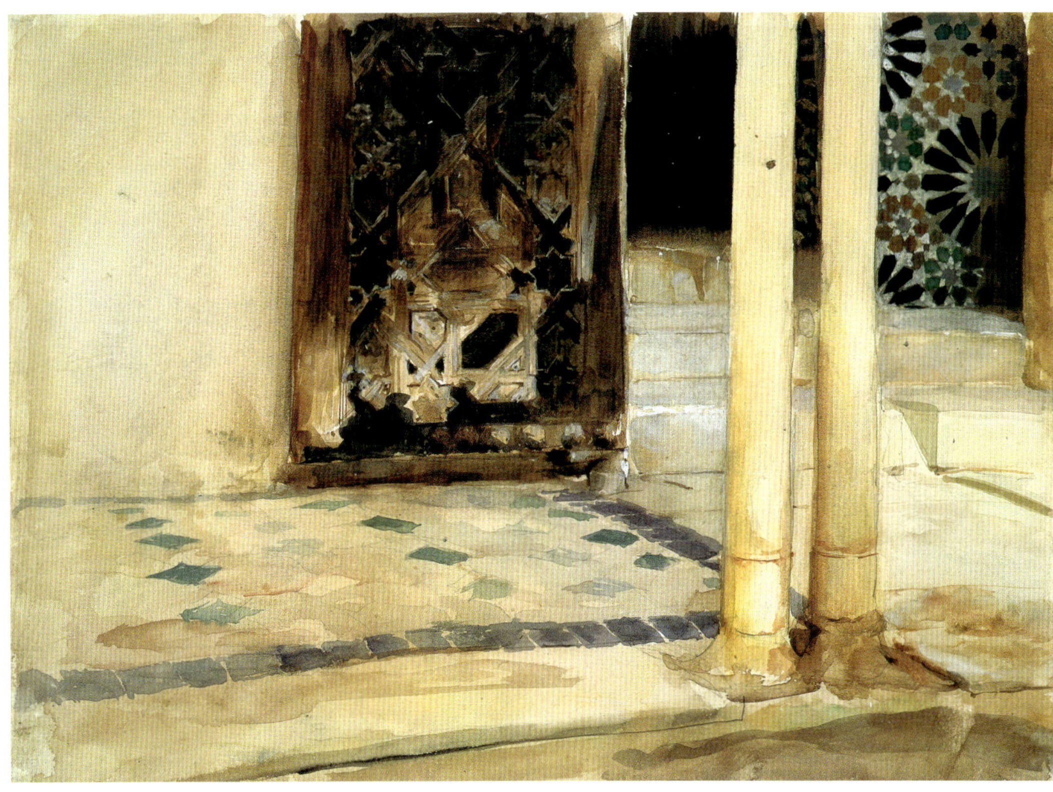

Moorish Patio c. 1880
Watercolor and pencil on paper
9 x 13 1/2 in. (22.8 x 34.3 cm.)
Trustees of the British Museum, London,
Presented by Mrs. Ormond

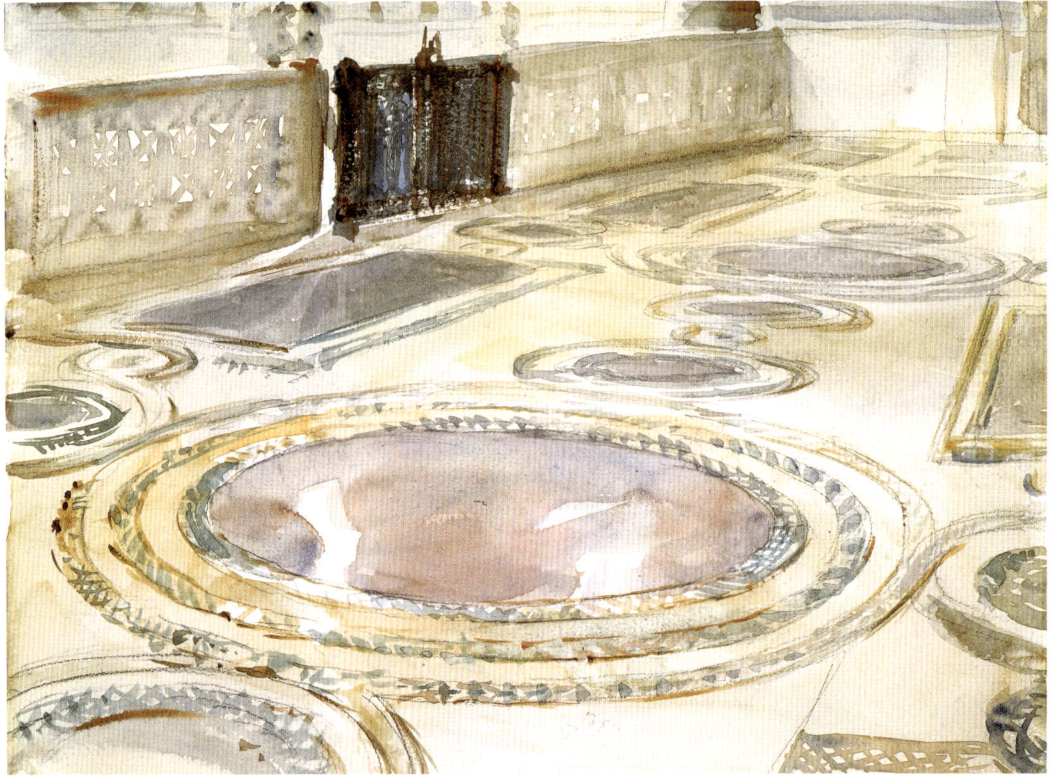

(bottom)
Colorful Pavements, Sicily c. 1901
Watercolor and pencil on paper
10 x 14 in. (25.4 x 35.6 cm.)
Courtesy Christie's Images

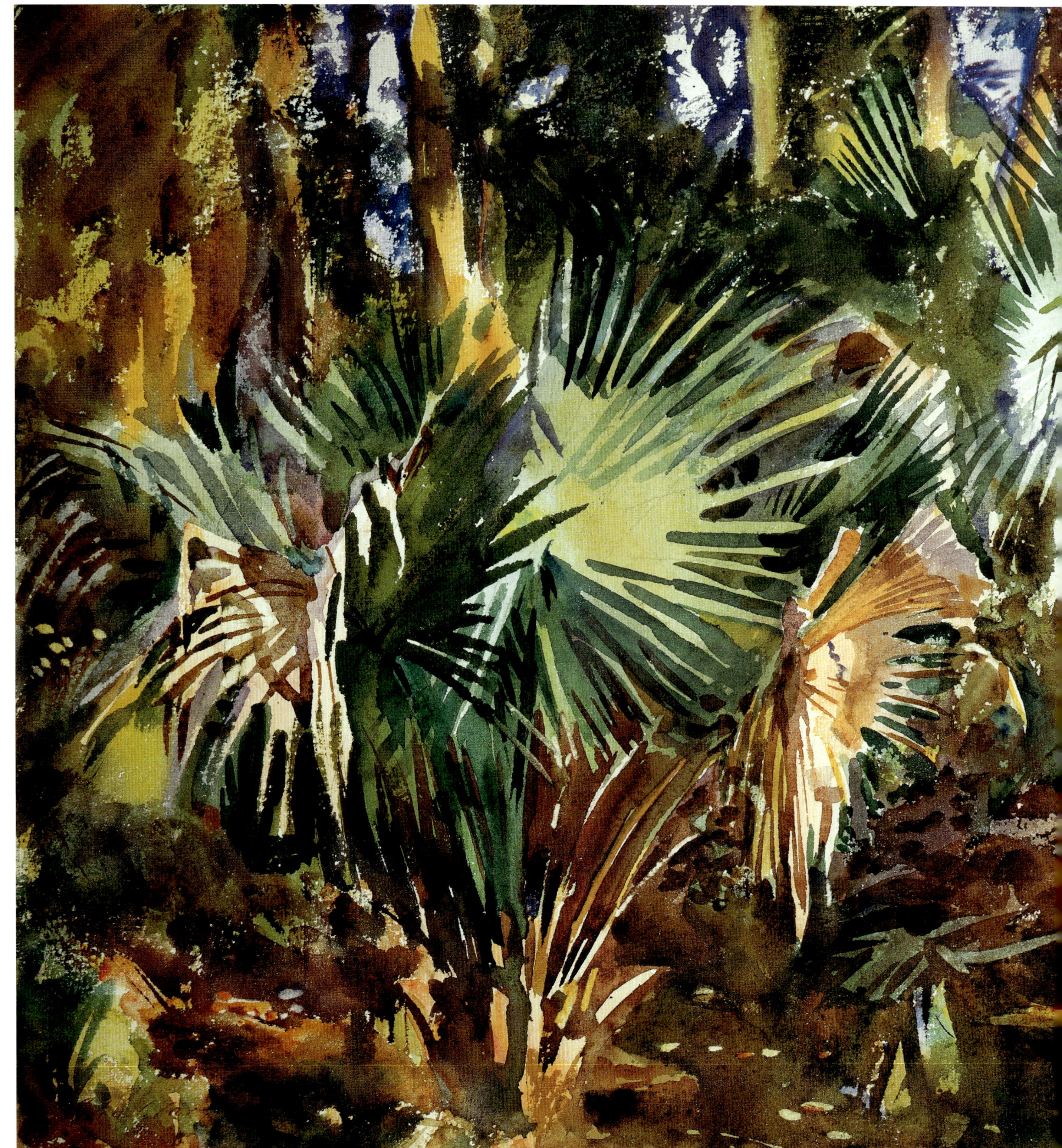

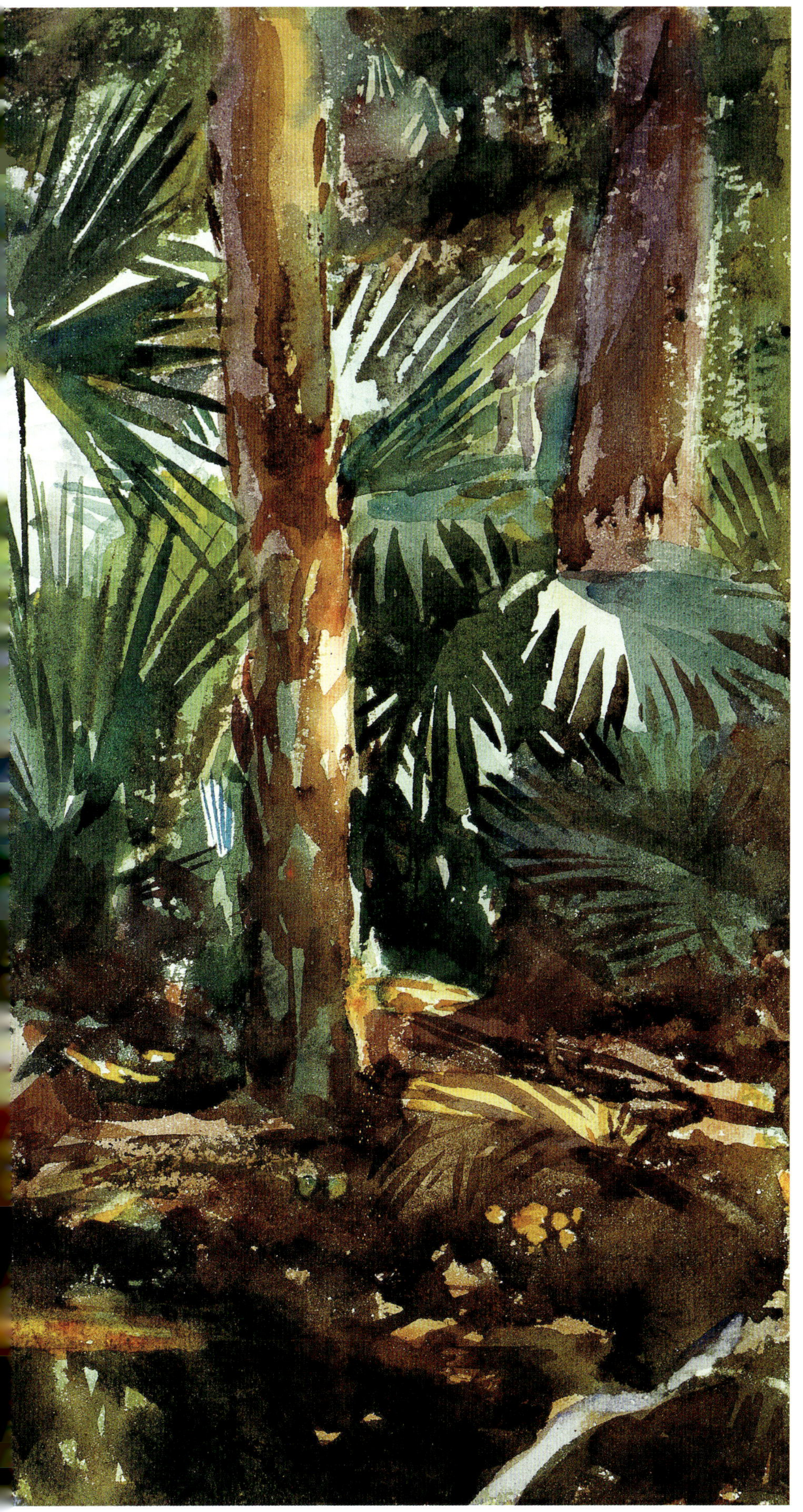

Florida

"It is very hard to leave this place," Sargent wrote to his cousin Mary Newbold Patterson Hale from James Deering's Miami estate, Villa Vizcaya, in the winter of 1917. He rediscovered elements of Europe in, of all places, Florida: "There is so much to paint....It combines Venice and Frascati and Aranjuez, and all that one is likely never to see again. Hence this linger-longering."

During his brief sojourn Sargent painted a series of brilliant watercolors, reminiscent of Winslow Homer's tropical works in subject matter, but having their own special flair—a wonderfully freeform yet controlled handling of the medium. The artist was drawn to the flora and fauna, but he also painted his palatial surroundings.

There is an expressiveness to the handling of the medium that seems new and fresh—as if Florida had liberated the artist from the cares of commissions and murals. Several paintings verge on abstraction and present color work quite unlike anything Sargent had dared before.

The Pool 1917
Watercolor over graphite on off-white wove paper
13 3/8 x 20 15/16 in. (34.5 x 53.2 cm.)
Worcester Art Museum, Worcester, Massachusetts
Sustaining Membership Fund, 1917.93

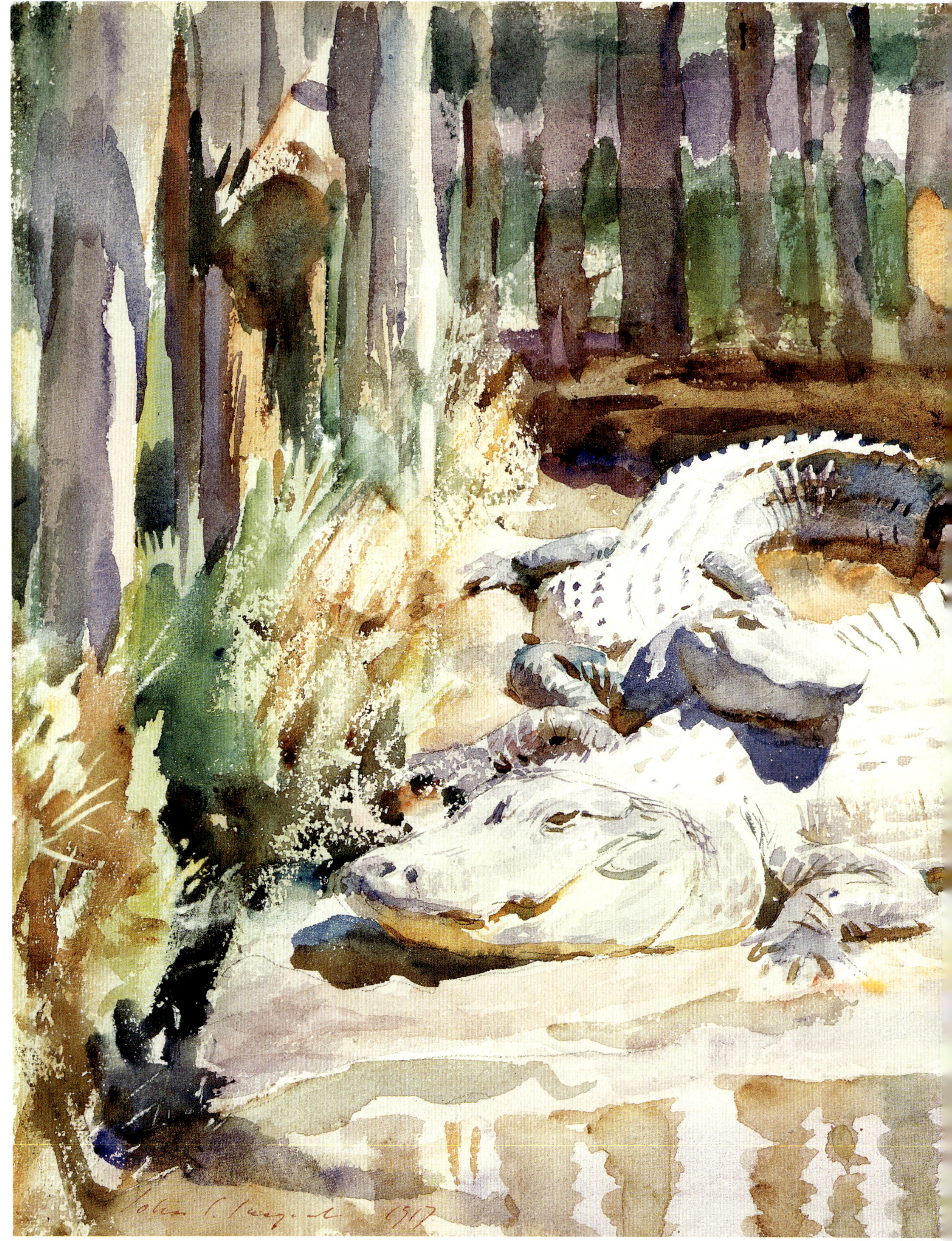

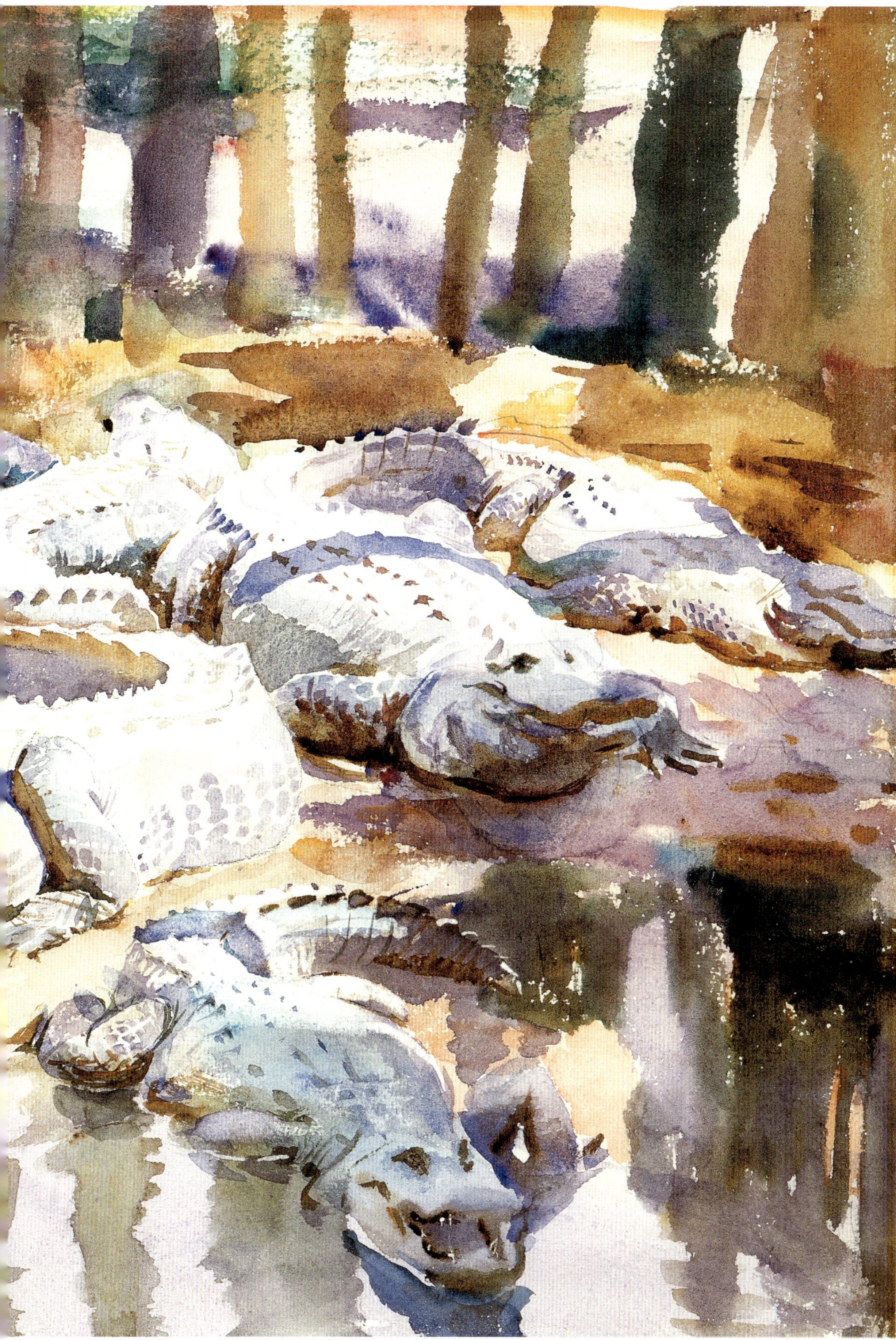

Muddy Alligators 1917
Watercolor over graphite on off-white wove paper
13 9/16 x 20 7/8 in. (35.5 x 53 cm.)
Worcester Art Museum, Worcester, Massachusetts
Sustaining Membership Fund, 1917.86

Palms 1917

Watercolor over graphite on off-white wove paper

15 3/4 x 21 7/8 in. (40 x 56.6 cm.)

Worcester Art Museum, Worcester, Massachusetts

Sustaining Membership Fund, 1917.89

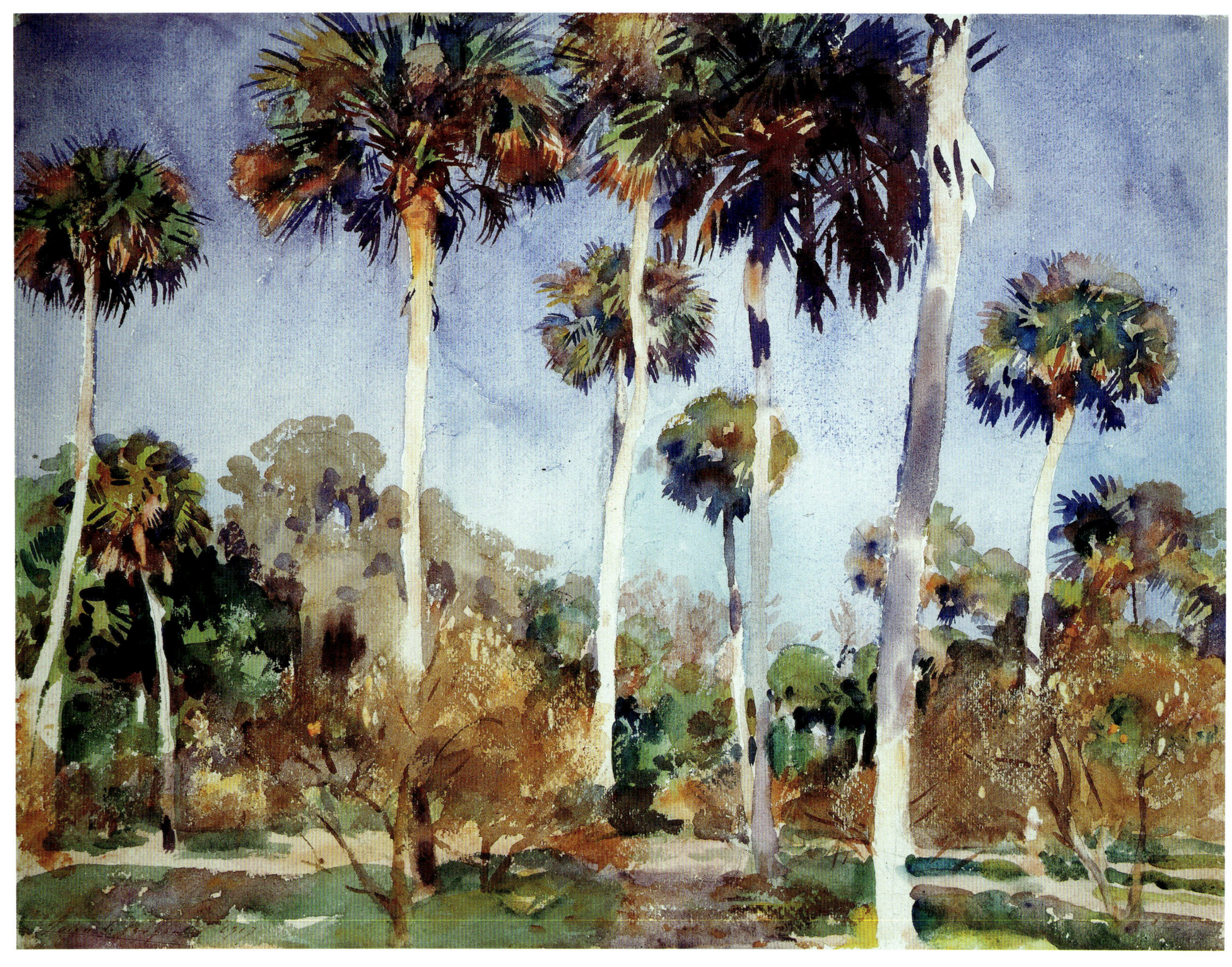

Shady Paths, Vizcaya 1917

Watercolor over graphite on cream wove paper

15 5/8 x 21 in. (39.5 x 53.3 cm.)

Worcester Art Museum, Worcester, Massachusetts

Sustaining Membership Fund, 1917.88

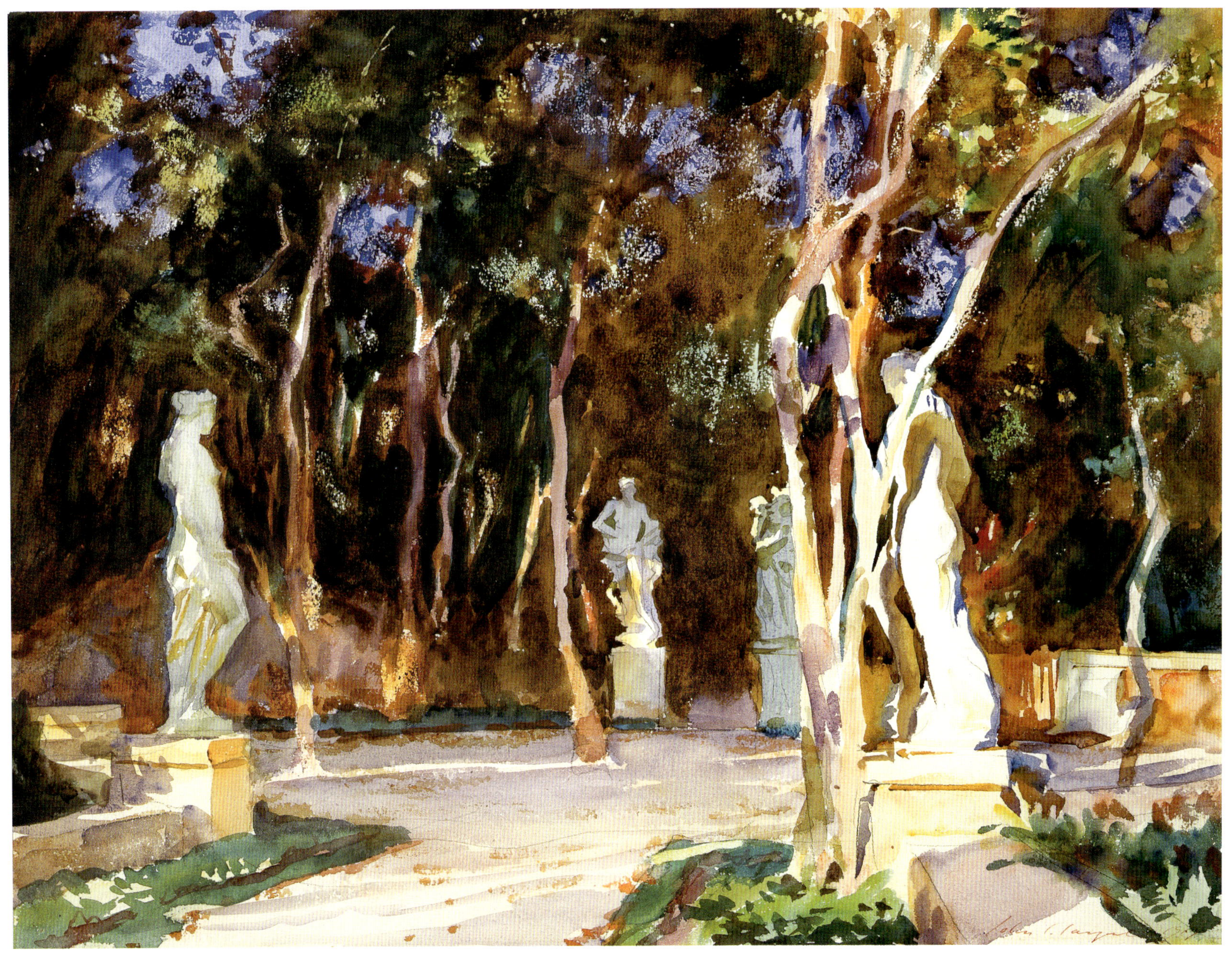

One feels vividly the heat of the day and the delightful sensation of relief and refreshment that these bathers are experiencing as they loll in the shallow pool, partly shaded by the surrounding trees. It is like a true momentary impression of something seen, instantaneous as a snapshot, but with nothing of the mechanical element.

—William Howe Downes, 1917

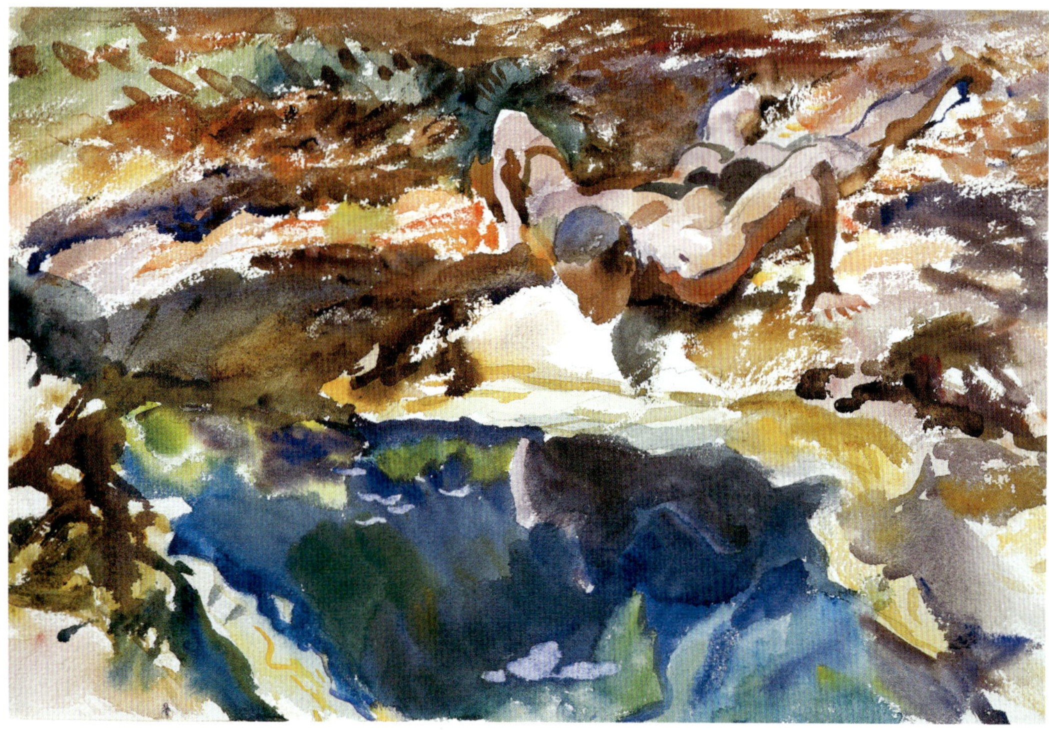

Figure and Pool 1917
Watercolor, gouache, and graphite underdrawing on white wove paper
13 11/16 x 21 in. (34.8 x 53.3 cm.)
The Metropolitan Museum of Art,
Gift of Mrs. Francis Ormond, 1950 (50.130.62)
Photograph by Geoffrey Clements
Photograph © 1989 The Metropolitan Museum of Art

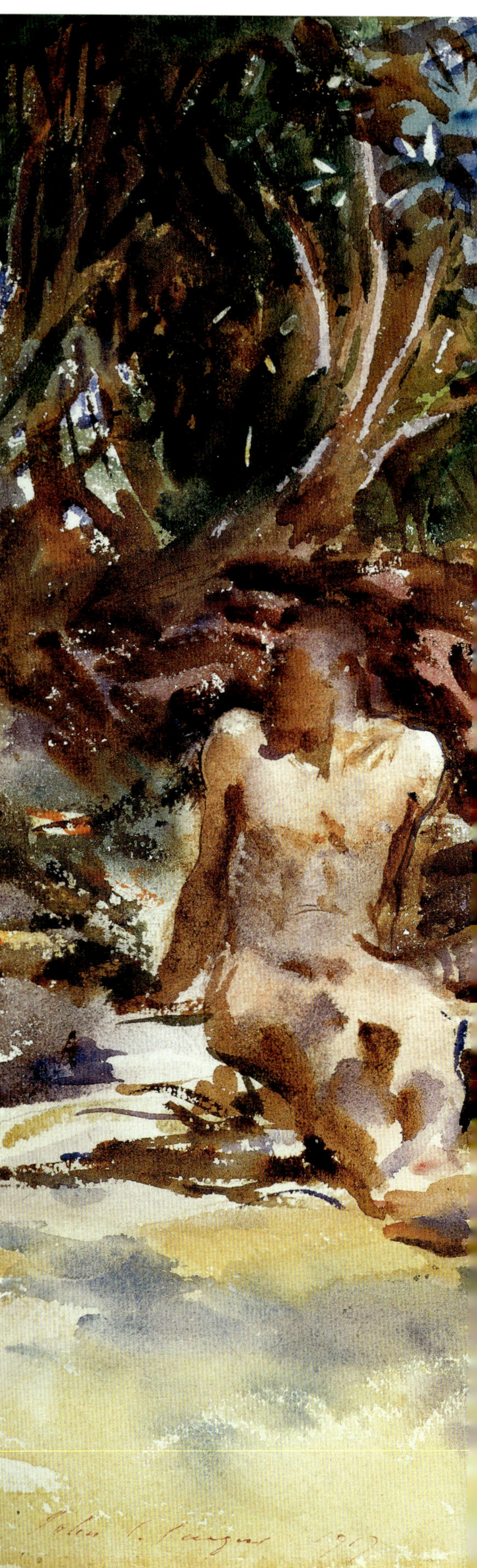

The Bathers 1917
Watercolor, gouache over graphite on off-white wove paper
15 3/4 x 20 3/4 in. (39.8 x 52.7 cm.)
Worcester Art Museum, Worcester, Massachusetts
Sustaining Membership Fund, 1917.91

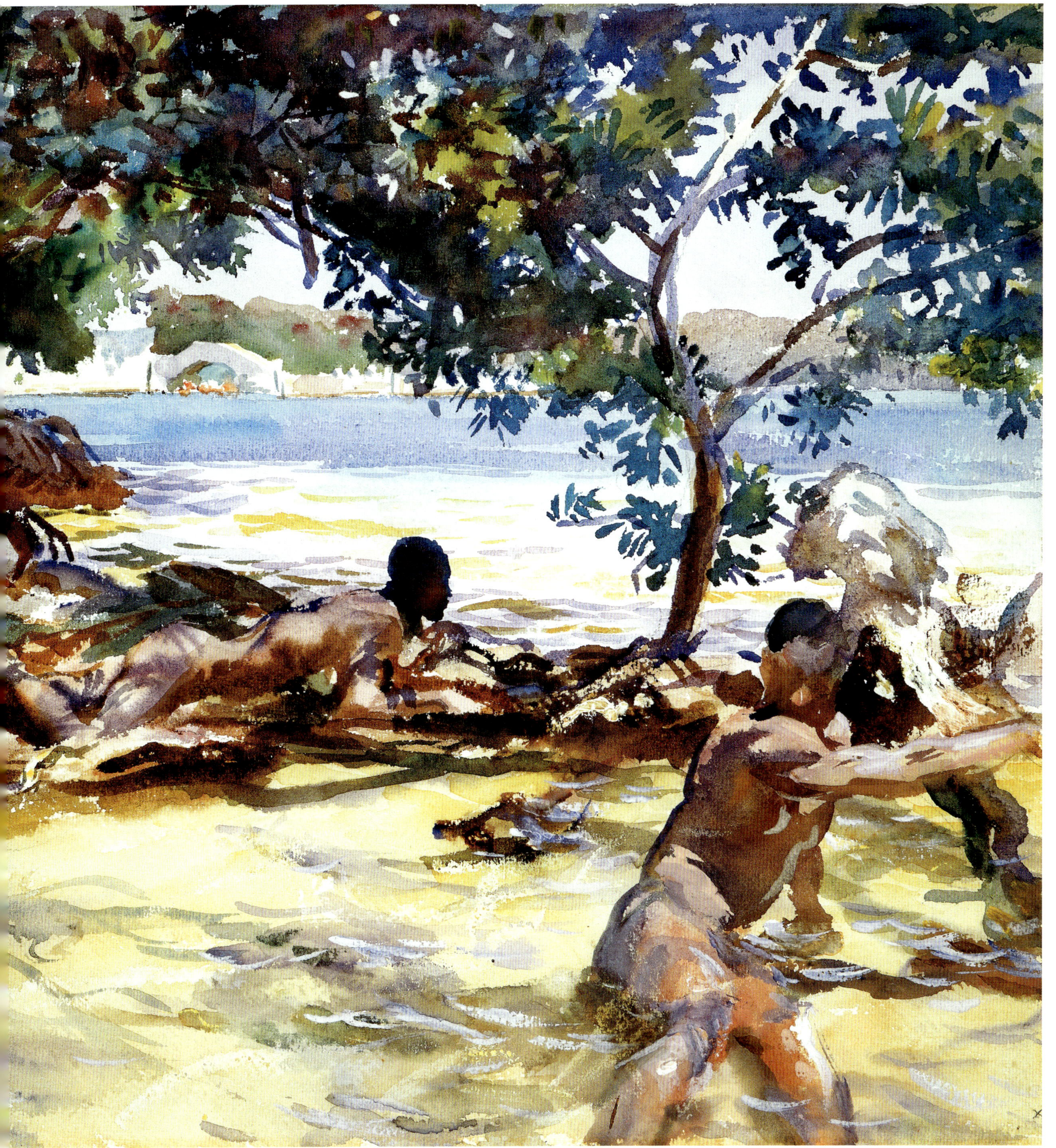

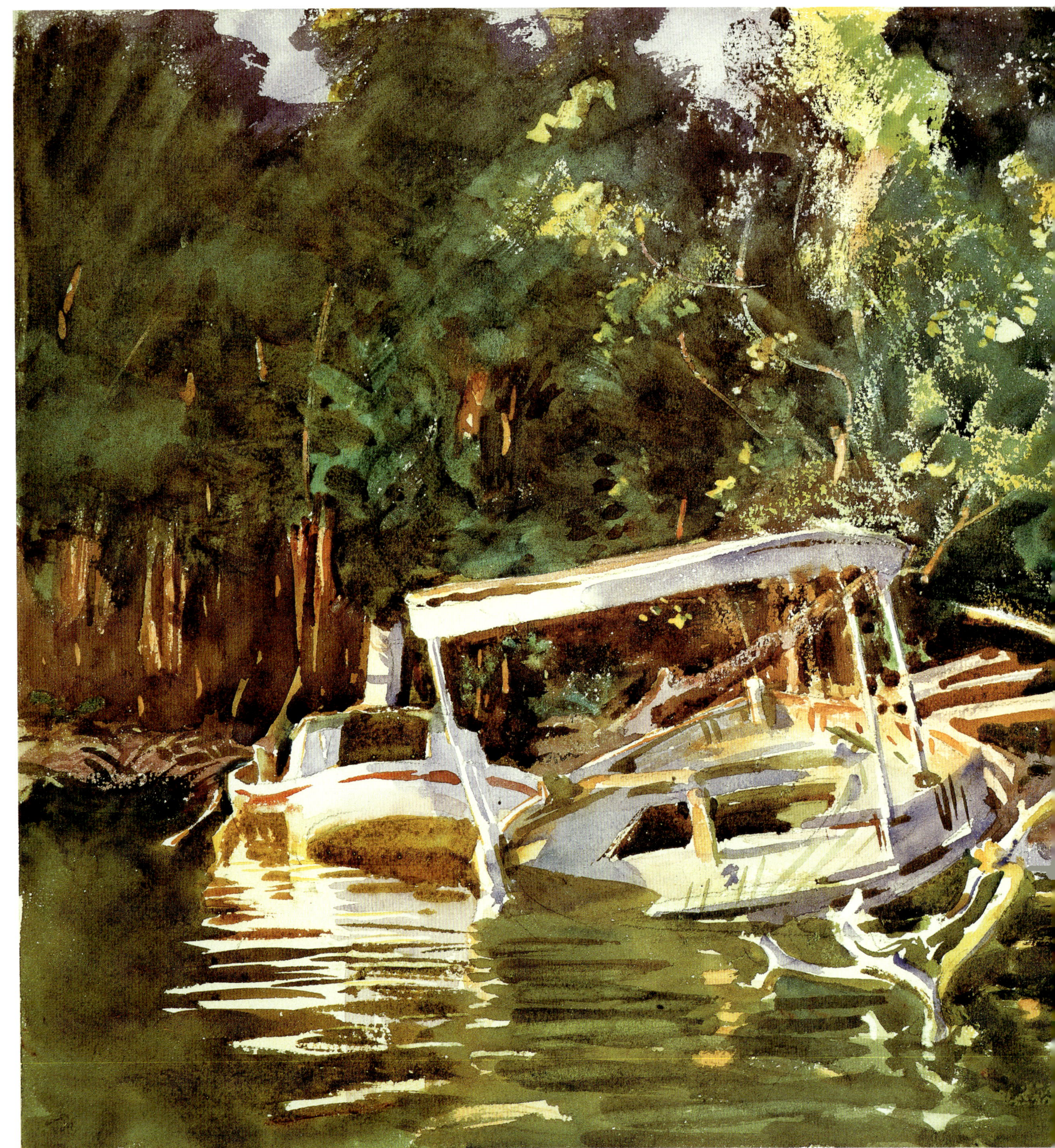

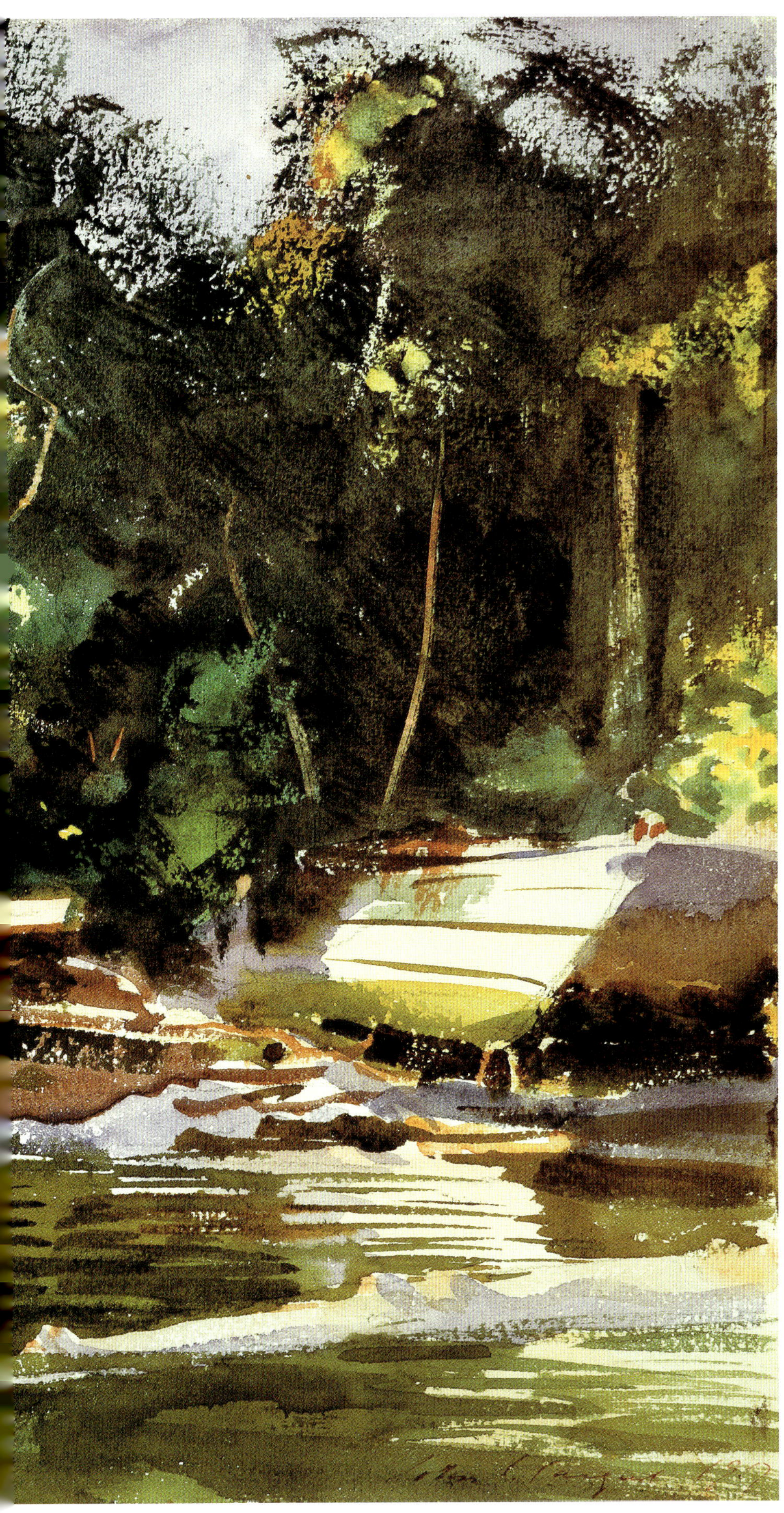

Above all things, get abroad, see the sunlight, and everything that is to be seen. . . .

—John Singer Sargent

Derelicts 1917

Watercolor over graphite on off-white wove paper

13 1/2 x 21 in. (34.5 x 53.2 cm.)

Worcester Art Museum, Worcester, Massachusetts

Sustaining Membership Fund, 1917.87

Landscape: On the Somme 1918
Watercolor
13 15/16 x 20 13/16 in. (35.4 x 51.3 cm.)
Museum of Art, Rhode Island School of Design,
Museum Appropriation
Photography by Del Bogart

Horse Line 1918
Watercolor
13 1/2 x 20 3/4 in. (34.2 x 52.7 cm.)
Imperial War Museum, London

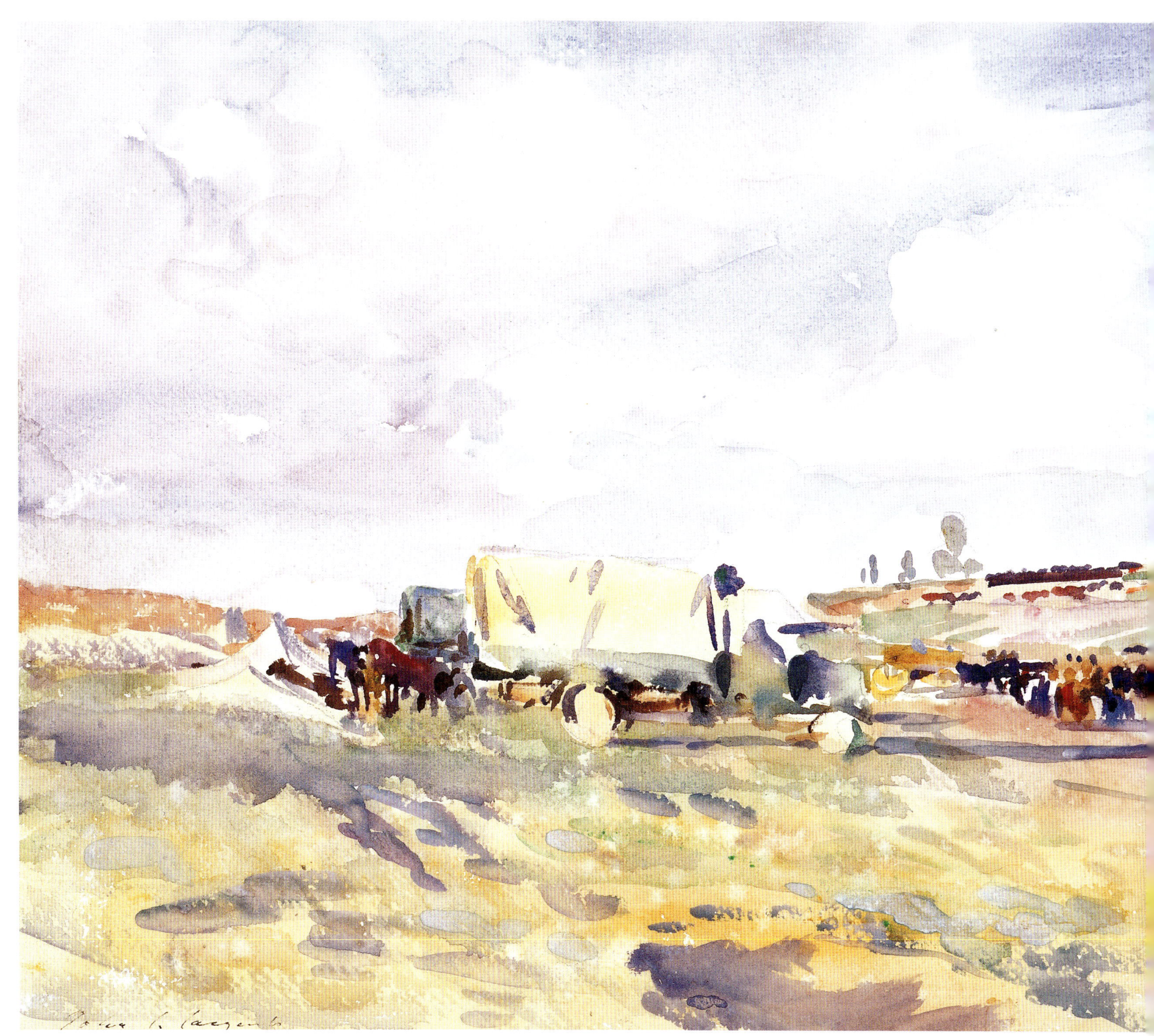

World War I

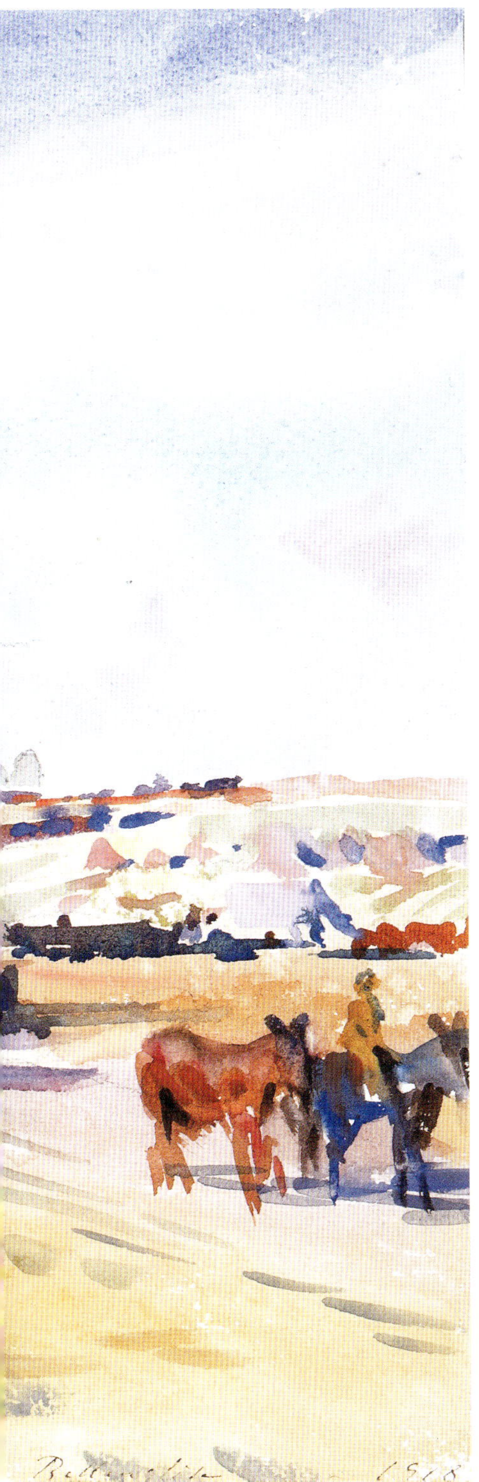

With alacrity but not without misgivings, Sargent accepted a commission in 1918 to paint the war in Europe. He took his assignment seriously, as attested to by the marvelous portfolio of watercolors he brought back to England.

The conflict presented new motifs: a camouflaged tank, troops on the move, a downed airplane. To each, Sargent brought all his powers as a draftsman, accurately modeling the men and machines with watercolor.

The artist who had been captivated by the architecture of Europe now was confronted with its ruins, and yet he managed to subsume feeling to the greater challenge of recording the scene. How at ease the soldiers seem leaning against a bombed-out building in Arras!

Sargent's empathy for the soldiers is most apparent in images of British troops—called "Tommies"—and Highlanders finding a momentary respite from the war, bathing or sleeping atop a pile of straw. In Sargent's hands, the interior of a hospital tent is a dim yet sheltering space that recalls those traveling homes of the Bedouins that he painted earlier.

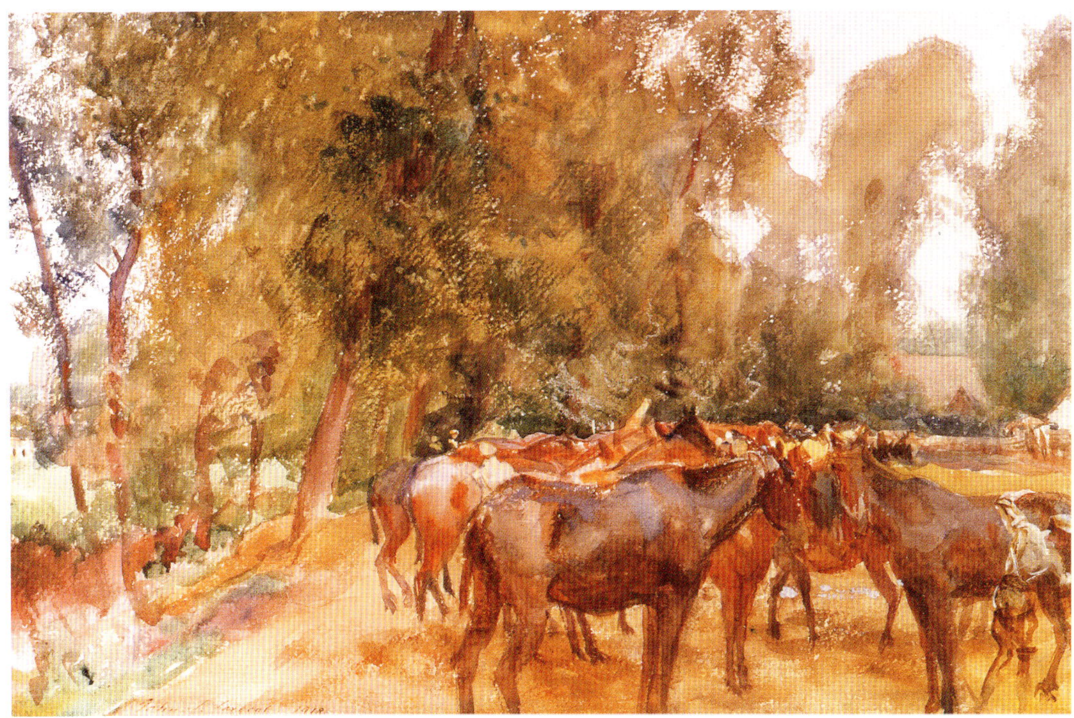

...Maybe to the very end of his days, I feel certain that his conscious endeavour, his self-formulated program, was to paint whatever he saw with absolute and researchful fidelity, never avoiding ugliness nor seeking after beauty.

—Vernon Lee, 1925

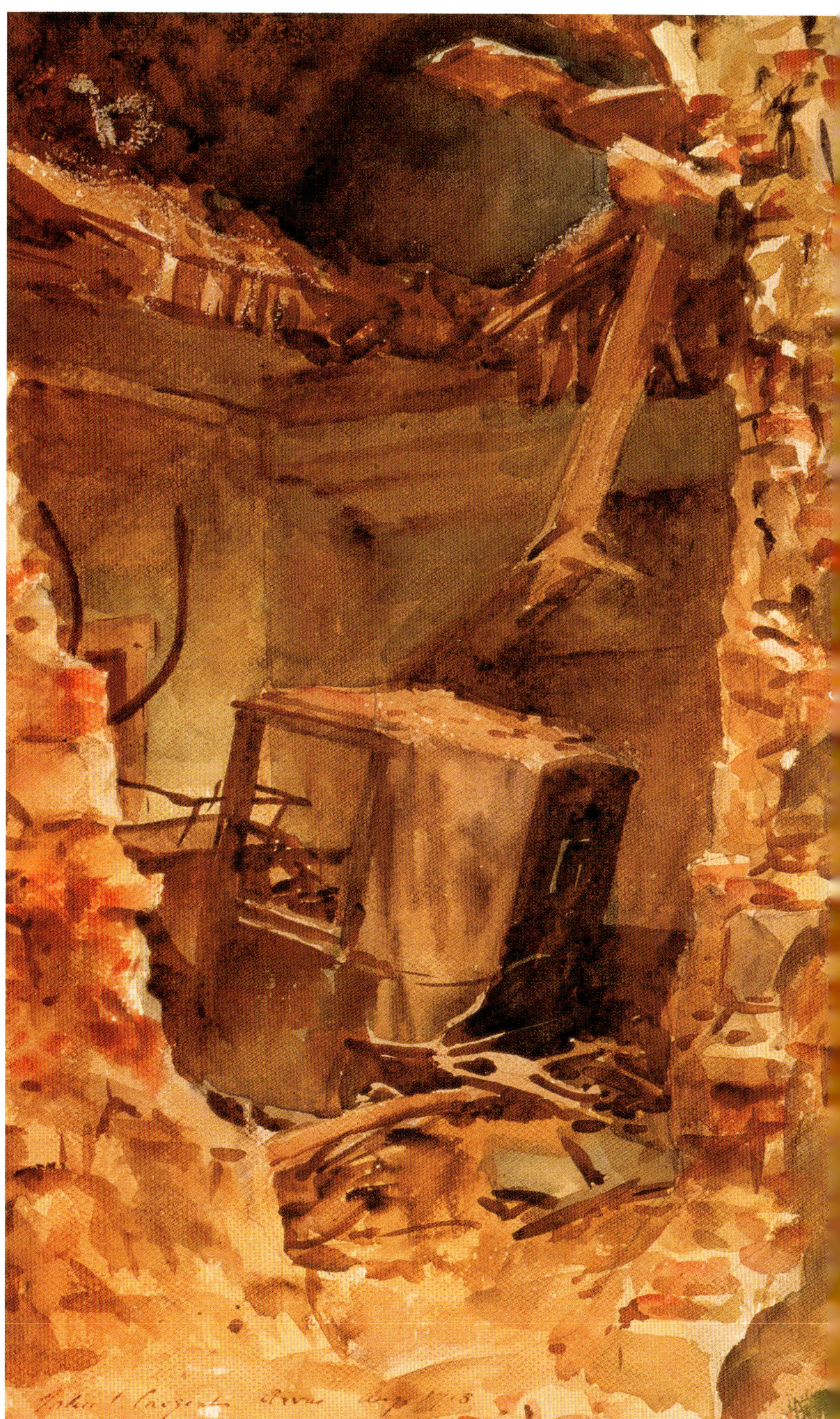

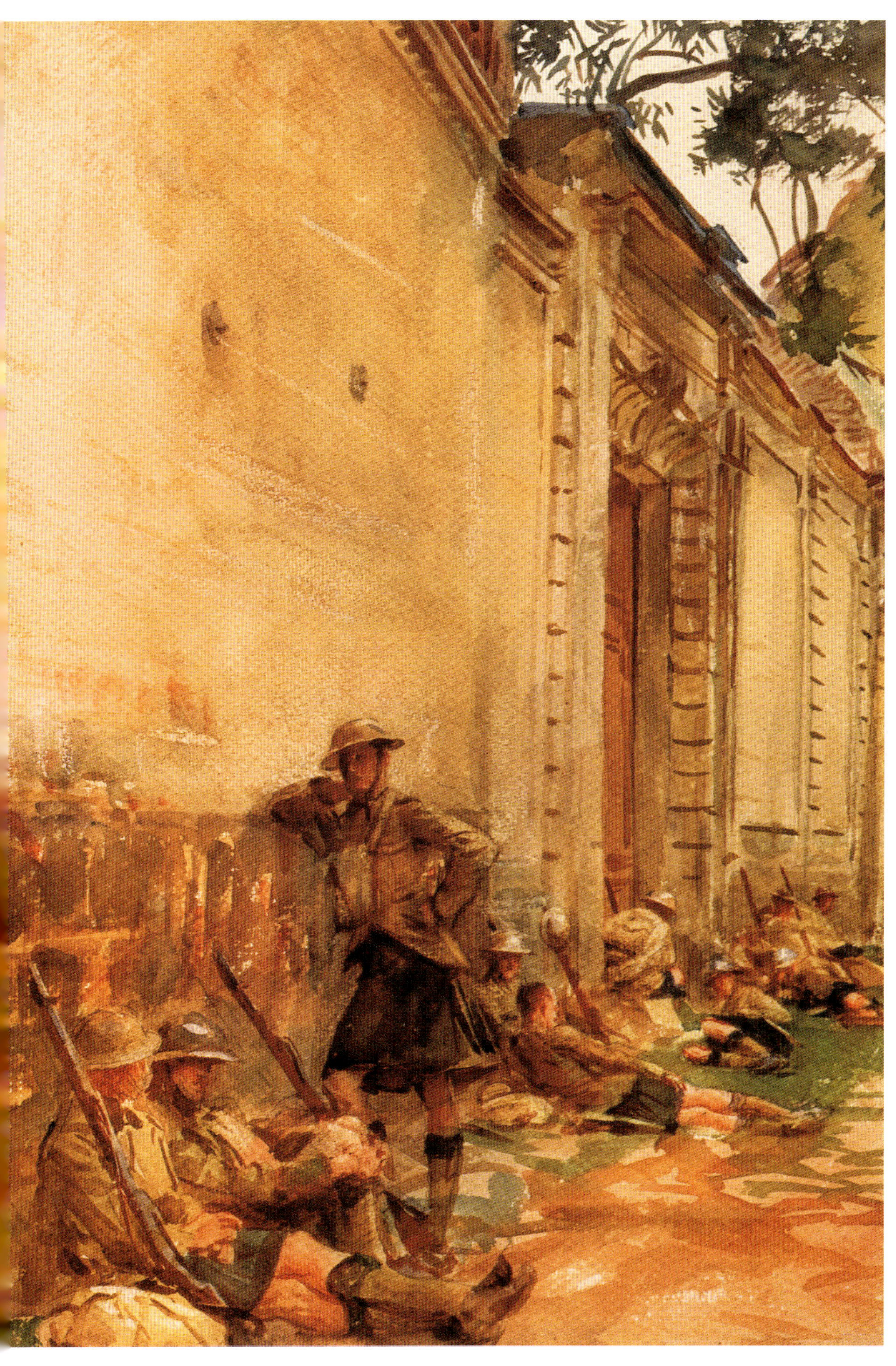

A Street in Arras 1918

Watercolor

15 1/2 x 20 3/4 in. (39.3 x 52.7 cm.)

Imperial War Museum, London

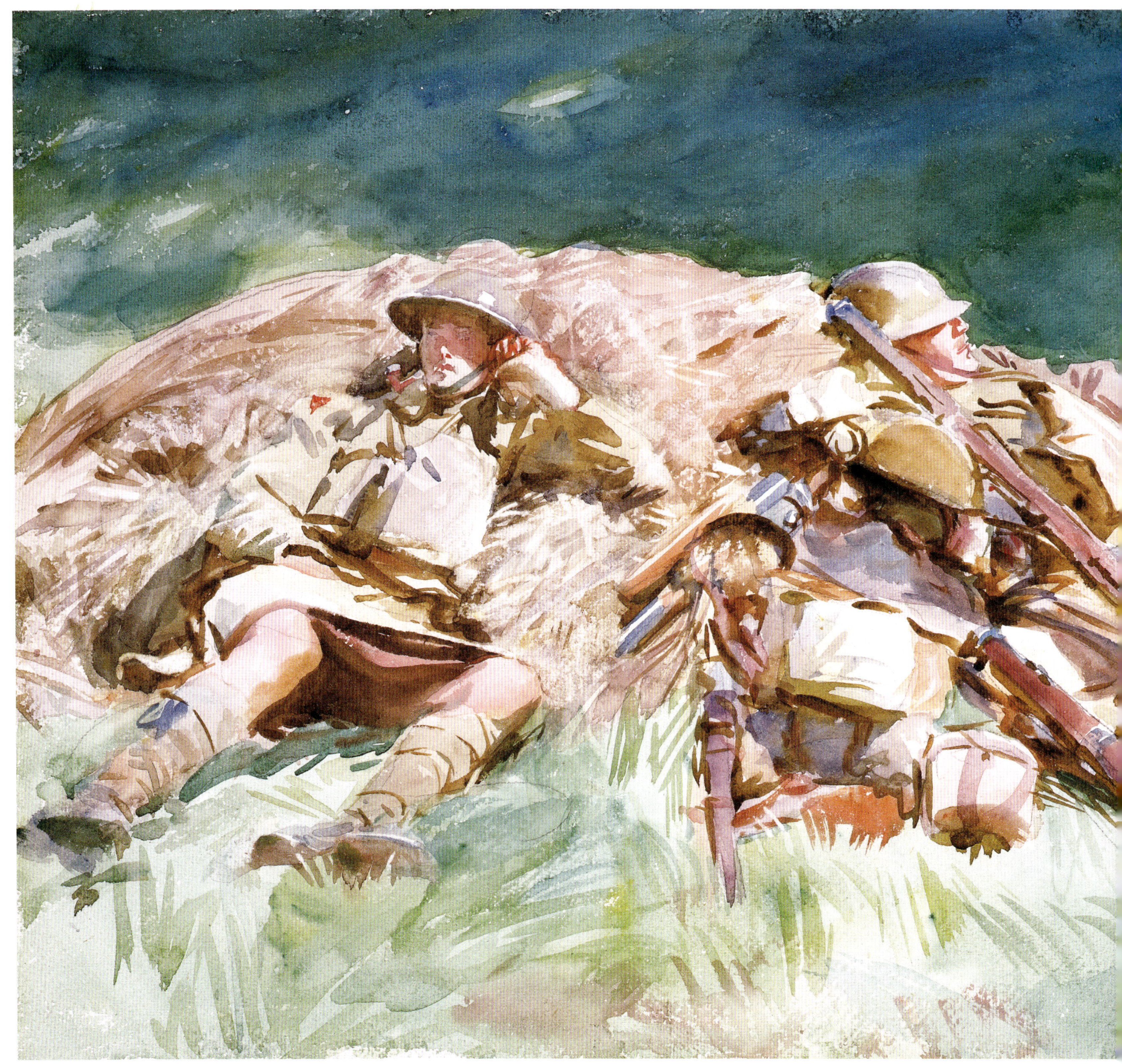

Highlanders Resting at the Front 1918

Watercolor on paper

13 1/2 x 21 1/16 in. (34.3 x 53.5 cm.)

Fitzwilliam Museum, University of Cambridge

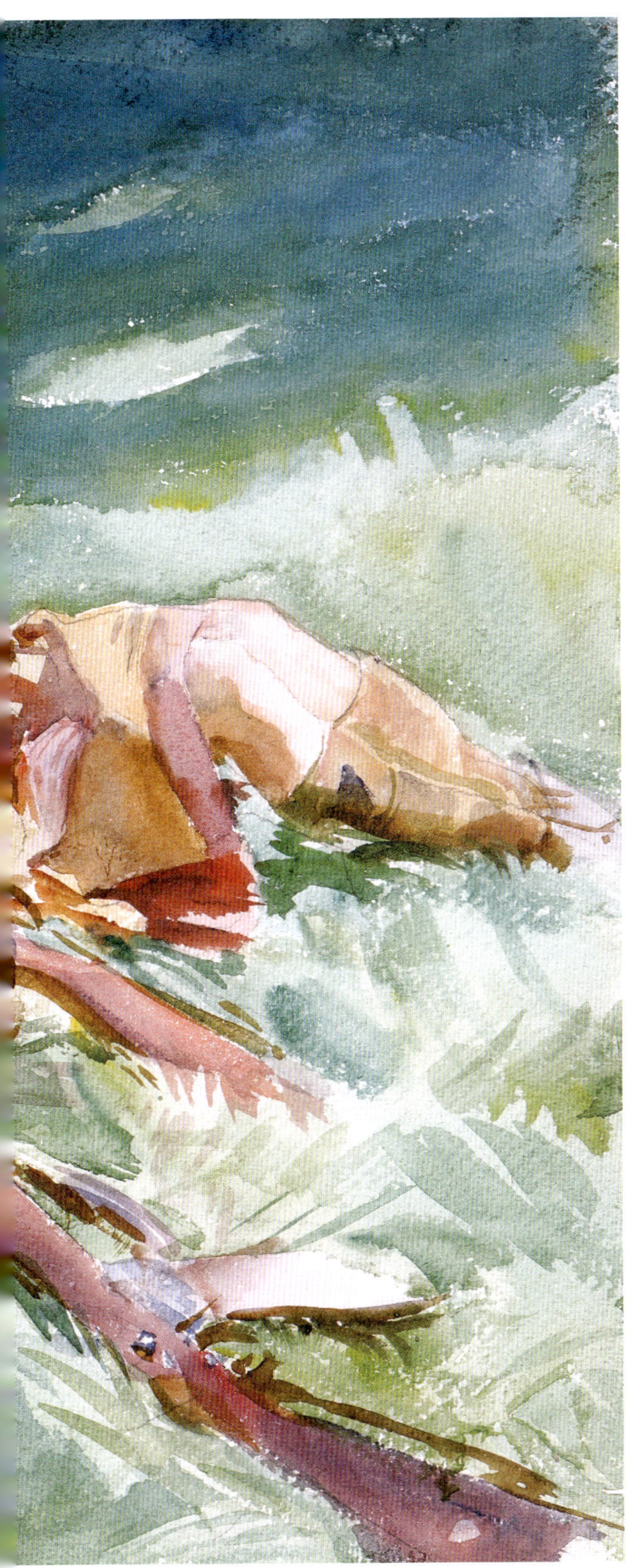

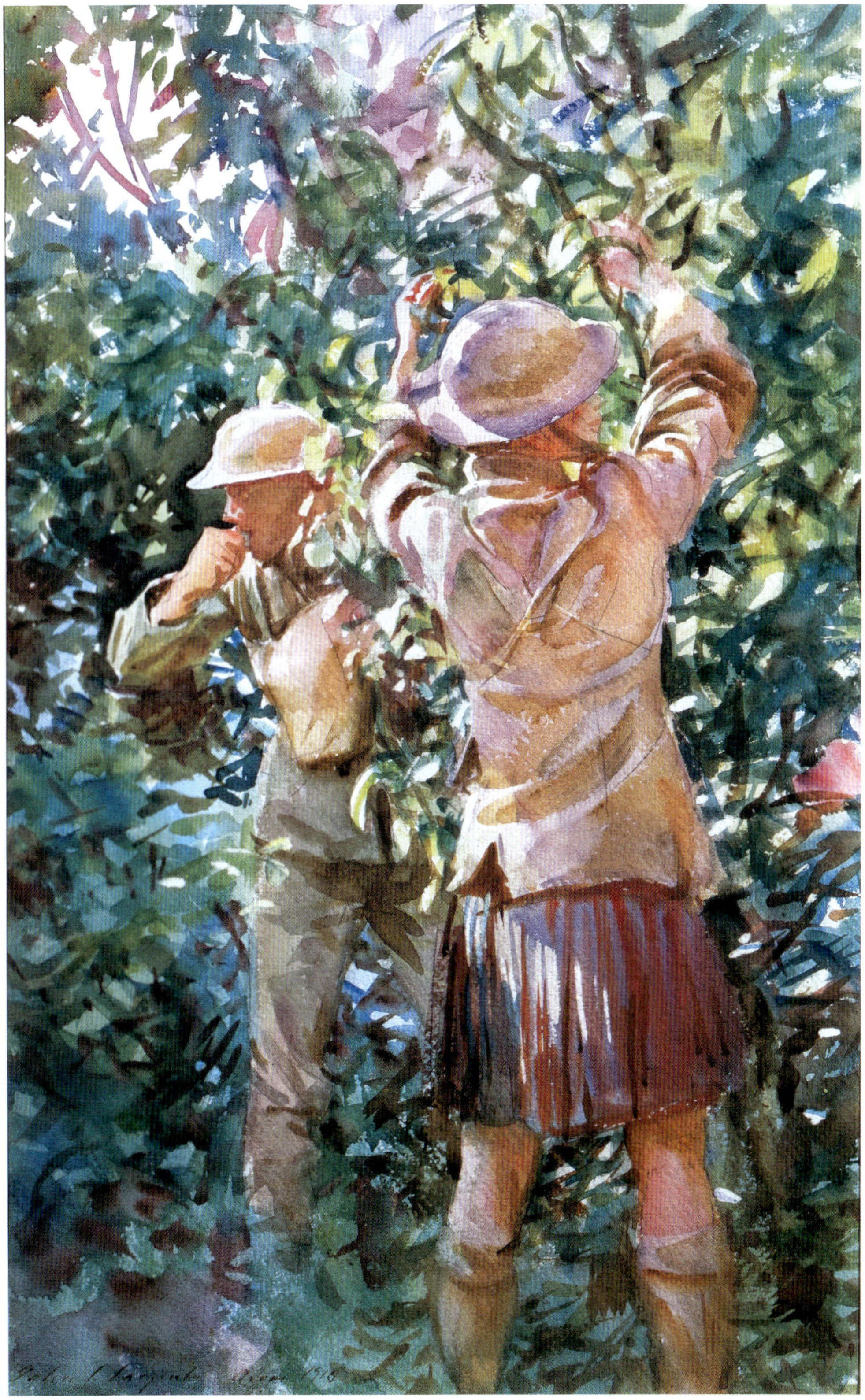

Thou Shalt Not Steal 1918
Watercolor on paper
20 x 13 1/4 in. (50.8 x 33.6 cm.)
Imperial War Museum, London
Courtesy Bridgeman Art Library

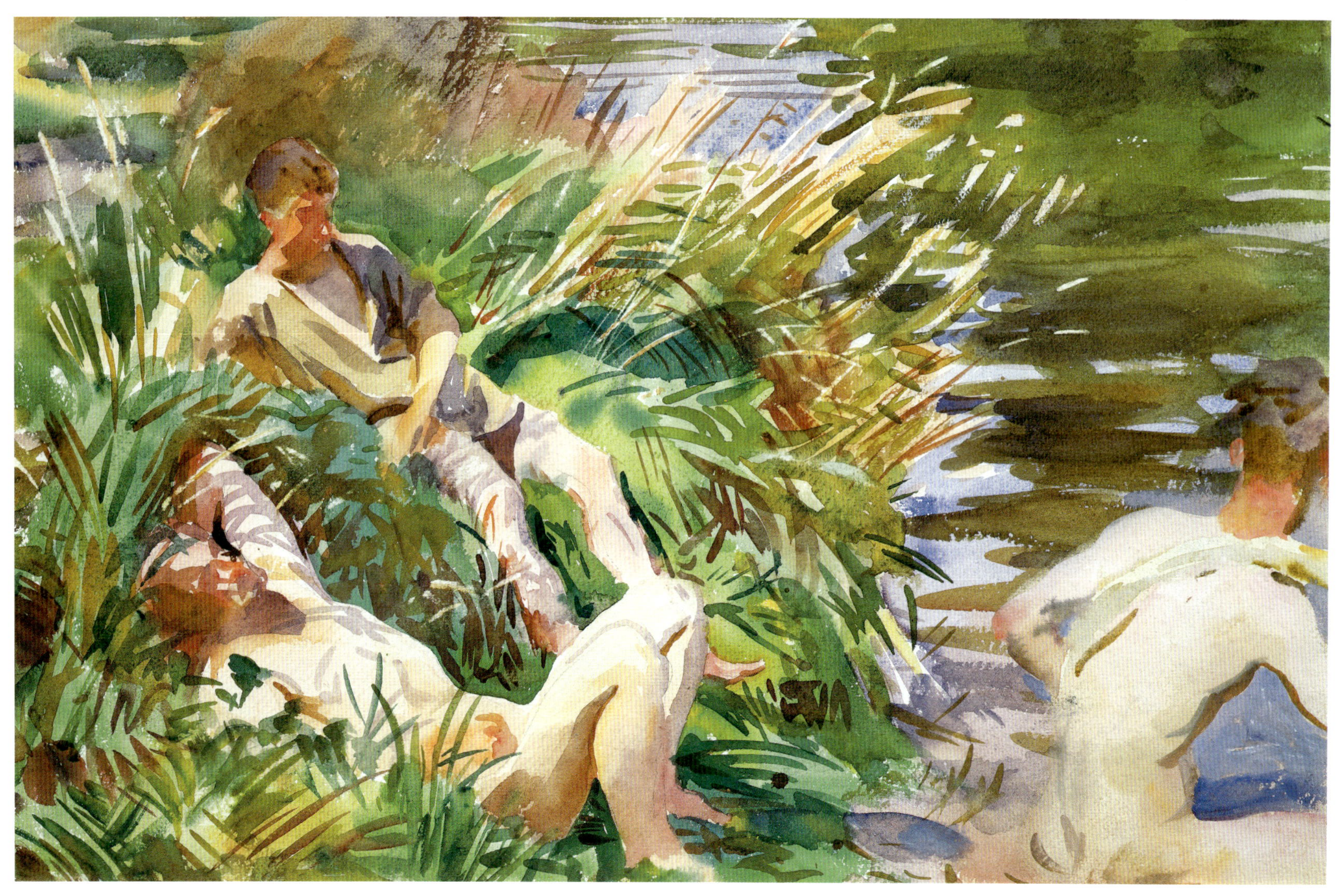

[The swift touches of his brush] are like those subtle moves in a game of chess leading up to the triumphant "checkmate" that comes with overwhelming unexpectedness.

—Martin Hardie, 1930

Tommies Bathing, France 1918
Watercolor, gouache, and graphite underdrawing
on white wove paper
13 3/8 x 20 7/8 in. (34 x 53 cm.)
The Metropolitan Museum of Art,
Gift of Mrs. Francis Ormond, 1950 (50.130.58)
Photograph by Geoffrey Clements

Tommies Bathing 1917
Watercolor and graphite underdrawing
on white wove paper
15 3/8 x 20 3/4 in. (39 x 52.7 cm.)
The Metropolitan Museum of Art,
Gift of Mrs. Francis Ormond, 1950 (50.130.48)
Photograph by Geoffrey Clements

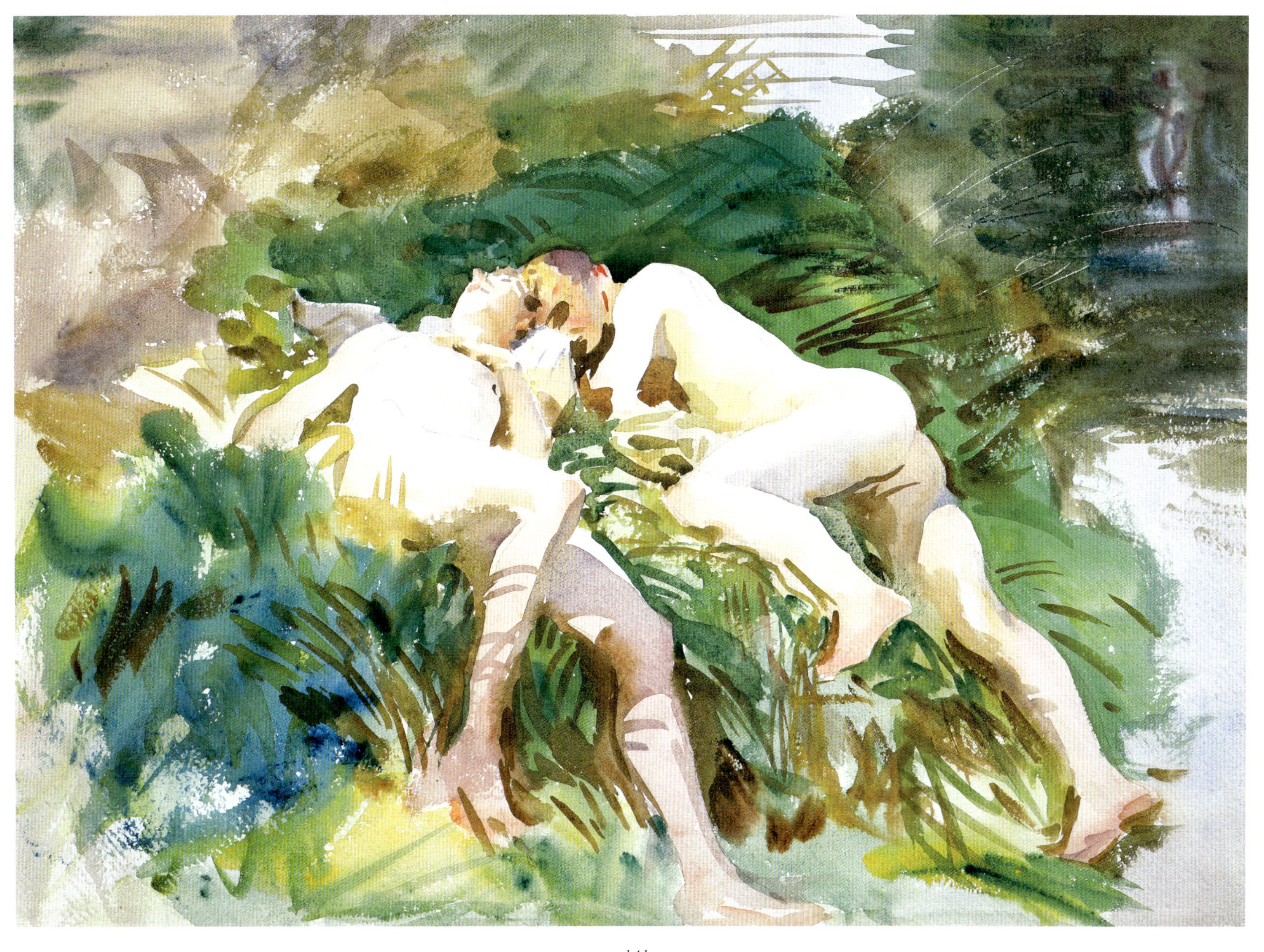

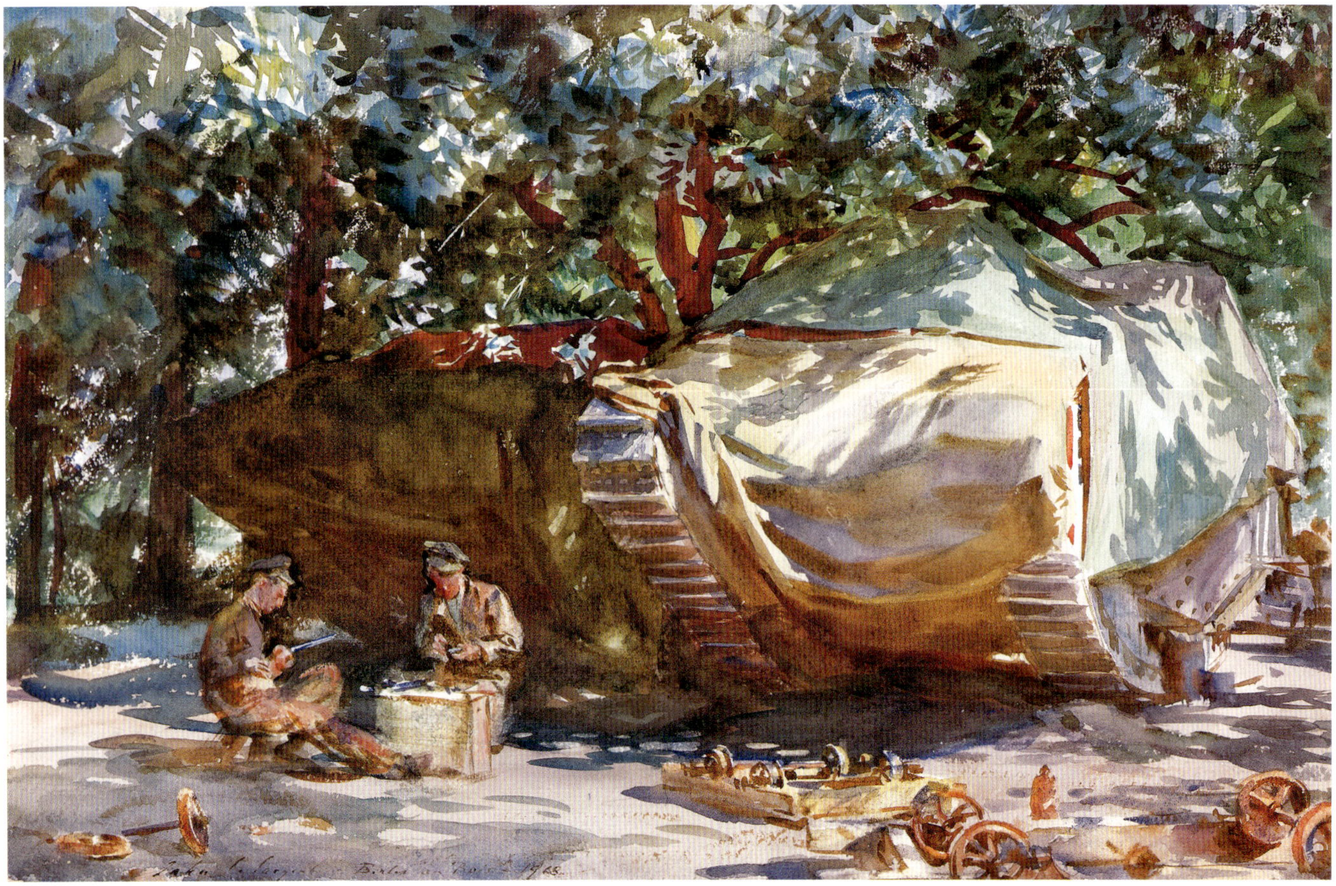

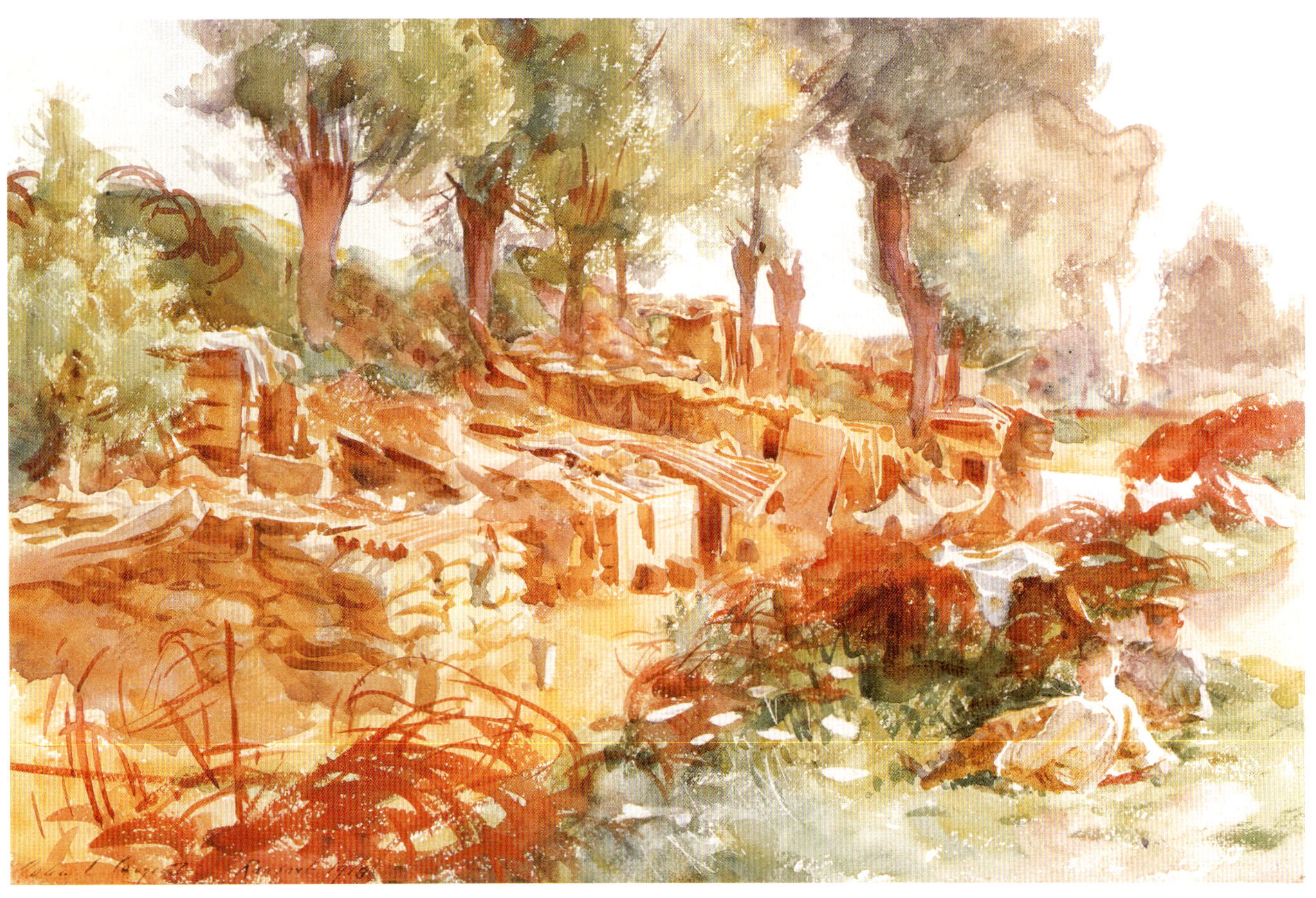

Camouflaged Tanks, Berles-au-Bois 1918
Watercolor on paper
13 7/16 x 21 in. (34.2 x 53.3 cm.)
Imperial War Museum, London

Interior of a Hospital Tent 1918
Watercolor on paper
15 1/2 x 20 3/4 in. (39.3 x 52.7 cm.)
Imperial War Museum, London

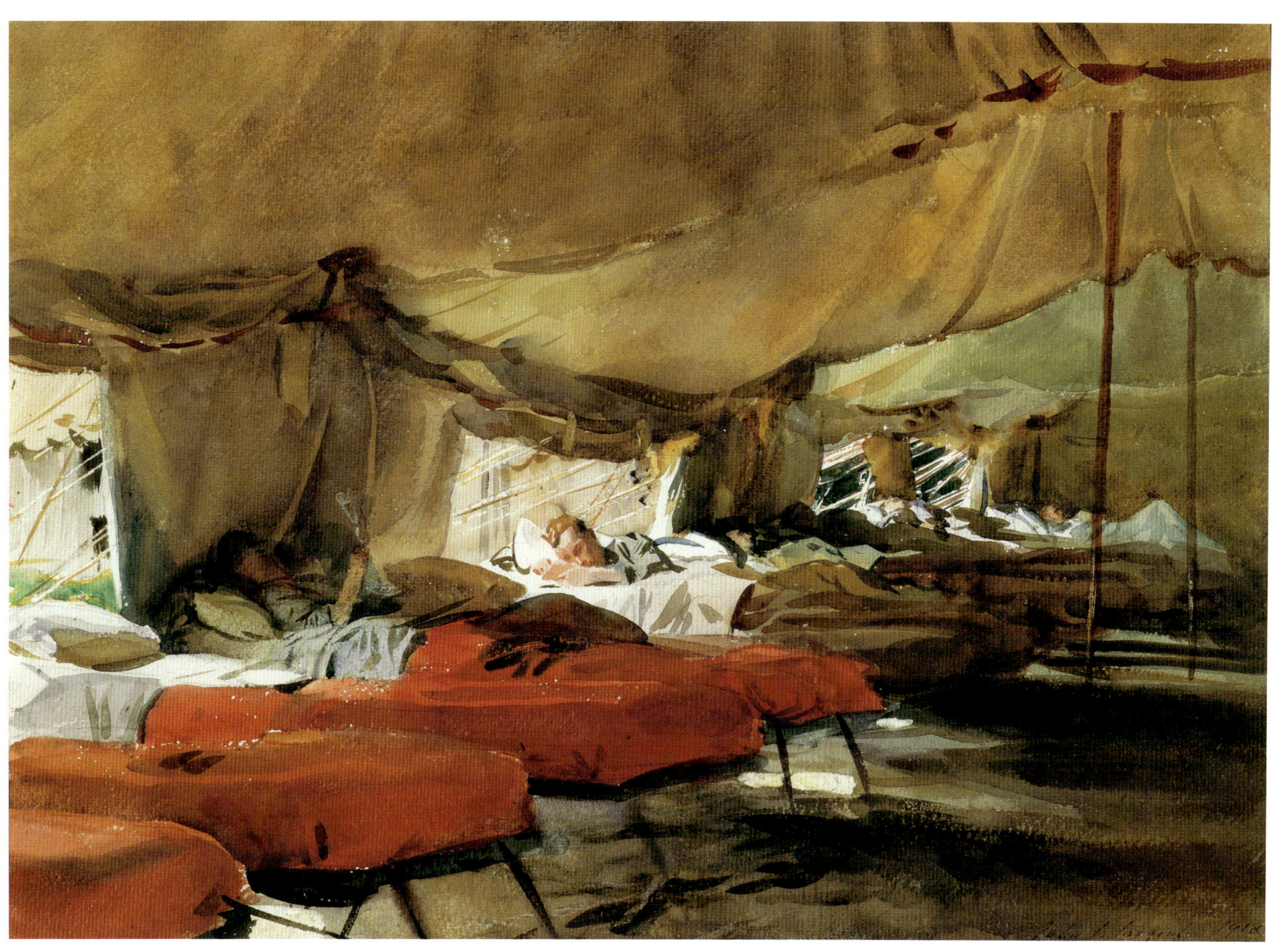

The Sunken Road, Ransart 1918
Watercolor
13 1/2 x 20 3/4 in. (34.2 x 52.7 cm.)
Imperial War Museum, London

He loved Plato's definition of beauty as "the splendor of the true." To that splendor he contributed, with the scrupulous yet generous spontaneity of his work, with the broadmindedness, the indulgence, the toleration, and the sincerity of his character. He leaves as an inheritance for the artists of all time the unstained record of a noble and laborious life.

—"J.H.H.," London Observer, 1925

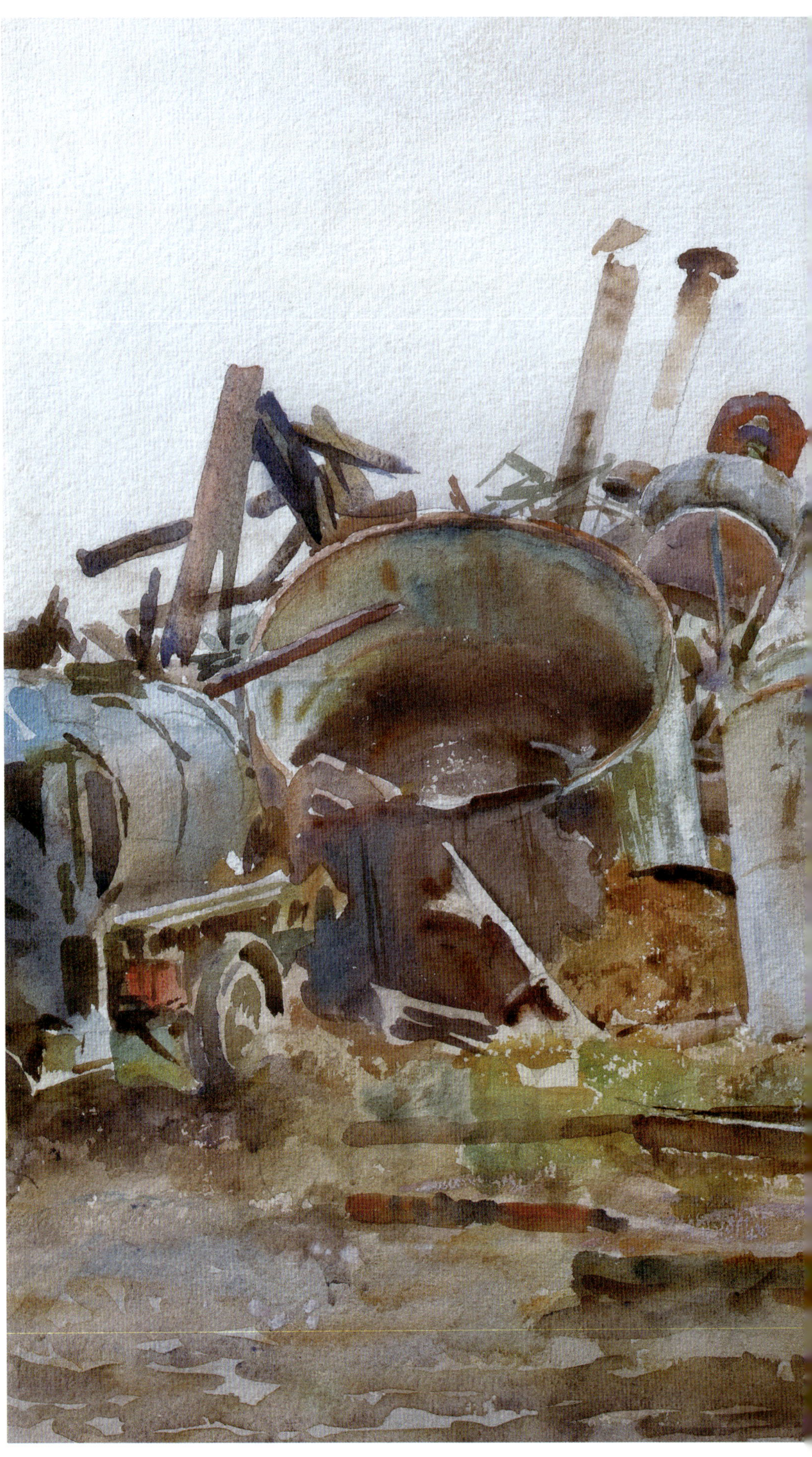

A Wrecked Sugar Refinery 1918
Watercolor on paper
13 1/4 x 20 3/4 in. (33.6 x 52.7 cm.)
Imperial War Museum, London

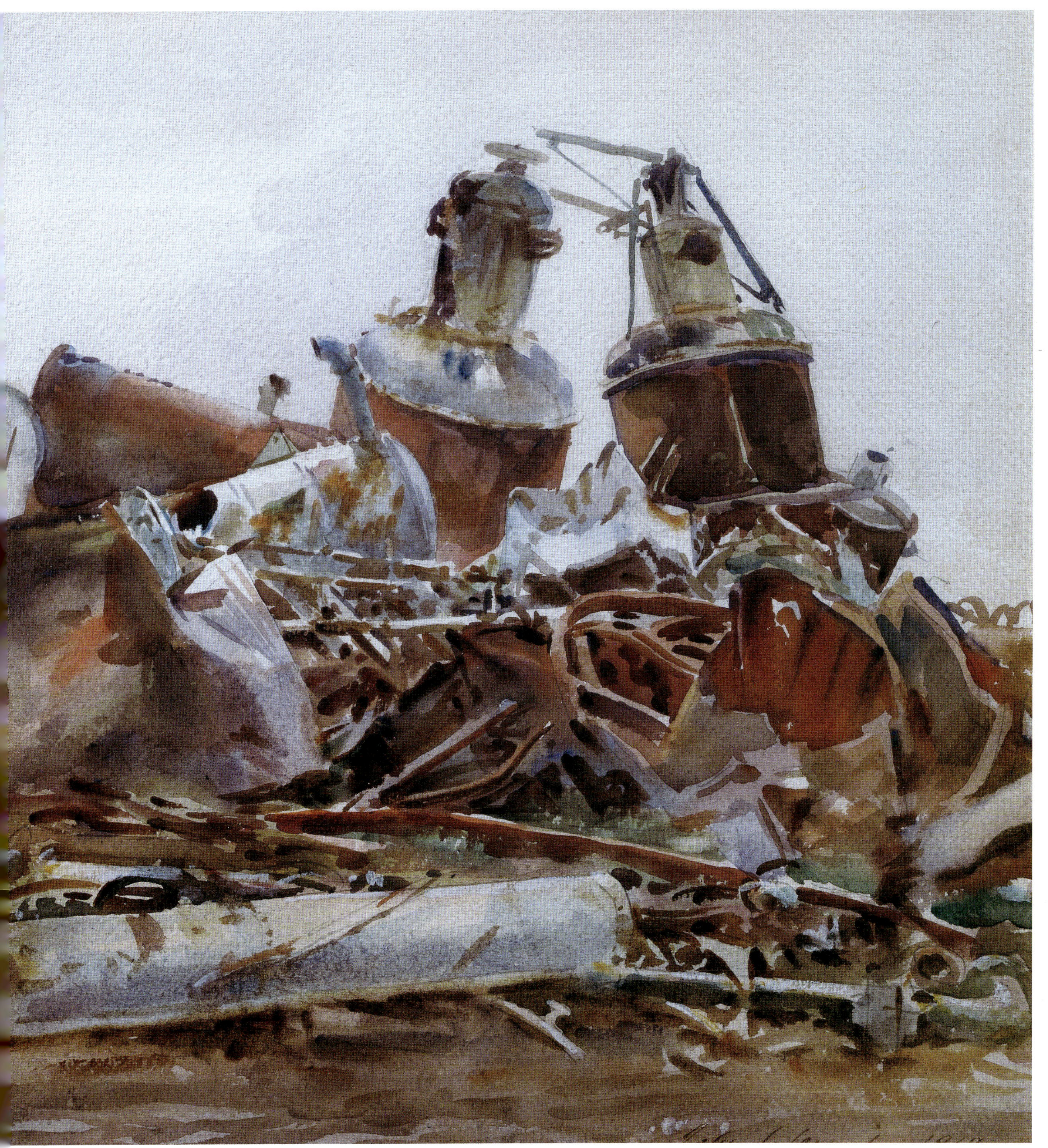

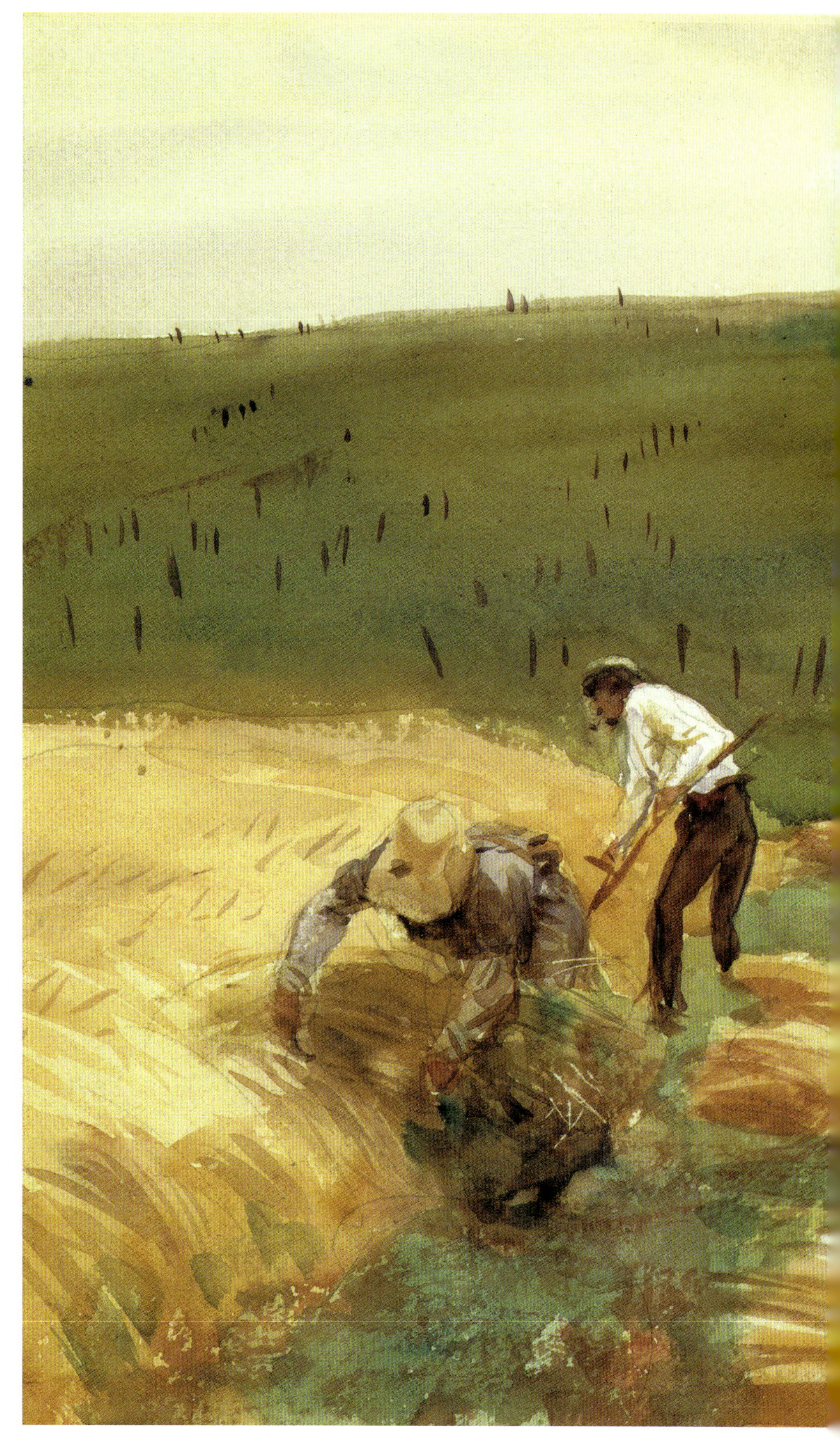

A Crashed Aeroplane 1918
Watercolor on paper
13 7/16 x 21 in. (34.2 x 53.3 cm.)
Imperial War Museum, London

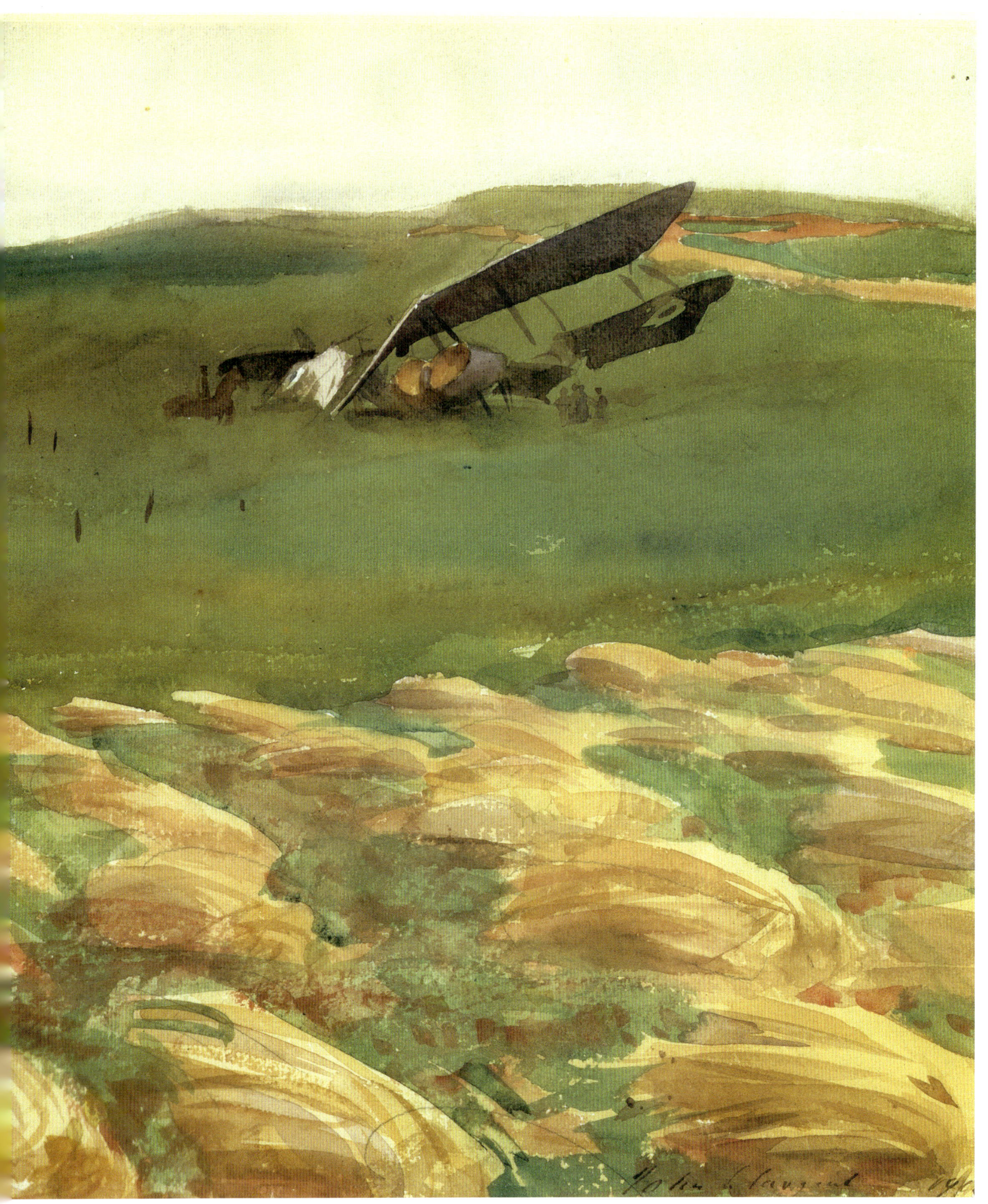

Lake Louise, Canadian Rockies 1916
Watercolor on paper
15 x 20 1/2 in. (38.5 x 52 cm.)
Courtesy Christie's Images

Lake O'Hara 1916
Watercolor over graphite on off-white wove paper
15 3/4 x 20 7/8 in. (40 x 53 cm.)
Courtesy of the Fogg Art Museum, Harvard University Art Museums,
Gift of Edward W. Forbes, © President and Fellows of Harvard College,
Harvard University, Photo: David Mathews

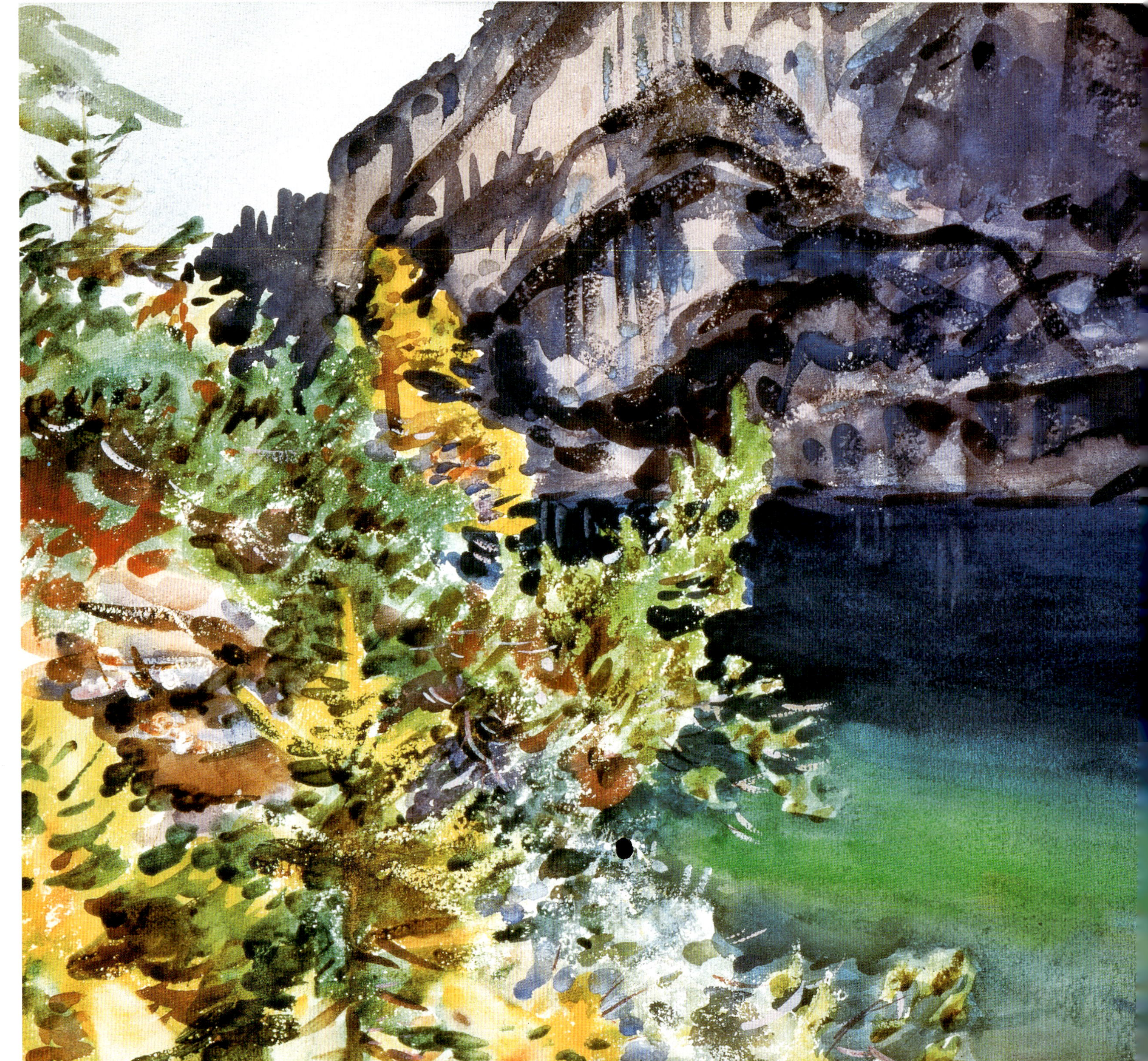

The Canadian Rockies and New England

Through his many visits to the Alps, Sargent had acquired a taste for cool climes. Taking a break from duties in Boston in the summer of 1917, he visited the Canadian Rockies, where he found the accommodations rather primitive but the painting opportunities first rate.

When not focusing on the scenery—Lake Louise and Lake O'Hara, among other landmarks—Sargent turned his brush to subjects most immediately at hand. In a wonderful series of watercolors, he painted the camp sites, taking special care in the rendering of the tents that served as the travelers' living quarters for much of the trip.

A few years later, in the 1920s, again on furlough, as it were, from Boston projects, Sargent visited relatives and friends in the Mount Desert Island region. Champlain's *Isle des Monts-Déserts* had already been made famous in the annals of art through the canvases of Frederic Church, Thomas Cole, Fitz Hugh Lane and other great 19th-century painters.

As was his way, Sargent found his own approach to this well-limned country of the pointed firs. A wharf, a stretch of sand, a schooner—he chose simple yet challenging motifs, his palette attuned once more to his surroundings. These Maine watercolors, which count among his last works in the medium, display no loss of skill or sharpness of eye. Sargent was at the top of his form.

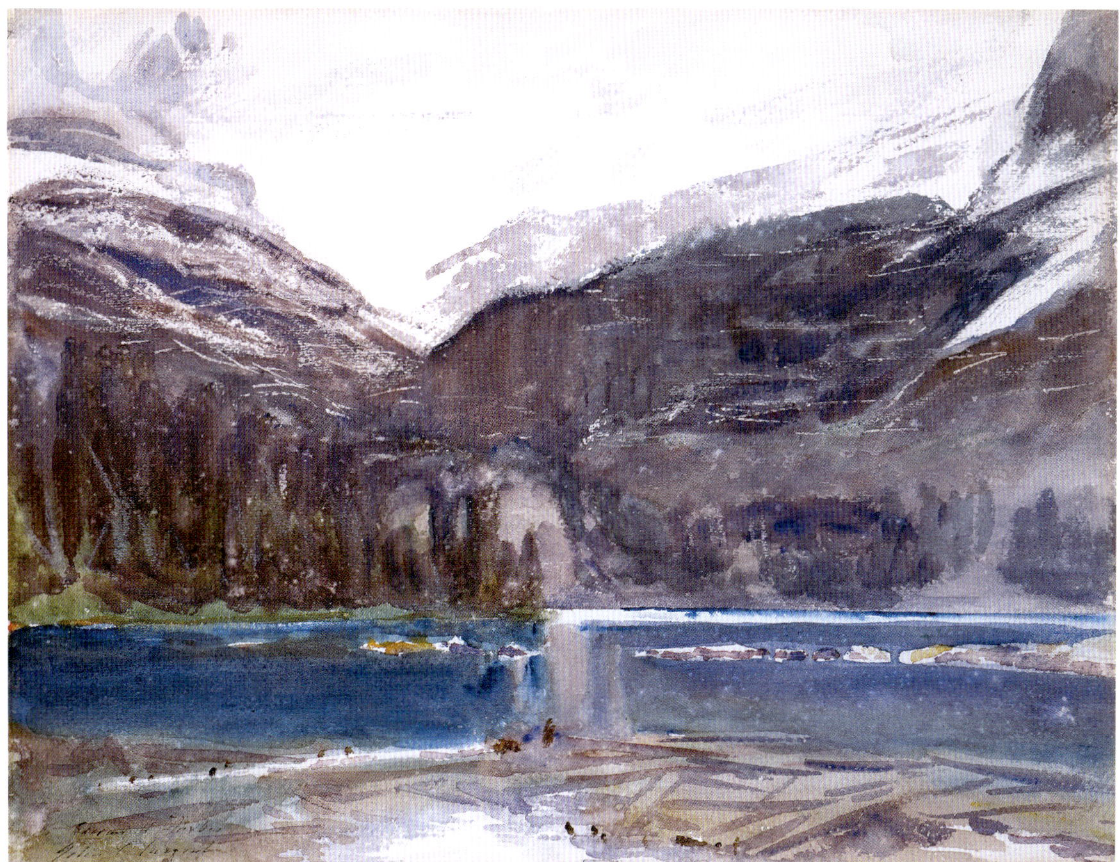

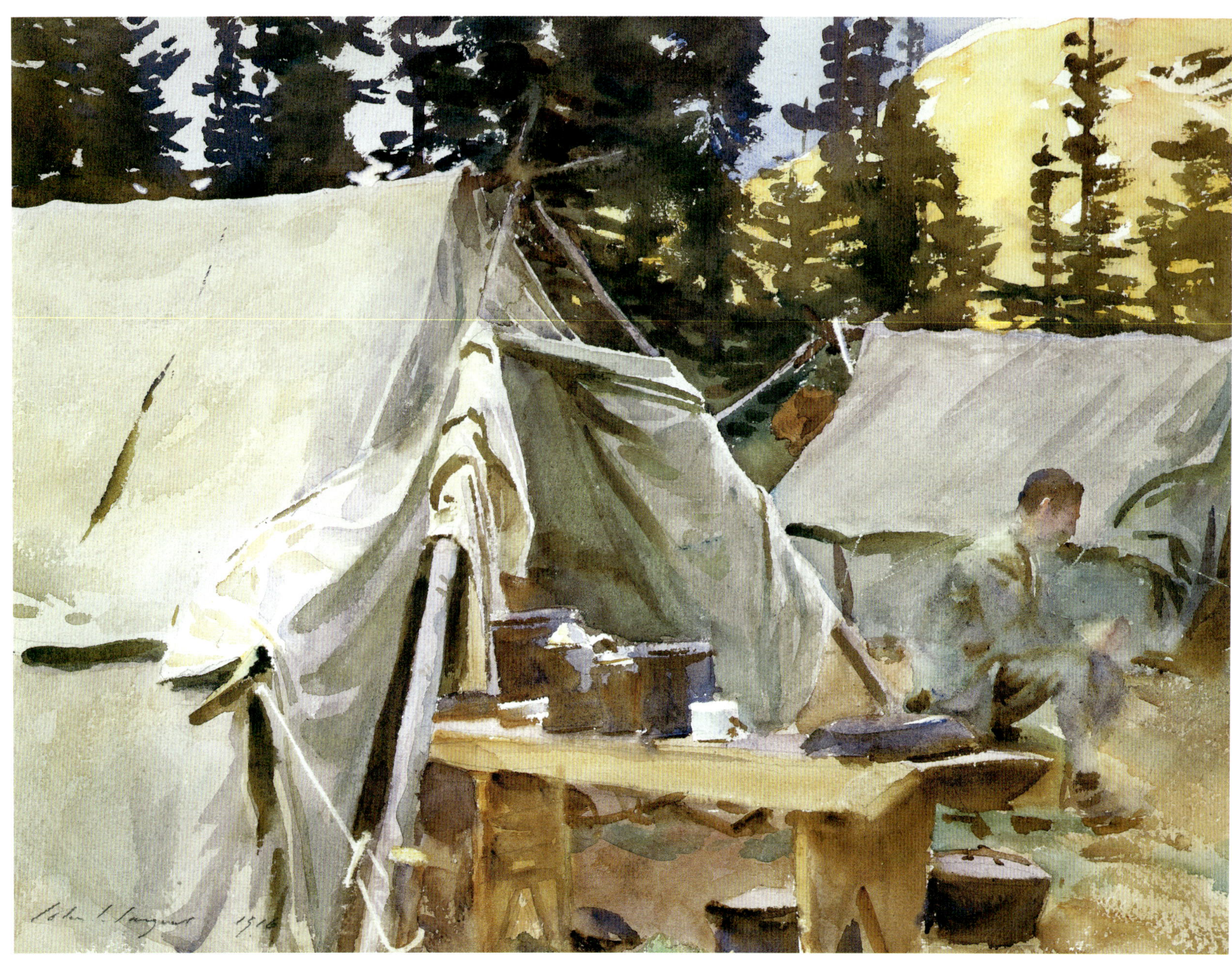

Camp at Lake O'Hara 1916

Watercolor and graphite underdrawing on white wove paper

15 3/4 x 21 in. (40 x 53.3 cm.)

The Metropolitan Museum of Art,

Gift of Mrs. David Hecht, in memory of her son, Victor D. Hecht, 1932 (32.116)

In the Canadian Pacific series of aquarelles the justice of observation, the swift and confident character of the handling and finality of the impression . . . go very far to place these studies in the top most rank.

—William Howe Downes, 1925

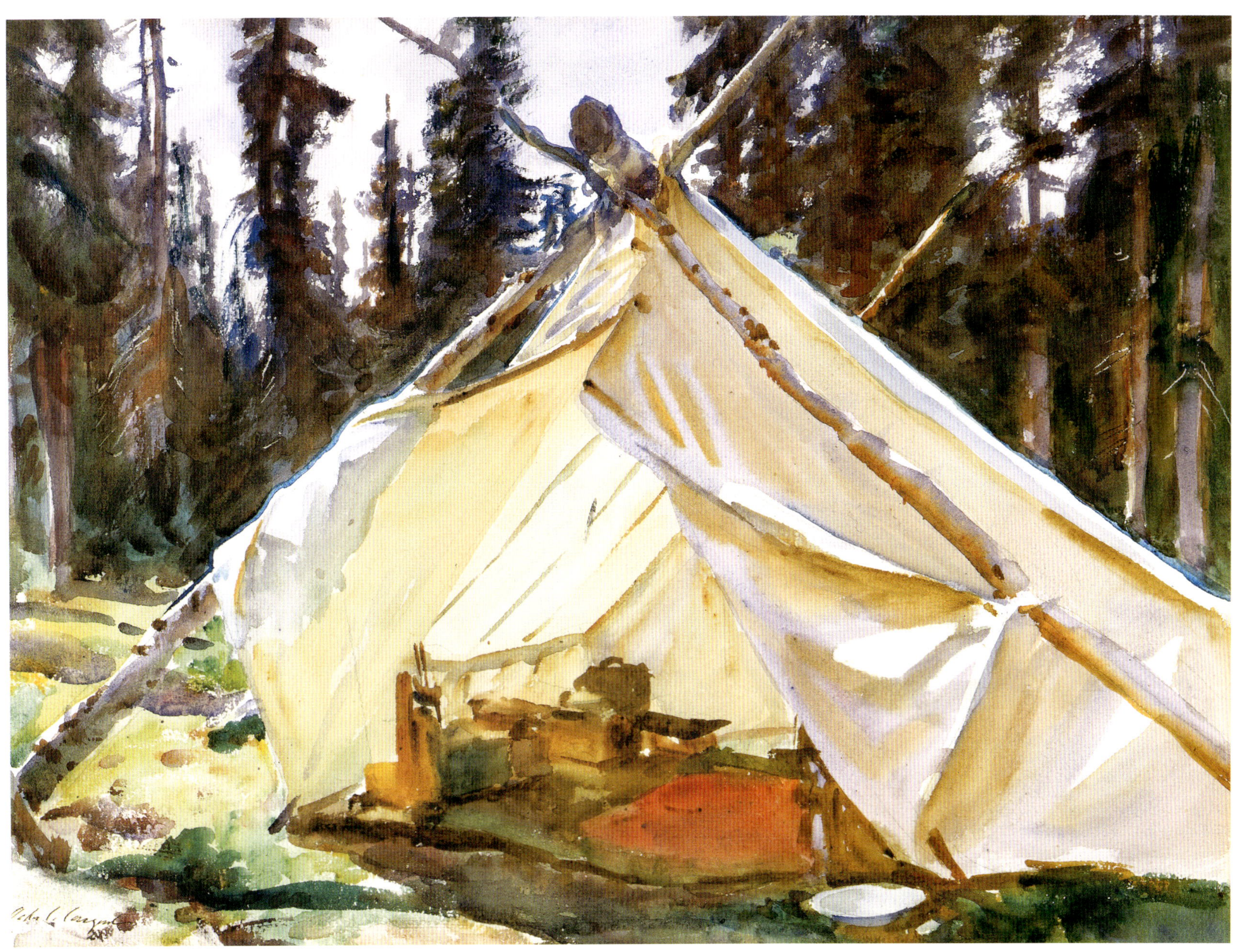

A Tent in the Rockies 1916
Watercolor on paper
15 x 20 1/2 in. (38 x 52 cm.)
Isabella Stewart Gardner Museum, Boston

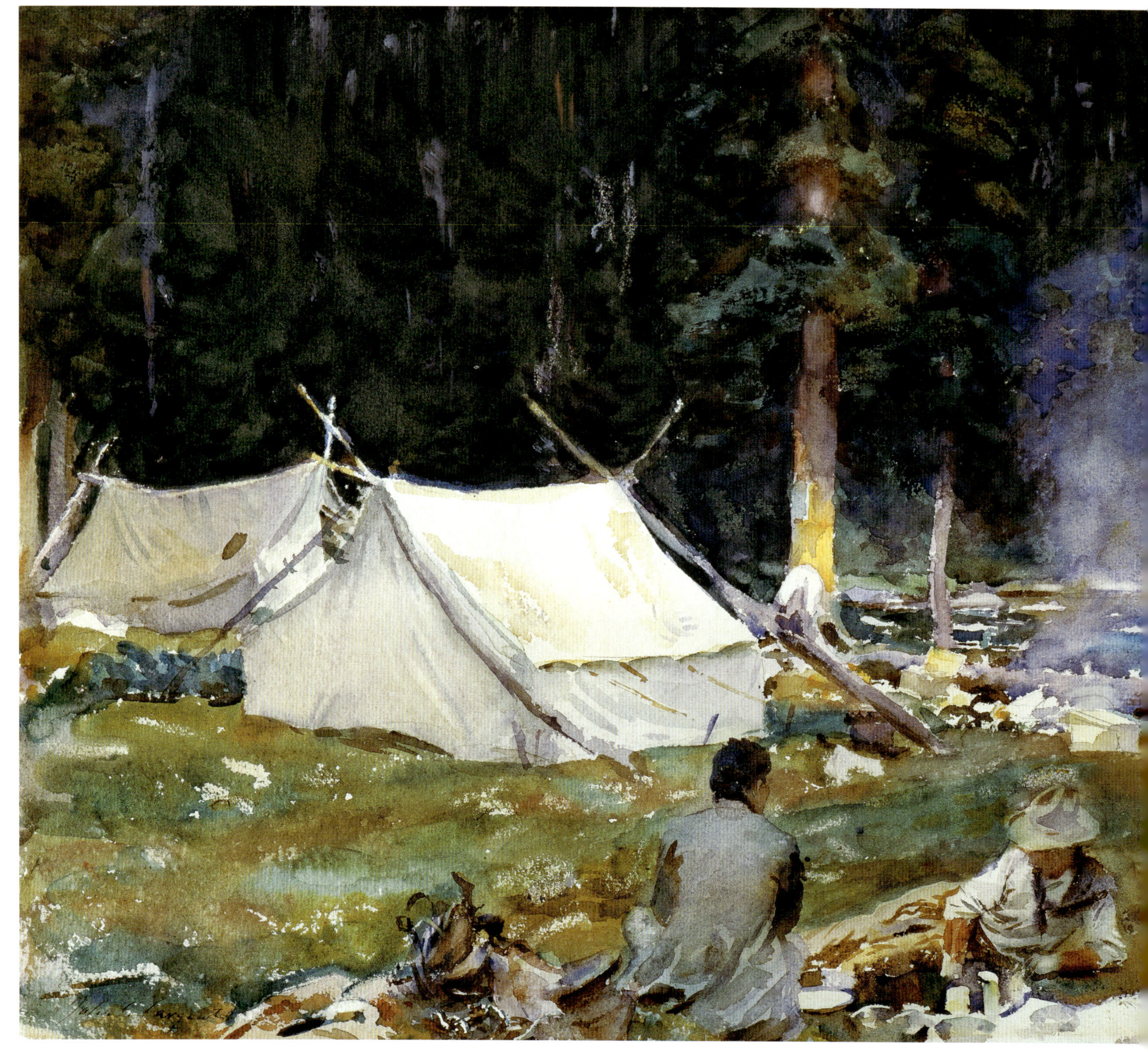

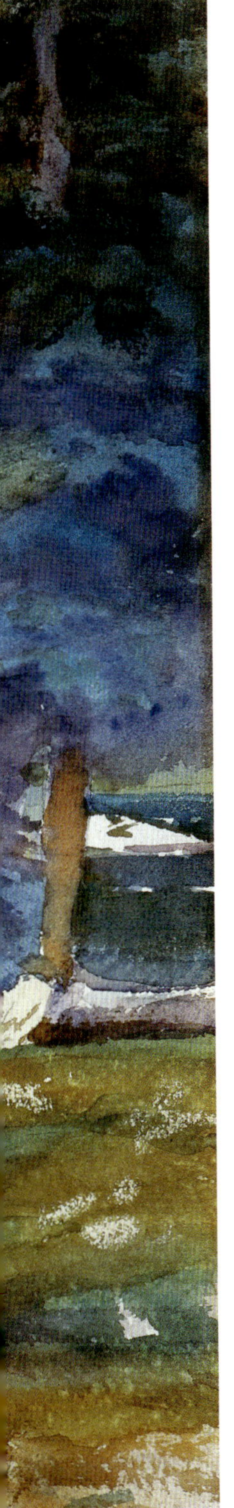

Camping Near Lake O'Hara 1916
Watercolor
15 3/4 x 20 7/8 in. (40 x 53 cm.)
Collection of The Newark Museum. Inv.: 57.86.
The Newark Museum, Newark, New Jersey, U.S.A.
Art Resource, New York

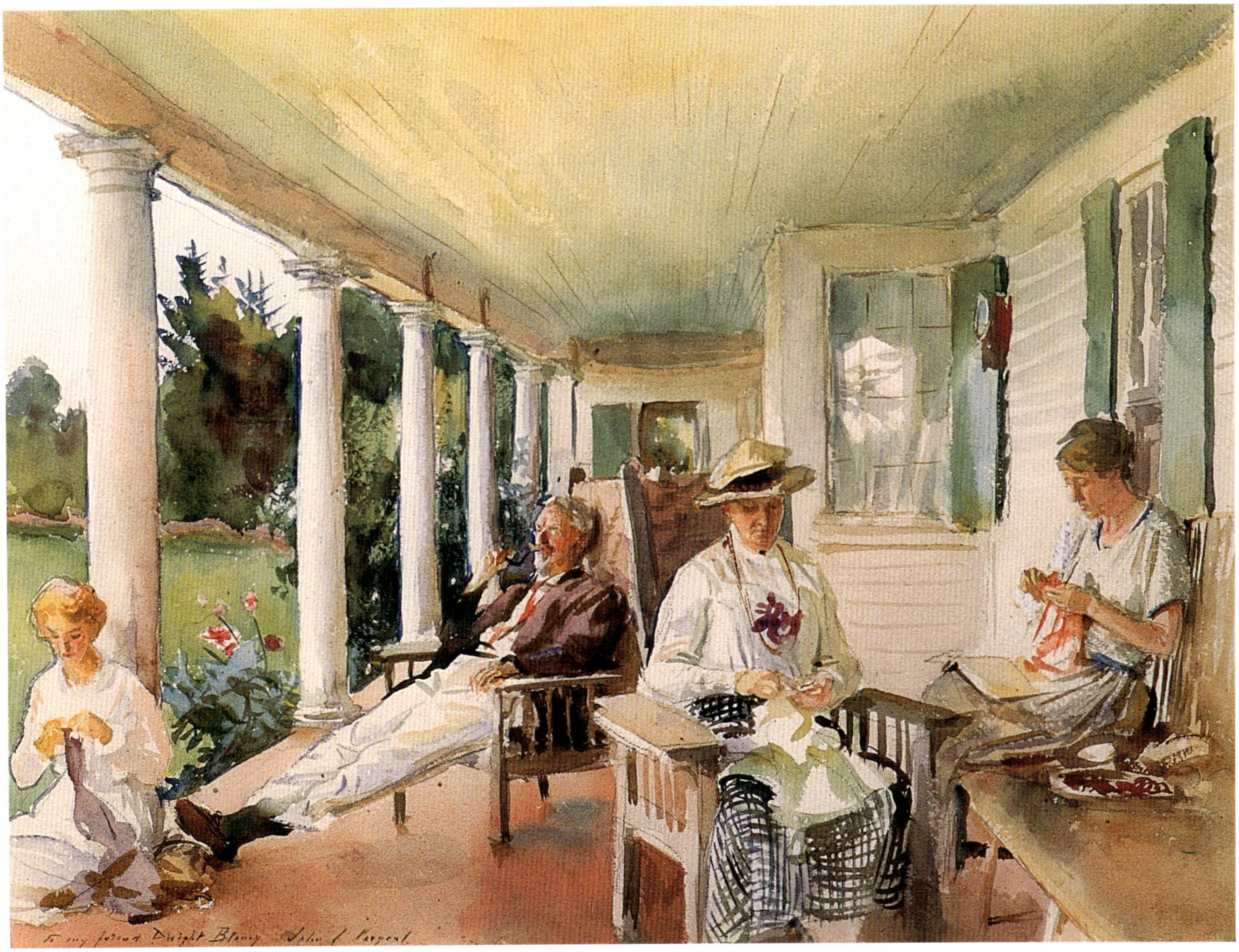

On the Verandah (Ironbound Island, Maine) 1922
Watercolor on paper
15 1/2 x 21 in. (39.4 x 53.4 cm.)
Private Collection

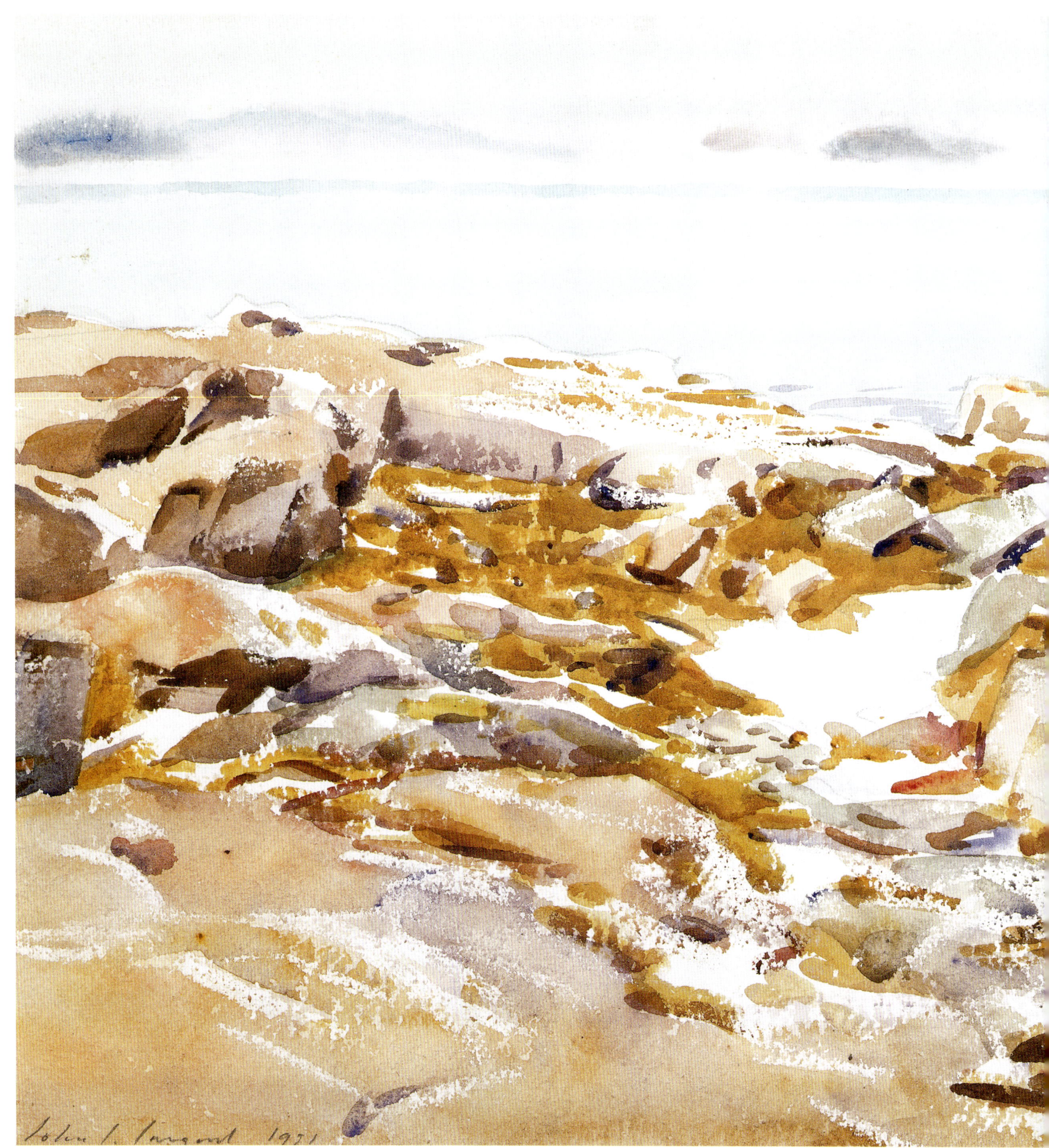

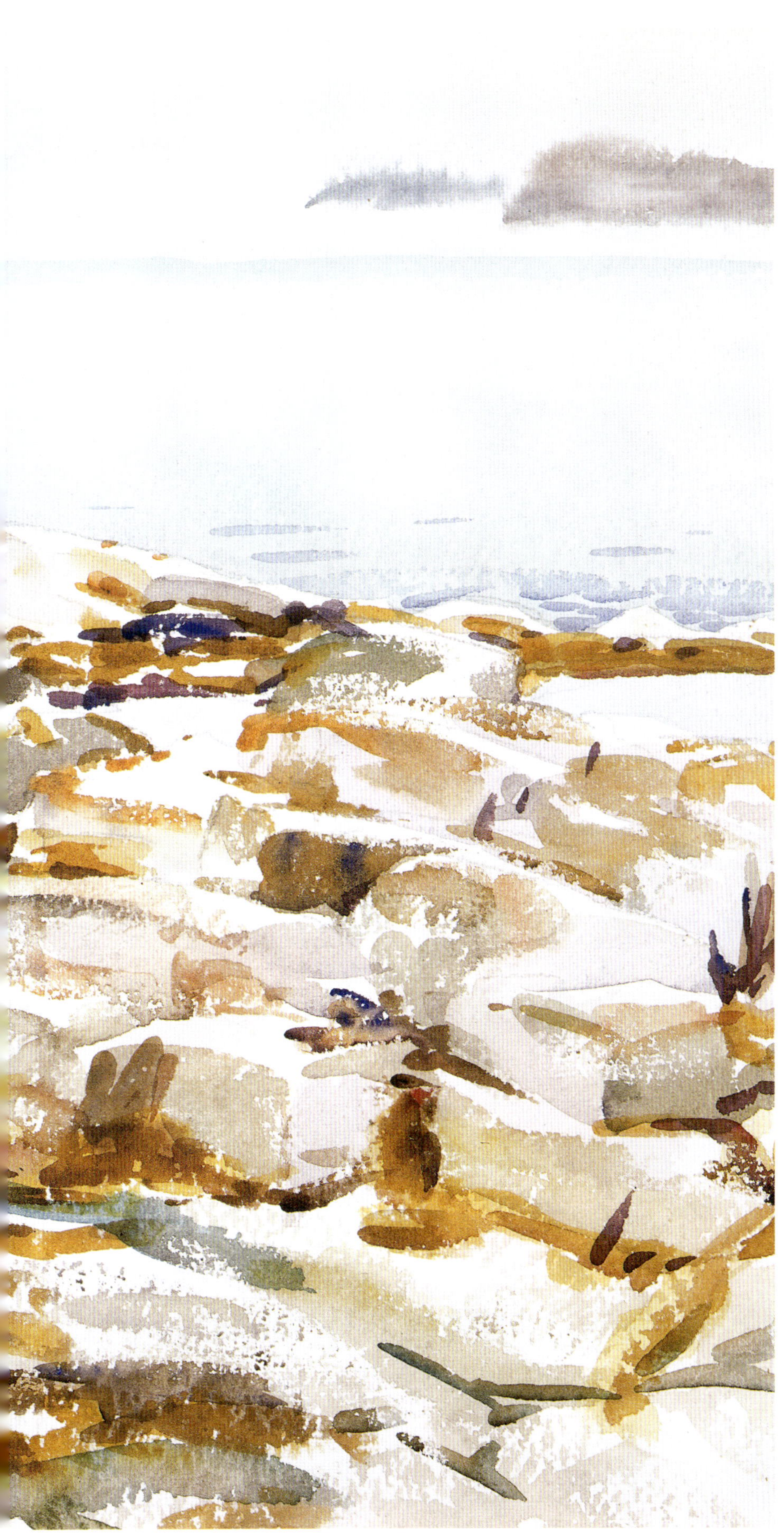

I should have liked to add that, besides significance, Sargent extracted and made visible the actual beauty of the world; and never so much as in the innumerable oil sketches and watercolours which make him one of the greatest of landscape painters.

—Vernon Lee, 1925

Rocky Coast Near Boston 1921
Watercolor over pencil
13 13/16 x 21 1/16 in. (35.1 x 53.7 cm.)
Museum of Art, Rhode Island School of Design,
Anonymous Gift
Photography by Cathy Carver

Change of light Sargent could understand and condone, but change of tide affronted him. When he was painting the Schooner "Catherine" and got the row-boats where he wanted them in the foreground, he was most resentful when the tide changed their position. He kept us hauling the "bestial boats" into place, and was afraid that we could not get them back in place the second day, as of course we did.

—Mary Newbold Patterson Hale, 1927

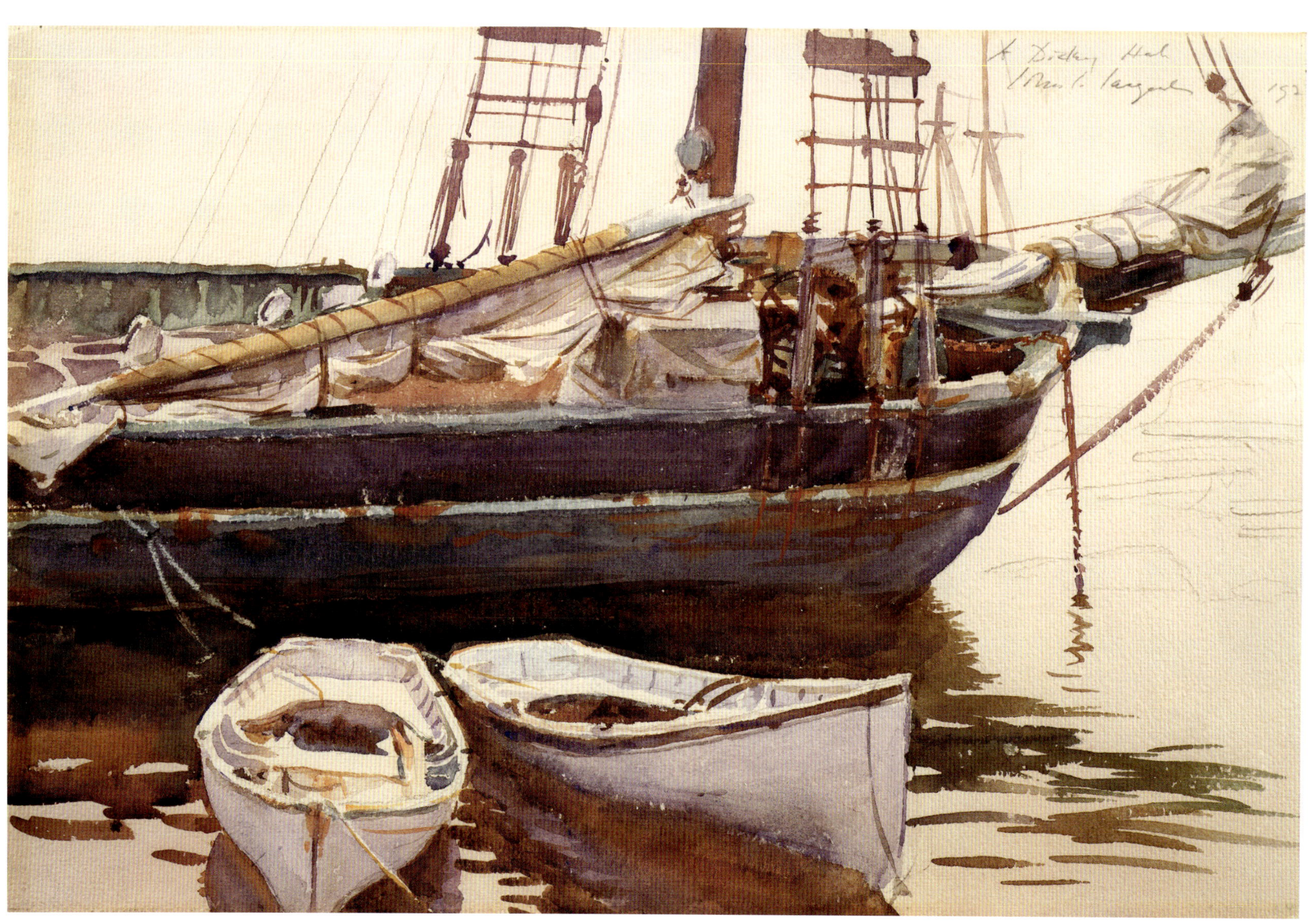

Schooner, Catherine, Somesville, Maine c. 1920–25
Watercolor on paper
13 3/4 x 21 in. (34.9 x 53.3 cm.)
Private Collection

Wharf at Ironbound 1922
Watercolor on paper
15 1/2 x 21 in. (39.4 x 53.4 cm.)
Courtesy Christie's Images

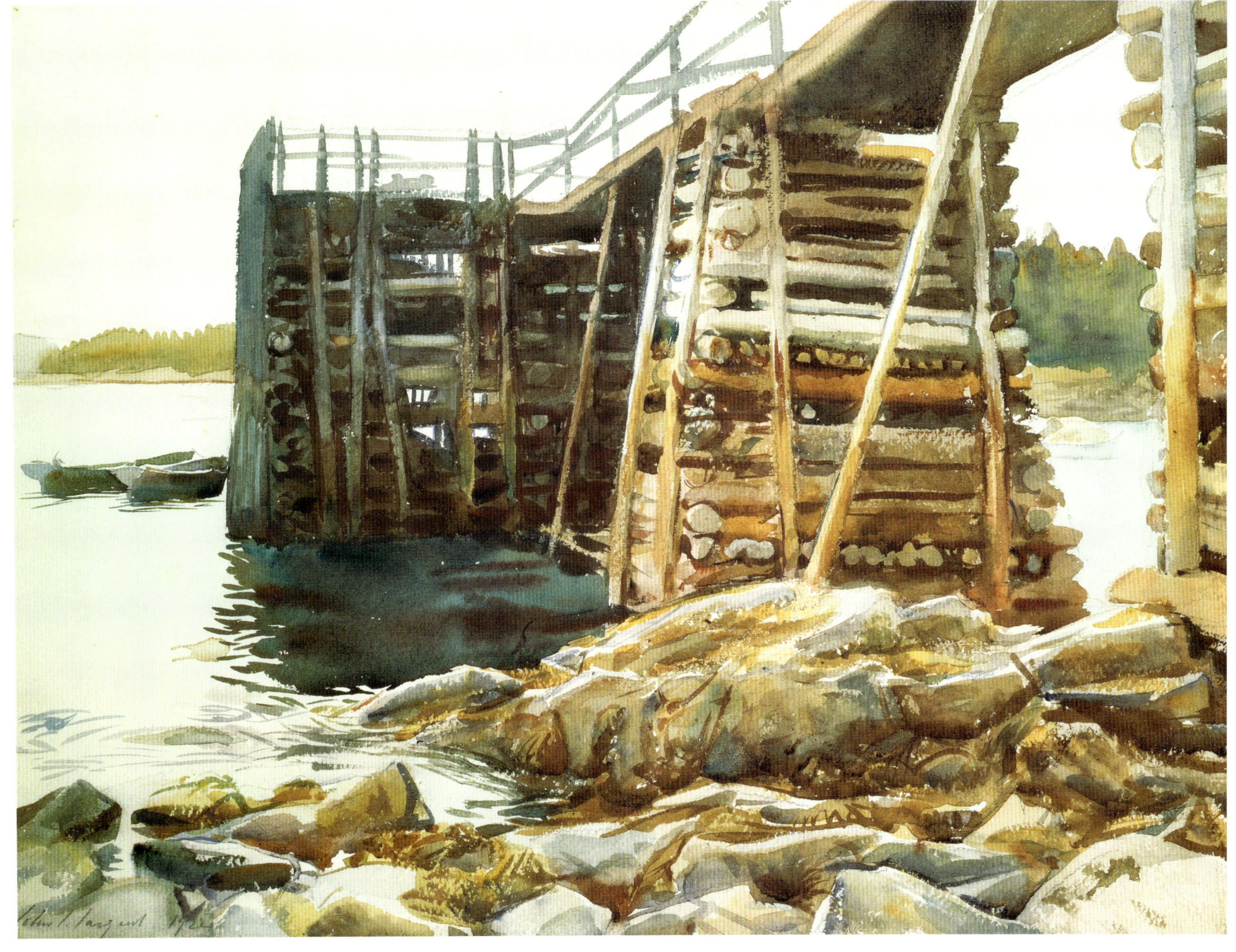

...Sargent's watercolors are just as beautiful as his portraits. They're actually better, aren't they? Watercolors are so hard to do.

—Andy Warhol, 1986

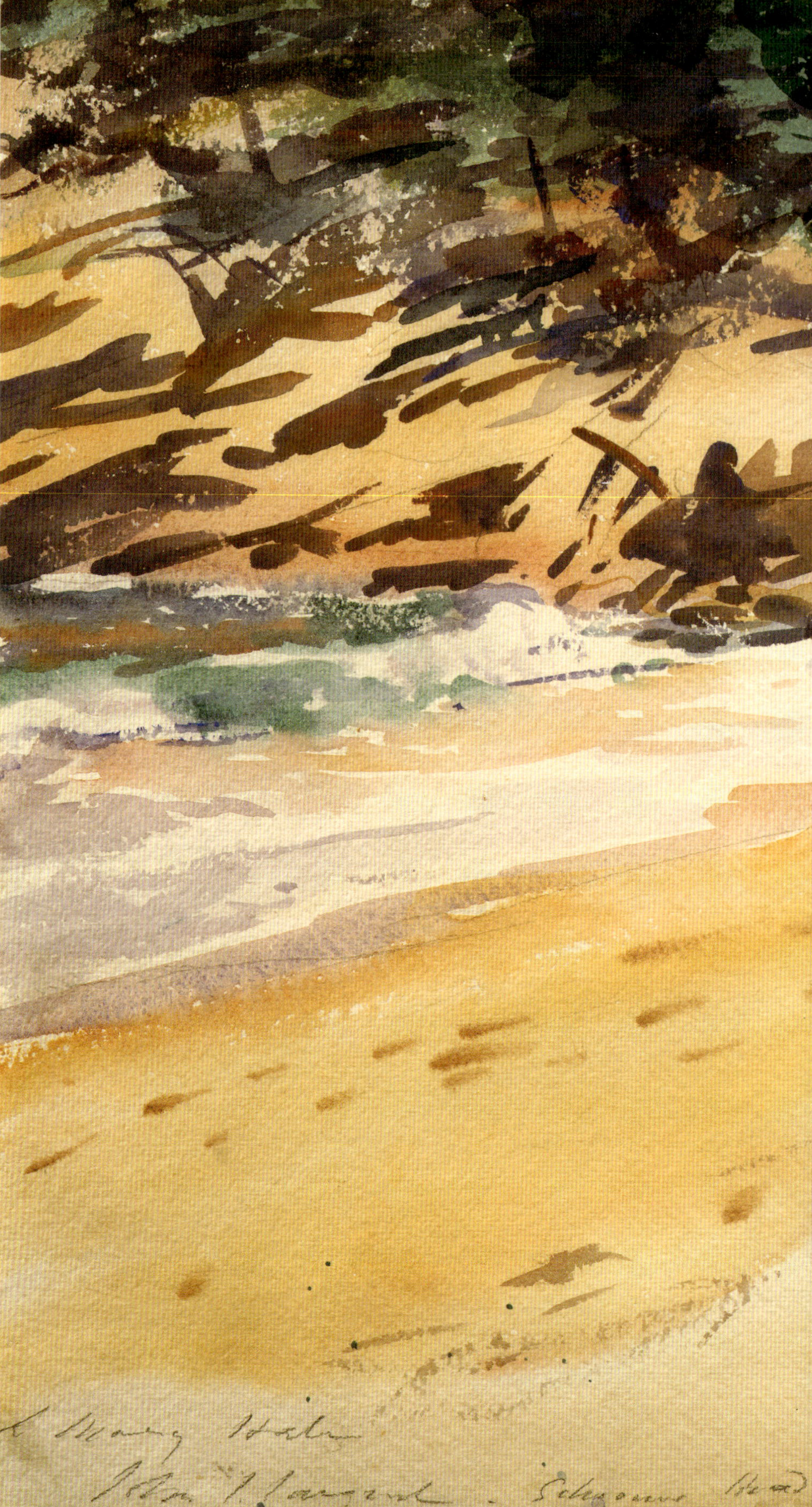

Sand Beach, Schooner Head, Maine 1921
Watercolor on paper
13 1/4 x 20 3/4 in. (33.7 x 52.7 cm.)
Private Collection

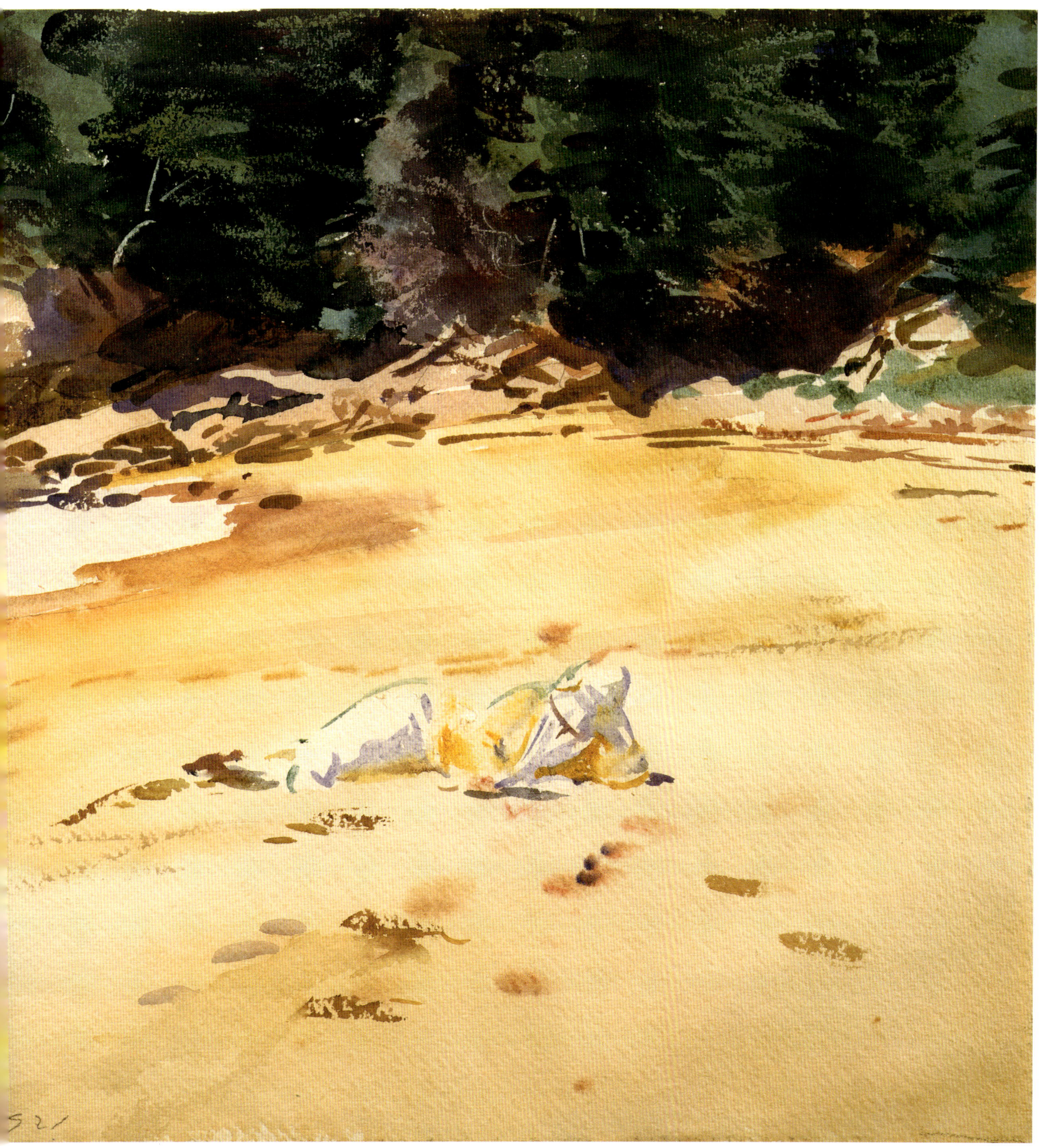

Sources of Quotations

P. 22: Evan Charteris. *John Sargent*. New York: Charles Scribner's Sons, 1927, p. 85.

P. 31: Charteris, *John Sargent*, p. 236.

P. 32: Charteris, *John Sargent*, p. 183.

P. 44: Henry James, "John S. Sargent," Harper's New Monthly Magazine, 75 (October 1887), p. 689.

P. 59: Charteris, *John Sargent*, p. 224.

P. 62: Martin Hardie, *Famous Water-Colour Painters, VII—J.S. Sargent, R.A., R.W.S.*, London: The Studio Ltd., 1930, p. 2.

P. 64: Philip Hendy, *European and American Paintings in the Isabella Stewart Gardner Museum*. Boston: Isabella Stewart Gardner Museum, 1974, p. 228.

P. 73: Charteris, *John Sargent*, p. 225.

P. 76: William Howe Downes, *John S. Sargent, His Life and Work*. Boston: Little, Brown, 1925, p. 63.

P. 80: Cited in Richard Ormond, *John Singer Sargent. Paintings, Drawings, Watercolors*. New York: Harper and Row, 1970, p. 70.

P. 85: Downes, *John S. Sargent, His Life and Work*, p. 107.

P. 90: Stanley Olson, *John Singer Sargent: His Portrait*. New York: St. Martin's Press, 1986, p. 20.

P. 95: John Updike, *Just Looking: Essays on Art*. New York: Alfred A. Knopf, 1989, pp. 58-60.

P. 96: Charteris, *John Sargent*, p. 225.

P. 98: Ferber, Linda S., and Barbara Dayer Gallati. *Masters of Color and Light: Homer, Sargent, and the American Watercolor Movement*. The Brooklyn Museum of Art/Smithsonian Institution Press, 1998, p. 127.

P. 102: Charteris, *John Sargent*, p. 224.

P. 106: *John Singer Sargent*, compiled by Nathaniel Pousette-Dart, introduction by Lee Woodward Zeigler, New York: Frederick A. Stokes Company, 1924, p. viii.

P. 109: Charteris, *John Sargent*, p. 95.

P. 110: Charteris, *John Sargent*, p. 225.

P. 116: Charteris, *John Sargent*, p. 85.

P. 125: Hoopes, Donelson F. *American Watercolor Painting*. New York: Watson-Guptill, 1977, p. 80.

P. 130: Downes, *John S. Sargent, His Life and Work*, p. 76.

P. 133: Olson, *John Singer Sargent: His Portrait*, p. 233.

P. 136: Charteris, *John Sargent*, p. 251.

P. 140: Hardie, *Famous Water-Colour Painters, VII—J.S. Sargent, R.A., R.W.S.*, p. 3.

P. 144: Downes, *John S. Sargent, His Life and Work*, p. 110.

P. 151: Downes, p. 71.

P. 155: Charteris, *John Sargent*, p. 254.

P. 156: Carter Ratcliff, *John Singer Sargent*. New York: Abbeville Press, 1982, p. 237.

P. 158: Trevor Fairbrother, *John Singer Sargent*. New York: Harry N. Abrams, Inc., 1994, p. 145.

Index of Watercolors

Above Lake Garda (at San Vigilio) 1913 105
Arab Gypsies in a Tent c. 1905–06 62
Arab Stable c. 1905–06 65
Arab Woman n.d. 57
Aranjuez c. 1902–03 103
Artist in the Simplon c. 1910–11 74
Base of a Palace n.d. 38
The Bathers 1917 131
Bedouin Camp c. 1905–06 63
Bedouin Mother 1905 57
Bedouin Women c. 1905–06 55
Bedouins c. 1905–06 54
Black Tent c. 1905–06 56
Boats at Anchor 1917 19
Boboli 1907 96
Boboli Gardens 1907 102
Bridge of Sighs c. 1905–08 44
Brook among Rocks c. 1907 71
Bus Horses in Jerusalem 1905 64
Camouflaged Tanks, Berles-au-Bois 1918 142
Camp at Lake O'Hara 1916 150
Camping Near Lake O'Hara 1916 152
Campo dei Frari, Venice 1880 50
Carrara: Quarry II 1911 84
Carrara: Trajan's Quarry n.d. 85
The Cashmere Shawl 1911 26
Colorful Pavements, Sicily c. 1901 123
Cordova, Interior of a Cathedral c. 1903 122
Corfu: Lights and Shadow 1909 111
Corfu: The Terrace 1909 94
A Crashed Aeroplane 1918 146
Derelicts 1917 132
The Desert from Jerusalem 1905 61
Doorway of a Venetian Palace c. 1901–10 42
The Eiger from Murren 1870 6
Feet of an Arab, Tiberius n.d. 14
The Fence 1912 87
Figure and Pool 1917 130
Florence: Torre Galle n.d. 114
Flotsam and Jetsam n.d. 107
The Garden Wall 1910 90
Gardens at Florence 1910 101
George Hitchcock c. 1880 22
Girgenti c. 1901 60
Goatherds c. 1905–06 52
Gourds c. 1905–08 118
The Grand Canal, Venice c. 1902 34
Grand Canal, Venice 1907 43
Graveyard in the Tyrol 1914 88
The Green Parasol c. 1910 30
Highlanders Resting at the Front 1918 138
Hills of Galilee c. 1905–06 53
Horse Line 1918 135
In a Hayloft c. 1904–07 25
In a Medici Villa c. 1907 97
In Switzerland 1908 31
In the Generalife 1912 23
In the Tyrol 1911 9
Incensing the Veil 1880 8
Interior of a Hospital Tent 1918 143
The Jetty at San Vigilio 1913 104
La Biancheria 1910 110
La Riva c. 1903–08 36
Lake Louise, Canadian Rockies 1916 148
Lake O'Hara 1916 149
Landscape: On the Somme 1918 134
The Library in Venice 1904 47
Lizzatori I 1911 82
Loch Moidart, Inverness-shire 1896 120
Melon Boats c. 1905 58
Mending a Sail c. 1905–06 59
Miss Reubell in Front of a Screen n.d. 32
Moorish Patio c. 1880 123
Mountain Fire c. 1903–08 66
Mountain Stream c. 1904–07 80
Mrs. Gardner in White 1922 33
Muddy Alligators 1917 126
Near June Street 1890 17
Olive Trees, Corfu 1909 113
Olive Trees, Corfu n.d. 112
On the Verandah (Ironbound Island, Maine) 1922 153
Palms 1917 128
The Piazzetta, Venice c. 1904 37
Pine Forest c. 1907–8 73
Pomegranates 1908 119
Ponte della Canonica c. 1903–04 40
The Pool 1917 124
Port of Soller 1907–08 116
Portrait of Madame Gautreau c. 1883 20
Rio di San Salvatore, Venice c. 1903–04 38
Rio di Santa Maria Formosa, Venice n.d. 41
Rocky Coast Near Boston 1921 154
Rose-Marie Ormond Reading in a Cashmere Shawl c. 1908–1912 29
Rushing Brook n.d. 72
Salmon River c. 1901 78
San Giuseppe di Castello, Venice c. 1903–04 41
San Vigilio, Lago di Garda c. 1913 108
Sand Beach, Schooner Head, Maine 1921 158
Santa Maria della Salute 1904 46
Schooner, Catherine, Somesville, Maine c. 1920–25 156
The Shadowed Stream c. 1884 121
Shady Paths, Vizcaya 1917 129
The Shallows n.d. 71
The Simplon n.d. 67
The Simplon c. 1910 67
Simplon Pass: Avalanche Track n.d. 68
Simplon Pass: Chalets 1911 87
Simplon Pass: Crags 1911 70
Simplon Pass: Mountain Brook n.d. 75
Simplon Pass: The Green Parasol 1911 76
Simplon Pass: The Tease 1911 77
Sketch of Cellini's 'Perseus' n.d. 14
Spanish Fountain 1912 15
Spanish Soldiers c. 1902–03 115
A Street in Arras 1918 136
Study for the Spanish Dancer 1882 21
The Sunken Road, Ransart 1918 142
Tangier c. 1905–06 60
Tarragona 1908 **(Tarragona Cathedral)** 99
A Tent in the Rockies 1916 151
The Terrace at La Granja c. 1903–04 or 1912 100
Thistles n.d. 7
Thou Shalt Not Steal 1918 139
Tiepolo Ceiling—Milan c. 1904 12
Tomb, Toledo n.d. 98
Tommies Bathing 1917 141
Tommies Bathing, France 1918 140
A Tramp c. 1900–08 24
Trees on a Hillside, Majorca 1908 16
Trout Stream Tyrol 1912 79
Tyrolese Crucifix c. 1914 89
Under the Rialto Bridge, c. 1909 10
Venetian Canal n.d. 48
Venetian Fishing Boats c. 1904 39
Venice c. 1902 49
Venice: La Libreria n.d. 37
View from a Window at Genoa after 1900 .... frontispiece
Villa di Marlia, Lucca c. 1910 95
Villa di Marlia: A Fountain 1910 92
Villa Torlonia, Frascati 1907 93
Vines and Cypresses n.d. 117
Violet Sleeping c. 1907–10 28
Wharf at Ironbound 1922 157
White Ships 1908 106
Woman Reclining c. 1908 27
Woodsheds, Tyrol 1914 86
Workmen at Carrara c. 1911 83
A Wrecked Sugar Refinery 1918 144
Zattere Rio Eremite, Venice 1904 51
Zuleika c. 1908 28